AESTHETICS

D1471345

AESTHETICS

AESTHETICS

1958/59

Theodor W. Adorno

Edited by Eberhard Ortland

Translated by Wieland Hoban

polity

First published in German as *Ästhetik (1958/59)*, © Suhrkamp Verlag, Frankfurt am Main, 2009

This English edition © Polity Press, 2018

The translation of this work was funded by Geisteswissenschaften International – Translation Funding for Humanities and Social Sciences from Germany, a joint initiative of the Fritz Thyssen Foundation, the German Federal Foreign Office, the collecting society VG WORT and the Börsenverein des Deutschen Buchhandels (German Publishers & Booksellers Association).

Polity Press
65 Bridge Street
Cambridge CB2 1UR, UK

Polity Press
101 Station Landing
Suite 300
Medford, MA 02155, USA

All rights reserved. Except for the quotation of short passages for the purpose of criticism and review, no part of this publication may be reproduced, stored in a retrieval system or transmitted, in any form or by any means, electronic, mechanical, photocopying, recording or otherwise, without the prior permission of the publisher.

ISBN-13: 978-0-7456-7939-6
ISBN-13: 978-0-7456-7940-2 (pb)

A catalogue record for this book is available from the British Library.

Typeset in 10.5 on 12 pt Sabon
by Toppan Best-set Premedia Limited
Printed and bound in Great Britain by CPI Group (UK) Ltd, Croydon.

The publisher has used its best endeavours to ensure that the URLs for external websites referred to in this book are correct and active at the time of going to press. However, the publisher has no responsibility for the websites and can make no guarantee that a site will remain live or that the content is or will remain appropriate.

Every effort has been made to trace all copyright holders, but if any have been inadvertently overlooked the publisher will be pleased to include any necessary credits in any subsequent reprint or edition.

For further information on Polity, visit our website: politybooks.com

CONTENTS

the experience of beauty • Not a definition • Idea • The
subjectivity of beauty • The imitation of the idea of beauty •
The aspect of danger in beauty

Interpretation of the *Phaedrus*, contd. • The paradox of
beauty • The image of beauty • Affinity with death •
Elevating oneself above the contingent world • Kant's theory
of the sublime • The sensual and the spiritual in art •
Force field

Ontology and dialectic in Plato • The relationship between
beauty and art • The aspect of ugliness • The aspect of
sensual pleasure • Aesthetic experience • 'Throw away in
order to gain!' • The meaning of the whole

Recapitulation • Enjoyment of art • The inhabitant •
Fetishism • Aesthetic enjoyment • The suspension
of the *principium individuationis* • Understanding works
of art

Reflective co-enactment • Aesthetic stupidity • Translation,
commentary, critique • The spiritualization of art •
Constructivism • The dialectic of sensual and spiritual
aspects in the work of art

Spiritual content • The structural context • Force field •
The allergy to sensual pleasure • Aesthetics without
beauty

Correcting the definition of the work of art •
Alienation • Reference to the object in visual art •
'Abstract' art • Form as sedimented content •
Loss of tension • Theoretical preconditions of
artistic experience

EDITOR'S FOREWORD

Adorno had been planning for some time to write a systematic book on aesthetics; his notes and drafts go back to at least 1956. A decisive factor in the genesis of the book, which was meant to become his central work, were the lectures on this subject that he gave a total of six times between 1950 and 1968.

The present course of lectures from the winter semester of 1958/59 is the fourth in this series. It is also the earliest to be documented in full by transcripts made from tape recordings at the Institute of Social Research. As the editorial traces in the typescript show, Adorno worked further on this text while preparing later lectures, and also while working on what would later become the *Aesthetic Theory*.

We have little information about Adorno's first aesthetics course after his return from American exile, except for the fact that it took place in the summer semester of 1950 on Mondays, Tuesdays and Wednesdays from 4 to 5 pm. As for the second course, from the winter semester of 1950/51, the Theodor W. Adorno Archive contains typewritten elaborations on key points, as well as a summary that indicates the range of topics discussed and a number of central theses. The third course, from the winter semester of 1955/56, is documented by handwritten drafts and notes, as well as a transcript elaborated from stenographic notes. Alongside the present fourth course, there exists also a complete tape transcript of the fifth, which Adorno gave in two parts in the summer semester of 1961 and the winter semester of 1961/62. The final course, also spread across two semesters – the summer 1967 and winter 1967/68 semesters – was given when large parts of the *Aesthetic Theory* had already been written and survives only in various drafts, notes, stenographic notes and partial tape transcripts. Excerpts from tape transcripts of a few lectures from the second semester were published in 1973 in an unauthorized edition that fell severely short of academic standards. The editor of this pirate edition, who signed his preface merely with the initials C. K., states that the quality of the tape recordings was 'extremely poor'.

The course of lectures from the winter semester of 1958/59 is instructive in several respects. It is a document of its time, intertwined in many ways with the artistic, intellectual and political confrontations that shaped life in West Germany during the Cold War. It documents a form of academic teaching that would be inconceivable in the framework of current BA or MA programmes. The unity of research and teaching, which, at the time it was practised, never required a word of commentary or discussion, can be reconstructively observed in these lectures at a distance of half a century. It did not consist merely in the professor presenting those elements of their research findings which they considered relevant; for Adorno, the course itself was a kind of laboratory in which he first developed his ideas, or could at least – due to the necessity of making himself understood – give them a structure and vividness that first had to be wrested from the complexity of the specific issues interwoven within them. The productivity of this 'gradual formulation of thoughts while speaking', as Kleist put it, becomes especially clear if one examines the relationship between the recorded sessions and the notes with which Adorno prepared his lectures, as well as the published texts to which he refers, and if one observes how Adorno himself went through the transcripts of his unscripted words, marking passages that struck him as particularly incisive.

Various topics that would later be elaborated in the *Aesthetic Theory* are mentioned, some of them developed in greater detail; fundamental motifs were already clear to Adorno, but some evidently reached a clear formulation only through the lectures themselves. At various points, the lectures go beyond what would later be taken up into the *Aesthetic Theory*. This applies not only to his engagement with Georg Lukács, which became a stronger focus during the autumn and winter of 1958/59 than he considered necessary while editing the texts intended for the *Aesthetic Theory*. One should especially emphasize Adorno's reflections on the theory of aesthetic experience, which are probably even more relevant now with respect to certain developments in philosophical aesthetics since the 1970s. Another notable aspect is Adorno's intensive engagement with the classical interpretation of beauty in Plato's *Phaedrus*, as well as the great interest he showed during the autumn of 1958 in the experiments of John Cage, which he evidently found somewhat confusing but deeply challenging and would later increasingly view as a questionable invitation to regression and 'ego weakness'.

This edition is based on 246 pages of tape transcripts preserved in the Theodor W. Adorno Archive under the numbers Vo 3497–3742. Marginal notes and other editing traces on the typescript attributable to Adorno are mentioned in the notes. While editing, care was taken to preserve the character of unscripted speech as well as Adorno's stylistic, lexical and syntactical idiosyncrasies. Obvious transcription errors were corrected as far as the content dictated. In a few cases, and only when there was no nuance of meaning involved, repetitions and phrase markers such as 'and', 'so' and 'now', as well as gap-fillers such as 'actually' or 'if you like', were removed. Occasionally, for the sake of readability, run-on sentences meandering via various associations had to be separated into two or more sentences. The punctuation, which had to be inserted by the editor, served primarily to make the structure of the sentences as clear as possible despite their occasional interruptions by passing thoughts. Gaps in the text owing to changes of tape or technical problems are marked with [...] and mentioned in the notes. Occasional omissions from texts quoted by Adorno are likewise marked with [...]. Additions to the text by the editor are indicated by square brackets. The notes are intended essentially as explanations of names, works and events mentioned in the lectures, as well as concepts which can perhaps no longer be taken as understood. In cases where a complex issue is touched on only in passing, or where Adorno's meaning does not become clear, references are given to correspondences in his published writings.

The lecture transcripts are followed by attempts to reproduce, as diplomatically as possible, the handwritten notes and structural outlines preserved in the Theodor W. Adorno Archive under the numbers Vo 4235–4255. The material comprises nineteen consecutively numbered sheets as well as two structural outlines without page numbers. The sequence of pages does not always correspond to the order in which the respective topics are treated in the lectures; some things were initially passed over by Adorno and taken up later. Accordingly, some pages show several layers of editing, indicated with smaller type and a restriction to the free space in the margins or between the lines. Dates in the notes usually refer to the day of the corresponding lecture. Two points where individual words or abbreviations could not be deciphered are indicated by [?].

The 'overview' provided is intended simply as an aid to the reader, not to impute a construction, much less any systematic approach, that is not actually there.

I extend my thanks to the Hamburg Foundation for the Support of Science and Culture and to all those who provided help and advice in the course of my editorial work. I would especially like to mention Michael Schwarz, Tilman Borsche, Lydia Goehr, Andrew Bowie, Christian Thorau, Marin von Koppenfels, Nikolaus Urbanek, Martina Seeber, Andreas Haug, Gesine Palmer, Christoph Ziermann and Michael de Groot, as well as Raimund Groß and Alena Gärtner.

LECTURE 1

11 November 1958

Philosophical aesthetics, which you will learn various things about in this course of lectures – I almost said: of which I hope to give you a few 'samples' in these lectures – has a difficult time, especially in the field of philosophy. It has, in fact, fallen a little into disrepute and, compared to the development of a large number of other philosophical disciplines, has received only a desultory treatment during the last thirty years. If you pick up Fischer's recently published *Encyclopedia of Philosophy* and consult the entry for aesthetics, which, as far as I know, was contributed by Ivo Frenzel,[1] you will find some explanation of the reasons for this. For we are told there that, on the one hand, philosophical aesthetics is infinitely dependent on prior assumptions, that it depends on the respective overall philosophies underlying it, especially the epistemological ones, and that it is swept up almost without resistance in the changes affecting these tendencies; but, on the other hand, that it never entirely penetrates the work of art in its concretion and, in a sense, always falls short of the work. Philosophical aesthetics, the author states, lacks the secure foundation of other philosophical disciplines. Now, I would argue that the secure foundation of the other philosophical disciplines is a somewhat precarious matter too; if you look at how many things are mere assumptions there – with the exception of the most formal and, I would say, the most meaningless logical theorems – one will surely encounter no less of a vacuum.[2]

I think that the peculiar situation of aesthetics is due rather to the fact that there is not truly an internally continuous tradition of aesthetic thought of the kind found in the area of epistemology and logic, at least in connection with the theory of science, that aesthetics has generally followed a more or less erratic course, and that it fluctuates between attempting to develop aesthetic theories from particular philosophical positions or, conversely, simply leaving the works of art to themselves and perhaps expressing descriptively what is the case in these works, and arriving at such an aesthetics in this way. Although I cannot promise you that I will present anything resembling a fully developed aesthetics here – for the very simple reason that my own aesthetic thoughts are in flux, and by no means in a state today that would permit such a codification, but also for the simple reason that an occasion like this course of two-part lectures would, for reasons of time alone, not allow me to provide you with such a fully explicit theory – I do think that these lectures can at least give you an idea of how a theory of aesthetics, a philosophical aesthetics, is possible, even today, that it is required, and, using some models of aesthetic problems, at least to elaborate on what the nature of such an aesthetics should be. The course is ambitious, to the extent that it seeks to expound the possibility of philosophical aesthetics, which I feel is a very urgent matter today; on the other hand, it is not ambitious at all, to the extent that it does not presume truly to carry out such a philosophical aesthetics.

As far as the dependence of aesthetics on great philosophy is concerned, and hence the connection of different philosophical aesthetics on philosophical theories, I would like to explain this briefly right at the outset in order to give you an idea of the problem that exists concerning precisely the connection between philosophy and aesthetics. Kantian aesthetics, the Kantian definition of beauty – or one of the Kantian definitions of beauty, at least – is, as many of you will know, that of 'disinterested pleasure'[3] – that is to say, some objects or other give pleasure to us as subjects without the involvement of any interest on our part, in the sense of our appetitive faculty or will. For example, as soon as we have the intention to eat a tasty apple, we no longer act aesthetically but rather animally or naturally, thus violating Kant's definition of the aesthetic. This is surely clear enough. As clear as it is, however, and as little as philosophy can dispense with such a definition as this Kantian one, it necessarily stems from a series of definitions that are truly specific only to Kantian philosophy. That means it first of all contains what one could call 'transcendental subjectivism'; the nature of beauty is recognized here from the perspective of the relationship between beauty and us as subjects, while the thought of something inherently beautiful, with a beauty that is independent from our specific forms of perception and only faces them autonomously, is not envisaged at all in this definition of beauty.[4] And it is, furthermore, a definition of beauty in which a formal criterion such as enjoyment – where some forms exist which our need for sensory perception views as satisfying rather than unsatisfying – is presupposed. I think you need only a second to consider whether the things we understandably call beautiful always have this sensually pleasing element – or whether this concept of the sensually pleasing, at least, does not perhaps undergo such incredible refinement and complication that nothing is left of this originally plain idea – and to call to mind that, because of this precondition of Kantian philosophy, so plausible a definition of beauty as the one he provides here ultimately loses much of its plausibility. This means, then, that aesthetics is here indeed swept up in the entire problems of philosophy.

By contrast, I will now give you the definition of beauty found in the *Aesthetics* of Hegel,[5] which, alongside Schelling's *Philosophy of Art*[6] and the third book of *The World as Will and Representation*,[7] is one of the most significant theoretical achievements in aesthetics that followed directly on from Kant under the banner of German Idealism. Hegel defines beauty thus: beauty is 'the sensual appearance of the idea'.[8] Here a concept of the idea is presupposed in an almost Platonizing sense as substantial, as something – one could almost say – given, as something that can appear; precisely this had been ruled out by Kantian philosophy, which forbade working with some idea or other as a finite positivity.[9] And only if you take into account something that you cannot simply know, of course, namely that Hegelian philosophy criticizes exactly this Kantian doctrine, that Hegelian philosophy claims the ability to construct and adequately recognize the idea or the absolute after all – only then does something like this assertion that beauty is the sensual appearance of the idea gain meaning at all. And, naturally, such a thesis as this superb definition by Hegel becomes infinitely less plausible in an intellectual climate where many people consider it simply dogmatic or deluded to posit a concept such as the idea as effective,[10] which does not help at all to gain an understanding of the actual work of art, in which such an idea is by no means always realized directly. I would like to say now, at the very start of this course, that I feel extremely close and indebted to the Hegelian approach in one respect at least: for when the aforementioned definition by Hegel mentions this 'appearance of the idea', or 'of the absolute',[11] it is already referring back – and this is once again due to the fundamental difference between the two great philosophies, the Kantian and the Hegelian – to the fact that beauty itself is not merely a formal thing, or merely a

subjective thing, but rather something in the matter itself. There is
no reflection on me as the observer or the effect that the art has on
me.[12] On the contrary: in his *Aesthetics*, Hegel treated this entire view
of aesthetics as a doctrine of art's effect, which was still inherited
from the eighteenth century, with withering disdain – and, I would
assume, with good reason; he starts from the assumption that beauty
is something objective, something substantial, something in the matter
itself, in the idea, which necessarily – to use the term in its traditional,
Platonic meaning for a second – possesses such a form of objectivity
compared to mere subjective consciousness.

Let me begin by saying that I will attempt to align the deliberations
on aesthetics we are carrying out here with this notion of aesthetic
objectivity, the notion that not only the nature of beauty but all aesthetic categories – and beauty, I would add, is only one aesthetic
category that, in its isolation, is by no means sufficient to open up
the entire realm of the aesthetic[13] – must be disclosed in their objectivity, not as mere effects on us as subjects. On the other hand, I am
very much aware that, in this context, I cannot simply posit Hegel's
objective idealism and objective dialectics as true. What I can attempt
is possibly and at most the following: to show you with an analysis
of the categories that something resembling aesthetic objectivity does
actually exist, and thus to do something that I increasingly recognize
as the essential approach to dialectical philosophy, namely to render
fruitful all the experience, the living experience that lies sealed within
dialectical philosophy and show it to you. In other words, quite
simply put: that objectivity of the aesthetic which I assume will
occupy us here can result as objectivity only from an analysis of the
facts, problems and structures of aesthetic objects – that is to say, the
works of art. There is no other path to this objectivity than to
immerse oneself in the works themselves,[14] and I will not hesitate to
show you at least with a few models how I think such an objectively
oriented aesthetic investigation should actually be carried out; here
our central methodological tenet should be – if I may use Hegel's
words again – to devote ourselves as purely as possible to the matter[15]
without adding too much of ourselves. And the more purely we
devote ourselves to the matter, the movement of the concept,[16] the
more emphatically, I would think, our own subjective needs will be
honoured.

On the other hand, it is clear – and I know I am here in agreement
with the critics of traditional aesthetics, for example Moritz Geiger[17]
– that it has been an idle pursuit when people constantly tried to
construct aesthetics from above, as it were, simply to delineate and
define the nature of aesthetic categories – let us say the tragic, as

ventured by Johannes Volkelt[18] – once and for all through decretory conceptual definitions. Those of you who have a relationship with living art would rightly harbour the greatest distrust towards such a high-handed subsumption of art. Usually this view from above, this observation in general terms, tends already through the character of formality that is implicit in its generality – that is, owing to its conceptual formality – to apply whatever entirely formal criteria for the purpose of recognizing beauty. For example, we are told that particular mathematical proportions dominate in art, or that the work presents itself to us as something gratifying in a particular manner, perhaps in the form of a surface line (or whatever one wishes to call it), as Hildebrand termed it,[19] and thus on the basis of whatever formal rules. I think I can advance the opinion, in agreement with Hegel, that all of these categories have something extremely inadequate and something extremely superficial about them in comparison to the living work of art. But please do not misunderstand me. I do not mean to say, for example, that these aspects do not matter, and when, later on, we turn to the problem of formal and contentual aesthetics, we will have to engage thoroughly with the fact that these two categories are mutually conditioned, that the so-called forms are sedimented content, and the aesthetic content, for its part, is something that is affected to its innermost core by the form, and by no means the same as what one appropriates as raw material from the empirical world and somehow stuffs into the work of art. It is undoubtedly the case, for example, that all the problems which have current relevance in today's art under the name 'construction', and which are now asserting themselves very energetically in all artistic media, would be inconceivable without something of these formal constituents, perhaps even mathematical proportions. So I do not want to eliminate this aspect here, only to tell you that, as soon as one isolates it, and does not see it in its living relationship – that is to say, its dialectic with the concrete artistic substance – one truly finds oneself in a harmfully formal view and ultimately arrives at the schoolmasterly attitude that presumes to judge if a work of art is worth anything or not, based on whether it fulfils some such formal proportions. To be sure, there will always be something of these elements in great works of art, but only in the way these elements present themselves in the specification of the aesthetic substance with which they are respectively dealing, and not as an abstract definition that can be separated from it and applied once and for all.

I would also like to tell you that it is not my intention to say a great deal about methodological matters in this course of lectures or to reveal much about the epistemological foundations of aesthetics. I could comfortably fill these lectures with such observations, and I know that there is no lack of philosophers who, when treating a matter such as aesthetics, would feel they were violating some standard of purity by going beyond the so-called preliminary considerations. Nor do I wish to underestimate this temptation; but I do wish to resist it. If you will forgive me for such declarations at this very early point, I too am a good Hegelian in the sense that I assert one can really become a smith only by working in the smithy; that is, one does not genuinely grasp a method, does not assure oneself of a method from the inside, by first of all representing it abstractly and then, as some eloquently put it, 'applying' it to whatever objects. This is already a dubious procedure in any area of knowledge; in relation to art, it also opens itself up to the suspicion of philistinism, and I will be sure to avoid doing any such thing. For here, in aesthetics, there is indeed no method that could be presented in isolation from the matter itself. I will attempt to acquaint you with the method I am using by explaining the individual aesthetic categories, instead of placing this so-called method abstractly at the start.[20] I do not rule out the possibility that some of you might have the impression of something rhapsodic and haphazard, as I am not laying out and applying this method fundamentally, once and for all, but all I can do to counteract that is to point out that, in my little books, I attempted to defend myself against precisely this separation of method and matter and to develop this motif – which, incidentally, is already prefigured in Hegel – from the perspective of contemporary consciousness. You can find these things, if they are of value to you, in the introduction to *Against Epistemology*,[21] as well as in the study 'The Essay as Form',[22] which probably goes furthest in this direction. But in these matters, too, I am not a rigorist; nor would I claim, of course, that I am simply drawing all the categories purely from the matter itself, purely from the works of art. Rather, as long as there exists a difference between subject and object, between the perceiver and the matter, there is naturally also no absolute or perfect coincidence of matter and method of the kind I have, with a little exaggeration, just stipulated. And, mindful of a certain liberality that is appropriate here, I do wish to point out that, at least on one occasion, I have given something resembling a short description of what I envisage as an aesthetic method: in the introduction to the Kranichstein lecture 'Criteria of New Music'.[23] While this deals only with music, it should not be difficult for you to extrapolate from the reflections you will find there in such a way that they can be applied to the aesthetic problem complex as a whole.

Here, of course, we are dealing in particular with a problem that, taking into consideration the need for epistemological justification, will immediately come to mind for very many of you, namely the old problem – already formulated by Kant – of the contingency or necessity of judgements of taste[24] – in other words: the problem of so-called aesthetic relativity, whose content we must also address in this course. And I would like to point out directly that the deliberations we will carry out are equidistant from both poles without being a thing in the middle. It is thus not my intention dogmatically to dictate or posit anything like absolute aesthetic 'values'; rather, the concept of such a philosophy of values, which proceeds from rigid, immutable values that confront the subject, strikes me as irreconcilable precisely with historical experience and in particular with the experience of what takes place in a binding form in art itself. On the other hand, I am equally disinclined to submit to the bourgeois convention of the contingency of the judgement of taste[25] – that is, the claim that art is a matter of taste where one person can like this and another person can like that. The reason I refuse to submit to this view – without wishing to examine its specific merits – is that, wherever this view manifests itself, it is never truly meant seriously. It is very peculiar that the people who claim most often that there is no accounting for taste are the ones who argue most about taste; and the man who says of a modern picture or a piece of modern music that he does not understand it, who exempts himself from the binding nature of a judgement, as it were, is usually the very person who thinks that, by not understanding something, he has already said something withering about the thing he has not understood.[26] But to share an even simpler thought on the same question with you: one can see how little serious is the idea of the relativity of the judgement of taste in, firstly, the fact that people are constantly caught up in disputes over aesthetic qualities,[27] which is taken to extremes in Germany; one can say that, in Germany, the greatest philosophical controversies, for example concerning Nietzsche's critique of Christianity, came directly from questions of aesthetic quality, namely that of Wagner's *Parsifal*.[28] In addition to this, one can say that, in general, no one would seriously claim that there is no such thing as tuition in art, that art cannot be learned, to a large part at least. And the possibility that I could give a person the most basic lessons in harmony, that I could show them when a chorale is harmonized well and when badly, when a counterpoint is placed properly and when it is not, or that someone with the necessary skill can demonstrate to a young person when the perspective in a picture is rendered correctly and when incorrectly – this alone already points to a decidability of aesthetic questions that is completely irreconcilable with the claim of that relativism. Well, if someone replies: 'Yes, naturally those are all mere questions of

technique, one can learn technique, but one cannot learn art', this is
just another of those idle platitudes that one hears repeated all the
time, and which I hope no one will repeat to me once they have had
the courtesy to listen to my lecture.[29] Concerning this idle platitude
– 'that is mere technique, but the absolute worth of the work of art
cannot be decided' – we can say that the separation of so-called
artistic substance from technique is something completely dogmatic
– that is to say, there is only such a thing as binding, objectively valid
artistic substance to the extent that the work in itself is technically
consistent in its execution. We can, furthermore, say that all these
aspects I have just named – those of harmony or perspective – are
elementary, and that a mature work of art, a mature composition, a
mature picture, naturally has nothing to do with that, for it is not
only permitted to override traditional harmony or traditional perspective but virtually obliged to do so.[30] Now, that is most certainly
true; but I would say – and I think this will at least give you a first
insight into the problem of the objective quality of the work of art
– that the path leading to a serious decision about whether something
is an autonomous and substantial work free from all school rules,
that this path is one which in fact leads on with a certain continuity
from those so-called elementary problems of being correctly harmonized or correctly drawn. This means that even the highest – I am
reluctant to say the highest, I want to be careful – but almost the
highest aesthetic questions can essentially be decided according to
categories of coherence [*Stimmigkeit*], which, though quantitatively
infinitely different from those primitive things I mentioned, fundamentally belong to the same level of decidability; and I hope that in
this course of lectures I can fully develop this very aspect for you,
which truly strikes me as the key to the objectivity of aesthetic judgement. At any rate, the question of the contingency of judgements of
taste will not trouble us. Allow me to say in passing, however, that
I am not referring to the empirical contingency of judgements of taste.
This means that, for any given work of art, what Mr X and Miss Y
think of it is indeed a rather contingent matter. And if one wished to
add together or take the logarithm of its aesthetic quality from these
subjective reactions, one would certainly not arrive at any objectivity;
for the only way to arrive at objectivity is through the inner composition of the matter, the categorial fabric, if I may call it that, which
every work of art constitutes in itself.[31]

I would like to add a few words about the widespread resistance
against aesthetic theory, as it will perhaps help our communication
somewhat if you reflect a little on a few of these resistances and do
away with them, and then perhaps feel more inclined to accept the

imposition that you will, however, face: namely that engaging with art is not a Sunday enjoyment but, rather, something very serious and very obliging – or, as Hegel put it, that art is a manifestation, a progressive manifestation of truth.[32] First of all, one must consider that, in the general, pre-philosophical awareness, art is viewed as something like a domain of irrationality, a domain of the unconscious, a realm in which the criteria of logicality do not apply. Let me say right away that the logic or stringency of the work of art, to which I referred earlier with the word 'coherence', naturally has nothing to do with ordinary logic, the ordinary extensional logic of the concept, nor should it be understood as a causal-mechanical logic; rather, it is a logic *sui generis*, the logic of an internally motivated complex of meaning, and that, if one speaks of aesthetic logic at all, one must address this specific nature of aesthetic logic.[33] On the other hand, however, I do wish to say that – although today, in the world of manipulated mass culture, controlled consumption, as it is termed, the thought of an 'irrationality of art' in general is really already abused to catch customers; that is, abused in order to make people stupid and lull them – I am far from overlooking the element of truth that even this notion of the irrationality of art contains. And during the next session, when we begin to talk about the relationship between natural and artistic beauty, I hope I can bring out this element of truth for you to some degree. This means that art is indeed largely the area whose substance includes those very impulses, forms of behaviour, feelings or whatever else that otherwise fall victim to the progressive control over nature and to the rationality that progresses together with it. Art, then, cannot simply be subsumed under the concepts of reason or rationality but is, rather, this rationality itself, only in the form of its otherness, in the form – if you will – of a particular resistance against it.[34] But, having conceded this, I believe that the fact of this element of irrationality in art itself – or, if I might indulge in a little pathos for a moment, the riddle character of all art[35] – to which we will return at the end of the lecture, does not automatically rule out a theoretical, reasonable engagement with art. This is no more ruled out than, for example, the irrationality of our inner lives initially rules out our examining, as reasonable people, our inner lives – that is to say, practising psychology. I believe that you can embark on theoretical aesthetic investigations productively only if you free yourselves from the fear – a fear that is certainly not limited to art, but which could be said to crystallize through art – that the fact of becoming aware will destroy the thing of which one becomes aware, that it is ruined, that, as soon as you gain insight into a work of art, this work will cease to 'give' you anything, as people say, or to make you happy. It may then lose certain qualities it has for the naïve awareness,[36] for example those qualities of so-called sensual enjoyment of which I have already spoken, and to which countless people cling. But it will gain other qualities at the same time, and whatever qualities it has must, if a philosophical awareness is appropriate to it, then be held, indeed truly preserved, in this philosophical awareness, not simply destroyed by it. For reflection on a matter does not immediately turn the matter itself into something reflected.[37] Some time ago, I had to give a lecture in Hamburg about 'Questions of Contemporary Opera Theatre',[38] and during the discussion someone rose to speak and said with great fervour that all these reflections I was engaging in were certainly not what guided Mozart; he never thought about any of all that – and, anyway, could I compose anything as beautiful as Mozart?[39] I replied to the man that unfortunately I had been asked to give the lecture, and that, if someone had invited me to speak theoretically about art, I could not be reproached for doing so. But I think that the fervour found here is genuinely so strong that the mere theoretical reflection on the work of art is already misinterpreted from the outset, as if it somehow referred to what had been going on inside the artist themselves while producing the works. For this reason, I think it is important – as banal as it is, and although I am almost embarrassed to say so – to point out to you in these lectures that, in my deliberations on art, I never say anything about artists, about the psychology of artists, unless some context expressly demands it; that I generally do not intend to speak psychologically here, not even in very specific contexts of a historico-philosophical character, and, above all, that none of the aspects I attempt to highlight as the objectivity of the work of art are the same as the so-called intentions harboured by the artists when they created them.[40] For the work of art becomes something objective precisely by asserting itself to the composer as an independent and internally organized thing. And I am almost inclined to say: the more fully it succeeds in this, the less it is a mere document of the artist, the more it is something that speaks in its own right – the greater the value of the work will be in general.

But I would add one more thing, namely the naïveté stipulated time and again in relation to art, which – largely because of the famous controversy between Goethe and Schiller, documented in Schiller's highly significant essay 'On Naïve and Sentimental Poetry'[41] – is almost a dogma:[42] historically, this naïveté has probably always been something quite problematic if one reflects on it in absolute terms. The artists were generally far cleverer than the operetta composers imagine when they speak about Mozart. Incidentally, the man who raised the objection was not an operetta composer, as I initially suspected, but was in fact the leaseholder of an operetta theatre, so I had not been far off in my guess about him.[43] That is to say: the view that the work of art is a pure expression of human naïveté is one that directly augments the interests of commerce or the administered world, or of the world dominated by mercantile interests.

But whatever the case may be – perhaps I can still say something to justify an examination of such theoretical questions as the one we intend here: in the current artistic situation, where literally all the conditions for artistic material have become problematic and there are no longer any substantial givens in art, where every artist instead finds themselves *vis-à-vis de rien*, one could say, the kinds of things one would describe as basic research in a field such as physics are urgently needed in the realm of art too. And I think it is better if such a theoretical consideration of art is carried out by people who imagine they know something about art and theory than by artists alone, for example, who do not, in fact, have the conceptual apparatus entirely at their disposal and consequently very often merely set up some apologetic support structures for their own practice, often drawing on rationalist theories that fall far short of what one actually finds in the works of art.

LECTURE 2

13 November 1958

To facilitate your access to theoretical aesthetics, I promised to say a few words about some of the forms of resistance against this discipline whose existence I presuppose as widespread; here I proceed from the conviction, hardly unknown in the field of psychology, that very often such resistance is overcome when one reflects on it oneself – that is to say, through a certain form of self-reflection. After the resistance I addressed last time, namely that against a theoretical consideration of art as a form of nature reserve for irrationality, I would like to discuss a second kind. But perhaps I can first add that you should not, of course, take the theoretical consideration of art or with aesthetic questions directly as a sort of instruction for how to act towards works of art, or as an immediate help in understanding difficult works. If these lectures are at all successful, I hope they will contribute something to this by removing certain blinkers and shaking up certain conventions, but, at the same time, you should not simply take that as a formula for how to view works of art. Although the question of one's individual response to the work is ultimately determined by the objectivity of the matter itself, it is certainly something different from the treatment of this objectivity, which is also clarified by a fact that I will still be addressing today in a different context: that some of the greatest theoretical achievements in aesthetics come from people who were quite distant from an immediate experience of art. So theoretical reflection on art and the direct understanding or perception of art are not the same thing, and theoretical reflection can perhaps contribute something to this living relationship, but must not be misunderstood, as some of you are perhaps doing because you know that I have a very close connection to certain elements of modern art – as if one were receiving a kind of instruction manual for difficult modern music or difficult modern literature here – otherwise you will be disappointed.

The second prejudice faced by the theoretical consideration of art – that is, theoretical aesthetics – is what one could perhaps call the 'individualistic' one, and it finds its starkest expression in the belief that art is something which depends substantially on both the talent of the one who produces it and that of the one who approaches it with some form of understanding. And if art is linked to this aspect that is contingent, and evidently beyond theoretical definition – individual talent – it seems as if, in the face of this individuation, any attempt to pursue more general reflections on art is something arbitrary. In response, I would say that, first of all, the deliberations on objective questions in the works of art and aesthetics we are carrying out address the matter, not the relationship of individual persons to this matter.[1] The tendencies of the observation found here are simply of an objective-aesthetic, not a psychological kind, otherwise I would be giving a lecture on the psychology of art, not a lecture on aesthetics. If I cannot rigidly separate the two categories, there are good reasons for this, and I dare say you will soon realize why that is the case. At any rate: the emphasis of what I am doing here – let me say it in advance – is, in contrast to the bulk of aesthetics, especially from the late nineteenth century, on observing the problems of aesthetic objects, not on reducing aesthetic objects to some way of viewing them. This is precisely what I feel the slackening of the theoretical aesthetic awareness I mentioned to you last time consists of: that, after Hegel and with the decline of Hegelian philosophy, theoretical speculation essentially no longer dares address the matter itself in this way, but has always attempted to reduce it to psychological forms of reaction. But as every work of art is in itself a strange union of objective and subjective elements – and this is the central topic for us to discuss – then that fact automatically rules out such a psychological reduction, and hence a reduction to mere talent.[2]

But that will probably be of little help to those of you who are coming here with this prejudice – and perhaps those who, for whatever reasons, do not consider yourselves specifically aesthetically talented. So perhaps you will allow me to say, at this point, at least a few words about a psychological problem, as it genuinely relates to the basic behaviour of humans towards art, and one can, after all, speak productively about the objective aesthetic questions only if there is some kind of living relationship between these individual humans and the concrete work of art. For it seems to me that the notion of talent is, in a sense, greatly overestimated in art. I do not mean to reason away this concept, and anyone who, as I do, has the opportunity to attend many music festivals – which today should instead be called modern music exhibitions – will become aware of differences in talent in an often very drastic manner. But what I mean to say is that one should not accept this notion of talent as something static, something immutable that has fallen from heaven, as it were, in the way that musicality is very often – and wrongly, in my view – viewed in analogy to mathematics as a form of definite natural talent. The talent for artistic matters is one part of the overall psychological constitution of humans, not some kind of specialist ability that has fallen to them. I think that, while one can have a good ear or a good eye, this alone is not at all decisive for one's artistic talent. In my life, I have known excellent, very important musicians who did not have an especially good ear, and I have known musicians with a legendary ear who could accurately sing sixth-tones, yet who struck me as essentially inartistic people. But genuine artistic talent is, in the end, a character of the person as a whole, one that is substantially defined by – if I may put it thus – a negative ability, namely the ability to emancipate oneself from the immediacy of existence, from entanglement in the immediate purposes and velleities[3] of life and – as it was expressed during the time of German Idealism in a single word that one barely dares utter today, but which still has some merit – to elevate oneself, in the same sense in which Plato referred to enthusiasm as the central precondition for philosophy.[4]

The one mode of behaviour absolutely ruled out by the relationship with art is the concretist approach, this being what I would call a damaged confinement to that which is and which places practical demands on us, and which exerts such dominance and provokes such feelings of guilt that, in a sense, one forbids oneself to partake of the happiness that is found where one does something that cannot claim any such purpose in the business of the individual's and society's self-preservation. It is not, however, as if a mere reflection on this condition for artistic talent were sufficient to cure people who feel a lack thereof. But perhaps this is enough to make them investigate the factors that make artistic experience foreign to them in the first place, and thus – perhaps in a form of self-reflection – to lead them to the deeper cause of that lack. Generally speaking, it tends – if I could just say this much of a psychological nature – to lie in the fact that they are people who (usually in earliest childhood) somehow had the principle of reality – that is, the practical activity of self-preservation – drummed into them by some strong authority, usually the father, in such a way that they have a sort of fear of anything which goes beyond that; they forbid themselves to venture there. And this fear is then often compensated for and rationalized by a certain kind of false arrogance towards what they now call tomfoolery and nonsense, and supposedly means nothing to them – an arrogance that has more than a whiff of sour grapes about it. I have very often ascertained that people who were extremely unmusical – incapable of learning to read music, for example, or simply repeating a sung melody correctly – that these were people who had somehow had it truly driven out of them by a strict father in early childhood. On the other hand, I have often observed how certain changes in a person's mode of existence can suddenly change their receptiveness to art. I know cases of people who, after growing up in a very musical but simultaneously authoritarian milieu, initially considered themselves unmusical – or were considered thus by their surroundings – and who then suddenly discovered their musicality, one could say. And these things in general are not so rigid or static. So that is what I mean when I warn you not to overestimate the question of so-called talent with regard to art. This overestimation also contains an ideological element: it is precisely a society which insists so strongly on that reality principle which so easily drives out of people the ability to react to artistic matters; it is precisely that society which needs an ideology of the absolutely natural, the irrational, which is entirely independent from the will and consciousness, as a form of compensation wherever it does not directly pursue its aims. I am almost inclined to say: the fact that musicality is a grace of God that falls from heaven and in which the individual has no part of their own is just as much part of the household of bourgeois conventions [5] as the notion that Papa goes to his office at the right time every morning and that one does not incur debts. These are all ideas that come from the luxury edition of Schiller's *Collected Writings*,[6] so to speak, and which – now that the education from which they once originated has long since fallen apart – still spook people and darken their minds, and which contribute to making it difficult or even impossible for people to relate to artistic matters in particular. I am pointing this out now not so much with reference to the psychological problem from which I began as to prepare you for something you will admittedly learn very soon in these lectures, namely that this very notion of art as purely sensual and thus independent from thoughts, effort and tension in general, which most of you are more or less likely to entertain – that this notion is untenable, and that the conception of a purely sensual art proves highly problematic in itself; it is an indispensable experience, incidentally, especially for understanding the authentically advanced contemporary tendencies in art.

You might [now] ask: after all that, who is supposed to occupy themselves with the theory of art if talent is not so important and if, on the other hand, what I conceded right at the start is true, namely that the weighty aesthetic tomes one finds in the libraries of philosophy departments contain an infinite amount of inartistic, even philistine, scribble that is especially likely to deter an artistically receptive person from dealing with so-called philosophical aesthetics? I think I must give you a slightly peculiar response here, namely this: here the truth evidently lies in the extremes that touch. I have the impression that there are two sources of aesthetic insight, as it were – or perhaps I should say two poles, where the spark sometimes leaps from the one to the other. One of these poles is the truly coherent theoretical idea, which often proves most fruitful precisely when it stays relatively far away from the specific aesthetic objects. This is the case in the great systems of aesthetics, especially in the *Critique of the Power of Judgement* and the *Aesthetics* of Hegel, but also in the aesthetic part of *The World as Will and Representation*. These three philosophers were surely not what one would term artistic people in a strict sense. They were surely not what one calls 'refined', but the power of their experience, their intellectual experience, was so profound that it also pulled other areas into itself, as it were, whose content was not yet so clear to them.[7] In fact, the most staggering thing about Kantian philosophy – if one is truly able to read it as expression, not merely as epistemology – is how, with Kant in particular, the power of the idea itself always extends, almost independently of the contingent nature of his person and even his specific experience, to all sorts of things which, if you will, he did not actually 'know' in that sense – in other words, how far Kant's knowledge actually extended beyond his own knowledge. That, one could say, is virtually the proof of Kant's genius, and at times it seems to me that things are not so different with Hegel, whereas in the case of Schopenhauer, strangely enough, whose entire perspective on life was probably more that of someone who enjoys art, this power of specific insight into aesthetic problems does not strike me as being developed in the same way.

On the other hand – at the other pole – one finds the people who are themselves involved in specific artistic work, who have specific experience of the material and may perhaps reflect upon it to themselves. There are people in modernity for whom this process of reflection goes so far that it can no longer really be distinguished from the process of artistic production. As many of you will have guessed, I am thinking especially of Paul Valéry.[8] So undoubtedly an engagement with art from within[9] – which always means an engagement with art according to its technological categories, that is to say the categories of its immanent production – is an equally legitimate source of artistic insight, albeit with the obstacle that it is relatively rare for artists with these experiences also to have the conceptual tools to make them theoretically fruitful; yet, at the same time, this ability is not quite as rare as it might seem. So I would think that a fruitful relationship with theoretical aesthetics actually consists in the communication between these two approaches – those of the 'highest height', as Goethe put it,[10] and the 'closest nearness'.[11]

But I would warn you with the utmost urgency of what can be termed the sphere of 'refinement', the sphere of the aesthetic aficionado, the sphere of the so-called sensitive man who collects Chinese engravings and is terribly fond of chamber music as long as it is not too serious. The deterrent example of this kind of middle-level 'refinement', which seals itself off from genuine, primary aesthetic experiences precisely because it refers from the outset only to what has already been transmitted to him through his education, is the œuvre of Wilhelm Dilthey,[12] at least where it relates to aesthetic matters. I do not intend to deal with it any further, only to encourage you in this context to have a look at *Poetry and Experience*, an enormously popular work among the teachers of the previous generation in particular, in which, among other things, he states in all seriousness that Hölderlin's language wraps itself in a purple cloak with deep folds, and more of the like.[13] We will simply avoid these things entirely and actually keep to those extremes which, to make them touch, we will try to bend towards each other.

I wish to say only one more thing before I get directly into the matter: perhaps you have all at some point had an experience I will mention here, because it sums up the theme underlying these lectures rather well, namely the experience – I will put it in stark and correspondingly heightened terms, as is my custom – that, in a certain sense, one cannot understand works of art at all. What I mean is this: either one is inside a work of art and aligned with it in a living sense, in which case the question of understanding the work or of the meaning of the work does not really arise;[14] or, on the other hand, through reflection or development – possibly even through something like disgust or an excess of artistic experience – one is now outside the sphere of influence of art and casts one's gaze on the work; and then – this is what I have experienced and still experience very often, and I would not be surprised if many of you had also encountered it at some point – then one suddenly asks oneself abruptly: so what's it all about, what is all this? The moment one is no longer inside it, where one is no longer aligned with it, art begins to withdraw in a certain sense, to close up,[15] and assumes what I earlier called its riddle character and will explicate in far greater detail later on.

If there is a justification for the philosophy of art – and I do not, after all, mean to attempt a philosophy of art with you without at least providing a more serious justification than the claim that aesthetics should form a part of the so-called philosophical sciences – then the justification for the philosophy of art lies solely in the fact that it alone can [cope with the experience] when one has felt that rupture in oneself, when one steps out of the work and it suddenly becomes foreign and mute, and one asks oneself: what's it all about, what's the point of it, what does it say?[16] This state, which surely forms a substantial part of every person's aesthetic experience, assuming they have not dulled their awareness of it through faith in education, this state of experience can probably be overcome only through a theoretical reflection on art. Now, I cannot explain that reflection to you immediately, in a word, like a shot from a pistol: 'Yes, that is the meaning of art; that is art; now I can hold it in my hands once and for all; now I know what one of those works of art is.' That would be presumptuous, and it would be fundamentally wrong to demand that theory provide such a thing. But through its totality, through the context in which it embeds its categories, it can do away with this foreignness and effect that reconciliation between the work of art and the one who experiences it which has become problematic at some point in any living relationship with art – and I would say especially in any authentic one.[17] It is only the art aficionados who find art unproblematic on all levels, which is why they have no need to reflect on art. But if this riddle character of which I will speak at length is truly inherent in art, then – and I would like to place this thought emphatically at the start of these lectures – the works of art themselves require commentary and critique for the sake of their own development and their own life. And while commentary and critique of art are elements of its own life, they cannot be halted, they push forwards, they cannot be stopped on the way towards a theory of art, which is where they must end.[18]

To be quite thorough, I would like to point out that the term 'aesthetics' is not necessarily limited to art. It comes from the Greek αἰσθάνομαι [aisthánomai], meaning 'perceive', and thus encompasses the entire realm of sensory experience; and Kant, as many of you know, and a number of German Enlightenment writers,[19] applied it generally to all forms of scientific conditions of sensuality – that is to say, the conditions for sensory perception. In more recent times, too, this use of the word 'aesthetics' is not infrequent; but I doubt that you have come to these lectures expecting me to speak about what Kant calls 'transcendental aesthetics',[20] which you will learn enough about in the epistemological courses and seminars. Rather, I will keep to the concept of aesthetics that is captured to some extent by phrases such as the 'doctrine of beauty' or the 'doctrine of art', though I should say in advance that none of these encapsulates all the things that aesthetics means. For the concept of aesthetics – like any philosophical reflection that views its object as living, not in a dogmatically hardened form – eludes such abstract definition; rather, aesthetics is then the content underlying the definitions that are brought together under this name. This correlation is really what constitutes the name, not some individual verbal definition[21] that one need only give for a hand to be raised and say that there is also something else that is aesthetics, but which does not fall under this definition. Once you have eliminated that, then all that remains of the conventional definition of the word 'aesthetics' in the most general sense is that, in aesthetics, one deals with the sensually perceptible – as one substantial element, at least – and when I get to my critique of the absolute validity of the reduction of the aesthetic to the sensually perceptible, this critique is only meaningful, of course, if one first concedes that in art, or in the realm of the aesthetic in a more general sense, one is not dealing with knowledge in the literal sense,[22] as used in the sciences, nor is it a practical behaviour, as I ruled out in my brief psychological excursus. For now, this sparse definition of the concept is all we hold in our hands.

If we continue looking at what the history of this discipline has produced in the way of important divisions, then the most extensive one we find is the difference between natural beauty and artistic beauty. The very strange thing here, which has perhaps not yet been recognized in its full scope, is that the relationship between these two disciplines has shifted in a peculiar fashion since the eighteenth century.[23] Kant still treated natural beauty and artistic beauty as having the same level of dignity. And, in Kant, one can even make the astounding observation that some of the deepest aesthetic definitions – indeed, that precisely those of his aesthetic definitions that point the furthest beyond his own time, and of which I will expound a few – are arrived at not in the aesthetics of artistic beauty but, rather, in the realm of natural beauty. This means that the second part of the 'Critique of Aesthetic Judgement', the 'Analytic of the Sublime', going by his own words, refers purely to natural beauty and not to artistic beauty, and thus, for Kant, only nature, not art, can be sublime.[24] This has now been reversed in a most peculiar fashion; and this reversal probably found its first conclusive manifestation in Hegel's philosophy.[25] The reason for this is the progressive spiritualization of the awareness of art as such, which began with the overall European movement of Romanticism, in which art increasingly moved away from the aggregate of mere sensual enjoyment to become a carrier of spiritual meanings or, to put it in the words of that philosophy, was viewed as the expression of an idea. At the same time, the formal aspect, which is connected to the idea of mere sensual pleasure or appreciation, necessarily receded. It is no coincidence that the transition from an aesthetics dominated by the concept of natural beauty to a theory of artistic beauty coincided with a critique of formal aesthetics, of the formal rules of the enjoyable, in favour of a content-based aesthetics, although – as I will say in a moment – even in these philosophies, the notion of what constitutes content in art is generally presented only in a rather raw and inadequate form.[26] And I would like to note right here that one of the themes we must examine is to reach a more thorough assessment of the contentual aspect, which stands in opposition to mere formal aesthetics, than is the case in the traditional systems.[27]

In order to give you a taste of this climate of turning away from natural beauty in aesthetics, I would like to read you a few passages by Hegel that I consider quite characteristic, and which I can perhaps follow with a few very brief thoughts. So, in the first, general part of his *Aesthetics*, Hegel writes: 'Now as the physically objective Idea, life in nature is *beautiful* because truth, the Idea in its earliest natural form as life, is immediately present there in individual and adequate actuality.'[28] Naturally this presupposes, as I already told you in the last session, that, for Hegel, everything is essentially idea, and that therefore – as the idea and beauty coincide for him – nature in its immediacy also has a piece, an aspect, of idea to it and, in so far as it has this, is beautiful. But Hegel immediately qualifies this. Here, following on from a discussion at the Hegel conference,[29] allow me to say that it would constitute a complete misunderstanding of Hegel to view him as uncritical, as a thinker for whom everything is grey in grey, for whom the mill of thesis, antithesis and synthesis goes clickety-clack; rather, the true substance of this motion in Hegelian philosophy is precisely, to an eminent degree, critique. If you really look at Hegel seriously, you will find that these famous movements of the concept that one finds there are, in essence, always a critique of something untrue, limited, false, dead or decayed. Consider the following example: 'Yet, because of this purely sensuous immediacy, the living beauty of nature is produced neither *for* [itself]' – that is, without any knowledge of its beauty – 'nor *out of* itself as beautiful and for the sake of a beautiful appearance.'[30] That means it is not there for the sake of its beauty, but it is simply there, and the beauty

it possesses is one that has not passed through this aspect of subjective spirit, nor thus through the aspect of spiritualization. – 'The
beauty of nature is only beautiful for another, i.e. for *us*, for the mind
which apprehends beauty.'[31] And for Hegel, whose aesthetics is substantially objective in its orientation, and who is thus concerned with
defining the aspects of beauty in itself, not simply to the extent of
their effects on the receptive consciousness, this definition of natural
beauty in keeping with Kant's view, namely that beauty here is only
beauty for the perceiving consciousness, is at once a very profound
and invasive critique of this concept of natural beauty. Or he says:
'The form of natural beauty, as an abstract form, is on the one hand
determinate and therefore restricted; on the other hand it contains a
unity and an abstract relation to itself. [...] This sort of form is what
is called regularity and symmetry, then conformity to law, and finally
harmony.'[32] So here, in Hegel, you find an expression of the idea I
hinted at earlier, namely that the belief in natural beauty and the
accentuation of natural beauty as opposed to artistic beauty is substantially connected with an emphasis on the merely formal – mathematical, if you will – conditions of art as opposed to their living
spiritual content. The force of Hegel's statement is that he therefore
considers natural beauty something subaltern, shall we say, and I am
fully aware that Hegel's manner here, this arrogance of the spirit
towards that which is not spirit, itself betrays an aspect of the narrowness of this philosophy; and I will draw the necessary conclusions
from this and attempt to move a little beyond this narrowness. Or
he says: 'The beauty of regularity is a beauty of abstract understanding'[33] – likewise consigning sensitivity to natural beauty, with a somewhat haughty gesture, to the rationalism of the eighteenth century,
when Baumgarten famously attempted to augment the philosophy of
Leibniz and Wolff in the spirit of such an aesthetics – such an *aesthetica formalis*.[34] The 'essential deficiency' of natural beauty – namely
that it possesses no 'ideal subjectivity' – 'leads us to the necessity of
the Ideal, which is not to be found in nature, and in comparison with
it the beauty of nature appears as subordinate.'[35] So here you literally
have the formulation of the subaltern that I just imputed. Or he says:
'Thus it is from the immediate deficiencies of reality' – and it is very
characteristic of Hegel that he does not stand still in such a critique
but, rather, uses the insufficiency, the inadequacy of natural beauty
to derive something like the necessity of art from it[36] –

> that the necessity of the beauty of art is derived. The task of art must
> therefore be firmly established in art's having a calling to display the
> appearance of life, and especially of spiritual animation (in its freedom,

externally too) and to make the external correspond with its Concept. Only so is the truth lifted out of its temporal setting, out of its straying away into a series of finites. At the same time, it has won an external appearance where the poverty of nature and prose no longer peeps through; it has won an existence worthy of the truth, an existence which for its part stands there in free independence since it has its vocation in itself, and does not find it inserted there by something else.[37]

So natural beauty, because of this element of chance, this aspect of not itself being pervaded by spirit through and through, is something – we would call it pre-aesthetic, he calls it 'prosaic' – for which the concept of beauty is essentially deficient, and this can be overcome only if the external itself, through art, is turned into the exterior of an interior. That is roughly what Hegel has in mind.

Now, I do not intend to revoke this development which Hegel's theory set off, nor do I wish to present you here with a theory of natural beauty – primarily for the simple reason that I myself have no such theory,[38] and because I have my doubts about whether it is possible, or whether all theoretical definitions of natural beauty, if one occupies oneself with them, would not lead inevitably back to that homeliness which the nineteenth century had in mind. On the other hand, I cannot ignore the fact that the investigation of the problem of natural beauty has actually been suppressed in a peculiar fashion and, one could say, reserved for the holiday weeks, meaning that there is something unfinished here[39] which theory has not properly addressed, and whose lack can in turn affect genuine theoretical aesthetics. The reason for that inadequate and questionable aspect presumably lies in a concept that stems from Kant and Schiller but was adopted by Hegel, namely the 'dignity' that is native only to humans, and which gives them a superior status in relation to everything else, which is accordingly reduced to mere material.[40] But if – as I consider inevitable in the light of current experience – one no longer feels capable of going along with this absolute supremacy of humans, this philosophical anthropocentrism, then surely one must at least consider the problem of natural beauty in its connection to artistic beauty and, even if one does not believe an explicit theory of natural beauty is possible, not stop at Hegel's verdict on natural beauty as subordinate, but assess the relationship between nature and beauty, which is far more dialectical than Hegel would have it, and which will simultaneously provide the first categories for a definition of what art itself actually is.

LECTURE 3

18 November 1958

Last time I spoke to you about the distrust that was increasingly shown towards the reflection on so-called natural beauty. And I think one needs to imagine only for a second how ridiculous it would be nowadays to reflect philosophically on a specific object of natural beauty, and say why a flowering apple tree is beautiful, to realize that this natural beauty has truly gone through the same thing that happens to very many concepts in philosophy: namely that their fate is sealed not so much by a rebuttal as by a strange antiquation; that they become unusable because the advancing historical consciousness has deprived them of their substance, as it were.[1] If you recall the arguments against basing theoretical aesthetics on natural beauty, or the arguments Hegel uses to term the concept of natural beauty per se 'subordinate', you will not be able to shake off the feeling that a motif is at work here which is familiar to those who are acquainted with Hegel's philosophy: the motif that the elusive, that which has not taken on a fixed form, which has not been objectified in a certain sense in order to be reconciled with the living subject again after passing through its objectification – that, I mean to say, anything elusive or ephemeral means little to this philosophy.[2] I do not intend to address the problems that arise at this point; that is a matter for a lecture on Hegel or dialectics, not for this session.[3] I will only say that, on the one hand, of course, this holds great power against the sentimentalism of a mere romantic mood, but that, on the other hand, this fundamental stance against – one could almost say – the power-less in Hegel's philosophy also sees the growth of that tendency which

ultimately drew this philosophy as a whole too much onto the side
of prevailing conditions. But with regard to art, or the question of
beauty in general, it is undoubtedly the case that this very aspect of
the elusive, the not-quite-graspable,[4] that which cannot be pinned
down, is its vital principle.[5] And perhaps it is good if I already say
now that – however great the progress made by Hegel beyond the
aesthetic formalism of the eighteenth century in aesthetics through
the subject–object dialectic and the incorporation of contentual definitions – this progress, even in his own work, comes at the price of
an aspect one could almost call inartistic, a surplus of materiality
which sometimes gives rise to the suspicion that, for all its greatness,
this philosophy of art has not, in fact, fully accessed the work of art
itself, which consists precisely in this ephemeral element. I think that
Hegel took the elusiveness of natural beauty – the fact that, in a sense,
natural beauty eludes definition by the spirit far more than the work
of art, which, as something already defined by spirit, is so much more
amenable to such definition by the spirit – took this elusiveness, this
impossibility of being pinned down, which belongs to the very essence
of beauty, and held it against natural beauty, whereas this is precisely
the point from which a reflection on the problem of natural beauty
should begin.[6]

The fact that natural beauty is so difficult to capture conceptually,
and that statements about it take on a formalistic or philistine character, strikes me far more as pointing to the unsolved problem that
thought has not yet mastered natural beauty than as suggesting we
should content ourselves with Hegel's verdict, which states that,
because we do not have any fixed, tangible form in our hands, the
whole matter of natural beauty should be considered subordinate.
But that, I believe, is of considerable moment for the constitution of
aesthetics as such, for without this element, which for Hegel makes
natural beauty something pre-aesthetic in the philosophical sense, one
cannot properly conceive of the work of art itself. I do not wish to
dwell on pointing out to you that someone who is unable to perceive
natural beauty – that is, who is not capable, already in the experience
of nature, of that peculiar separation from objects of action from
practical objects that constitutes the aesthetic – that such a person is
probably not genuinely capable of artistic experience either. I would
rather tell you that natural beauty has a very specific model character
for artistic beauty, and that it is therefore unacceptable to exclude all
thoughts of natural beauty from an examination of beauty, as the
whole of recent philosophy has done, because the conception of
artistic beauty itself, in its most intrinsic meaning, is entwined with
natural beauty and – as I hope to show you – with nature itself.[7]

Let me demonstrate this using two examples. Those of you who took part in the seminar on the sociology of art heard the presentation on Benjamin,[8] which discussed Benjamin's concept of 'aura' as the special character of the here and now, the unique, that forms around a work of art, and which [Benjamin] ties to the 'cult value' of the work of art, and which he assumes was certainly decisive for the traditional work of art. I cannot believe it a coincidence that this concept of aura, which Benjamin introduced in his study on 'The Work of Art in the Age of its Technical Reproducibility',[9] is explained using not a work of art but something in nature – that is to say, the phenomenon in works of art that he means to describe here is actually a phenomenon that is revealed in the observation of landscapes.[10] Let me read you the lines that refer to the aura – a passage that also points to natural beauty, without pursuing it very far:

> Perhaps we should illustrate the term 'aura' as proposed above for historical objects by the concept of an 'aura' of natural objects. The latter we define as a unique manifestation of a remoteness, however close it may be. Lying back on a summer's afternoon, gazing at a mountain range on the horizon or watching a branch as it casts its shadow over our reclining limbs, we speak of breathing in the aura of those mountains or that branch.[11]

This concept of aura, which is thus very close to what you all know as the 'atmosphere' of a work of art, or what was later, borrowing Heidegger's terminology, termed its 'attunement' [*Gestimmtheit*], this aura is hence itself a natural phenomenon, namely the special character of distance even in what is closest. This character of distance even in what is closest is undoubtedly connected to the special element of the transient, the ephemeral, the impossible-to-pin-down and the not-quite-graspable, which forms a substantial part of both the work of art and our experience of nature. And in these two aspects, the normally so opposing categories of nature as an object of our perception – I am not speaking of nature as an object of the natural sciences – and the idea of artistic perception seem to be in agreement.[12]
Let me add a second thing: I think that what is also central for accessing a work of art, for experiencing a work of art as a work of art in the first place, is that one is met with an experience of – how should I put it? – 'meaning' as something objective. I understand a work of art at the moment when – I almost followed on from a different Benjaminian expression and said that a work of art lifts up its eyes[13] – I understand what it is itself saying as something it says to me, not as something I am projecting onto it, something that has

come only from me. One could almost say that this is the threshold
between the pre-artistic experience of works of art, like the housewife
who reads a novel so that she can identify with the figures in it – I
once knew a monster who said she could not read Proust because
there were no figures in Proust with whom she could identify, where-
upon one of her people said very aptly that this was not the idea – I
would say that this is precisely the threshold on which the artistic
experience of a work of art sets itself apart from the pre-artistic or
merely material experience, when one becomes aware of that quality
in the work that inheres in it as an objectivity, as something spiritually objective that does not extend beyond the subject viewing the
work.[14] But the primal phenomenon of this – the source from which
we can gain this possibility of aesthetic experience at all, and a form
of behaviour that probably remains fixed for each work of art – is
likewise found in the relationship with nature.[15] I think only someone
who understood – and I would almost think: in their childhood – that
when one says, 'It is a melancholy evening', it is a mood not of the
observer but rather of the evening itself, admittedly in a constellation
with the observer, that is melancholy[16] – that someone who has never
had this decisive experience, this 'freedom to the object',[17] one could
say, this experience of self-forgetfulness before the object, has no idea
what a work of art is. And the barbaric forms of behaviour towards
art that we see so often today are substantially due to the fact that
the matter-of-fact attitude, the *terre-à-terre* attitude produced by the
positivist spirit as a whole, also extends to the works of art,[18] such
that they are perceived either as materials or as psychological projec-
tions of the observer – but no longer in the way that the evening can
be experienced as an inherently melancholy one.

Let me add that this same objectivity of spiritual content, that
which is not limited to the subjective reflex, strikes me as providing
the deepest reason why concepts such as 'mood', which come from
Jugendstil or a form of impressionism already somewhat corrupted
by journalism, seem so thoroughly questionable and suspicious in
their current philosophically rehashed form too – of which, in aesthetics, Kommerell[19] has not been innocent – because they dissolve
into a merely subjective definition that very thing whose perception
within the matter itself constitutes the specifically aesthetic in the first
place. If what I have tried to communicate to you here is the case,
then one could conclude from this, or perhaps go further to the idea
that I will expound to you in greater detail, that art, which stands in
a certain opposition to all nature because it is man-made and already
a spiritual manifestation of existence, is at once mediated by nature
in a certain sense and vindicates suppressed nature, meaning that the

theory of artistic beauty, precisely because of this dialectical relation-ship with nature, is actually inseparable from a theory of natural beauty.[20]

First let me try to show you a little more wherein this mediation, this relationship between natural and artistic beauty, actually con-sists. The unthinking view, as you all know, simply treats the natural world and the historical world as opposites,[21] and even the passage by Benjamin which I read to you earlier does not break with this habit.[22] I will pass over the question of how far this is true, and how far the separation of nature and history is itself a context of delusion that should be resolved in both directions.[23] This too would belong in a lecture on dialectical logic or dialectics, not a specifically aesthetic one. But I do think that one can use so-called natural beauty itself to show how it is mediated by history and thus reveal propaedeutically a certain affinity for artistic beauty; here I do not intend to occupy myself with ambivalent, allegorical phenomena such as the ruin, which one could almost call a historical thing that acquires its histori-cal expression by creating the impression that it is part of nature.[24] For now I really mean only that, in the realm of aesthetic experience, there is not as radical a difference as is thought between φύσει [phýsei] and θέσει [thései], that which is given by nature and that which is made by humans.[25] It is a fact that has perhaps been observed on occasion, but as far as I know has not been taken as seriously as should be the case for aesthetic theory, that those areas of nature which are central to our experience of natural beauty, for example high mountain ranges and the sea, really took on that meaning only through late historical experiences. So the beauty of nature as some-thing untamed and infinite came about only in a world where the social fabric had spread so far that the contrast to this, namely that which had not been completely taken, not completely dominated and domesticated, was properly perceived in its beauty for the first time;[26] and, similarly, it was only the discovery of the principle of subjectivity as something infinite that allowed humans to feel a kinship with the same infinite quality in nature, where it had previously been perceived only as frightening and uncanny. Kant's aesthetics of the sublime, which I shall address later, could be described as standing on the threshold – that is, both the fear and terror of nature in all its pathos are still palpable but, simultaneously, associated with that feeling of the sublime on which the experience of the beauty in these aspects is based.

A statement like Verlaine's that 'The sea is more beautiful than any cathedral'[27] is an extraordinarily late one. That is, only in a world where the cathedrals have ceased to be what they once were and

become a piece of education, something to be found in a museum –
only in that moment does the sea take on a form of beauty that it
undoubtedly did not possess in the High Middle Ages, when the
cathedrals of the Île de France were built; just as perceiving the beauty
of the sea or the air, for example, would probably be inconceivable
without the simultaneous aesthetic experience of Impressionism,
which made it at all possible to objectify artistically the gradations
found in the sea, on the surface of the water or in the atmosphere,
meaning that our experience of natural objects is itself really a reflex
of our aesthetic experience. Or, rather, both – let me put it more
precisely – point back to a third element, namely the apperception of
the concrete world, which has its own historical status.[28] And you
could all see how next to the devastation of the bombed-out cities,
anything resembling order – a well-arranged garden, a house that was
still standing, a hundred things that seemed anything but beautiful
before in the intact bourgeois world – suddenly took on a certain
quality of beauty that consisted only in their status alongside this
destruction. And one can certainly assume that, as long as nature was
more powerful than humans, as long as humanity was locked in a
blind struggle with nature in which it did not have freedom to the
object, as I called it with reference to Hegel, in relation to nature, it
could not really perceive natural beauty at all; rather, the perception
of natural beauty as something innocent, not disfigured by humans,
became possible only once people no longer needed to fear nature,
once nature became weaker than humans and they had to make a
kind of amends. So the thing which seems to have come first in our
relationship with beauty – namely that relationship with nature – is
actually something late, and presupposes a distancing process in
which the entire historical confrontation between humans and nature
is contained as a constitutive element. In this sense, it is no coincidence that the theory of natural beauty draws significantly on theories
from the artistic domain.[29]

Here I would like to point you – especially in this context of the
confrontation between humans and nature, which is really the key to
that peculiar dual character in the relationship between art and
nature – to a splendid passage from Kant's *Critique of the Power of
Judgement*, in the chapter on the 'dynamically sublime', in which,
unlike the aestheticians who came after him, he ascribes the category
of the sublime purely to natural beauty. Here you will see how the
idea of infinity, the idea of the confrontation with nature, and the
idea of subjectivity are intertwined in a remarkable fashion. Beyond
this, you will also notice – and I think this is what makes this splendid
passage in Kant so extraordinary – that, in the name of natural

beauty, Kant points to aspects that in fact became decisive for the idea of artistic beauty in subjective – or, as Hegel says, romantic[30] – art, which largely developed after Kant. This means that the quality he ascribes here to the sea or the mountains is the same thing that entered art itself as the new[31] – for example in Beethoven's music – which Kant could obviously not have known about:

> Bold, overhanging, as it were threatening cliffs, thunder clouds towering up into the heavens, bringing with them flashes of lightning and crashes of thunder, volcanoes with their all destroying violence, hurricanes with the devastation they leave behind, the boundless ocean set into a rage, a lofty waterfall on a mighty river etc., make our capacity to resist into an insignificant trifle in comparison with their power.[32]

One could say that this is the phase in which nature is so much stronger that a feeling of beauty does not arise. But now, when the viewer pauses for thought, we see the strange dialectic to which Kant refers: 'But the sight of them only becomes all the more attractive' – that is, it is now beautiful – 'the more fearful it is, as long as we find ourselves in safety; and we gladly call these objects sublime because they elevate the strength of our soul above its usual level, and allow us to discover within ourselves a capacity for resistance of quite another kind, which gives us the courage to measure ourselves against the apparent all-powerfulness of nature.' It is notable, furthermore, how much – I say this for the literary historians among you – Kant's language, which is usually taken simply as part of the language dimension of the Enlightenment, approaches the *Sturm und Drang* movement in such passages. But the central element to which I want to draw your attention here, and which I think should indeed be incorporated into a philosophical aesthetics, is that of resistance. [Kant] says that the feeling of the sublime – and what he means here would meanwhile be considered fundamental to the constitution of the aesthetic – actually consists in the party which is destined to be the weaker – the human being, as nature – is nonetheless capable of resisting the stronger by becoming aware of itself as spirit and, as I tried to express earlier, becoming aware of the similarity between the infinity of the spirit and the infinity of nature, as it were. One can perhaps extrapolate and go a step further, and say it is an objective part of all beauty that we feel the happiness of beauty wherever we feel that, through the purpose of the spirit – even if we stay within a picture, within the realm of semblances – we are free, and stronger than the context of mere nature in which we are otherwise embedded.

In other words, this feeling of resistance against mere existence actually contains the utopia where mere existence does not have the last word. And this pictureless picture of utopia, this expression of a utopia that does not utter itself but conveys itself only in the feeling that something is stronger, or that we feel stronger than the world as it is: that, at any rate, is one of the categories which I would like to think are generally characteristic of beauty.[33] Directly after this, Kant writes: 'In this way, in our aesthetic judgement nature is judged as sublime not in so far as it arouses fear, but rather because it calls forth our power (which is not part of nature) to regard those things about which we are concerned (goods, health, and life)' – this is very reminiscent of the hymn by Luther; you can see how certain theological categories – 'Let goods and kindred go, this mortal life also'[34] – could be said to have migrated into the basic categories of aesthetics – 'as trivial, and hence to regard its power' – to which we are subject in the light of this, however –

> as not the sort of dominion over ourselves and our authority to which we would have to bow if it came down to our highest principles and their affirmation or abandonment. Thus nature is here called sublime merely because it raises the imagination to the point of presenting those cases in which the mind can make palpable to itself the sublimity of its own vocation even over nature.[35]

Consider for a moment the contrast between the two passages of Kant I read out to you: on the one hand, this somewhat philistine, petit bourgeois passage stating that one can perceive the beauty of nature only if one is in safety, and then this feeling of sublimity as the inner moral awareness, which for Kant means freedom removed from the control of nature. So this actually gives you the exact polarity that I want to point out by explaining something about the character of natural beauty. Namely: in nature, there is, on the one hand, that element which is stronger than we are, and which does not really permit us to contemplate beauty any more than was possible in earlier times, before the increasing domination of nature; but, on the other hand, after nature was harnessed to a degree and lost its horror, this awakened the self-awareness of humans, and a kind of second affinity, a form of symbolic reconciliation, was brought about with nature, which humans had subjugated, but to which they had done an injustice in the process.[36] Kant expressed these experiences so deeply – though they do not appear in his reflections – that he described this feeling of the sublime elsewhere as a trembling-in-oneself, a form of movement in the consciousness[37] that fluctuates between this feeling of powerlessness and being overwhelmed, on the one hand, and the feeling of resistance and being in control of oneself, on the other. And, in so doing, he unwittingly expressed the fact that aesthetic experience – the only kind that is still possible after that time – is actually dialectical in itself – that is, it is not simply the harmonic experience of something sensually enjoyable, as he formulates it in his aesthetics of artistic beauty; rather, it is caught within such a tension, such a coincidence or balance of opposites, namely that between something stronger and something weaker. And if all art since then, in order to be beautiful, to give any happiness at all, has necessarily and inescapably had to include dissonance, then this fundamentally dissonating character of all comprehensively modern art is in fact an expression of the dialectic which Kant encountered in natural beauty, because it was not yet present in the art of his time, but which already transcends the realm of natural beauty and points to the realm of artistic beauty, which is its only proper one.

The stance Kant demands for art as a whole is that of 'disinterested pleasure', and this is echoed in his definition of the sublime. This means that, as he so touchingly writes, only if we 'are in a degree of safety', so if there is no reason for us to have a personal interest in the overhanging rock not falling on us and the waves not consuming us, only then are we – according to him, at least – at all capable of experiencing natural beauty. This view of the disinterested experience of natural beauty has dominated the entire aesthetic discussion. And I think it is very difficult to avoid adopting it; for I believe that, as soon as one enters a practical relationship with an object, as soon as one, simply put, wishes to consume or possess it, then this specifically aesthetic relationship is either completely non-existent or fundamentally disturbed. But it should give us pause to think that there is such a severe taboo on this relationship with the desirable in art. I do not consider that this view falls prey to psychologism, but rather that it lends genuine expression to an aspect that explains, in a veritably dialectical fashion, the strength of this ban on showing direct desire towards the aesthetic. What Freud once said of the uncanny – that it is only uncanny to us because it is all too familiar[38] – surely applies equally to all so-called disinterested pleasure. The quality that makes the works of art seem beautiful to us, and which, in its very beauty, simultaneously keeps immediate desire at a distance, is intimately connected to the fact that desire is contained in them as a necessary but subsequently devalued condition. And perhaps I may close today's lecture by saying why I consider a renewed reflection on the concept of natural beauty so extraordinarily important for aesthetics: because only thus can one become aware of that strange interplay of forces between desire and the prohibition of desire which, in fact, essentially encompasses all beauty since Plato's definition in *Phaedrus*.[39] And if this element of desire is not contained within the idea of beauty in a negated form, then the concept of beauty itself becomes stale and empty. Furthermore, I will show you in the next session that this establishment of the aesthetic sphere as one lying beyond desire is always precarious, and that the tension between these aspects is actually present at every moment of an aesthetic experience and keeps concerning us anew; so it is from this perspective that we must understand in what sense nature cannot be driven out – even out of artistic beauty – with a pitchfork.[40]

LECTURE 4

20 November 1958

In the last session we turned to the problem of the relationship between the realm of natural beauty – and thus, in a broader sense, nature as such – and that of artistic beauty and art. And we had arrived at a thought that is perhaps central to this complex: how artistic beauty, in the sense of disinterested pleasure, is connected to natural beauty in the sense of a desire. We had emphasized the observation that the very thing which arouses disinterested pleasure is something that had originally aroused the very greatest interest, namely the object on which desire, the capacity for desire, directed its most immediate focus. And I think there is no sensation of beauty that does not, with a special kind of pain, have an element of that separation between the desired and the desirer that is originally expressed in the experience of beauty, but perhaps even of the pain that lies in the concept of beauty because, in order to be perceived as beauty at all, it is pushed away from desire, withdrawn from desire, and thus gains that character of inauthenticity, of a special aesthetic sphere,[1] that inhabits everything one usually refers to as aesthetic semblance.[2]

Now, I would not want you to misunderstand what I have said about these things as espousing a psychologistic theory of art – that is, as if I simply viewed everything aesthetic, or even beauty itself, as nothing but a somehow modified or diverted sexuality. Certainly the formulations used in psychoanalysis have, at times, created such an impression.[3] But that not only stems from the inartistic character of most psychoanalytically oriented doctors who have spoken about

these things (and, in this sense, Freud himself should be considered
primarily a doctor), but is connected *a priori* to the psychological
angle of enquiry, the fact that, when a psychoanalyst examines artistic
questions, they are simply interested most in the psychodynamic elements contained in the experience of beauty – in the aesthetic realm
in the sense both of the observer and aesthetic production – and this
direction of their interest does not tell us anything about the objectivity itself. Perhaps we can come a little closer to the matter at hand
by saying that only this strange removal of immediate desire from
the object provides a clear view of the specifically aesthetic quality,
or that this aesthetic quality contains in itself – one could almost say
– that liberation from objects of action which is described in the Kant
passage[4] as the feeling of resistance against the compulsion of sheer
nature. Perhaps one can say that, on the one hand, the sphere of the
aesthetic object is only isolated, only leaves the totality in which it
was originally a mere stimulant, through this strange withdrawal of
desire from the object; but that, on the other hand, the energies resulting from such a transformation themselves also enter the perception
of beauty and constitute the special aesthetic element. One can say
that precisely in the taboo placed on desire by the work of art, precisely in the refusal of every work to be touched, consumed or in any
way appropriated, lies that element of nature which was present in
desire – but now sublated in its negative form. In other words, the
energies that originally wanted to take it, absorb it and directly
possess it now actually serve to posit, to constitute, beauty as a form
of special sphere in relation to the sphere of mere immediacy.[5]

If I may say one more thing about the psychological side of this
phenomenon: to be sure, the drive energies that need to be transformed in order to arrive at something like an experience of beauty
are essentially of a sexual nature; there is no doubt about that. But
what specifically happens to these drive energies – and psychoanalysis
certainly saw this accurately – is that, when an experience of beauty
takes place, they are not repressed, suppressed or diverted by force
but rather, to use the psychological term, 'sublimated';[6] this means
that they are retained and preserved in a certain sense, but in such a
way that what was originally immediate desire becomes mere imagination, mere representation. This transformation of something desired
into something imagined is, if you will, one of the original phenomena of aesthetic behaviour as such – though, at this point, I am not
even distinguishing between the aesthetic behaviour of the observer
and that which is sedimented in the work itself, because what I want
to describe to you here takes place prior to the realm of an already
objectified artistic sphere. I think it is this peculiar process of

sublimation – which leads to something desired being transformed into something that is merely imagined, and in this strangely altered form brings happiness – that, at least from the subjective point of view, constitutes the precondition for the spiritualization of art – the element that makes art something sensual and simultaneously more than sensual – which we will find again in the definition of beauty, and which we already encountered when, by way of prelude, I reminded you of Hegel's definition of beauty as the sensual appearance of the idea.[7] This removal of desire, this transfer to the imagination, this form of sublimation itself is already a process of spiritualization; and, at the same time, this process is also what in turn enables the work of art, as an objectivity, conceivably to become the carrier of something spiritual. It must be said, however – and I think this is central to a precise notion of artistic beauty in its complex relationship with nature – that this process of sublimation, like all such psychological processes involving the strongest drives we have – and art must rest on incredibly strong drive impulses to wield such power over humans as it asserts time and again – that there is nothing definite about such a process of sublimation. Its nature is precarious, one could say; at any stage, at any moment, it can be cancelled. This means that the element of immediate desire – or, as Kierkegaard would have called it, of sensual immediacy[8] – can flood it again at any moment. So there is nothing solid here; rather, because of this character, every work of art itself constitutes a form of tension field between the sensual and spiritual aspects, which keep working away at each other and never arrive at anything definite. My justification in showing you the relationship between art and nature so emphatically is – and this is the specific reason for giving it such significance – that, in the usual forms of aesthetics,[9] the distinction between the imagination and the desired – or, more generally put, between art as a sphere of semblance and beauty as a sensual reality – is treated as something that has been made once and for all, an act of creation that gave birth to art, as it were, and that the question of the relationship between art and nature can now be considered settled and is no longer of concern.[10] But the saying that nature always returns, even if one drives it out with a pitchfork,[11] seems to apply here too. This means that the tension between the aspect of sublimation and the aspect of immediate desire, a conflict one can construct as belonging to the sphere of artistic prehistory[12] in the sense of an ideal prehistory of art, in fact applies time and again to all layers and stages of art, and each time with the same force. The ultimate reason for the weakness of so-called formal aesthetics is probably that they claim this endlessly self-reproducing tension has been dealt with once and for all, and then retain nothing except, on the one hand, an abstract concept of the spirit that determines the work of art and, on the other hand, an equally abstract notion of the sensually pleasing that no longer reveals any of the tremendous force that is inherent in the sensual in art.[13] But the ultimate reason for this ambiguity is that, in the end, the phenomenon of sublimation – which not even psychology, furthermore, has managed to distinguish with absolute stringency, with absolute clarity, from the aspect of repression – always has an element of need to it. This means that because, for natural and social reasons, we cannot entirely fulfil our desire and have to spiritualize it in a certain fashion, with all the heightening of spiritual powers that only then becomes possible, and all the tremendousness that the experience of the artistic owes to those powers, there is also, if I may put it very brutally and crudely, something of the substitute about this. That means that in a certain sense reality, full and real fulfilment, is ultimately greater as an ideal than the ideal of spiritualization. But this does not imply a standard one can apply to art from the outside, in the sense of saying, 'Well, life is more than art; life matters more than the picture', and so forth. Such choices between two options are rather unfruitful – whether it is more important for Reims Cathedral to be left standing or a certain number of soldiers to stay alive[14] – they are choices of whose fruitfulness I am scarcely convinced. But I think that the problem we are currently discussing is revealed in the works of art themselves, just as I generally think that the question we are tackling here can only really be answered by decoding specifically aesthetic matters. And then one encounters a very peculiar phenomenon: the dignity of the works, in fact, always depends on something living inside them which is more than merely art; that they are neutralized, and become impoverished in a sense, if they are not – by fulfilling their own formal laws – always simultaneously more than form, and thus do, in a certain sense, refer after all to that aspect of reality that they have excluded and to which they can refer only by exclusion.[15] In the critique of Aldous Huxley that I included in *Prisms*, I tried to make this state of affairs clear with reference to a play such as *Romeo and Juliet*.[16] Certainly such a play – or *Antony and Cleopatra*, or any of Shakespeare's great erotic dramas – certainly these plays have nothing whatsoever in common with so-called tendentious plays.[17] And if, shall we say, one tried to interpret *Romeo and Juliet* as a plea by the incipient bourgeoisie against the feudal bonds of love between individuals, this would be nonsense, if only because the so-called early and rising bourgeois society had incomparably more taboos in erotic matters than the feudal class ever did. Furthermore, you need only read Shakespeare's final drama, *The Tempest*, to see how little his work in turn favoured the rise of Puritanism during the poet's later life. [...][18] But even in *Romeo and Juliet*, on the other hand, the song of the nightingale and not the lark[19] – the last great aubade in medieval poetry[20] and, one could almost say, the first great love poem in modern literature – would be inconceivable, it would lack its sweetness and indescribable power, if this play did not, in spite of all, hold the living utopia of something like boundless fulfilment, like a love that is undomesticated, untamed and unblemished by objective conditions. This is not part of Shakespeare's agenda, it is not espoused by the play; the play does nothing except to follow its own internal law, namely to show with a *voilà*! gesture how things are for love, how love and immediacy fare in a mediated world. But if this aspect were missing, if, with this, something more than aesthetic had been posited in the play itself, then the play as such would still be aesthetic – and not what it is. And I would say that, if one were to criticize the notion of *l'art pour l'art*[21] – and no one could be more careful about criticizing the ideal of *l'art pour l'art* than I am[22] – but if one seriously intended to criticize it, it could only be by saying that the work of art, in being sworn completely to its pure immanence, in having anything cut out of it which is somehow a reference, which points beyond it – that the work itself must wither as a result. But one must immediately add that in a world where precisely that connection between works of art and the capacity for desire has in turn been manipulated by the market, and in which the sensually pleasing, that which appeals to people, has long served to devalue the works of art and cheat them of their utopia – that, under such circumstances, a concentration on the pure immanence of form, namely the principle of *l'art pour l'art*, has been extremely justified.[23]

Nonetheless, one can say that art, by distancing itself from nature and thus no longer making itself the immediate object of desire but, rather, transferring the happiness of immediacy to the mediation of the imagination, always tries through this very act of immanent constitution to come to the aid of nature, to preserve something of nature, to give back to nature some of what belongs to it and is taken from it by the historical world. I am well aware how significantly these two elements – nature and history, or the human and the artificial – are mediated by each other. Let me add, however, that, even if two categories are mutually mediated, any thought that simply rejected these categories because of their mediatedness would be invalid; for only if they are retained in their determinacy, only – to speak of nature and art – if one holds on to their ideas as such, is one capable of correctly understanding their mediation, the way in

which each produces the other. And I therefore consider it right if I
now leave aside for a moment the mediatedness of nature, which I
told you enough about in our last session, and say that art in particular is no less mediated by nature than vice versa.[24] I hope I have given
you an accurate impression of this aspect. I think we can draw a
conclusion from this which may be indispensable for the experience
of modern art, contemporary art. What I am talking about is the
aspect of sensual happiness. You all know that, in a very broad sense,
modern art has increasingly moved away from what is sensually
pleasing. In painting, one could perhaps date that back to Manet,[25]
where the pleasing harmony of colours is ruptured by the extreme
contrasts of colour. One can see it above all in music, in the increasing predominance of so-called dissonance over consonance, which
ultimately means that this preponderance of the dissonant renders
the old, traditional distinction between dissonance and consonance
– one could almost say, between beautiful and ugly in general –
extremely problematic. At this point, where the concern is to apply
the question we are addressing to genuinely concrete matters of
artistic experience, I would like to say – and I reject the option of
postponing this application until hell freezes over; I believe in making
hay while the sun shines, and aim to carry out the application as it
results concretely from our deliberations – I consider it a mistake to
attribute this predominance of dissonance in the very broadest sense
simply to the awareness of suffering, or the abstraction and spiritualization of art. If what I said earlier is true, namely that the separation of art from nature is nothing definite, but that the confrontation
– let me call it the dialectic – between these two aspects is reproduced
at virtually every historical moment and in every partial aspect of the
work of art itself, then this also means that the aspect of the sensually
pleasing does not simply disappear but is, rather, sublated and preserved in the work, though now in the form of that dissonance. Let
me put it like this: the harmonization of a work that dispenses with
everything that, according to the traditionalist, now outdated rules
of harmony, is considered beautiful, euphonic or consonant does an
incomparably greater honour to its own idea through the consistency
of this renunciation – that is, by excluding, by negating this beauty
in the traditional sense – than if it were simply to produce this pleasing quality in an immediate sensual form, for one can truly say that
it has long since degenerated into a commodity brand and a factor
in the mere manipulation of humans. The ears and eyes of artists
register the phenomenon I am referring to very accurately with the
label 'kitsch'. Whenever we speak of kitsch, it refers precisely to the
experience of that layer, namely that sensual happiness is preserved

in art where it is negated by it, not directly striven for, but that it is betrayed where art itself presents it as such. It has often been said, and I have no intention of denying it – I think I have said so myself too – that the dark, shocking, alienating and in many ways repulsive aspect of today's aesthetic forms is connected to the constant threat of disaster under which we all live and that, in the face of this threat, a harmonistic art, an art that simply idealized existence with its forms, would inherently take on a quality of impotence and nullity which any art seeking to be a genuine manifestation of truth must rebel against with the utmost vehemence.[26] But it would be a disastrous misunderstanding and a highly dubious restriction of the experience of modern art if one were to take an approach like that of the late Klaus Mann[27] when he wrote in an essay – a very reactionary one in aesthetic terms, incidentally – that, well, the world of today is ghastly, and it is surely not the task of art to be even more ghastly than the world and merely imitate this ghastliness of the world; rather, the task of art is to depict what is better and more beautiful[28] – though, as transpired from one of his own biographical novels, his ideal of the better and more beautiful was represented by the symphonies of Mr Tchaikovsky.[29] You can see from that how questionable a matter such ideality is. No, that is not how things are. The experience of the artist who draws on dissonance – to apply this oft-misused word, and to try perhaps to give it a slightly more decent meaning – the experience of what is dissonant or pleasing, is infinitely multi-layered. If an artist, for example a composer, places their dissonances today, they are doing so not in order to duplicate the horror of the world – though something of that horror is always present in these dissonances, their exclusivity and their constructive treatment – but rather, first of all, because every such dissonance, merely through its deviation from established contentions, and far more through its unused quality, its newness and expressive charge, also has an element of happiness.

I told you that one of the substantial intentions of important works of art is not only to push nature away, to distinguish themselves from the merely natural through sublimation, but also to give nature back what belongs to it. In a sense, this happens in every dissonance – using the term in its broadest sense, beyond its limited musical meaning. One could say that every dissonance is a small remembrance of the suffering which the control over nature, and ultimately a society of domination as such, inflicts on nature, and only in the form of this suffering, only in the form of yearning – and dissonance is always substantially yearning and suffering – only thus can suppressed nature find its voice at all. And dissonance therefore contains not only this

aspect of an expression of negativity, of this suffering, but always at
the same time the happiness of giving nature its voice, finding something not yet taken, drawing something into the work that – if I could
use the word again – has not yet been domesticated, something akin
to fresh snow, which thus reminds us of something other than the
ever-same machinery of bourgeois society in which we are all trapped.
That too, I think, should already show you at this stage what the
whole purpose of the dissonating aspect is. The dissonating aspect is
pain and happiness at once, like the stroke of genius in the lilac monologue from *Die Meistersinger*, where Hans Sachs sings '*Lenzes Gebot,
die süsse Not*' [Spring's command, sweet need] over an indescribably
poignant and sweet dissonance.[30] Now, the need has certainly
increased, but perhaps the sweetness has increased with it; that is how
it seems to me, at least. And perhaps I could also add that the widespread belief that the dissonant element in art is identical to the sensually displeasing, the sensually ugly, is itself a form of superstition. For
it is part of that dynamic between nature and history or art which I
am describing to you in these sessions that the aspects of so-called
sensual pleasure are also revolutionized, that they are in a state of
constant change. The fact is that sounds which were taboo at a particular time, in the sense that they were considered ghastly, can become
sensually pleasing. Furthermore, it is part of the composer's art, the
technical mastery of a great composer, to deploy even the most dissonating chords, when they are required, in such a way that they
indeed possess this sensually alluring aspect, this element of happiness,
which is precisely what most people say they lack. And I think that
understanding truly current art – and a lecture on aesthetics can hope
to be more than an antiquarian affair only if it tackles the questions
raised by the most advanced art, in God's name – a truly adequate
experience of modern art, does in fact require that one also understand
the complex of the dissonant in relation to all these aspects.[31]

To the extent that art too, with all the traits I have tried to unfold
for you today, is a manifestation of natural behaviour, it is something
older than rationality and embodies or represents that which, in the
meantime, has essentially given way to the rational. And this perhaps
leads us to something like a philosophical prehistory of art, the kind
that, in my view, would have to replace mere verbal definitions, which
remain arbitrary and non-binding. Let me point you here to the
theory of art as mimetic behaviour, which Horkheimer and I formulated in depth in the *Dialectic of Enlightenment*, in the introductory
chapter on the concept of enlightenment,[32] and which I shall refrain
from expounding here because our time is awfully short. But I think

it would help you to look up these things, which, to a certain extent, actually give the theoretical answer to what is at issue at the point we have now reached. Art is a mimetic behaviour that is captured, preserved in an age of rationality.[33] There was a time in the history of mankind when mimetic behaviour – that is to say, direct imitation in general – was one of the primary behaviours. We know how decisive a part mimesis or mimicry plays in the survival of primitive creatures; without a doubt, it played an equally central part in the lives of primitive humans, ultimately leading to the practice of magic, whose underlying idea is essentially that one can gain control of nature by imitating some natural phenomenon or other – as when the magic priest goes 'psh psh psh' and believes that, if he does so for long enough, it will rain. These forms of behaviour then gave way to the process of de-mythologization, the process of enlightenment, in a very complex and difficult manner that I cannot describe to you now[34] – in a manner, if I could just say this, in which the so-called mythologies themselves already constitute a stage of enlightenment by transferring these mimetic practices into narratives, and thus rationalizing them. If you look at the chapter about the *Odyssey* from the *Dialectic of Enlightenment*,[35] you will find a great deal about this transition in particular. But while this process of progressive enlightenment saw humans, on the one hand, becoming ever freer and more powerful in relation to nature, they increasingly reduced nature, on the other hand, to what is known in psychological gestalt theory as an 'object of action' – that is to say, the practical object.[36] So, in other words: in this process whereby humans removed themselves from the threat of forceful nature, they always did nature an injustice too. And art, by clinging in a certain sense to the mimetic process, to this archaic, older phenomenon rather than the rational one – and, in this, I would almost say that all art is childlike, infantile, because it truly still has the notion that it can take full control of reality through the image, not by intervening in reality with thought and action – by clinging to this aspect, art always tries at the same time to do justice to that element of suppressed nature. This strikes me as the more comprehensive historico-philosophical explanation for the circumstance we have discussed in general terms today, namely the return of nature in art. That is why nature returns in art, that is why art means the restoration of nature in a certain sense, because it is part of the prehistory of art itself – the idea of art itself, if you will – that that which would otherwise perish because of rationale, law, order, logic, classificatory thought, because of all these categories, finds its voice and receives its due after all.[37]

In our last few minutes here, let me say a word about the concept of imitation, which was so central to the description of art in earlier aesthetics. From the perspective of modern art, it is easy to say that art does not imitate but is, rather, expression, or something spiritual, or whatever one wishes to call it. On the other hand, if you read an author such as Vasari and see what tremendous significance this great historian of Renaissance painting still assigned to the element of imitation[38] – and he was surely no fool – then one does feel a little ill at ease dealing with this problem of imitation too quickly. I would say that an element of imitation is indeed a central aspect of art, but with one qualification: not as an imitation of something, but as an imitative impulse, an impulse of mimicry – the impulse to turn oneself into the object one is facing or to turn that object into oneself. In other words: art is imitation, but not the imitation of an object so much as an attempt to restore through its gestures and its overall attitude a state in which the difference between subject and object did not really exist, where instead a relationship of similarity and thus kinship prevailed between subject and object, rather than the antithetical separation of the two elements we find today.[39] Schoenberg's apt statement in his preface to Anton von Webern's Bagatelles for String Quartet, op. 9, that music can say something which can only be said by music is a very precise expression of this.[40] It means to say that music or art in general says something, expresses something, one could say imitates something, yet without imitating it as an object, without replicating it, but rather making itself similar in its entire mode of behaviour, its gesture – its being, one could almost say here – in order thus to reverse the leap. By comparison, however, the common view of art as an imitation of something is already – and I think this follows quite directly from what I have said to you today – a form of pseudomorphosis. This means that, in this view, the mimetic behaviour which is actually the concern of art is already rationalized, is treated as if it were a behaviour relating directly to the concrete world; one could call it the enlightened misunderstanding of mimetic behaviour in art.

That brings me to the topic that will occupy us in the next session. For it would be a mistake if you now thought that art is nothing but archaic, nothing but mimetic, nothing but a restoration of the natural state; rather, it is always also – and substantially – interwoven with the historical process and is itself involved in all categories of the progressive mastery of nature. And this other aspect, namely the part of the mastery of nature in art itself, and thus the dialectic between the rational and mimetic elements in the work of art, will be our focus in the next session before we finally determine the upshot of all these reflections for the concept of beauty.

LECTURE 5

2 December 1958

Today I mean to conclude, at least provisionally, the fundamental reflections on the relationship between natural beauty and artistic beauty – or, as we can perhaps say more broadly now, the relationship between nature and art. Let me repeat once more that this relationship should be understood very much as a dialectical relationship, not a simple contrast; but neither, as the sentimental view would have it, is it in the sense of a direct relationship, as reproduced in the platitude that perfect art is perfect nature,[1] and such like. I will attempt to present this dialectic – that is to say, this unity of opposites or this identity in non-identity – theoretically as vividly as possible. Art, at least in the way we have experienced the concept historically, initially stands in contrast to nature, in so far as it is taken out of the natural world and occupies an area that does not coincide directly with the real world; indeed, we consider it a failing in works of art if this line of demarcation from empirical reality is not drawn. For example, it was interpreted – by the cultural historian Friedländler, to name one author – and I would say with good reason, as a symptom of incipient barbarism in the days of the Roman Empire that the classical Attic tragedies were staged in some sort of Latinized versions, but that those heroes who were destined to die were played by slaves who were then genuinely killed on such occasions, as painfully as possible, resulting in a form of synthesis between gladiatorial games and tragedy.[2] I think this is sufficient to show you what I mean by this demarcation line, and it belongs to an essentially similar, albeit initially less bloody, area, that today, within so-called popular art, there is an increasing tendency to blur this boundary and give the work of art a kind of justification, a *raison d'être*, by adding that it is based on true stories. On a side note, I think that this decline in the ability to observe a sphere without this sphere identifying itself directly in relation to empirical reality is also the reason for the unspeakable poverty of so-called biographical novels, which were originally associated with the names of Emil Ludwig,[3] Herbert Eulenberg[4] and Stefan Zweig,[5] but have meanwhile become such a lucrative business that there seem to be few people who, after losing their posts as journalists at some point, would not try their hand at looking for a great man to use as the subject for such a hybrid product of art and reportage.

This fact that art is removed from the world is not the main thing, however; after all, it shares this trait with the sphere of games in the broadest sense. It is a feature of every game in existence that it is not initially part of immediate empirical reality, that it has no purpose in a certain sense, and that one does not directly pursue any advantages by playing it; when the latter does happen, it is only through some back door. You can tell from the sophistic distinctions between the amateur and the pro how strong is the awareness of this separation from empiricism; that is, even when the game, namely sport, has long become a source of income, one might hide this in order somehow to remain faithful to the idea of the game; and that a sportsman falls out of favour, to an extent, if he directly seeks to earn money with his activity. But, on the other hand, art does differ very substantially from the sphere of the game in a particular character that I would like, for now, to call its image character – though without examining this image character, this character of the imaginary, more closely than last time, when I told you a few things about the mimetic root of art. Here too, furthermore, the distinction between art and games that comes into play is not absolute, of course; there are countless games that also have mimetic character, for example children's games, where a child is a locomotive, a confectioner, an aeroplane or a Sputnik[6] or whatever else; naturally they have this mimetic character too, but the mimetic character is not as fundamental as the character of a certain activity. Categories such as those of art and games, incidentally, can only be kept apart through their extremes; it goes without saying that there are an infinite number of transitional phenomena between art and games, and it is surely genetically true that one can trace the origins of art far back into games, perhaps even – if one is to believe the claims of Groos[7] – back to certain behaviour in animals, to animal mimetism, animal imitation. But one can generally say, I think, that art sets itself apart from nature by constituting a special area characterized by two poles: on the one side the game aspect I just underlined, where the activities developed in art are not viewed as directly real but placed in parentheses, as it were, taking place in a separate realm; but on the other side the aspect of semblance – that is to say, the aspect that the work of art as a whole, to the extent that we understand it as art in the true sense, has an intention, that it means something, that something appears in it which is more than the mere appearance itself. And that, it seems to me, is the categorial element which distinguishes it from the game. One could certainly write a theory of art in which one organizes the elements of art around these two poles, and in which one establishes, for example in drama, how the two aspects of play [on the one hand] – for there is playing, people are playing and pretending to be others – and semblance [on the other hand] – for here a whole appears as if it were the sign of something standing behind it, something ideational – [face each other]. In this way, then, one can indeed treat the sphere of art as a tension field between these two aspects, play and semblance, which are both separate from empirical reality.[8] One should perhaps add that this separation is a form of secularization. This means that the origins of art on the one side are surely those of the game which I have touched on; a different sphere – and I do not intend to indulge in speculations about which is most important, and whether there are others – would [relate] to the rhythms of work, for example, and everything associated with them. Such questions about the origin of art are always a little futile, and one immediately finds oneself in the sphere of 'Yes, but ...'.[9] This much seems certain, however: the demarcated, separate sphere of art, whose violation we actually view as the negation of art as such, is initially nothing other than the secularized form of a sacred area sanctified by a taboo, an area that one cannot touch, as it were, without exposing oneself to some kind of unpleasant consequences. And the shudder in the face of the work of art, the concept of the sublime which you already encountered in the first sessions with reference to Kant, is unquestionably rooted precisely in the fact that something of this sacred nature of the untouchable, something of the presence of the *mana*,[10] the great divine power in such a domain, has remained in art.

I said a few words to you earlier about art's roots in games, and one can certainly see this element as the root of what, in the language of philosophy, has been termed the element of the 'idea' in works of art. The idea, by which I mean that very feeling of life which leaps out at us from a work, is the sacred sphere that has passed through the subject, through reflection, through human freedom, in which this *mana*, this force that spreads among everything existent, is then concentrated.[11] At the same time, however, this aspect I am describing to you, this aspect of the shudder, which is connected to the separate sphere of art that must not be touched, as it were, this element of recalcitrance in every work of art against communication with empirical reality – this aspect also contains something else. For this *mana*, this spirit that is meant to manifest itself in the work, always amounts also to a claim to totality. I think one can say that every work of art, even the most wretched, even one produced for the most pitiful profit, always seeks to be something like the whole, the absolute, the totality, the absolute fulfilment – objectively, by its own structure, even against its own will, even if its maker's consciousness would not dream of any such thing. And only this aspect, the fact that every work of art essentially promises us it is the absolute – under all the conditions of empirical thought, as it were, to which we find ourselves chained and of which we will speak later today, in an entirely different context, as an antipode of art that must be taken from us – and that we must, to a degree, be able to experience the unfettered, boundless whole: this aspect – and here too, you can see how much the same side of art I am emphasizing to you here is connected to the side of semblance – is what Schopenhauer, with particular reference to music, spoke of in art as 'the world once again'.[12] Every work of art is, in a certain sense, 'the world once again', namely the world cleansed of immediate purposes; in relation to the sacred sphere, however, it is at once a secularization, in that – as I once called it – the separate sphere of art, removed from the empirical realm, is freed from the lie it contains in the sacred sphere: the lie that there is any claim that this special, separate area, which is set apart in the world from the world, is actually real.[13] In this sense, one can say that precisely the aspect of aesthetic semblance, which, compared to the immediacy of the game, entirely suspends reality itself, in turn honours reality especially because the mythical belief in the omnipotence of the idea – namely, that the idea is directly one with reality, that it even exerts a magical power over reality – that this aspect is negated from the outset in art.

And thus we come across a state of affairs that will still occupy us a great deal, and which strikes me as decisive if one is to avoid overly primitive notions of the conception of art. For if art, in a certain sense – to which we shall return shortly – looks after the interests of nature against the control over nature, then it does so not in some arbitrary way but specifically by always constituting some degree of enlightenment in itself. So this fact that – I would like to repeat this, for I believe it is central to understanding what one might call the nature of art – the special area, the aesthetic circle, as it were, no longer appears as a magical agency, but as something distinct from reality, does preserve, if you will, the memory of the old taboo and thus the memory of the stages of the relationship with nature that humans, in their history, left behind; but, at the same time, one no longer wears the countenance of the magic priest and behaves, within this separate sphere, as if one had any direct power over the world. In this manner, the semblance is freed from the lie of being real. And with this, the semblance also has what is initially an entirely immediate relationship with the truth that, as Hegel splendidly puts it, keeps on unfolding; for Hegel said that art is neither a pleasant nor a useful plaything but, rather, itself an unfolding of the truth,[14] and I think you would do well to measure what I am putting forward to characterize the aesthetic against this statement by Hegel, which, in a certain sense, I have taken as my canon.

So now I have already touched on the opposite of what I demonstrated to you first of all, namely that art is separated from nature as 'the world once again' and stands in opposition to it. For it is precisely by opposing the entire workings of the empirical world – and this applies in an additional sense to the one in which I spoke to you just now of the relationship between art's semblance and the claim to magical truth – that it acts in the interest of nature in a certain sense. This should be understood in the sense that the social process as a whole – and allow me to remind you of some thoughts from the *Dialectic of Enlightenment* that you will find expounded particularly in the first part about the concept of enlightenment,[15] and which I will therefore restrict myself to hinting at – takes place primarily under the banner of the progressive rational control of nature. The old mimetic behaviours are replaced by a progressive alienation from nature; and, because the knowledge of like by like – to use the classical metaphor[16] – is increasingly replaced by the motif of knowing like by unlike,[17] the control of nature becomes possible to an ever higher degree. And it is precisely this process that, in a very broad sense, one calls the process of enlightenment – or, if you prefer, the process of rationalization. Every conceivable thing falls victim to this process – starting from the actually and genuinely suppressed natural world mangled by humans, and extending to the infinite abilities of humans themselves, such as all the abilities that were once mimetic abilities and which we perceive in ourselves only in a scattered, fragmented state. One could say that art is an attempt to do justice to all that falls victim to this ongoing concept of control over nature, to give nature its due, albeit for now only a symbolic portion – namely the portion of memory, the memory of the suppressed, of that which becomes a victim, and also the memory of all those internal human powers which are destroyed by this process of progressive human

rationalization.[18] To that extent, there is even an element of truth to
the philistine platitude that art addresses the emotions rather than
the intellect. It is very easy to mock it, and if one considers how
cleverly petty bourgeois art has exploited this aspect in particular,
how much it has lent itself – out of people's craving for what the
ongoing process of rationalization has expunged from them, one
could say – to carrying out a rationalization of its own, namely sup-
plying commerce and people with heart-warmers, then, God knows,
one can approve of the hatred towards the conventional view that
art serves the emotions; I certainly do. But there is also some truth
in it, in the sense that art is the sphere in which those behaviours that
were destroyed in us are kept and preserved. Now this is very closely
connected to the aspect of art's removal from empirical reality. For
in empirical reality – that is to say, the world in which we live as
active, 'practical' people, pursue goals, use other people to achieve
goals, and commit God knows what other atrocities – this world is
indeed ruled by the reality principle, namely the principle that one
behaves in such a way as to master this reality as comprehensively
as possible. And the behaviour of art is fundamentally a negation of
this reality principle – fundamentally in the sense that it constitutes
a sphere whose ambition is essentially to be the semblance and the
representation of a total area that is certainly independent from the
reality principle, and hence an area one cannot 'get something out
of' in the same practical sense as with most things in this world. And
whenever people invoke the platitude of the liberating quality that
inheres in art, I think this is not so much because of the so-called
exhilaration which some crusty classics are meant to awaken in us
with their virgins; it is far more probably because art promises
through its mere existence to exempt us from the omnipotence of that
same reality principle, the omnipotence of a mechanism of self-
preservation at the expense of everything else that exists in the world.

This is, of course, closely connected to the fact that great art, as
so many individual cases illustrate, could be said to stand with the
victims; that history goes against the grain;[19] that it is not history
from the perspective of the victor, one could say, but rather the
unconscious historiography of the ages, historiography from the perspective of the victim;[20] and that what calls out from works of art is
in fact always the voice of the victim,[21] and that there is no art which
cannot truly do this.[22] So, because of its very principle, it is primarily
on the side of whatever is suppressed, and it thematizes the suppressed time and again. I think that the element one generally terms
'expression' in art, which has a very difficult dialectic that I do not
wish to hide from you, that this element is connected precisely to the

fact that art is the voice of what is suppressed, for, essentially, expression always amounts to an expression of suffering.[23] Compared to the significative-rational element, the mere sign, expression itself is a mimetic residuum from the outset, an aspect that is left over from an otherwise tamed nature, yet manifests itself vividly there in a remarkable fashion and can thus be included in the process of progressive differentiation. In that sense, one could say – if you will permit the dialectical exaggeration – that, on the one hand, art exits the realm of nature, and in that sense constitutes the absolute opposite of everything merely natural. If one watches a play and there is a smell of apples on stage, then this is essentially already the negation of the work of art itself, to put it crudely; and anyone who has first not experienced the antithetical position of art in relation to the natural world is a barbarian, just like people who go to see a play and then talk about it in the past tense as if it had been a real event, as they do not grasp this contrast. On the other hand, art is itself the manifestation of nature in a world where nature has alienated itself through a mighty and irreversible process. It is, one could say, the self-alienated manifestation of nature; but this also means that, in keeping with such alienation, art is more loyal to nature – not because it panders to it in any way or behaves as if it were nature but, on the contrary, because it dispenses with the semblance of the immediate, the merely natural, at least in the guise we find today.[24]

I do, however, want to protect the definitions I have given here from a very logical misunderstanding. This misunderstanding would be to take what I have just told you as a sort of phenomenology of the relationship between art and nature – as if it were like this once and for all – and that, if one follows the definitions I have given, one knows what art and nature are. I am sorry that I must once again behave in the way that evidently befits this idea, that I first attempt with some effort to expound the concepts clearly and distinguish between them, and then once more take away what I have gone to some lengths to give you and must tell you: that things are not so simple after all. What I mean is the following: this relationship between nature and art which I just outlined to you is not a static thing; there is not once and for all the sphere of nature on the one side and the sphere of art on the other. Rather, these two aspects are constantly in a state of mutual tension – and probably will be for as long as there is such a thing as art – and the relationship between these two aspects keeps changing at every stage of art history. There can even be stages – just to define things from one of the utmost extremes – where a particular form of aesthetic sensibility, directed against the sphere of cultured chit-chat and the affirmative-cultural,[25]

virtually demands of the work itself that, in order to remain a work
of art at all, to remain faithful to its purpose in opposition to the
world, it must revoke that very cultivatedness which defines its special
area and then engage once more with elements from empirical reality
after all – as has been the case time and again in the collages, in the
montages, as the whole of surrealism has shown, and as you can still
find today in the most recent works of the great painter Picasso,
where the need for a perpetual metamorphosis of some elements or
other taken directly from nature plays such a major and far-reaching
part.[26] So you should not take something like the idea that the aesthetic realm is removed from empirical reality as an absolute definition; rather, you must also take it as an aspect that is subject to
historical dialectic and is precarious – precarious in the same way I
told you in one of the previous sessions that so-called disinterested
pleasure is a precarious thing,[27] which means there can be no such
thing as a work of art that is not rooted in sensual pleasure and does
not refer back to this sensual pleasure, even if negatively so. But this
means something very fundamental for art that one must establish
with reference to the poles I mentioned to you earlier, and it means
touching on an element that we must not neglect if we are to avoid
reducing the polarity at which I have attempted to hint to what could
be termed a form of 'nature reserve of culture' – in the way people
imagine that, in a world that has grown as cold, alien, hard and evil
as the world of today, it is fortunate that we can still read some
sincere writers who will warm us and make us feel as comfortable as
we supposedly did in earlier times, when it was probably not the case
either. That is not what I meant, but practically the opposite, and I
will try to show you very simply why: because art, as an attempt to
create such a special sphere and to help the suppressed, that which
is not rational, to find its voice, is involved in the overall process of
enlightenment and in fact cannot exempt itself from this overall
process. I told you earlier, at the start of the session, that the mere
distinction of the special area of art from the special sacred area is
already a piece of enlightenment, in the sense that this special area
no longer claims to be true reality with an influence on the empirical
domain but in a sense something powerless – one could almost say,
as powerless as nature – and this already hints that this overall
process of art's separation is pervaded by the process of enlightenment itself. In other words, art's attempt to object to the ever-
advancing control of nature itself involves an element of that control,
and as a very substantial, a truly central aspect.[28] Essentially, what I
am telling you here is the same as the specifically aesthetic experience
of a fact that philosophy, especially Hegel, but all sorts of others too,

has referred to time after time and with great emphasis, namely that the path humanity might find to a realm of freedom – that is, a realm in which oppression and violence, both towards humans and against nature, finally cease – that such a domain cannot be created through some *retour à*, through a return to something that supposedly existed once, as first formulated programmatically by Rousseau in his famous prize essay;[29] rather, both art and social development are only defined by the idea of nature to the extent that humans learn to control nature just enough so that they no longer blindly obey it.[30] So what I mean is that a work of art approaches the idea of giving a voice to suppressed nature only once it manages to free itself from the heteronomy of nature – that is, once it is no longer dependent on some materials that stand outside the artistic process as something unilluminated, blind and unpenetrated, and which exercise a power over humans that they perceive as heteronomous, as foreign, as other. In other words, then – and I would say that this is really the true dialectical key to the relationship between nature and art: the aspect that nature is salvaged in art is inseparable from the fact that art is increasingly able to control nature, yet, as long as it is blind and powerless in the face of whatever materials, it lacks the power to make nature as a whole speak within itself; then it falls victim to something blind and unilluminated, to a kind of mythology. And I would say that the tension between these two aspects, the idea that the progressive control of nature can at once help it to achieve freedom, this is the tension that truly distinguishes the artistic process and thus defines the meaning of the work of art in the first place.[31]

The concept that is responsible here, and which I must introduce at this point, which is as constitutive of all art as it was in Greek times, when one word applied equally to two things, is the concept of technique. No art that can seriously be termed art is without a technical element – that is, without the aspect of moulding its material sufficiently that, by the very fact of being removed from its natural form and melted down into an intention, into something human, it becomes the bearer of this intention, which in turn essentially belongs to nature. It is in this inescapable necessity of technical accrual that art's fundamental intertwinement with the process of enlightenment lies – precisely in the name of lending nature a voice, as I attempted to describe to you.[32] Incidentally, it is probably a sociologically plausible consideration that art, whose special sphere remains a special sphere within the whole – that is, within the totality of society – cannot somehow remain static in itself but must rather – in so far as it has an interactive and antithetical relationship with this reality – take part in this reality.

I think that these reflections allow us to say a few words about the concept of progress in history. Supposedly there was once a so-called naïveté about progress in art, a 'naïve faith in progress' – though, for the most part, I always heard more squabbling about this faith in progress than expressions of this faith in progress itself. I can only say this: it would have been better for the general aesthetic awareness if there had been a greater faith in progress, namely faith in the development of technique and craft, especially here. And, on the other hand, we keep hearing: yes, it is simply a naïve enlightenment attitude to assume that art is making progress. And a number of very significant people, for example Hegel,[33] then independently of him Carl Gustav Jochmann[34] and also Karl Marx, have repeatedly said with great emphasis that there is actually no such thing as progress in art. This means that, for us, as Marx writes in one famous passage, Homer's poetry is just as canonic, and in Marx's view we are just as capable of 'enjoying it', as was the case when it was written, and it is impossible in the age of gunpowder to place anything alongside the *Iliad* that equals it.[35] Nowadays such thoughts seem worn out, for example in arguments that are occasionally wielded against me when people claim that, when it comes to music, I simply have a faith in progress, but that there are powers of being that remain natural and untouched and have nothing to do with dialectic. I will refrain from discussing these things now. But I do think that we can say a few things here – I would indeed say, with good sense – on the basis of what we have clarified for ourselves. Namely this: there is such a thing as progress in art, but only in a very specific sense, namely the progressive control of nature. This process of progressive control of nature, progressive control of material, progressive technique, is irreversible in a very peculiar way,[36] in a way that can be fully understood only if one has something resembling first-hand artistic experience. So, anyone who attempted to compose using Beethoven's methods or to paint with those of Monet would not produce works with the dignity of Beethoven or Monet but, rather, turn out tedious conservatory pieces or decorative hotel paintings,[37] that seventeenth-rate impressionism which one finds so often in hotels and which would even make me choose a Defregger reproduction[38] instead. But, on the other hand, the quality of a work of art, the truth content of a work of art, is by no means directly connected to this progressive control of material. There are works from earlier phases in which the control of the material was not developed to a remotely similar extent, but which nonetheless stand their own through a particular unity between their content, namely the truth they express, and the manner of their formation, though this does not mean that any person can turn back the clock of that progress in the control of the material, for it has a peculiar – I would almost say demonic – power which the individual will is powerless to defeat. In this sense, one should really speak of a progress in art, the control over its material and the absolute necessity for every artist to be capable of using the most advanced techniques of their time. On the other hand, one should not equate this progress in control of the material undialectically with the progress of art itself, where this aspect, in relation to what is controlled and what it actually expresses, is only one aspect and by no means the whole.[39] This is the sensible meaning one should give the concept of progress in art, which would be both free of a kind of animal technocracy of art and, conversely, free of the obscurantism which believes that, to preserve nature, it must isolate itself from progress.

LECTURE 6

4 December 1958

On the lectern I find a question that resulted from a brief conversation I had with one of you after the previous lecture; it reads: 'Why does art express only what has been destroyed in us?' Naturally I would like to correct myself here – and it is the achievement of this question that it has led me to such a correction: I did not, of course, say that art expresses *only* what has been destroyed in us.[1] I would say, however – and this perhaps induced me to use formulations that led to this question – that, in the current situation, the task of art as such is almost entirely to express what has been damaged, or – as Samuel Beckett said to me barely a week ago[2] – to express the powerless and oppressed parts of humans, not the power and glory with which, at least on the surface, official and officially recognized art has usually occupied itself. But I do not, of course, mean that art should express only what has been destroyed in us. That would result in a narrow view of art as such that would, in its way, be no better than the narrow view roughly corresponding to the classicist or academic concept of beauty. I meant to say, and I would like to define this a little more precisely, only that there is really no art that does not have, as a substantial element, the aspect of giving a voice to what has been muted or suppressed – not necessarily destroyed – in the process of the progressive control of nature. It is only really through this perspective of the radically destroyed or damaged that art in our time proves it is worth taking seriously at all. And, to avoid any misunderstandings on this point, I would like to say and repeat what I attempted to expound to you in the last session, namely that art cannot be reduced undialectically to a catchphrase like 'the voice of nature'. If, as I told you, art opposes the immediacy of nature largely through the constitution of its special area, then it always already contains the opposing force, that which controls nature – in a certain sense, the triumphant element. And if one is very sensitive to these matters, one may even suffer due to the fact that the might of lordly rule is greatest precisely in the most authentic works of art, namely the works that hold the greatest power over humans, and, in these so-called authentic works of art, this might turns into a certain suggestive force, a certain element of not letting one go, of coercion, that to some extent mirrors the coercion to which humans have subjected both external nature and internal nature – that is to say, themselves. I do, at any rate, think that, if one's eye or sensorium for the works is sufficiently developed, this aspect of giving a voice to the other, to the suppressed, will also reveal itself in what we call positive, authentic and suggestive works of art.

In the last session, the one among you who kindly reminded me to address this point once more today asked me about the nude figures mastered by classical sculpture. For these figures, he felt, showed no trace whatsoever of mutilation or suppression. My response to this is that, yes, naturally one does not see it directly – and it is generally one of the difficulties of productive aesthetic reflections that, on the one hand, they are of use only if they can lead into the concrete problems of art, but, on the other hand, they should never be taken too literally. In other words, what we are dealing with here – this aspect of helping to give the suppressed a voice – should not simply be imagined as something material, as if every work of art somehow expressed advocacy for something suppressed; rather, this aspect can potentially lie – and usually does, in fact – in the principles of artistic design, not in the immediate material substance. Indeed, it may even crawl away and entrench itself behind the choice of any objects at all. I would not presume to answer this question truly precisely in the context of classical sculpture, but it does seem to me that this sculpture, which, as you all know, flourished in the classical Athenian city-state, the polis of the fourth and fifth centuries BC, was connected to the urban citizens to the extent that it incorporated, one could say, the protest against – how shall I put it? – the harming of the human body within the civil process of life. It is certainly true that the free citizens of Athens at that time did not perform manual labour themselves, and that they consequently remained free of the bodily deformations that the work process so easily inflicts on other humans. At any rate, that was precisely the period in which the great philosophical movement of Sophism truly

worked out the opposition between that which is settled, made, artificial, that which is θέσει, and that which is φύσει, that which is
naturally meant to be. The whole of Sophism, after all, essentially
rests on voicing the protest of this suppressed nature against the
human rules imposed on it. There is certainly something of this assertion of *physis* against *thesis* in the restoration of the body that was
aimed for in the great Greek sculptures, and then attempted time after
time. I was asked how it is with situations like a battle: did people
not fight naked too, and was such a situation not restored? I would
say, that generally speaking, battle is not exactly the authentic situation in which suppressed nature receives its due; on the contrary, it
tends to be damaged there in quite a literal sense. What is true,
however – if I am correctly informed – is that the Spartans, the hop-
lites, namely the heavily armed Spartan soldiers, cast off their clothes
during battle and fought naked. But, in doing so, they would have
exposed themselves to considerable discomfort. Moreover, this was
far more a kind of archaic ritual – one could say the symbolic restoration of a state preceding civil conditions – than an expression of
the actual historical situation at the time of the Peloponnesian War,
for example. So one could almost say that the Spartans, who did not
especially distinguish themselves in matters of aesthetic sublimation,
attempted to realize with their own bodies, if only symbolically, what
the great art of the same period was trying to achieve in its representation of the naked body. I think that precisely the transition to a
form of representation which faithfully captures the anatomy of the
body is a function of suppression that this same body experienced in
the conditions of the Greek city-state through civil conventions and
clothes and everything connected to that; in other words, that the
progress found in so-called realism, which one usually observes in
the classical rather than the archaic period of Greek art, is on the one
hand a progress of rationalization, of the more faithful and precise
control of means, but on the other hand it also corresponds to a
protest against the suppression of that very body whose voice is found
here – whereas the function of representing the body, namely the body
as the bearer of a divine purpose, or whatever else it might have been,
was something completely different in the archaic period.

I would like to remind you of what I told you in the previous
session: the opposition between the aspect of nature and the aspect
of art, or the relationship between nature and art as both opposed
and identical – this relationship should not be understood as a static
one; it is not fixed and immutable once and for all, as if some form
of treaty long ago had removed art from nature, and it could now
settle down comfortably in its little garden until the end of time.

Rather, I attempted to show you how it is a central feature of art that, at all stages, it keeps developing anew the tension which I have sought to describe. I think it is useful, and I like the idea of it, to give you now a concrete model if this kind of tension, to attempt to show you how, in a particular artistic development, the aspect of nature and that of the control of nature interlock and enter a form of dialectic. For this, I will go completely against academic customs and choose a model from the present – the most immediate present. Let me briefly justify this choice, because it so radically contradicts most of what you will learn if you read one of the philological tomes. For it is quite normal in the writing of these so-called aesthetic interpretations to stop at contemporary artistic products and more or less to assume that one cannot know exactly how things are with 'modern' works, while the view of older, traditional art, by contrast, has become clearer, and one can thus make value judgements about traditional art comfortably and with a [...].[3] In no way do I agree with this widespread view. If one holds the view – as I described to you somewhat dogmatically, but which I hope you have been able to develop much more concretely – that art is genuinely an unfolding of the truth, as Hegel states,[4] then this naturally means that the truth content itself also unfolds; in other words, even the content of those works already created is not a static content, not something we gaze upon once and for all as a finished object, but rather something that transforms itself and even reaches a certain threshold at which we can no longer experience it at all. In this sense, I would say the notion that one can understand older works of art better than new ones either expresses a fear of overly exposing oneself in modern matters, and saying something that conflicts with the rules of the game, or simply points to an already reified relationship with art – that is, a relationship that only really includes those works that have already been codified and removed from any living connection. To put it in extreme terms, I hold the view that, in a deeper sense, even the most difficult and complex artworks of one's own time are easier to understand than relatively simple ones from a fairly remote past, as the latter always require a sort of detour of empathy, the construction of an inner state, the reconstruction of a historico-philosophical topos of which we are no longer capable. If it is true that the substance of Johann Sebastian Bach's work lies in a very particular constellation between well-ordered churchly devoutness and pietism, then a truly direct experience of this substance would require us to think ourselves back into such a thing, into such an inner state, as was believed in Romanticism, whose promotion of this view famously opened the doors to artistic syncretism. In reality, I would say, even people who are incapable of appreciating a very difficult modern piece, let us say by Boulez,[5] in the way that they think they can appreciate a piece by Bach because of its relative simplicity, can nonetheless, simply by having the same historico-philosophical conditions – as the young Lukács would have said: the same 'transcendental place',[6] meaning those *a priori* inner preconditions of any experience at all which it shares with such a modern work – grasp this work, which they believe they cannot understand, incomparably more accurately than the older one. Comprehending the older work, on the other hand, is burdened with never-ending problems, as shown by the fact that histories of literature attempt to 'acknowledge' famous works of the past – let us say the seventeenth century, think of a novel such as *The Asian Banise*[7] – because one no longer has any use for them, because they have become unpalatable, crudely put, and to think that, in doing so, one can arrive via an educational detour at what, to use a highly questionable term, one calls 'aesthetic pleasure'. I think that the entire view which is manifested in this attitude is fundamentally wrong. And I think that, if engagement with theoretical aesthetic questions is to have any purpose, and not simply to remain a profes- sorial matter in the worst sense, then it must draw on the most immediate experiences of the most advanced art corresponding to one's own level of awareness – rather than spending its time measur- ing how exactly the Golden Section was applied to some or other Renaissance picture.

Now that I have said this, I shall address the dialectic of nature and art within art itself, as currently [revealed] in two [categories] for modern art – and I am taking music, the art closest to me, as a model – namely the categories of expression and construction.[8] Let me first say a few words about the specific concept of expression with which we are dealing in this dialectic. Naturally, art has expression in infinitely many layers and at every possible stage. The gesture in a drawing by Manet can be as expressive as a phrase in a Beethoven quartet, or probably as much as some gesture in a Hellenistic sculp- ture. But if we speak of expression in the way that has truly become relevant and concrete in modern art, we are thinking first of all of the movement of expressionism. I would say, incidentally, that – in opposition to the widespread habit of inveighing against 'isms'[9] – I consider terms such as 'expressionism' quite good and useful, because they testify to the fact that even seemingly extraordinarily individual and specific manifestations of artistic consciousness have their own historical status; this means that they are in reality collective move- ments sustained by collective powers, however much they might stylize themselves as merely individual. If you think of the expressive ideal of expressionism – that is, the art which, especially in Germany, dominated painting and poetry, as well as music, almost exactly forty years ago, and which, I would say, is still more or less open to direct experience by us – then you will find that, here, expression always means exactly what I was referring to in the last session, when I said that, in a certain sense, art helps what is suppressed and suffering to find its voice. Expressionism consists first of all in the protest against hardened social and conventional forms, both the social hardenings in the fabric of the state, or even the apparatus of war, and the hardened forms of art itself, which were viewed as no longer binding in the face of the immediacy of human suffering. The attempt has been made to let suffering itself speak directly, as it were, without placing a third element between expression and artistic manifestation, without inserting a form of stylizing principle, a mitigating or surrounding factor. If I might take the liberty of a dialectical remark here, I am pointing – if I am not mistaken – quite precisely to the threshold between two artistic movements that also, from today's perspective, have far more in common than a superficial view would suggest, namely the threshold between *Jugendstil* and expressionism. For, in a sense, *Jugendstil* is also an art of expression, and suffering because of convention is infinitely strong in it. The attempt to assert the status of the free, autonomous human being, the 'free noble man', as Ibsen puts it,[10] against conventions could be considered the innermost motif of *Jugendstil*; except that this motif of expression in *Jugendstil* remains tied to the notion of some supposedly universally binding, predetermined formal categories – precisely those categories which, after the expiry of the academic ones, people thought they could discern in the pure ornament. So, in other words, people thought at the time that, through pure will, they could discern something resembling a style for this expression of suffering, the emancipation of resistance to convention, while the shift from this movement to expressionism took place at the very moment when people discovered that, as a language of expression – as a word for what one suffers – even those formal elements far removed from prevailing conventions, for example the expressionist flower ornament, which seeks quite directly to emphasize suppressed nature in opposition to conventions, were no longer entirely viable. The specific aspect for the concept of expression in expressionism is an element that it now – if you think for a second of the problems of *Jugendstil*, and if you are not bothered too much by expression – shares with another, earlier movement, namely naturalism, to the extent that, as I just told you, the *principium stilisationis* is essentially discarded[11] in favour of an attempt to derive something like aesthetic form purely from expression itself. In other words: the intention in expressionism is to arrive at an aesthetic form through expressive transcripts of a kind, by allowing expression to present itself as directly as possible, without mediation. [...] The most authentic documents of expressionism are probably those which express this idea without anything intermediate, and which come closest to shaping form from expression itself, without drawing in any external categories. To the extent that it aims at producing documents, transcripts – the surrealists later spoke of 'automatic writing'[12] – of emotional states, expressionism strives for the ideal of a pure immediacy. In that sense, one can say that expressionism constitutes an extreme in the attempt to give suppressed nature – that one pole of which I spoke to you before – its due. And this, of course, is connected to the fact that, through the overall social dynamics, the notion of a secure bourgeois canon of forms in the social and aesthetic sense had come to an end with the close of the Edwardian and Wilhelmine eras.

But now [it transpires] – and that is the dialectic between this aspect, that which is φύσει and states once again: 'Humans are good', and that which is θέσει, the aspect of construction, if I might introduce the term here, the aspect of control over nature – between these two aspects one can already see, in pure and stringent expressionism, a very specific kind of tension. Here one can think of several problems in which this tension is manifested; first of all, in artistic work – for which, in modernity, it is central that it must not rest on its laurels, and which has become incredibly sensitive to any form of reification – it is constitutive that it remains itself only by changing. What I mean is this: for this type of sensitivity, which really forbids repetition and must modify itself, it transpires very quickly, very early on, that it is impossible to stay at the sheer point of expression. The pure 'this-here', the art that seeks to present the pure 'this-here', the pure moment of expression, the absolute sound, so to speak, as absolute nature – this art approaches in an almost literal sense, one could say, the threshold of silence. It cannot unfold in time or in space and cannot actually objectify itself at all. In fact, all it could do would be what Dada – which is rigorous on this point – utters in its name, namely to say 'Da' [there], really just to take a breath. For everything beyond that would be a kind of betrayal of this pure sound, and consequently the need is aroused – if one is not to fall silent entirely – to go beyond this pure 'there', a need that was felt as early as around 1912[13] among the most radical expressionist artists, for example Anton von Webern, and which – I am trying to be cautious – was probably also one of the impulses for what was termed synthetic cubism.[14] But it is those artists, and precisely the most profound and important ones – and, when I speak of experiences, I always mean the compulsion exerted by the matter itself, not the psychological experiences of the individuals; I am completely uninterested in the psychology of art here – at any rate, in this objective sense, it is precisely the most rigorous and integrous artists who experience that this absolute immediacy they pursue in expressionism is a form of illusion. You can see that in a number of aspects. One of these is what I once tried to define using the term 'dialectic of loneliness',[15] which actually already applies to *Jugendstil*: that the situation of loneliness so characteristic of this whole atomistic consciousness in the late bourgeois phase, that this situation of loneliness is itself a universal situation, that everyone is so lonely, and that what one considers the absolutely immediate – the individual person's being-only-for-themselves – that this is itself mediated, which means it is something that actually contains the law of a totality which presses for atomization.[16] A further aspect of this kind is that – and it is one of the strangest aspects one can encounter in the experience of modern art, an aspect that gives the philosophy of art a great deal to think about – that this anti-conventional art, which expressionism was everywhere, must evidently produce something like certain conventions from within itself. At the moment when expression becomes art, where it is truly not just the immediate, living sound but strives in some way for objectification, it is evidently possible only through the development, the sedimentation of a language based on the agreement that certain colours, certain gestures and certain configurations are carriers of one expression and no other. It is very peculiar: one can examine this symbolism in detail – the literary historian Mautz has done so, for example[17] – with reference to the colour symbolism of the great German expressionist poets Georg Heym and Georg Trakl; probably one could even trace it back to the forefather of modernity, to Arthur Rimbaud.[18] One can equally show that, in radically expressionist music too, certain configurations have the tendency to keep returning, and that the anti-conventional, simply through the consistency with which it is used, with which it must be used in order to express at all what it is meant to express, and not to disintegrate into the insubstantial and completely indeterminate, itself contains [something] like a *principium stilisationis*. And, after all, the important artists of this particular expressionist phase experienced, likewise very early on, differently in the various countries – this aspect was more evident in France than in Germany or Austria – the aspect that I shall term 'aesthetic contingency'. By this I mean the chance nature of such a pure expressive language that, precisely because it constitutes a kind of internal agreement that this or that gesture, colour or pitch sequence is meant to have this or that meaning, always has an element of arbitrariness to it, and could in a certain sense also be different; and that the matter itself therefore objectively contains the demand to be objectified, to be shaped in such a way that it realizes through itself what it is meant to realize, rather than leaving this aspect to chance and preference.

This situation which I have tried to describe to you based on the inner problematics or dialectic of expressionism is precisely the situation in which the concept of construction comes into play for modern art as a whole; it is the point at which construction is demanded. It is very important here for you to grasp correctly – and I think this is generally fundamental to comprehension in questions of modern art – that you understand correctly that construction, in the very strict sense in which I am using the term, has nothing to do with the conventional and philistine view of form. I mean that the key aspects of problematics of expressionism I have just elaborated for you cannot be solved by saying: one cannot remain on the mere point, one has to return to forms, for otherwise, if one does not return to forms, it does not amount to anything. Firstly, this is a reactionary tendency – that is, a tendency which would truly deny that element of protest against convention, the emancipatory element. At the same time, however, there is a historico-philosophical impossibility in this; for it is in the nature of artistic forms that they are only possible because of the historico-philosophical conditions of their period. And Hegel's view that, in modernity, which meant the Romantic phase of music, the artist was free in relation to their object in the sense that they had the choice to select any form that suited or pleased them – this view of Hegel's, I am sorry to say, is very much an inartistic one, very far removed from the inner laws of these things. So if you wish to understand correctly the concept of construction towards which I wish to guide you, you must realize that there is a power being exerted here over the material in order to articulate this material completely, and to do away with those dangers or problems that arose from expressionism; but not – and I think this is the decisive aspect here – a form of power that is inflicted on the material as something foreign, through recourse to constraints, through stylistic will or the like, but rather an articulation that grows from the matter itself – even from the logic of the material itself, if you will. This construction is necessary because the forms no longer dictate with naïve immediacy, because they are no longer what Hegel termed 'substantial' in his aesthetics with reference to what he considered the great times in art.[19] The concept of construction, then, if I am to indulge in some very philosophically ambitious claims, essentially means nothing other than the effort to extract, purely from the matter and purely from the postulates of the matter – but through all efforts of the organizing artistic awareness – that objectivity which was once guaranteed by the established forms dictated to artists, whether truly or only supposedly, without borrowing from anywhere else. The term 'construction' – which means that the artist or the subject must by construction complete the organization of the material, in contrast to the concept of form, which dogmatically presupposes this act as already performed, one could say – points very clearly, if we examine this linguistic fact a little, to what I wish to express here. But the 'result' – if one can call it that – of expressionism, in fact, itself supplies the precondition for this transition to construction. For, on the one hand, expressionism cleansed the material, in a sense, of all merely conventional bonds. The material is now at the direct disposal of the subject. One can observe here what Heidegger called 'destruction'[20] – and Heidegger's philosophy in general, alongside many other things, also contains aspects of the expressionist legacy precisely in this meaning of destruction, namely the removal of some or other forms placed over it θέσει, leaving behind something like naked substances – although it then transpires, I would like to emphasize right here, that these purportedly naked, pure substances, which expressionism brought to light and which subsequently became available for construction in all the arts, are not naked or pure at all; rather, they always already contain an infinite number of mediations, philosophically put – that is to say, an infinite amount of spirit, of sedimented human elements. It is one of the strangest phenomena in modern art, one to which we may later return for a closer look, that this very aspect of linguistic character, this aspect of the human, which is still present in the apparent materials, resembles a vulnerable point that stimulates the artists, and that they actually remain utterly faithful to the expressionist impulse in this sense by attempting to eliminate ever more of this linguistic preformation of their material and the forms tied to this material, because the technically immanent state of procedures arrived at today no longer corresponds to this pre-dictated linguistic element.

In addition, expressionism supplied the preconditions for construction by carrying out that emancipation of the subject from predetermined forms which now permits it to control the material confidently and freely. Here you can really see quite precisely how seriously the concept of dialectic must be taken in aesthetic matters, that it is not some turn of phrase I use because I am accustomed from philosophy, alas, to thinking dialectically, but something that actually comes from the matter itself. In what can broadly be termed expressionist art, the subject attempted to express itself purely, without making art merely a semiotic language of its inwardness or its stirrings – it need not even be inwardness; one could almost say its nature – and, in so doing, to eliminate everything that heteronomously obstructed it. Thus, as I stated at the beginning of the lecture, one could say that it represented the cause of suppressed nature. By representing this cause, however, precisely by investigating this relationship with nature, by attempting to turn art directly into nature, namely the nature of the subject, it became autonomous in relation to its material and, through this autonomy – that is to say, by breaking down the heteronomous and everything standing in its way – gained a freedom or a new ability: the control over nature, the opposing aspect within the parallelogram of forces that works of art simply constitute, to highlight this opposing aspect all the more by reducing its material to the pure sound, the pure colour, the pure expressive value. By making it pure nature, [the artist] simultaneously turned it into the pure substance which they, as the artist, now have more or less at their disposal; hence the very fact that, in the expressionist movement, nature gained such a pure voice became the precondition, indeed the force, which demands and makes it possible for the opposing principle, namely the principle of construction, to take effect from within nature itself.

LECTURE 7

9 December 1958

In the last session, we attempted to address the problem of the relationship between nature and art – or, rather, the return of the natural aspect in art and the specific engagement with this aspect – by way of a central problem in contemporary art, namely the relationship between the aspect one can call expression and that of construction. In general terms, we had described the aspect of expression as a returning aspect of nature and that of construction as the artificial, as what one does to nature. I think that, after everything we have already discussed here, I do not really need to point out to you, and do so only out of conscientiousness, that, when I say expression is an aspect of nature in art, I do not mean that it is a piece of static, untransformed nature that remains as it is. Rather,[1] of course, this aspect in art is itself also subject to a historical process; indeed, one can virtually retrace – and that is what I was primarily doing in the last session – how, in modern art, this expressive aspect, this aspect of nature, this aspect of the not-quite-grasped, and also of the mimetic, hence the direct announcement of a feeling, went through an extraordinarily long and difficult process before it became capable of manifesting itself at all. In a certain sense, one can say that the emancipation of this aspect is itself a very late, artificial product, and that the purity of expression in general stands only at the end of a historical process in art, not its beginning; and this obviously means that, compared to a pure natural material of expression, this expressive aspect also went through an extraordinary internal transformation – transformation in the sense of differentiation. What distinguishes this natural aspect from original nature, then, is that, by finding its way into art, a differentiation takes place between feelings of the most varied kinds and between the finest shadings. Indeed, it seems as if the restoration of what can be interpreted as the voice of nature is essentially tied to this differentiation process; this means that, only when art is capable of the utmost specificity, of that which has not yet been mangled through classificatory impositions and generalization, when it truly attains specific difference – and that is only a very late result – does it actually become capable of being the voice of nature. And it means that the pure sound or the pure colour in art creates itself as a carrier of expression only when it is simultaneously defined, in a sense that will not be pursued at all, as a here and now, as something that is here and is unique. And perhaps that also gives you a sense of that idea of nature – the nature which, in the dialectic of art, is dominated and simultaneously restores itself – which differs entirely from the superficial concept of nature 'lyricism', for example, from nature painting, and from the superficial notions of what is termed 'natural' art. For, in reality, these traditional ideas of the natural in art presuppose certain conventions, certain generalities, as valid. Usually they refer – just think of all the bad nature novels – to the *concept*[2] of nature in the abstract, instead of yielding to that impulse which I have tried to show you is in keeping with the true ideal of expression. Hence one could practically say that the concept of nature in art, as I developed it for you in the previous session, is the precise opposite of the notion of an art deemed 'close to nature', as cherished by the cultivated philistine and displayed time and again by the enemies of modern art – although, on a side note, I think their basic reasoning error is that they view some states, whether forms of artistic expression or some prevailing conventions in art, as if they were themselves φύσει, as if they were naturally there, instead of recognizing their own historical character.

So, I had shown you last time that expressionism, if you treat it is something dynamic rather than static – and one could easily show that expressionism has its own developmental tendency, and a very strict, implacable one – led, on the one hand, to the material being cleansed of preformations and thus directly becoming construction but that, on the other hand, the subject also gained, in this phase, that freedom from all possible ties to convention which allowed it precisely to gain construction; here we had arrived at a concept of construction which stood in a certain opposition to that of form, in its traditional character. This means that construction is in fact the liberated form imprinted on the material by a free and, if you will, sovereign subject, whereas traditional form is one in which the separation of subject and object, and hence in this context the emancipation of the subject, has not yet taken place at all. Although, on the other hand, one certainly can say retrospectively, from the perspective of the artist's constructive freedom gained today – and I want to add this too, so that what I am showing you does not become too simplistic – that great artists of the past, such as Mozart or, as I just read in a very fine article published by *Akzente*,[3] Raphael, used forms from tradition yet were at once great constructors. So this form – aside from its traditionalist air, from those aspects in which it does not yet appear imprinted purely by the subject upon its content – is internally structured in such a way that, beneath the shell of convention, it already exhibits everything that one must demand from a liberated and autonomous construction; except that, back then, these forms were initially predetermined and the construction took place *within* the forms or beneath the surface, whereas today the problem of construction has become absolute, no forms are predetermined, and the form is consequently supplied purely by the subject that controls its material. At the same time, this control of the material by the artist – I tried to show you this too – consists simply in leaving this material to itself as far as possible, gaining freedom to the object and thus, one could say, completely becoming the executor of what the material demands in every single one of its aspects.

Perhaps I can use this opportunity to tell you that, among conventional notions of art, from which it is rather important for someone who reflects theoretically on artistic questions at all to emancipate themselves, one of the more important is the idea of the artist as a creator essentially independent in relation to their work, somehow drawing everything out of themselves; some secularized theological notions then found their way into this idea of the creator-artist. The artist thus becomes a form of little God, as one no longer really believes in the big one. Then one imagines that – if it's not to be found anywhere else any more – the artist performs such an act of creation.[4] I think that, by seemingly elevating art and the artist to such an excessive degree, one actually wrongs art and the artist in a way, not only by demanding too much of them but also by failing to do justice to the matter itself. This means that one describes it as something arbitrary, whereas it is generally the fact that the artist, albeit not every artist, if they – let me say this – have talent, if there is really something there and if they approach their object in true freedom, actually creates a disproportionately small part of it and does not in any case have that freedom, that creative power, everything the layperson attributes to them; rather, to an infinitely higher degree, they must obey the demands of the matter and cannot posit it purely in accordance with their own will. And when I say that one is wronging the artist by failing to recognize this, what I mean is simply that art's claim to objectivity – that is, its claim to be something like a manifestation of truth, not a mere game or something merely arbitrary – is directly connected to the fact that the so-called creative act actually shrinks to something infinitesimal, to the crossing of a boundary that can certainly not be thought away, but which essentially means the freedom to submit without arrogance or vanity, and with the utmost concentration, to what the matter wants purely of its own accord.[5] It is in this alone, not in the production of a so-called objectivist mindset, that I see any possibility for art to attain something like objectivity, especially in the present situation, but not through the artist's undertaking, in some archaic manner, their own efforts to shape the work of art as if anything resembling objectivity could be guaranteed from the outset.

It is unquestionable, however, that the tendencies towards the transition of expression – that dialectical shift of expression into construction which I attempted to reveal to you in the previous session – correspond to certain qualities on the subjective side, the side of the artist's own need to express or shape, and these are clearly qualities that are by no means predominant only among the artistically productive: they are exceedingly strong and exceedingly present among today's younger generation in general. That is why I feel a kind of duty to say at least a few things to you today about this subjective aspect which sets itself against expression. For one could say that there is a kind of allergy to expression in general, or – to put it a little more precisely and artistically – that the young generation, especially young artists, feel a kind of aversion to all those elements in the process of artistic production which can be termed speech-like. In this sense, language itself, if you will, is tending today towards de-lingualization, towards a rejection of its expressive elements. On the other hand, it is clear, for example in painting and quite especially in music, which is the art I can say most about, that the efforts of the young generation of composers ultimately amount to eliminating everything in music that recalls language, which they consider alien to it, and that any reminders of language whatsoever bother them. I already pointed out that this cleansing process, if you will, this puristic process within the act of artistic production, first of all undoubtedly contains the element – and I would call it an entirely legitimate element – of feeling that now, in the face of the radically emancipated material with which artists in all areas must reckon with today, whatever trace of language is still found within these materials is like a rudiment of something older. Thus a certain contradiction arises between the speech-like or, if you prefer, expressive traits and the historical state of the material itself; they behave as if there were still something predetermined, as if one could still rely on something that speaks from the material itself, so to speak, whereas the result of the young artist's conscientiousness is precisely that one can no longer rely on any such thing but genuinely faces a kind of *tabula rasa*, and the incredible paradox of every seriously current artistic production lies in the fact that one is confronted with a void of forms and specific materials, yet is still meant and compelled to draw from this void the particular characteristics through which alone the work of art gains a binding form. For if they do not come from the material, if they are simply imposed on it from without, then they have something arbitrary from the outset, an element of randomness which one resists extremely strongly. But I think there is something else here that is very characteristic of the current situation, and which one perhaps cannot necessarily encapsulate in the principle of the historico-philosophical state of the production process itself, but which should be understood more in terms of a dialectical anthropology: the aversion to expression as such. This aversion seems based first of all on the fact that any expression is, to an extent, considered vain in both senses of the word: firstly, the powerless individual, essentially meaningless alongside the overwhelming facts of the world in which we live, attempts through expression to claim that it is something after all; it gives itself airs that it is something substantial, as if anything depended on it, when everyone knows that nothing depends on it. But vain also in the other sense, namely that any such endeavour to effect, through recourse to the specific individuality expressed in each work of art, any meaningful changes in the state of awareness in which we live, let alone the state of the world itself, is doomed to futility; that when this individual, after withdrawing purely to itself, expresses itself, it no longer possesses the power to express anything substantial at all, but rather, by expressing itself, really expresses only something entirely transient, entirely ephemeral and insignificant, to which it clings only because there is nothing else, because, without relation to anything objective, individuality in itself is always null and void. That, I would say – so first of all this aspect of shame, if you will – is a central component of the hostility to expression.[6] But I think one should not make things too easy for oneself with this aspect. Do not forget that – and this is explained at length in the *Dialectic of Enlightenment*[7] – part of the signature of our entire civilization from a very early stage has been to place a sort of taboo on stirrings of expression; that, compared to the claims of the rationality which controls nature, every mimetic feeling that [deviates] to an extent from the straight path of the rational, which famously always views the shortest paths as the only and true ones, that everything which strays from this is essentially another Fall of Man, something uncivilized – one could almost say, something cultureless. Anyone who has lived in English-speaking countries for an extended period, as I did, has probably experienced this aspect even more strongly – this aspect of the mimetic taboo – than someone in Central Europe, or even France, would easily do, because in English-speaking countries this taboo is genuinely so strong that it is really viewed as a form of indecency to show feelings too strongly, rather like the way people in our culture already find it indecent if one speaks to strangers of private matters too quickly, too willingly, too uninhibitedly. Just as every expressive gesture, every sign of strong grief, especially every sign of pain – and the stirrings of expression are really always stirrings of pain – is subject to a kind of taboo: 'That isn't done.' It is essentially always the gesture of that famous governess who, when Gustav Mahler reached port in New York and his children became terribly excited, called out to them: 'Don't get excited! Don't get excited!'[8] – because, from this governess's point of view, mere excitation was already a sign of bad upbringing. Getting excited is something for common people, so to speak; those who are brought up properly, the gentleman and the lady, do not really get excited. But this aspect, this fear of expression – and one must surely think this through here – is clearly present in the current allergy to expression, and it seems to me to indicate – although this aversion to expression also contains those elements I tried to present to you as legitimate – that there is something harmful about it. This means that this civilizational consciousness, which art probably has a greater duty to protest against in the administered world than ever before, is suppressed, and that people thus have an allergic reaction to expression only because it reminds them of things that, under the current dominion of the civilizational principle, can hardly come to life properly any more. It is as if one can only bear it if one avoids speaking about it, if it does not even manifest itself in a sign. Firstly, I would quite simply say here that the strongest aspect of this allergy to expression prevalent today is fear, real-life fear, which has become so great that any art which reveals too much thus becomes unbearable to people. The objectivity demanded today contains both: the attempt to avoid all now illusory expressive elements and connections and also, negatively, the fear of letting in some of what is usually kept beneath the surface. The greatest works of art today will probably always be those in which the construction principle is very radically taken to its conclusion yet which, often through the very hardness of the construction principle, no longer submit to this ban on the expressive sphere.[9]

But we must also recall the problematics of the concept of individuality. If a great many people show a tendency to view this individuality as something meaningless, random and purely private – for example, upon encountering some picture or daring music – 'My goodness, that expresses his feelings, but it cannot really objectify them, cannot transform them into something general or convey them to me; he cannot communicate it, it is his private affair; and why should the expectorations of such a private person concern me? It is really simply indecent for him to bother me with that' – then, I would say, such a notion of the self-expressing subject in turn also rests on a certain naïveté. If one levels the accusation at this self-expressing subject that, in fact, it is not simply itself but actually null compared to objectivity, then this statement also contains something positive: namely that, while it is null as a mere individual, the principle on which its individuation rests – the fact that it is this powerless, suffering, needy human being who is standing here and nowhere else, and wants to express themselves – is itself an expression of that objective situation. It is objectivity, it is ultimately the character of society itself, that reduces people to that minimum which, on the other hand, is then meant to forbid them to express themselves in the present world. If that is the case, however, then the question of justification must also be posed quite differently. That is, the expression of this 'minimum', this very reduced thing that remains of each person at all, and is really little more than what Anatole France meant when he said that humans 'are born, suffer and die'[10] – then that is itself brought to a certain kind of objectivity, and by virtue of this objectivity it has the right to exist after all. An additional factor in the aversion to expression is undoubtedly that the expression of fear and everything connected to it falls short of real-life fear, whereas the mimetic taboo means that what is required for adaptation to rational society would have to be lost again.[11]

When I refer to the aspect I have just mentioned, namely of artistic fear falling short of real-life fear, I am thinking of something like the embarrassing, scarcely bearable nature of certain attempts to deal somehow with the horror of the 'Third Reich' on the theatre stage,[12] attempts that – however well they are meant, and although I do not wish to deny that they may have some humane effect, namely to remind people of some of the things they repress – fall so short of what happened that the mere fact of basing a play on whatever, let us say Anne Frank or the murder of children in the gas chambers of Auschwitz,[13] that the translation of these things into the aesthetic medium is a kind of injustice towards the dignity of the horror that took place there.[14] And if one shies away from expression as a whole today, then surely an element of this is that, in fact, one feels that one should be ashamed of any expression in the face of what happened in our world, and no doubt continues to happen, and whose nature really consists in the impossibility to find expression.

But I will not keep insisting on this point; let me rather tell you simply that, after what I have tried to lay out for you, the criticism of expression in the current artistic situation is at once true and false. It is false in the sense that it demands a direct positivity of the objective, a positivity that, if it does not contain – in whatever form – this subjective or expressive or natural aspect, in fact loses all tension and has the tendency to degenerate into mere wallpaper. On the other hand, however, the criticism of expression is true to the extent that it raises the problem of contemporary art – the problem of randomness – extremely seriously, and recent works have taken this bull by the horns, as it were: they thematize the problem of randomness itself to an extent.[15] One could say that, in the present situation, the absolutely purified material – that is, material cleansed of all predetermined categories of meaningfulness – has become caught up in something like a crisis of meaning.[16] This means that it no longer provides any meaning of its own accord, while the artist themselves, on the other hand, cannot breathe into it a meaning, something positively meaningful.[17] This results in what I would like to call the 'fetishism of methods',[18] that overvaluation evident in the entire development of contemporary art of technical procedures, which have been perfected to an extraordinary degree, in relation to the *terminus ad quem*, to the τέλος [télos], to – if I am to put it plainly – the *raison d'être* of the work of art, the cause for such a work of art to exist at all. And those are precisely the phenomena that have been described by the most different sides – and by no means always the most sympathetic ones – as a 'loss of tension' within modern art.[19] If I might be allowed to exaggerate very antithetically for a moment, I would say: until the most recent past, the question with which art as such was confronted was really whether a meaning can be realized in art. In the whole of Romanticism, for example, the question of how the aggregate of a series of experiences, how they [were articulated], especially in the great Romantic philosophy of Schelling, of Schopenhauer, but also of Hegel, how such experiences of something meaningful could now concretely find their way into the artistic form. And the fragility of most things in this period of art lies in the fact that it stopped at meaningful ideas more or less inserted into the artistic form from outside, without these ideas becoming substantial on their own terms, in the sense of organizing the work of art completely of their own accord. Then the result is something like the worldview art – let us say, of the highest standard – of Richard

Wagner,[20] but also someone like Hebbel[21] or, if you will, even in a certain sense the worldview art of Flaubert,[22] who was certainly infinitely superior to either of these in purity of design, but in whose work the rupture between intention and the actual material content nonetheless emerges, although this rupture itself is really one of the main thematic elements of Flaubert's writing. In comparison, the situation faced by contemporary art today has been radically inverted. For it precedes a critique of the illusory nature of aesthetic meaning, as it were incorporating the liquidation of all these Romantic and worldview-based conceptions. It no longer asks: how can a meaning realize itself aesthetically, truly realize itself completely, without infiltrating art as a worldview? Today, by contrast, it asks this: how can a pure material, how can pure material processes then become meaningful?[23] So the question of the relationship between idea and appearance[24] – if I could use these two terms here for a moment – has been radically inverted in contemporary art. For art today, the point is no longer how an idea can be made to appear – that was really a dominant notion from German classicism until expressionism and beyond – but rather the opposite: how can the appearance, by virtue of the artist leaving it to itself positivistically, as it were, without reserve but also without adding any meaning, how can such an appearance, and thus all organized material processes, become meaningful?[25] I would say, however, that it is very easy to mock this line of questioning. It is very easy to say that a fine art is one which starts from its material, but which must then also ask how this material can become meaningful. A spiteful person could say, 'So it is an art that says something but does not know what it has to say, and which is really always in search of what it actually has to say – whereas, in supposedly better times, art always knew what it had to say and was only unsure at times how to say it.' I think that this dismissal of the problems which I have just improvised for you would be very superficial, for that crisis of meaning which I initially described to you as a purely aesthetic one is, in fact, also the crisis of the state of the world itself.[26] I am not in the same fortunate situation as the aesthetician Lukács, who claimed that the worldview of 'diamat'[27] consisted, among other things, in viewing the course of the world in total as a meaningful one moving towards the best end[28] – if only because even such a hope could not for a second take away or console mankind for the boundless suffering and boundless injustice of history so far, even if it were only a prehistory. Today, reality itself is in a very serious crisis of meaning. So there is not only no longer a binding order, a binding worldview or anything similar which is given so that one could react by searching, with greater or lesser success, to find another such binding worldview to hold onto; rather, the very meaning through which the experience of existence would organize itself has become as problematic as the hope that this disastrous course of the world could one day be changed. In this, the situation today is radically different from the situation formulated historico-philosophically by Hegel and Marx.[29] And if art finds itself in the absurd situation of having to search for a meaning in its material processes, as it were, where – if I may repeat this – it says something without knowing what to say, then it is in fact expressing the current state of the world spirit with absolute purity;[30] and if it has the possibility to go beyond this state, to transcend it at all, it is probably only by expressing itself in this way.[31] In that sense, I believe, this crisis – as absurd as it might seem today, and however much it provokes the resistance of the critical awareness – is an inevitable consequence of the historical-philosophical state of things.

On the other hand, however, it must be said that the attempt at a pure construction – the attempt to breathe meaning into the material purely by surrendering to it completely unreservedly – seems itself doomed to fail, primarily because this material one is dealing with is not like some [natural material]. That is indeed the error made by many material fetishists among my young artistic friends, who think this material is itself a natural material, and that one need only make it speak, as it were, for nature itself to speak purely.[32] This marks the limit of construction, for construction, as I told you, is the attempt to surrender completely to the material by, if you will, crossing out the subject. But because, not being nature, it does not produce the material in a pure state of its own accord, because this material is also historical, such attempts to yield unreservedly to the material themselves display an element of the arbitrary, the random. They treat as a pure natural force something which is only a human will concealed from itself. In this way, it is the extreme anti-subjectivism of today's constructivist art that finds itself especially caught up in a form of subjectivism. This means that the self-unaware subject overlooks its own presence in the material – as if it were the actual force that posits meaning.[33] The material itself is never pure and entirely material, nor does it guarantee any meaning on its own. So this is how the problem of randomness has entered art today – a randomness that concerns not only the individual aspects within the works of art but also the construction, the formal principles themselves, in which, the more rigorously they are executed, the more there is also a degree to which they could equally well be different. And that is why the problem of the aleatoric, and thus in a sense a purely scientific category – if you will: the idea of statistics – has now infiltrated art;[34] and that is the present state of nature in this dialectic of art and nature.

LECTURE 8

11 December 1958

I was posed another two questions by members of your group today, and I am glad to be able to answer them, despite receiving them only just now, and hence lacking the necessary time to think through the problems touched on, which are certainly not very simple. The first question concerns what I mean by the crisis of meaning in reality, and especially by the change in the situation of art with reference to this problem of the crisis of meaning. The question in its original wording is as follows: 'It was not clear to us what you meant by a "crisis of meaning" in our social reality, or how this reality has differed in concrete terms from other historical realities since the time of expressionism – e.g., the time of the late nineteenth century.' I think it would be too much for me if you expected an immediate historico-philosophical analysis of the change in the objective historico-philosophical situation since that time. I could not provide that. But one can certainly say this much – and I will try to keep a little more closely to the specifically art-theoretical problems – that, in the time of expressionism, the horizon of experience was incomparably more open to the assumption of an aspect of meaning, be it transcendence (to which people are open, as is evident from the special status of religious motifs in the poetry of high expressionism) or be it the notion that the world itself must be shaped as a meaningful world (as in the recent book by Lukács, which resembles a final recollection of that age) – I think I touched on that in the last session – and contains the somewhat pathos-laden, almost confessional formulation that he or his like simply believed that the process of the world was meaningful, that it moved towards a meaningful τέλος, and that any art which did not partake of this meaning through its perspective was consequently bourgeois and decadent.[1] I really have no intention of raising the question of how far reality's chance of coming into itself, as Hegel would have said,[2] of becoming a meaningful reality or not, has decisively changed since the time of high expressionism, though I tend towards the opinion – as you asked me for my opinion – that, in this aspect too, there have been very far-reaching changes in the last forty years. But I think I can at least justify telling you this much: both the awareness of a principle that gives meaning to life in an absolute sense and the concrete hope that people will thus gain control of themselves have faded to such a degree that substantiality no longer has the power to carry art as something objectively binding. There is no longer an art movement today, and it is really very difficult to imagine an art movement that drew its strength from assuming such a meaningful aspect as positively given. As in all historico-philosophical cases, the situation is hence that, in retrospect, one can also observe elements of the problematics we face today in the previous, the older phase.[3] This means that, if one looks at how the name of God is bandied about in Werfel's work, for example[4] – I will not even discuss Rilke, as it is debatable how far he can even be called an expressionist – one can already sense very clearly that referring to such categories here already has something hollow, something no longer tenable about it; that these categories, then, should really be ruled out by a strictly self-aware literature or art in general, as in such great and genuinely theologically inspired art as Kafka's, in which one can search in vain – fortunately, I would say – for any such direct allusions to a divine meaning.[5] So, in this sense, the question is justified. Perhaps this side of things has not changed fundamentally since the time of expressionism; but this, in retrospect, could be considered a judgement on expressionism itself, whose weakness, whose powerlessness, whose – how should I put it? – 'frozen' manner of the exclamation mark comes from the fact that every fibre of it still acts as if a meaning were present in a positively embodied form, when in reality it is already absent. If one wished to salvage expressionism at all today, this could probably happen only in the sense of decoding it as a powerless invocation, as a desperate attempt at invocation, yet one already scarred in its desperation; not, however, in the sense of asserting these primal words in which it believed itself – these 'phaenomena', as the young Werfel called them[6] – as something directly present. One can say, at any rate, that – let me just use this ghastly expression for the sake of clarification – the 'underlying sense of life' among the artists – I would describe it more

precisely as the historico-philosophical place, the *a priori* preconditions on which all production rests – is such that nothing so positively
meaningful is given by it. And the situation of crisis I have described
to you purely in terms of the technical dialectic, namely that the
material could be said to ask how it can become material – this is
explained by that very historico-philosophical situation. This, first
and foremost, is my answer to the question of what I meant to
express.

Now for the second question: 'At a different point you mentioned
that, in a work of art, radical alienation demands an adequate representation, but that the work simultaneously possesses truth because
unmutilated nature, which would no longer find a voice in actual
society, is able to speak through it. My question: how can immanent
critique be used to reveal the aspects of alienation and unmutilated
nature be concretely in the individual work of art?' I will try not to
make things too easy for myself by simply saying that, on the one
hand, one cannot provide any formula for such things, while attempting, on the other hand, to reveal such aspects to you as best I can in
a concrete analysis; for it is always a little too easy to deal with such
questions, which always express a degree of genuine unease, using
such declarations. So I would rather attempt, even if the question
itself does not seem entirely to identify precisely what I meant, to do
justice to its intention and thus answer it nonetheless. If I said that
the task of art in every period is to allow unmutilated nature to speak
in actual society, then this was genuinely a slip of the tongue, a
mistake, and I must apologize to you for it. One cannot make unmutilated nature speak, for this unmutilated nature, a pure nature – that
is to say, a nature that has not gone through the mediation processes
of society – does not exist. On the other hand, I believe I tried so
emphatically in my lecture to tell you this – in the last one too, where
I warned of all attempts at a direct representation of the natural –
that I dare say you can easily correct this misunderstanding yourselves if I made any such misleading statement. I would rather say
that it is the task of art to give a voice to mutilated nature, meaning
nature in the respective form in which it exists through its historical
mediations at a particular stage in history, not that it should dwell
on the chimera of such a pure form of nature.

Now you say in your question, and that really strikes me as very
rigorously thought out: I am actually demanding two contradictory
things of art. On the one hand, I claim that art must articulate the
state in which we, humans, mankind, every individual finds themselves historically, and this state simply happens to be that of alienation. On the other hand, however, I demand of art that it give a

voice to suppressed, mutilated nature, meaning the exact opposite of alienation. So am I not, in a sense, demanding both freedom of press and censorship from art in the same breath? I think it is truly good to think about this seriously for a second, for here you can really take a little course in dialectic. You see, I would say that, if what I tried to lay out for you in the last session – that pure, untouched nature in its immediacy can neither be recognized nor crafted by art – then the only possibility to give a voice to this suppressed force is negativity – that is to say, the very expression of alienation itself.[7] So what I mean is not that one can give a voice directly to nature in its manifestations, however they may be transformed, but rather that only by casting a veil of silence over what lies beneath, which art can never lose, after all, and showing nothing but the form of alienation itself, by excluding it, by refraining from taking the side of this nature in some illusory or deceptive manner, only by confronting its very deformation, if I can formulate it very starkly – only thus can one express at all what might, at best, be meant by the category of nature today. If you recall the concept from philosophy of 'determinate negation',[8] meaning that the abstract form of truth is not given to us, not *'verum index sui et falsi'*, but rather *'falsum index sui et veri'*[9] – that is, by measuring and confronting every phenomenon with what it claims to be, we can thus arrive at its untruth and, by negation, if we want, also at its truth. If you hold on to this idea and view it as constitutive for art too – and here, I believe, art and philosophy truly form a radical unity – then I think you will understand that it is precisely through the expression of complete alienation – the fact that every corner of pure nature is excluded from art, that art does not pretend nature is still present in it – that, precisely because of this, the aspect of nature which, as I said, consists in suffering and negativity is captured and can only be expressed at all in this manner.

Perhaps I could characterize this idea a little more closely for a second in the way that befits aesthetic reflections, namely with a technical examination: through the concept of defamiliarization [*Verfremdung*].[10] For the alienation of the world can be clearly reproduced only in the work of art – and I think that Brecht, as a theorist, saw something very significant here – that one refrains from presenting the familiar, because it is something conventional and preformed, as familiar.[11] The task of art is, in fact, to defamiliarize the familiar, which allows it to be seen from a perspective that is the perspective of its essence, no longer the mere appearance. Through this aspect of defamiliarization itself, however, something happens that communicates, if you will, with the concept of nature in an extraordinarily profound sense. For this dismantles the conventional, it dismantles everything that mediates between the matter itself and consciousness. So, through the fact that the object is defamiliarized, through the fact that the artistic formulation does justice radically to the actually existing alienation between the subject and the object, the object is, in a certain very delicate sense, changed back into nature; not into an ahistorical nature that faces us once and for all – you know I ruled out such a notion very thoroughly – but rather changed back into that which is, one could say, freed of its ideological ingredient. [And that actually comes] very close to what I meant when I said that mutilated nature – namely, what the world has largely done to us and to nature[12] – is meant to be given a voice in this manner in the work of art. So one could genuinely say that, on the dialectical level of estrangement we inhabit, the consistent technique of aesthetic defamiliarization somehow restores the view of nature. And it is no coincidence that very important artists using the defamiliarization technique, like Brecht, but above all Samuel Beckett,[13] by taking this process of defamiliarization extremely far, by completely doing away with the self-evident certainty of what one terms 'realistic experience', end up with something that, in a sense, [evokes] natural conditions, eating, drinking, sleeping, illness, physical harm[14] – that a kind of naked nature remains in these works, but that this naked nature is precisely not the mythicized, idealized, eternal, so-called all-nature,[15] but rather that to which humans – in keeping, one could almost say, with the process of historical mutilation to which they are subjected – are ultimately reduced.[16] I think this does perhaps give you a concrete idea – which I readily admit I did not provide adequately in the lecture – but you can see here how the dialectic also refers in a very particular fashion to the categories I myself presented to you. This means there is not nature over here and alienation or defamiliarization over there; rather, the categories of nature and alienation are themselves mutually mediated, they necessarily refer to each other and necessarily depend on each other in the situation of contemporary art. I hope this answers the question to some extent. Should this not be the case, I would ask the gentlemen who posed it to say something about it.[17]

In the last session, while dealing with the concrete dialectic between the aspects of expression and construction, which here stood in for the aspects of nature and spirit in art, we came up against a particular limit, namely the limit which is imposed on construction and which today applies in artistic experience per se. Hence this limit to construction – perhaps I could just repeat this – comes from the fact that construction itself is not literally construction in the realm of art. It is perhaps good if one examines this idea, which I swallowed up somewhat in the last session, more precisely. The term 'construction' was taken up into art theory from the language of technology, and, in technology, construction refers to a rational standardization of a number of given elements, and its law is quite simply that the object in question which is constructed in this manner functions correctly. The construction is good if it adequately fulfils the task assigned to it in reality with the smallest possible expenditure of power, with the smallest possible use of material and with the most durable results, and whatever other criteria there might be. If you recall – which you must not overlook for a second if you are to avoid falling out of aesthetic reflection, so to speak – that art does not serve this kind of real practical purpose but is, rather, separate from the realm of purposes, then you will immediately find that no such literal construction exists in art. And if certain theorists, for example the Cologne music theorist Eimert, have taken the position that art must reach the point where one no longer asks today whether a work is true or untrue but, rather, whether it is correct or incorrect,[18] then this does show a particular tendency, namely the binding, responsible moulding of the material; yet this aspect of a work of art's 'correctness' is, of course, not given in the same way as in mathematics. You cannot literally prove a work of art in the same way, cannot literally construct it the way you can construct a piece of reality. And great artists of radical modernity such as Paul Klee and Juan Gris – God knows both of them were constructivists – emphasized time and again that, in truth, the constructive work of art begins only at the point where its own so-called laws are suspended.[19] As I tried to show you, however, the truth is that the critique of the expressive aspect, the tendency to strip away everything that is not itself construction through the totalist demands of construction, which comes at the expense of everything that opposes it in the artistic material and the artistic shaping; that, as a result, art is almost compulsively driven into the position of following its own constructive principles to the letter, and thus understanding itself as if it were truly something like a suspension bridge or a similar object. This means that, through its own art, if you will, art is shifted into a kind of conflict with the aesthetic principle itself, with non-literal being, with the principle of semblance. On a side note, you can see very clearly something that strikes me as being of considerable importance for the physiognomy of the current situation, namely that certain regressions of consciousness – a certain infantilization of the overall consciousness which can be observed in every nook and cranny of our world today – do not come simply from the fact that people have become so weak, so stupid, so foolish or whatever; rather, it is that this infantilization, this regression of consciousness, one could almost say, is implicit in the principle of progress itself. That is, at the moment when the construction principle is truly taken to its logical conclusion in art, this aesthetic stringency will produce a result as if a work of art were ultimately a mathematical exercise, and thus bring it down to the level of literality, a crude factuality that opposes the very principle of art – but we do not have the right simply to dismiss this development with a certain condescending arrogance, for it is contained in the matter itself. It is similar, if you will permit the comparison, to the way in which it is easy and convincing to see that positivist philosophy, which essentially cuts off all true philosophical questions as meaningless and pointless, ultimately arrives at complete tautologies and formalisms – indeed, it constitutes a total regression of consciousness in relation to the interest that philosophy has in any substantial questions – yet that, nonetheless, there is in epistemology, which is the reflection of knowledge upon itself, a certain satanic necessity that leads precisely to these positivistic constructions. I think it is good for you to appreciate that in all its seriousness, so you do not think that one can deal with these extremely difficult things by having a good attitude, as it were, and by feeling what would be better. One can deal with them, if at all, only by grasping them in their necessity and then in turn criticizing this necessity. Whatever there is to be said about that, it follows from what I have told you, at any rate, that construction in art reaches its limits as a result of this – a twofold limit, in fact: on the one hand, because the concept of construction in art really becomes meaningless when there is nothing left to construct. In contrast to the empirical realm, where the concept of construction makes good sense, as I have tried to outline for you, construction in art really *cannot* mean anything but the organization of something otherwise diffuse and manifold that no longer has its own principles of organization, and would truly degenerate into senselessness, but is now held together.[20] But if, as modern art genuinely intends in a certain sense, this construction principle is elevated to an absolute, if the non-identity of this identity[21] is underlined because, as some composers have wanted, the stipulation of the note-row for a composition would make the entire course of this composition predetermined, every single rest and even all its instrumental aspects[22] – I can reassure you: in reality it is not – yes, if that were truly the case, then the construction would become meaningless for lack of meat, crudely put. That is to say, there would then be nothing to construct, and the construction would potentially cancel itself out as a result. On the other hand, however, the second reason why one reaches one of the limits of construction is that the construction principle itself is not justified on its own terms – or its relation to the purpose, namely by the thing driving or working in whatever fashion – but the construction is rather divorced from any criterion of its own truth or untruth, as it were: it is self-sufficient, one could say. And if it seriously has to offer a proof of its truth, a proof that it can truly only be thus and no other way, then the construction principle always reveals an element of randomness.[23] A few young music theorists have even seen fit to enlist Heisenberg's concept of the 'uncertainty principle';[24] I think it would have been better not to do so, but I thought I would at least mention it to you as a curiosity. At any rate, as soon as the construction principle is truly applied in earnest, when it asserts itself as something literal, it transpires that it is not anything literal, as one is not actually dealing with pure mathematics, a pure logic of the matter itself, but always to a certain degree with the arbitrary decisions of an aesthetic subject. And that is how the aspect of randomness which I mentioned to you finds its way complementarily into the construction, randomness in a twofold sense: on the one hand, the aspect of randomness in whatever individual detail still appears in this construction, which is random because it is essentially no longer there at all and only called by the construction to its respective location, where it no longer identifies itself concretely as something meaningful; and, on the other hand, also an element of randomness in the construction as a whole.[25]

I think that the most recent efforts of a so-called aleatory[26] approach, which you can observe in music in the most peculiar fashion and the most diverse places independently of one another – in America with Cage,[27] in France with Boulez[28] and in Germany with Stockhausen,[29] though the American Cage deserves priority – that this aleatory principle is really a form of self-awareness of this state that, in art, any use of rules that is driven to the absolute and fetishistically exaggerates itself simply turns into something random.[30] But I would like to share a few deliberations with you that might contribute to unsettling you with regard to a number of concepts we have to work with here, but in which I must also unsettle you for the sake of a defamiliarization, namely the defamiliarization of art itself. For the experience one encounters when faced with these constructs is such that something begins to unravel which all of us – myself included, before I experienced this – nearly took for granted in art: the notion of musical meaning as an aesthetic criterion. Though I can at least cite the extenuating circumstance that I have already treated very extensively with the crisis of meaning in *Philosophy of New Music*,[31] and that at the end of that book I even raised the question of whether music might ultimately have to forfeit the aspect of its authenticity, its having-to-be-such-and-no-other-way, if it seriously wanted to end its servitude to the ruling culture.[32] So the uncanny element, and that which, if I am not mistaken, also causes art itself to lose something of that aspect of naturalness and self-evidence which it still had until our time, is twofold. First of all, it is evidently the case in art that whatever is treated with absolute rigour takes on a kind of meaning through this rigour. In other words, meaning is not necessarily something that art can express; one has only to [follow] some principle, even if it is the principle of a schoolteacher gone wild or a watchmaker; even if one uses such a principle to organize some work of art in an utterly intractable, stubborn and paranoid fashion, and does so for long enough and goes far enough, then its sheer stringency alone permits the work to present itself as if it were actually meaningful. I had an opportunity to observe this already thirty years ago in several artistically rather childish experiments by the Austrian musical tinkerer Joseph Matthias Hauer,[33] who used a self-devised and truly abysmally primitive system of so-called tropes to produce an equally primitive music. But because he did not depart from this principle for even a second, these constructs did exude a certain kind of suggestive power; and naturally this is the case to an even higher and more extreme degree with the incomparably more advanced organization of the constructions one can encounter in contemporary music. For now, this really means only that the compelling force, the suggestive element, the element in a work of art whereby one can define its meaning in the first place – that it constitutes a kind of context with a kind of logic one cannot escape – that this element itself should, in fact, probably never be taken entirely literally in art, that no work of art is a real complex of meaning, but that every work of art is actually only the fiction of a complex of meaning; that it pretends to be a complex of meaning; that it evokes the semblance of a self-contained and integral whole but cannot really preserve this integral wholeness in itself. And now it is called to order for this, as it were, by these aleatory structures; it gets its comeuppance. So it transpires that, if one now dispenses with this semblance – this semblance of embodying a meaning – and instead focuses purely on stringency, that something resembling meaning will nonetheless arise, except that this meaning is itself cursed with the aspect of randomness of which I tried to show you how it finds its way into these things in the first place.[34] On the other hand, however, and this is one of the experiences I have had with the works of John Cage in particular, whose quality I do not even intend to assess, as their nature is such that the question of aesthetic quality would truly be out of place and would miss the point entirely: in a sense, they do not aspire to be works of art, and indeed they are not through-composed pieces. But in these compositions, which are the antithesis of the pure construction principle shifted to the extreme, the principle of chance has been elevated to the only one that still applies. This means that, in the instrumental parts of a composition such as his piano concerto,[35] which are really only sketched and arbitrarily recorded, there is no rule, no structural connection except for the absolute prohibition of any relationships, thematic or otherwise, between the elements that appear in it. The only rule is that, amid the universe of notes at every moment and in every colour, each note has the same chance to have its turn. It really is the principle of chance taken to its limit. If you listen to this peculiar thing, then you too – and that is really something that gives much food for thought – will certainly not have the impression of something meaningless but, rather, through this negative principle, have the impression of an extremely integrated quality, if you will, even a very strong necessity. And you will even perceive, through this complete surrender to chance, a form of expression – a desperate utterance of wildly protesting expression – that goes very far beyond what one knows from traditional expressive works of art.[36] I am aware that one does not generally speak about constructs like the piano concerto by John Cage in aesthetics lectures. Following the principle at which I hinted to you, however, namely that I believe one must extrapolate theory from the most advanced tendencies of development, not vice versa, I do not wish to keep these things from you.

You can see here that the category of meaning which I have presented to you is not a final, isolated one that can be taken as the measure of all things; rather, one must think it in such a context oneself, like the context of the categories I just laid out for you. But at any rate, what applies for now is that, today, the subject is confronted by construction in its reified and external form – construction that has become absolute. And that aspect of the loss of tension, which all of us probably observe in so much modern art, and which precisely those who identify with it, not those who make a great fuss about the 'loss of the centre',[37] have most reason to observe – this aspect of the loss of tension within modern art seems to stem from the fact that, very often, the absoluteness of the construction principle eliminates the aspect of tension between the construction and the constructed, one could almost say between the subject and the object, and that, as a result, these purely subjectively posited laws simultaneously reveal the force of their arbitrariness. The upshot of this for the concrete work of art and concrete artistic shaping is to work against these things, to counteract this 'fury of disappearance'[38] in construction in a certain sense, and to strive anew for something unambiguously crafted. The problem, which is really the fundamental problem faced by contemporary art as something to be achieved, [is] no longer one of construction alone but, rather, the problem of formulating characters, characters that are inalienable, unmistakable, that give each individual element a specific quality, and which are then the factors enabling the construction principle to find its justification again, if at all.[39] You can, if you [take up] this idea of rediscovering characters – and the problem of characters also has a long history in art[40] – then you can perhaps observe in the general philosophy of history in art, or in aesthetics, that, if art history does not proceed in a straight line, if there is no such thing as straight and uninterrupted progress, but possibly categories such as expression or the characterization or shaping of the individual element are instead taken up again at a certain point, this does not necessarily imply any heteronomous demands brought to the work from without; rather, such leaping, such a zigzag or spiral, follows the dialectic of presenting artistic problems from the perspective of this presentation itself. In other words, the schema of two-dimensional progress is not the same as the movement of the spirit itself, which cannot be imagined except as a dialectic.

LECTURE 9

16 December 1958

It is my intention to introduce the consideration of the central aesthetic concept, namely the concept of beauty, which we must now address, by discussing with you one of the first major texts to contain something like a theory of beauty. The text in question is a section from Plato's *Phaedrus*, approximately chapters 30 to 32 according to the famous Stephanus pagination.[1] Now, you could say first of all that it is rather strange to begin an examination of the concept of beauty by drawing on a passage of a somewhat mythological, dogmatic and certainly pre-critical character such as this one by Plato. For it is really an explanation, a continuation of one of the most famous Platonic myths: that of the charioteer from the *Phaedrus*.[2] If I have chosen this passage nonetheless, it is because it demonstrates that Plato was a philosopher after all, not a mythologist; that is, all the decisive motifs which later appear in the philosophical theory of beauty are collected in this exegesis and continuation of a mythological reflection, somewhat akin to the way that, in the introductions to certain great symphonies, the most important themes are presented as if under glass and are then developed in the course of the symphony itself. So I can here present to you *in statu nascendi*, as it were, in an almost prehistoric form, the motifs that dominate the discussion of the concept of beauty. And I think I can, at the same time, carry out a kind of test – if you will permit the term – of the fruitfulness of what we have developed together so far, as I will elucidate a large part of the motifs that are now found here, and later return in the philosophy of beauty, in aesthetics – indeed, I would almost say, take away some of their mythical foreignness – with the aid of concepts we have already used.

At any rate, I must at least say a few brief words about this dialogue by Plato so that you know what you are actually dealing with here. It is a dialogue which has had an exceedingly strange fate in intellectual history. In Schleiermacher's time, people assigned it to Plato's youth; if I am not mistaken, it was even taken for the first, the earliest Platonic dialogue.[3] Then, for many long decades, it held its place as one of the four so-called classical dialogues that lay out Plato's theory of forms, which also include the *Republic, Symposium* and *Phaedo*.[4] And finally, during the last decades, this dialogue was even taken up into the body of Plato's late works because, if I am correctly informed, of exclusively philological considerations, primarily word statistics.[5] Perhaps I could just take this opportunity to say that the inclusion of this dialogue among the late dialogues strikes me as extremely problematic on account of its content, despite the philological evidence that might support it, because the theory of forms, which is indeed the focus of this dialogue, is not presented here in its revised, mitigated state – which characterizes the later Plato – but in fact appears substantially in its classical form and directly recalls formulations from the *Phaedo*, very often down to specific conceptual motifs. Otherwise one would be confronted with the extremely peculiar fact that the aged Plato, as it were forgetting the revision evident in such dialogues as the *Statesman* or the *Laws*, had fallen back on his middle-period, classical, starkly dualistic theory of forms.[6] It seems more likely to me that this dialogue is composed of several layers, that it was originally one of the so-called sophistic dialogues, the critical confrontations of subjectivistic atheism, and was then merged with the theory of forms; and it is certainly conceivable that, as is usually the case with such problem children, it occupied him for his entire life and he subjected [the text] to reworking in the end. In its structure, at any rate, the [*Phaedrus*] is one of the thinker's most complicated and enigmatic works, so complicated that it is almost impossible to point to a general theme of this dialogue. It begins as a discussion of a sophistic speech about love in which a starkly sophistic claim is made, namely that the only true lover is the one who does not love himself.[7] This thesis, which is presented to Socrates by a youth, a young student of the Sophists – Phaedrus – is then corrected by Socrates, one might say, in the sense that he immanently criticizes it and outdoes it in a speech that is both more internally rigorous and more virtuosic.[8] This, however, is suddenly followed by a magnificent rupture. The entire approach up to that point is abandoned, and we are instead offered a doctrine of love that corresponds to Socratic theory itself, and which is mostly based on the motif of re-remembering, or anamnesis.[9] And let me say it already: what the Platonic theory of beauty essentially states is that the power of beauty comes from the fact that we recognize the Form – or whatever it is – in the objects or people we have reason to call beautiful.[10] It is this splendid motif of pain and longing, which seizes people in the face of beauty, that was formulated for the first time and in the most outstanding fashion in this dialogue.[11] This interpretation is then followed by a third part, which also has a very typical Platonic form that I would like to place in the category of return. This means that now the soul, saturated with the experiences gathered by philosophy after turning towards its highest objects, namely the Forms, returns to the earth and now brings the sublime – to use one of Kierkegaard's terms[12] – into the pedestrian.[13] This Platonic motif, incidentally, went on to play a tremendous part in German classicism too; one need think only of Faust's 'I weep, I am for the earth again'[14] to understand that. The meaning of this return – which is also hinted at, incidentally, at the end of the *Symposium*, and which is highly characteristic of Plato's middle period – is now that the elements of the theory of forms as presented in the great parable of the palinode, which really constitutes the middle section,[15] are then applied to the issues relating to the rhetoric at the beginning. One can say that this dialogue intertwines motifs such as the critique of sophism, the attempt to make rhetoric objective, to base it on the truth content, namely the forms, and then the theory of forms itself, which found some of its most powerful formulations in the palinode, and finally also something like a Platonic aesthetics[16] and a Platonic doctrine of love at the same time. And all these aspects are so artfully interwoven that really one thing always conditions the other. In a certain sense, the dialogue is comparable to the *Symposium*, in that it does not present a single thesis but, rather, expresses its idea – or its content – purely through the constellation of the aspects contained within it.[17] But the structure, if one can put it like this, is even subtler, even more artful than in the *Symposium*, because here one does not simply have a steady build-up of the concept – that is, a dialectic from which the searched-for concept emerges ever more purely as the result; rather, these elements are all treated separately at their respective points and actually reveal their content far more like threads of a carpet[18] than as things which can be understood through such a uniform process of development.

I would strongly encourage all of you, if you occupy yourselves at all with aesthetics and the matters we are dealing with here, to read this dialogue, the *Phaedrus*, in its entirety; for one must simply recognize it as one of the greatest basic texts in the whole of Western metaphysics, and you can also learn something about the problem of philosophical representation as an integral aspect of philosophical truth itself. For if talk of Plato's art of representation is more than a mere school platitude for any work,[19] and rather justified by the structure of the idea, then – aside from the *Symposium* – it is this dialogue. One of its central 'themes', it must be said, is the relationship between reason and madness;[20] the position of reason – Hegel would say, of 'reasoning' or merely reflective reason[21] – is essentially equated with merely sophistic reason, and the actual transition to the middle part, which is accompanied by a very abrupt shift, takes place at the moment when Socrates – referring, perhaps in mild jest, to nymphs – shows himself seized by enthusiasm and leaves the rational realm.[22] There is an entirely systematic reason for this, if you will, in Platonic philosophy. Platonic philosophy as a whole has a peculiar twofold character, for it is rational or, to use its own terminology, dialectical, meaning that it consists in the definition and development of concepts – both the abstraction and the classification of concepts – yet is not limited to this but rather – so that the concept indeed becomes what it really is, namely the objectively valid idea – since it is joined by that very aspect of ἐνθουσιασμός [enthousiasmós], divine madness, which Plato deems the element in which the highest truth discloses itself, albeit only as a sudden flash:[23] until, having experienced it, we carry out that return which is so fundamental to Platonic philosophy. And it is from this defence of madness against rationality – one could almost say: against stupidity, so-called female wisdom or equally male wisdom, which believes it can take possession of what it loves through especially clever and devious efforts, instead of throwing itself to the ground and surrendering to ardour – it is from this justification of delirium, and really an erotic delirium, that Plato's theory of beauty follows on. He presents intense emotion in the face of beauty as one of those forms of madness which is wiser than the usual wisdom of reason. I had to tell you this much so that you would understand what I will now read you, and then interpret in some detail. So, we read in chapter 30:

'Now we reach the point to which the whole discussion of the fourth kind of madness was tending. This fourth kind of madness is the kind which occurs when someone sees beauty here on earth and is reminded of true beauty. His wings begin to grow...' – this 'his wings begin to grow' is a reference to the central parable that precedes this,[24] but which I shall not discuss now –

> ... and he wants to take to the air on his new plumage, but he cannot; like a bird he looks upwards, and because he ignores what is down here, he is accused of behaving like a madman. So the point is that

this turns out to be the most thoroughly good of all kinds of possession, not only for the man who is possessed, but also for anyone who
is touched by it, and the word 'lover' refers to a lover of beauty who
has been possessed by this kind of madness. For, as I have already
said, the soul of every human being is bound to have seen things as
they really are, or else it would not have entered this kind of living
creature. But not every soul is readily prompted by things here on earth
to recall those things that are real. This is not easy for a soul which
caught only a brief glimpse of things there, nor for those which after
falling to earth have suffered the misfortune of being perverted and
made immoral by the company they keep and have forgotten the sacred
things they saw then.

– That almost sounds like Hölderlin.[25]

When the remaining few, whose memories are good enough, see a
likeness here which reminds them of things there, they are amazed and
beside themselves, but they do not understand what is happening to
them because of a certain unclarity in their perceptions. But although
the likenesses here on earth (of things which are precious to souls, such
as justice and self-control)...

– in the catalogue of Platonic virtues, these are among the cardinal
ones; δικαιοσύνη [dikaiosúne], justice, is the highest virtue, and
σωφροσύνη [sophrosúne], which is here termed 'self-control', is really
the ability to maintain a balance between the extremes of the other
virtues[26] –

...lack all lustre, and only a few people come to them and barely see,
through dim sense organs, what it is that any likeness is a likeness of,
yet earlier it was possible for them to see beauty in all its brilliance.
That was when – we as attendants of Zeus and others of one of the
other gods – as part of a happy company they saw a wonderful sight
and spectacle and were initiated into what we may rightly call the most
wonderful of the mysteries. When we celebrated these mysteries then,
we were not only perfect beings ourselves, untouched by all the troubles which awaited us later

– that is, on earth – 'but we also were initiated into and contemplated
things shown to us that were perfect, simple, stable and blissful. We
were surrounded by rays of pure light, being pure ourselves and
untainted by this object we call a "body" and which we carry around
with us now, imprisoned like shellfish.'[27] The final parable, incidentally, is a kind of aesthetic variation, one could almost say, on one of
the most famous passages in the *Phaedo*, to which the whole of

Christian theology then referred back, namely the doctrine of the body as a prison from which the soul must be saved, from which the soul must flee.

I will now try first of all to highlight a few aspects of this exposition. Beauty appears here as a form of madness. If you think of the definitions we arrived at earlier, you will perhaps recall that we said the aesthetic realm, or the experience of art as such, is the suspension of the so-called reality principle; that we behave aesthetically the moment we – to put it quite bluntly – are not realistic, the moment we do not wisely consider our advantage, our progress or whatever goals we may have but, rather, surrender ourselves to something that is-in-itself, or at least presents itself thus, without regard for the context of purposes. It goes without saying that this behaviour, which I had characterized positively to you, always has the aspect of folly as its negative, of that which falls short of reality; and when a well-known politician, namely the interior minister of North Rhine-Westphalia, recently saw fit to warn of aesthetic experiments which the majority of people consider over the top,[28] this phrase 'over the top' in fact encapsulated precisely the very element which gives life to art. So as soon as what appears here as madness – that aspect of not staying on the middle path of reason – is not suspended, as soon as there is no enthusiasm that elevates itself above attachment to purposes and where people are concretist – then something like art does not actually exist. But something else is closely connected to this: the fact that this madness seizes people only because they are not themselves in control of the unconditional thing which they imagine beauty to be. In other words, then, the conditional nature of humans is the precondition for the specific experience of beauty as such. The relationship with beauty could then be understood – and we will find a very specific definition of this in Plato – as a state of tension between the conditional and the unconditional, as that emotion, that movement which seizes conditional beings in the face of the unconditional and now lifts them above the vicinity of conditionality itself, at least temporarily, for as long as they observe beauty. In all this, of course, one already finds a clear prefiguring of such motifs as Kant's 'disinterested pleasure' – that is, a pleasure which is not directed at goals, at practical aspects within the context of self-preservation and control of nature but, rather, goes beyond all that.

And if I mention here the aspect of pain, which is one of the fundamental components of any experience of beauty, then the reason for this pain in the sense of Plato's theory – and this too is a very intense experience – is that, in the face of beauty, namely in the experience of the possibility of something unconditional, humans become aware of their own conditionality, their own fallibility. This pain and suffering is, in a sense, the only form in which we, as conditional creatures, can think, feel or experience utopia at all – for, as Plato says, we are not in control of it. If we were to see beauty in its primal image, our entire life would be suspended; we can experience it only in a state of yearning, only in the form of the rupture separating us from it, and herein already lies, beyond a substantially dynamic aspect to the experience of beauty, precisely this: that suffering, pain and dissonance are fundamental parts of beauty, not simply acciden-tal. You can see from this how far a classical thinker – and if the term 'classical' was ever rightly applied to a philosophy, it is surely Plato's – is superior in the impulses of his thought, how far beneath him are the things one generally associates with the notion of the 'classical'.

I would also like to point out to you that Plato does not define beauty at this point, and I can already tell you now that the passages I will subsequently read to you and interpret further likewise contain no such definition. With a philosopher who took the art of separat-ing, forming and defining concepts to such a high level as Plato, this is already extremely notable, though here too I can perhaps add the general philosophical observation that, if one looks at the Platonic dialogues – including those from his earlier period – which seem to move towards definitions, one will always find that they ultimately withhold the definition and end with a *non liquet*, with an element of openness. So Plato's faith in definitions was evidently not remotely as great as the definitory method he chose would suggest. One could almost suspect that – with certain exceptions, of course, like the definition of courage as the midpoint between foolhardiness and cowardice – Plato's definitions are geared more towards thwarting the definitory procedure than affirming it. If things were indeed as I am hinting to you, then Platonic philosophy would be a dialectical philosophy in a sense that already goes considerably beyond what one usually has in mind when speaking of Platonic dialectic, by which people generally mean little more than a method for acquiring insight.[29]

But nonetheless – and this strikes me as decisive, and of the utmost import for the theory of beauty in particular – such a concept does not remain vague in Plato's work, not indeterminate; rather, he brings together a wealth of aspects through whose constellation one could say beauty sustains itself. I have told you about a few of them, such as self-elevation, madness or all these things; there is another crucial element referred to here in the text I read to you, known as being 'initiated'.[30] This initiated status – and here I can reuse something we developed earlier – quite simply means that the realm of beauty is characterized by being a secularized magical realm; that is, it removes itself from the everyday context of effects into a form of taboo area and, in this context of effects, it is something autonomous that one needs to have experienced, needs to have entered, to see at all what is going on in a work of art. Anyone who approaches a work of art directly with the categories of everyday life, with the thoughts, feelings and impulses one has at some moment without, I would almost say, carrying out a kind of reduction, without entering this circle and leaving their jacket outside, as is rightly expected of us at the theatre, will thus deny themselves the experience of art as such from the outset. What I mean to say to you is the following, which is perhaps quite important for Plato and the theory of forms in general: the Form, or rather the Idea,[31] in the very emphatic philosophical sense in which Plato uses it – and which actually still clings to it if we are speaking truly philosophically and not using the term in a completely debased fashion – is not a concept that can be defined simply as the entirety of however many objects encompassed by it that share one attribute; rather, it draws its life from within, it is the life of the matter itself.[32] And the things which are named in order to concretize this concept, to fulfil it, are not the defining qualities that distinguish it; rather, they are all elements of this movement that takes place inside it, which I have already mentioned and which we will hear much more about, which forms its true substance.

Plato defines beauty here by its – if I should speak of definitions at all; let me correct myself: Plato seeks to determine the concept of beauty at this point by its effect, namely the effect it has on us. You could call this paradoxical – and say that Plato, in that sense, belongs to the domain of aesthetic subjectivism, the critique of which we will pursue in detail in the next sessions, because I feel that this critique is the most decisive element in a reformulation of aesthetics as such. One could think that Plato was here already at the start of that tradition which seeks to define art by explaining the affects and emotions it causes, and which we still encounter in the *Critique of the Power of Judgement*, where the starting category is meant to serve an understanding of aesthetic beauty, of artistic beauty, of the enjoyable. Now, Plato certainly does not lack this subjective aspect in the explanation of beauty, and I would say this is because the idea of beauty itself eludes definition and can, in a sense, [be defined] only indirectly through this effect.[33]

But on the other hand – and you must take this into account too, if you want to understand this theory of beauty we are dealing with here as a complexion of aspects, not as a definition of beauty – this very fact that we feel beauty only through its effect must be shown with reference to its objective nature: its character as an archetype and its special position within the realm of ideas. What I have just told you, and what initially sounds like a rather philological observation – namely that, on the one hand, Plato seeks to explain beauty only in terms of its effect, but, on the other hand, beauty is supposed to be nothing but the imitation of the idea of beauty, and that is what you will hear later – this seemingly merely exegetic remark on the Plato passage is, if I am not mistaken, of the most central imaginable significance for the establishment of an aesthetics. For it means that neither can we explain the idea of beauty or the idea of art as such in directly objectivist terms – that is to say, without reflection on the spirit, without reflection on humans and their attitude towards objectivity – nor, on the other hand, is this idea of art or this idea of beauty limited to the context of effects that it imposes on us; rather, it is essentially objective and has an objective aspect. In other words: if I could already formulate here the polarity which one encounters in Plato, if one does not wish crudely to impose an inconsistent theory on him, one must say that the underlying conception of beauty itself here is a dialectical conception of beauty. This means that beauty itself, by its own nature, presents itself as mediated, inherently as something like a tension between subjective and objective aspects.[34] And when I told you that all the motifs of aesthetics that ever unfolded in later times are already present here, as if in a kind of sacred foundational text, then this is primarily what I had in mind. For even at its highest peak, at the Hegelian peak, aesthetic speculation did not get any further than that definition of beauty which termed beauty itself – instead of calling it being in a static, object-like sense – just such a state of tension between subjective and objective aspects.

But I would at least like to say a word about the characterization of the effect of beauty which Plato provides here. For this description indeed differs fundamentally from the modern, Christianity-based description of beauty in that it does not similarly make disinterested pleasure – that is to say, the elimination of desire from the object of beauty – a self-evident precondition for the experience of beauty.[35] In this, Plato is simply closer to certain primary experiences of beauty – which withdrew ever further and, if you will, were repressed ever more in the further formation and development of art – such that he openly admits the relationship between beauty and desire of which I spoke to you at length when we discussed the relationship between nature and art. First of all, beauty for him is directly an object of desire, and only the result of a process that takes place within the concept of beauty itself, if you will, which at the very least takes place in the experience of beauty, namely that that sublimation occurs – that abstention of the experience of beauty from immediate erotic appropriation – which is already predetermined for us when we believe we are acting aesthetically. So here you gain insight into a piece of the hidden prehistory of beauty, one could say, into a process that is present in the later conceptions of aesthetics – I am thinking primarily of Kant's, of course – in a congealed, an object-like form, in a sense only in the form of its result. If I said to you that, with the supposedly static, ontological Plato in particular, the theory of beauty is substantially dynamic and, indeed, envisages beauty as something trembling or in internal motion, one should not least consider that he describes the experience of beauty itself as, one is inclined to say: an inalienable and constantly self-renewing process of sublimation. At the same time, you can see here whence that aspect of danger comes that plays such a large part in Plato's theory of beauty: it is seen in what I hinted at in very different words – and very harmless ones, if you like – when I told you, albeit in agreement with contemporary psychology, that the sublimation which characterizes the realm of beauty is a very precarious one – that it never fully succeeds, and that precisely that taboo domain separated off from reality which we experience as the domain of beauty is problematic, for the most profound reasons, namely due to its inner character, and that it can end again at any time. In a sense – at that moment of sublimation, in its distancing from the realm of the immediacy of purposes – the potential for collapse is inherent in the idea of beauty itself: that the aesthetic distance is not maintained, and that the aesthetic subject either falls back into the sphere of the merely existent, the sphere of self-preservation, of immediate desire, or that it indeed loses itself in that madness of which Plato very rightly says that it is an integral aspect of the experience of beauty as such.

LECTURE 10

18 December 1958

I will continue with the treatment of the Plato passage we examined in the last session, and I hope I can be reasonably concise, as I actually went a little further in the interpretation of chapter 30 of the *Phaedrus* than was directly justified at that point, which means several of the motifs I discussed then do not need to be discussed again now. I think it is best if I begin by briefly reading you the following chapter and then add what may not have been said last time after all: 'Let this be my tribute to memory; it was remembering and longing for those past events which has made me go on rather too long now.'[1] Here, if I could just insert this, you already find the motif of the connection between the representation and the matter. That is, he now justifies – ironically, of course, with a certain Athenian coquetry – his own comprehensiveness in the treatment of his subject by saying that this subject captivated him so greatly that he could not free himself from it, as it were; so the representation is viewed as a function of the matter. 'But turning to beauty, it shone out, as I said, among its companions there' – namely the archetypes which the charioteer with his team of horses espied once on his heavenly journey – 'and once here on earth we found, by means of the clearest of our senses, that it sparkles with particular clarity.' – 'Here' refers to the return, namely to earth; and now we find a sort of hierarchy of sensory organs that is probably not the last reason why the theory about the essential visual character of Greek culture developed. For now, among the sensory organs – in this anthropology, then – primacy is assigned to the eye; and perhaps, before I examine this, I could just say that, of the sensory organs, the eye is really the objectifying one, the organ that most enables us to assure ourselves of objects in their objectivity, in their materiality, such that the eye has, in a certain sense, been most closely associated with rationality, with illumination, with the principle of controlling nature – unlike the ear, which does not clearly know any such concrete relationship; and all the more unlike senses such as taste and smell, which are really far more archaic, far more mimetic senses, and presumably gradually wither away in the development of civilization. There can be no doubt with the sense of sight. 'For the keenest kind of perception the body affords us is the one that comes through seeing, though we are not able to see wisdom.'[2] Here, of course, wisdom is the λόγος, objective reason, the reason that, according to Platonic doctrine, governs things themselves; Hegel would have called it 'the absolute'. The German word *Vernunft*, of course, like all terms in modern languages for what is meant here, is so subjectively inclined that initially it seems odd that reason is not visible to us and yet it will set off mighty pangs of love. If, for example, one recalls logistics[3] and imagines it setting off mighty pangs of love when it becomes visible – that is asking a little too much. But what Plato means here, of course, is this: if the objective in-itself of reason, the reasonable nature of things themselves – essentially, the true order of being – were to become visible, humans would be seized with such longing that they could no longer bear to live in the conditional world. In general, if I may add this, whenever you encounter such terms as 'reason' in Plato, you can understand what is meant only if you bear in mind that we are dealing with an essentially objective concept of reason, that for him the concept of the reasonable is always something objective, judged with reference to the idea of truth, and that reason here is thus not the same thing we usually mean by reason as the instrumental reason of our mere consciousness. In Plato, this is complicated somewhat by the fact that this reason also has its subjective, one could say its subjective 'shadings',[4] that it is conveyed to us through subjective reason, through our thought, but this thought is ultimately legitimized only by partaking, only by the μέθεχις [méthexis] of scattered things in the objectivity of reason itself.[5] This is simply to make that slightly odd-sounding passage a little clearer to you. '[...] as with everything else that is an object of love, wisdom would cause terrible pangs of love in us if it presented some kind of clear image of itself by approaching our organ of sight.' By 'everything else that is an object of love', of course, what he means is none other than the forms, the archetypes of things themselves, which he envisages as objectivities of this kind. Now comes the specific formulation about the nature of beauty, which distinguishes it in multiple ways from the other forms in his account: 'But as things are, it is only beauty that has the property of being especially visible and especially lovable.' And here the words 'only beauty' naturally refer once again to the archetypal. Of all the forms that exist, then – and this is the essence, if you will, of Plato's aesthetics – of all the forms there are, the only one that is directly observable (and we should take 'observable' very literally in the sense of observation by the eye), the only one that possesses this intuitive nature is the form of beauty; and – if I may anticipate – everything that is beautiful, every individual beautiful thing is a mimesis, an imitation of the idea of beauty itself. If you wish to understand my subsequent interpretation, keep this in mind for now as the true centre of this theory. 'Anyone who was initiated long ago or who is corrupted is not given to moving rapidly from here to there, towards beauty as it really is.'[6] Then comes a passage which reproduces the process I interpreted for you last time: that, for Plato, the idea of beauty is not radically separate from interest – that is, from the capacity for desire; rather, it is a process of sublimation that is supposed to lead us to this idea – today we would call it pure aesthetic beauty – and this is shown at various levels where he begins with primitive, unharnessed sexuality and then of the sophisticated, refined kind. 'But when someone who has only recently been initiated, and who took in plenty of the sights to be seen' – who has not long returned from the world of archetypes to which he raised himself –

> then sees a marvellous face or a bodily form which is a good reflection of beauty, at first he shivers and is gripped by something like the fear he felt then, and the sight also moves him to revere his beloved as if he were a god. In fact, it is only concern about being thought completely insane that stops him from sacrificing to his beloved as if he were a cult statue or a god. Following this sight, the kind of change comes over him that you would expect after a shivering fit, and he begins to sweat and to run an unusually high fever, because the reception through his eyes of the effusion of beauty causes him to get hot. Now, this effusion is also the natural means of irrigating his wings. His heat softens the coat covering the feathers' buds, which had been too hard and closed up for wings to grow. A further nourishment pours in, the quills of the feathers swell and begin to grow from the roots upwards and to spread all over the underside of the soul, because previously

– when it elevated itself to the divine – 'the whole soul was winged.'[7]

To follow on from the latter part: this shiver of emotion, which fluctuates between pleasure, enthusiasm, displeasure and suffering

– as familiar from Cherubino's famous aria in Mozart's *Figaro*,[8] and as later interpreted by Kierkegaard as virtually the essence of erotic beauty[9] – this shiver is taken [by Plato's Socrates] to mean that touching beauty once more brings forth the feathers with which humans elevate themselves above the concrete, the merely existent; and he describes this growth of feathers in a playful, naturalistic way as a kind of itch, as if one's feathers were growing again, which he identifies as the reason for the aversion which seizes the humans in this parable in the face of beauty. I promised to show you how this passage in Plato is a little like certain magic boxes among variety artists, from which the performer can extract everything that might be inside, that the essential constituents of the later philosophy of beauty are actually all gathered here. This applies above all to the concept I mentioned in passing earlier, namely the notion of beauty as a sensually intuitive idea or form. In Plato's theory, then, beauty is characterized by a certain kind of paradox. And it has been said, not without reason, that whatever one rightly finds beautiful somehow exhibits a paradoxical quality.[10] The paradox inherent in beauty is that it is at once the bearer of something absolute, something spiritual, of the idea and also something sensually present; that the idea itself, as philosophy later expressed it, is for us in its immediacy, namely as an intuitive idea.[11] Hegel's definition of beauty, which I have already quoted for you – that beauty is the 'sensual appearance of the idea'[12] – is really no different from the description Plato gives here, taken out of its mythological casing and repeated. It is really the same theory that was then reproduced by objective idealism – and not by chance, for only an objective idealism was capable of bringing together these two elements: the objectivity of that which appears to us and its sensory aspect, which is very much a defining characteristic of ourselves. Plato does not show how these two elements are connected in the idea of beauty. Aesthetics followed him in this – not to its advantage, I would say – by generally contenting itself with saying that beauty is the idea in an immediately intuitive form, not an implied or mediated one – or, as it was generally expressed, that beauty had the form of the symbolic, and hence that the spiritual was implied by something sensual. And this meant taking the easy way out, by positing in this concept of the symbol, which was not further reflected upon, a unity that cannot in reality be imagined as such an unambiguous, positively given unity.[13] Plato may have caused that with his formulation, but he went far beyond it in the description of the effect of beauty I just read to you; for he described this effect – and I really cannot emphasize this enough, you will see why later on – as a process, I would say a dialectical process that is in itself the unity of attraction and repulsion, a process between the conditional and the unconditional, a process between pleasure and displeasure [...].[14] I think he took this much further than in the definition of the sensually intuitive nature of the idea itself. For this sensual intuitiveness of the idea is not something that simply is, and faces us as such; rather, this thing which confronts us in the form of the beautiful is in itself always in motion, it is in itself a process, just as the genuinely aesthetic form of behaviour, namely so-called disinterested pleasure, the *amor intellectualis* of the idea, as I showed you, is described by him as the result of a process. I would like to draw your attention to the somewhat paradoxical quality of the formulation that the beautiful is an image of beauty. For common sense would be more inclined to assume, on the contrary, that the concept of beauty is the generality which, as the unity of all individual beautiful things, of the properties of all individual beautiful things, subsumes the individually beautiful under itself; crudely put, the common view would be more that beauty is the image of all beautiful things, not that the beautiful is the image of beauty. But I think you should here recall an aspect that I attempted to develop theoretically for you first of all, and that would have been incomparably more natural for a semi-archaic philosopher like Plato, or at least one still on the threshold of the archaic, than for us, who require strenuous philosophical reflection to revive that aspect of the aesthetic at all, namely the aspect of the mimetic.

One can say that all art indeed has an element of imitation to it, but not the imitation of a particular thing, not the imitation of anything concrete. Rather, it is the imitative behaviour itself: the behaviour of identification, one could almost say, the identification of the entity with that which it is not, with another entity, but without this act of imitation having any quality of objectification, of materializing imitation to it. And that, it seems to me, is what Plato captured in the paradoxical and cryptic formulation that the beautiful is the image of beauty. That is, he recognized in everything which appears to us as individually beautiful that something is the same, that it refers to something, that it touches on something, one could almost say – that it exhibits such mimetic behaviour. At the same time, however, he also noticed that this aspect of similarity in the beautiful is not a similarity to anything particular, but that, if I might use so speculative and extreme a formulation, it is a 'similarity in itself' – the aspect of similarity as absolute similarity – without having a specific *terminus ad quem*. And this absolute similarity, this quality of similarity in itself, without a similar object being meant, this is the aspect he sought to capture in the paradoxical formulation that the beautiful was the image of beauty or similar to it – not, I should add, to a beautiful thing, but rather the attempt at that imitation which once, originally, was a response to the shiver caused by its contact with being.

This idea of beauty as similarity is profoundly related to that of beauty as pain. In one of the most splendid passages from the late novel *Indian Summer* by Stifter, who was a student of Goethe in the higher sense, and can therefore be called a Platonist, and for whom a category such as return, which I expounded upon in the last session, played such a large part – in one of the strangest passages of this novel it transpires that the hero once saw his beloved before, at the start, in a theatre, and that for him she had always borne the character of similarity, yet this similarity had never revealed itself; simply put, he did not know where he had seen her before, yet always regarded her as a being that he somehow already knew.[15] And the particular pain that accompanies love, as in Frank Wedekind's Lulu play, where one stage direction describes the young Alwa Schön, who falls hopelessly for his father's wife, closing his eyes almost blinded.[16] So this aspect of pain seems to be a part of the internally dynamic, processual nature of beauty, which exists between attraction and repulsion. One can surely say that, where there is no beauty, where beauty does not touch the wound, where beauty does not manifest itself by simultaneously embodying utopia and distance from that utopia, and thus absorbing all suffering and all the contradictory character of existence – that one cannot speak of beauty there. Perhaps you can see in this an aspect that was emphasized in the now much maligned *Jugendstil*, and which played a major part in the poetry of the godfather of *Jugendstil*, the poetry of Baudelaire,[17] but also in Richard Wagner, and which tends to be lost today along with the general loss of the capacity for aesthetic distance:[18] that the concept of beauty is simply irreconcilable with the concept of health, and that it is essentially impossible to conceive of a beauty that, being such an affliction, does not have a certain kind of affinity with death.[19] I would say that the inartistic quality in the relationship with art and beauty is that it establishes itself as if beauty were something wholly positive and harmless – something that is in agreement with life, as it were, something which perhaps encourages the business of life, without also positing that distance from life whose own idea is the thought of death, and no other.

Let me also say that the innermost motif of any doctrine of beauty – namely that beauty can only be conceived of as the manifestation of utopia[20] – is, in Plato's theory, likewise very closely connected to the thought of the feathers, the thought of elevating oneself, where this elevation is synonymous with a self-elevation beyond the entire world of contingency. But utopia here also means that this self-elevation above the contingent world – and therein, if you will, lies the fatality or the element of resignation in the concept of beauty – cannot actually succeed, that it can only succeed as semblance. If one were to search for a metaphysical theory of the emptiness of aesthetic semblance, the only place to look would be in the fact that art captures utopia as something present among us, albeit at the cost of its reality. And herein lies the twofold nature of art: in so far as it is critical and does not betray the absolute, as it were, it opposes reality; yet at the same time, by refraining from realizing that absolute quality, it becomes embroiled with – not to say degraded by – reality, and then in turn becomes part of the merely existent, of mere reality. And that, if you will, is really the moral question that can be put to art and the justification for art, especially the justification for art today.[21]

The theory of unease is developed further by Plato in the following chapter, which I will not read to you now, where he describes the particular character of the itch as the unity of pleasure and displeasure in the face of beauty. I would now like to fulfil the last part of my promise, as it were, namely to show you that this Platonic theory actually contains the entire theory, at least the entire traditional theory of beauty, and wish to show you that this aspect of ambivalence – the fluctuation between negativity and positivity in beauty – already appears in Kant's theory, not of beauty, admittedly, but of the sublime, by reading to you a passage from the *Critique of the Power of Judgement*, from the theory of the mathematically sublime: '.'[22] This theory, incidentally, is the corrective – albeit not in the realm of artistic beauty but only that of natural beauty – of the traditionalistic, essentially still eighteenth-century Kantian doctrine of beauty as the sensually enjoyable, which he has already left behind, in fact, by no longer viewing beauty as something enjoyable but rather seeing it as a field of tension, a tension between the enjoyable and the repulsive; in this we also find the polarity of the spiritual and the sensual that appears in Plato, and which is only conceivable as such a field of tension. One can recognize the great aestheticians by the fact that they refrained from using some sentimental concepts to dilute and deny this tension between the spiritual and the sensual; that they tried instead to view the concept of beauty itself as such a concept of tension, as such a dialectical concept. In both cases, in Plato and in Kant, the tension is the same, namely the tension between the contingency of sensual nature and the absolute. In Plato and in Kant, the purely sensual aspect, the human element that conspires with mere existence, is put into a state of unease by being presented with that which goes beyond it, while the spiritual part, on the other hand, experiences joy at the moment when it can gaze on beauty. But – and I think this is fundamental to the theory of beauty with which we are dealing – you must not reduce the nature of beauty, as conceived in those passages from Plato and Kant, to the banal opposition of the sensual and the spiritual, as if art were the manifestation of something spiritual that affects us negatively by opposing the sensual aspect and positively by embodying the spiritual. Neither author is close to espousing such a view, for the simple reason that – if I could just emphasize that once more in the Plato passage – the beautiful itself is described by Plato first of all as an intuitive, observable element. So it is not the case – and I think this is central to any theory of beauty at all – that the spiritual simply stands in opposition to the sensual, that the sensual falls away, so to speak, leaving the spiritual; rather, it is fundamental to the beautiful that the spiritual itself becomes sensual in it, that it appears, and that the sensual, on the other hand, is at once spiritualized in its sensuality as the bearer of something spiritual. Let me be clear:

The difficulty and the real problem of a genuine philosophical theory of beauty, which is simply the central issue of aesthetics, can perhaps be formulated thus: one the one hand, it is impossible to construct a concept of beauty in such a way that the tension between these aspects – the sensual and the spiritual – is simply done away with by bringing the two together in an unbroken unity, as has repeatedly been attempted with the concept of the symbol. On the other hand, it is equally impossible to polarize the concept or the idea of beauty in such a way that you say: 'the beautiful consists of a sensual and a spiritual component, where the sensual is the mere bearer of the spiritual.' The essence of the definition of beauty seems to lie rather in the fact that, while these two aspects exist as distinct, and hence in a state of tension towards each other, each is mediated by the other. That is to say, there is nothing spiritual in a work of art that is not also sensual, and nothing sensual that is not also spiritual, though without the two ever simply subsuming each other. And understanding a work of art in these terms really means realizing the constellation or dialectic that obtains between these aspects, understanding how the sensual is the spiritual and the spiritual sensual, always keeping the two apart yet conceiving of them together.[23] Someone who can see only the sensual side of the work without at once perceiving its spiritual aspect is essentially in a pre-aesthetic or, as I like to call it, a culinary state.[24] They treat the work of art the way one treats a dish, and here I must voice the suspicion that, especially in the current situation, which, as I said earlier, can barely summon the power for aesthetic distance, this circumstance also prevails with works of art that do actually have a spiritual aspect. On the other hand, anyone for whom a work of art is nothing but the intricate written form of something spiritual, anyone who simply reduces works of art to their meanings without recognizing that there is no meaning, no spiritual aspect in a work that is not mediated by the sensual, and which does not become the spiritual thing that it is only through its sensual manifestation – they indeed fall prey to what one could call the intellectualization of art in the negative sense. That is, they confuse the so-called intentions, the meanings of the works, with what one can call aesthetic substance, and which constitutes itself only in this state of tension. And expressing this tension in its various stages and making it ever more concrete – this alone could be the task of a developed philosophical aesthetics.

I think I have now arrived at a result which differs very radically from the notions with which most of you have probably grown up, though this difference may not be fully clear to you yet; I would therefore like to end the session with a few words about that. It is generally assumed – and this is connected to the nature of our entire culture – that beauty is a kind of being,[25] and that the more a work of art transports of that being, or the more it is itself a being from which every notion of process has been driven out, the higher its standing. Nietzsche already criticized this view very harshly when, in one of his late writings, he poured scorn on the view that the perfect must never be something which has become[26] – thus going against what I would call the phantasmagoric view, in which the work of art must present itself as absolute being, like a piece of the creation. In the phantasmagoria chapter from *In Search of Wagner* I attempted to highlight this very aspect in the nineteenth-century concept of appearance, and perhaps I might suggest that you take a closer look at it.[27] Now the concept of being has attained a disastrous dominance in current aesthetics, albeit no longer in the form of demanding that a work of art appear as if it were absolute being – which was the ambition of Wagner's *Gesamtkunstwerk* – but in the sense that being itself speaks through the work of art.[28] And what, then, does being say through the work? Being simply keeps saying 'being' through the work. I will refrain from discussing the decisive objection to this theory of art, namely its indescribable meagreness, which truly equals that indifference on Schelling's part of which Hegel once said that, in it, all cows are black,[29] meaning that all art simply says one and the same thing over and over again, and that this one thing it says cannot be defined, that it actually has no content. Naturally such a claim is impossible to disprove on account of its complete generality,

and a part of it – namely that the work of art means the unconditional, in opposition to the limited and the absolute – is not without
truth; but if aesthetics is to offer more than simply a sentimental sense
of the cosmic and, rather, immerse itself in the phenomena themselves, then it must not stop at such a definition. But I think the
reflections we have now carried out, and which have now reached a
temporary conclusion, have led us to overturn these notions via an
entirely different route; for I think I have shown you that, because
of its own constituents in the aesthetic process, the work of art is a
force field, is itself in motion, is in itself a process, and that the experience of the work of art is therefore connected to, or consists in, the
fact that the work – which initially appears as a being in its closed
domain – comes to life beneath our gaze. That is, we suddenly, instan-
taneously, become aware of the work as a force field, in the way
described so magnificently in the very important allegorical poem
'The Tapestry' from Stefan George's cycle *The Tapestry of Life*.[30] And
perhaps I can add that, if one is looking for the aesthetic criterion
– that is, if one asks when a work of art can reasonably be called an
important one – that the decisive criterion is how far a work is
capable of taking up the contradictions of its own real and formal
conditions in itself as such a process, working through its contradictory nature and, by perhaps settling this contradictory nature in the
image, pointing both to its irreconcilability in reality and, ultimately,
to the potential for reconciliation envisaged in the concept of utopia.[31]
So I think one can only move beyond the poor, merely bourgeois,
contemplative concept of beauty, which is content simply to let a
work of art be blessed in itself – as Mörike puts it in a fine poem[32]
– if one is capable of recognizing through the observation and experience of important works of art, not through an intellectualization
and interpretation after the fact but through the experience of their
inner constitution, the elements of which they consist, recognizing
them as the play of forces that they are by their very nature, and
which is not external to their concept of beauty, but in which the
very substance of their own beauty lies.

LECTURE 11

6 January 1959

Before I go on to show you by means of an elaborated dialectic – that of beauty itself – what I consider to be the central task of a lecture on aesthetics, I would like, at least in brief, to address an intervention from your circles that reached me at the end of the last session. I was guilty – and it is very easy to become guilty in one's efforts to explain specific aspects of a problem to you – of passing over self-evident and general things, things that are known about the topic, which naturally results in a skewed perspective. I am referring to Plato's view, and I was rightly told that I had presented – one could say – a radically dynamic or dialectical interpretation of the view of beauty in the *Phaedrus*, whereas the first tenet of the idea of beauty – and of all the ideas, or forms, in Platonic philosophy – is that it is eternally self-same and unchanging. In other words, that Plato's aesthetics too is a static ontological theory. This is true, of course. That is to say, Plato's theory of forms also extends to the *Phaedrus*, and one must insist on that all the more if, as I do, one wishes to contradict the prevailing philological view that the *Phaedrus* is from Plato's revisionist late period. I simply took this aspect for granted and wanted to show you instead that, in his, if you will, phenomenological effort to reproduce the experience of beauty as precisely as possible, Plato himself was actually pushed by the structure he had developed beyond that aspect of static ontology which, as we say, naturally remains the systematic foundation at least of classical Platonism. However, I would still like to say – although it does not really belong in a lecture on aesthetics, but as I have engaged with Plato, I do perhaps owe it to you to say a little about it – that one must not label philosophers too easily, and accordingly one should not believe that the whole of Plato can simply be subsumed under the category of a static ontology. For while it is true that this character of eternal self-sameness and immutability is ascribed to the forms, Platonic philosophy nonetheless, despite its doctrine of objective reason, the objective being-in-itself of the forms, was always dealing also with the problem of mediation, the problem of how these objective forms – the forms in themselves, Hegel would say[1] – become something for-us, and how – to use a Platonic expression, albeit taken from a different context – we can participate in the forms.[2] And because he views the nature of humans as a fragile and imprisoned one[3] – today we would call it finite and problematic – that faces the infinite nature of the form's being-in-itself, there is already a dialectical relationship between these forms and our knowledge of them; in Plato, however, it is a dialectic that takes place largely on the side of the subject, not of objectivity. So it is no coincidence that, in keeping with the old division of educational disciplines, Plato refers to the theory of knowledge – which for him is synonymous with the theory of forming concepts – as dialectic.[4] In his own view it constitutes a movement, one that is not even absolutely continuous but which, as I have just attempted to show in the *Phaedrus*, contains an element of a qualitative leap, a sudden transition: that same aspect which Plato describes with such categories as frenzy (ἐνθουσιασμός)[5] or divine madness (μανία).[6] I do think, however, that because we can only know about the forms by means of our own knowledge – through those aspects of concept-formation that Plato highlights – Plato's ontology is not as indifferent, compared to this so-called Platonic dialectic, as one usually and trivially imagines; rather, because we cannot know about the being-in-itself of the forms, unlike their being-for-us, according to Plato, and as we ascend to them through the mechanisms of our own knowledge – by which he always means our own thinking – they are actually affected in their being-in-themselves by the process of appropriation, as Kierkegaard calls it.[7] And that is what I really wanted to show you in the last session: how far the subjective aspect of the experience of beauty, as represented in that passage from the *Phaedrus*, does also, *contre cœur* – against the official static-ontological doctrinal content of platonic philosophy, so to speak – affect the objective concept of beauty itself.

I am telling you this today because I think it may not be entirely irrelevant to the questions with which we must now begin our main reflections. For now I will focus mainly on laying out the problematics of the concept of beauty for you, in so far as it is a problematics

of subjective behaviour towards the beautiful, and I think that this
will lead me to emphasize the objective aspect very strongly in relation to aesthetic subjectivism. This makes it all the more important
– so that you do not shift towards the opposite extreme, namely a
dogmatic objectivism – for you also to recall the subjective aspect
necessarily connected to aesthetic objectivity which I highlighted in
those passages from Plato, but with the addition that I have made
today at your suggestion. So I would like to start by saying something
about the concept of beauty itself, and about the relationship between
beauty and art. Now this is a peculiar matter. On the one hand, if
one were to be roused from one's sleep and asked what the nature
of art is, based on the education one has fortunately or unfortunately
received, one would be inclined to say: 'My goodness, art – that is
the area of beauty as a whole, and not just natural beauty, but rather
that special area which developed from the magical one and which
we have discussed in such detail.' On the other hand, especially if
one has one's own aesthetic experience of works of art – and we are
now emphatically referring no longer to natural beauty but, indeed,
to art, and in the second half of the lecture we will occupy ourselves
exclusively with aesthetic questions concerning – if one knows what
a work of art really is, if one feels that, then one will be very uneasy
about the concept of beauty, and what will happen – I cannot recall
if I ever told you the story – is the same thing that happened to me
at the Hamburg lecture,[8] when a man energetically objected that, in
all my very complicated reflections, I had forgotten the simplest thing
of all, namely beauty, the eternal beauty of works of art, to which I
responded that this sort of criticism was chiefly voiced by operetta
composers; it then turned out that the gentleman in question, though
not an operetta composer, was in fact the retired leaseholder of an
operetta theatre. In telling you this, I mean to sketch the sphere in
which the current experience of the concept of beauty generally takes
place. I dare say that, at first, unless we come directly from the coun-
tryside, we would all resist equating the experience of art with the
experience of beauty. The idea of doing so would call to mind the
toothpaste faces from advertising pillars, or even the grinning of
advertising film stars, and we would tend to feel cheated of the main
substance of the work – whatever it might be – when it confronts us
directly with a claim to immediate, sensual beauty. I would like to
point out that the experience to which I am referring is by no means
as new as it seems to each subsequent generation; rather, it has come
about countless times throughout history in an ever-changing fashion.

    I would like to remind you above all that dialectical philosophy,
even Hegel's school, highlighted very emphatically the concept of

ugliness as a necessary aspect of beauty, and that one of the most talented and important of Hegel's students, whose work – unlike that of most others – continued to have an effect well into the nineteenth century, namely Rosenkranz, expressly wrote an *Aesthetics of Ugliness*.[9] Yet I also wish to tell you that, if one is well aware of the limits of the concept of beauty in art, a certain historical differentiation is necessary. It is not as if so-called ugliness – whatever that might be – always simply constituted an aspect of art in the same way, as the meaning of this aspect itself significantly changed. I think it is also important, if you are to understand what we will subsequently develop concerning the critique of the ideal of beauty as something sensually pleasing, to understand this change in the relationship with ugliness as a historical one. Think of the importance of so-called ugliness in the great Dutch paintings of the seventeenth century, for example Frans Hals's *Malle Babbe*, which, if I recall correctly, used to be exhibited at the National Gallery in Berlin.[10] It is a depiction of an ugly, grinning and laughing old woman; but the depiction itself shows such a mastery of antithetics – it highlights this ugliness so humorously, one would say, it distances itself so strongly from this ugliness through its expression – that this ugliness is, in fact, indirectly taken up into a harmonistic ideal of beauty; naturally this is also evident in the picture's composition, in what one generally terms the formal elements of painting, which in this work – as in countless other Dutch depictions of so-called ugliness – integrates this aspect, takes it up into the form, and in this way precisely reinforces the victory of the beauty principle by showing that it can also incorporate the aspect of ugliness. If you look at contemporary depictions of ugliness, for example those found in virtually all of Samuel Beckett's work, which almost exclusively contains repulsive things – the most primitive bodily functions, physical defects, semi-putrefaction, dementia and the like[11] – then you will, of course, no longer directly have this feeling that the shadow of ugliness here serves merely to underline the triumph of the self-possessed shaping mind all the more strongly. Nor do we find here any compositional approach that points beyond this ugliness and has a kind of affirmative meaning in relation to it; rather, the aesthetic element here lies in the power to endure those utmost experiences captured in the images of ugliness without glossing over them. I think it would be an undertaking that I can mention here, in order to prevent references to the significance of ugliness in art from being limited to an inferior generality, to trace the changes in the ideal of ugliness undergone by art;[12] but, on the whole, aestheticians and cultural historians only like to chatter about the changes in the ideal of beauty. Instead of pursuing this aspect further, however, I would like to take on the critical question of beauty after all, and start by attempting to unfold its negative aspect for you.

Generally speaking, the concept of beauty we resist in art is indeed a subjectivist concept. This means it is synonymous with the sensually pleasing – be it the mere harmony of some formal properties that are meant to accommodate some primal need for harmony in us or the sensually pleasing in the sense of the attractive, the enticing, the enjoyable, or an image removed from erotic beauty in the widest sense. What I aim to undertake here, and what I shall now begin, is another attempt at immanent critique. This means I will not attempt – as I certainly could, and to which I shall return later – to show you positively in what sense the true substance and nature of works of art come only from their own objective constitution; rather, I will take the opposite approach and seek to show you how far the aspect of subjective enjoyment falls short of what, in our genuine aesthetic experience, we encounter as beautiful. In other words, I intend to take aesthetic subjectivism at its word. First of all, I will truly keep to the subjective experience of beauty or art and examine it a little more closely than is done in the usual forms of aesthetics, and I hope that, in so doing, I can also point out some things regarding the concept of beauty that would not otherwise be apparent. Allow me to remind you of what I attempted to show in my explanation of the difficult and by no means stable concept of disinterested pleasure: that works of art – the important works of art – do not lack aspects of sensual stimulation, but rather – as the sphere of art as such is a product of this interest in sensual stimulation, which never stands rigidly and abstractly opposite the sphere – that, at all its stages, time and again, it is always in a state of tension with this sphere. I would ask you to note this first of all, so that you do not lapse into the opposite extreme of – how should I put it? – cheaply spiritualistic aesthetic observation. But here you must also bear in mind that, in true works of art, these sensual stimuli appear only in a scattered form. When I say 'scattered', I am not referring to anything quantitative; I do not mean that they appear only sparsely here and there; there are surely great and important works that correspond in their entirety to the concept of the sensually stimulating, even if we have particular difficulties with such works of art today. What I mean to say is rather that, even where these aspects of sensual pleasure appear in the works, they are actually accidental; they do not constitute the nature of the work itself but are only scattered in comparison to that element which actually carries the work, namely its organization, its unity of meaning. In specific aesthetic experience, we will only really find those sensual stimuli adequate, we will only be able to identify with them as aesthetically experiencing individuals, if we see them in relation to the meaning they carry – but not if we view them as such in isolation, as valid in themselves.[13] So if a work such as Alban Berg's *Lulu*[14] constantly strives for a very particular form of sonic beauty and, one can certainly say, achieves it, this is connected to the fact that, in this work itself – if I can put it like this – the idea of sensual beauty and its allure, that entire dialectic between nature and control of nature, is at the heart of things, and that sensual beauty is here essentially the carrier of this idea and by no means a thing that stands in itself.[15] I think it is relatively easy for me to make this plausible to you. I told you that the sensual elements of art as aspects of stimulation and pleasure become false and questionable the moment we isolate them. All this means, however, is that they then become culinary elements, values of taste. We then literally approach the work of art in the way we approach a good dish – or perhaps I should say a very fine wine. We consume the work as if it were physically real, so to speak, and thus violate the taboo which is the very law of art, namely – and here, too, I can refer to what we have already studied – that it constitutes a sphere which is removed from the sphere of mere empirical existence, which is not directly one with our own existence but separated from it like a sort of magical area.

What follows from this is something that I may not yet have told you in so simple a form, and which you are all the better equipped to understand at this point: that the nature of art as spiritual is, in fact, in direct union with that removal of the aesthetic realm from the empirical realm. Because we do treat works of art not as physical aspects of our existence but, rather, as aspects which are separated from us in a certain way, which are not directly part of our existence at all, and we can only experience them in a special way, namely through what has been called 'aesthetic attitude',[16] this already removes them from the sphere of mere sensual immediacy. And this removal from empirical immediacy is itself necessarily an element of spiritualization, meaning one can say – and I think this is very important – that the spiritual aspect of art already lies in the immediate perception of a work of art as a work of art, and is not added afterwards through some spiritualistic act that only considers the so-called spiritual content of works of art *post festum*. By taking up the distance that accompanies my decision to view a work of art rather than eat an apple, I have already brought into play that entire process of spiritualization which reaches completion when I face a composition by Anton von Webern or a picture by Klee.[17] By comparison, the culinary is always the atomistic, by which I mean that individual stimulus which becomes something physically real and sensually pleasing, and which is spiritualized precisely through its relation to the whole as defined by the formal law. And if I might adopt a schoolmasterly tone for a moment and provide you with a rule or a little aid to your own aesthetic experience, I would say this: it is really the decisive aspect in the experience of works of art that they understand the individual sensual element never as an individual sensual element but rather in relation to the whole, which makes it more than merely the isolated sensual manifestation as which it appears in the here and now. So if in the first movement of Beethoven's 'Eroica', for example, a certain very emphatic motivic element in semiquavers intervenes in the events,[18] then primitive or culinary listening, atomistic listening, will grasp this theme in the same way as all the other individual themes; perhaps it will be remembered and, if one has heard it often enough, one might perhaps whistle it and recall it as a so-called musical 'idea'. I have no wish to denigrate this. And I believe that, if one has not gone through this stage of sensual-atomistic behaviour towards works of art, if one perceives the work purely as an abstract whole, so to speak, without ever abandoning oneself to these individual sensual aspects, then one certainly does not know what a work of art is. But you will only understand the 'Eroica' at the precise moment when you do not hear this intervening motif as one idea alongside however many others but, rather, relate it to the totality; that means noticing that a kind of heteronomous force here intervenes in the movement's progression, that you really experience this specific theme as an intervention rather than a mere continuation – and hence that you are really capable of experiencing the difference between an exposition that progresses and develops and one that is antithetical, in which an element appears that seems not to have been planned and first obstructs the interplay of forces, but is finally reintegrated through the ongoing development of the whole. I think that, in so far as you are being trained in individual philologies or in musicology, you will be made aware of such individual phenomena – this is certainly the case in recent literary history – and then be given these as categories of stylistic critique and shown how individual aspects of the works of art relate to the respective whole. But what I wish to teach you here is actually something less harmless. I do not so much want to contribute to your education and show you, for example, that Beethoven's style does not consist simply in a stringing together of ideas but in the fact that these ideas are actually determined by one another and gain meaning through their functional context. Rather, I want to tell you what artistic experience is, namely that subjective aspect with which we engage in our critique of the sensually pleasing, and that you can only understand the work of art at all, only come close to it at all, if you perceive these relations between the individual element and the whole. This means that you will only truly understand a work of art if you perceive all its sensual details concretely and specifically, to be sure, but so much in relation to the other sensual aspects and to the whole that they accordingly become carriers of a structural meaning, and at that moment cease to be mere isolated sensual stimuli. The simple example of this is really that one cannot understand a music – if it is a highly organized music – as long as one perceives only individual beautiful passages in it, which may even become a virtual wall blocking one's access to an understanding of the work itself. If you add up an important musical work for yourself from such beautiful passages, what you are really making of this work is nothing but a potpourri of itself – or you are moving it in the direction of a smash hit. Incidentally, if I might add this, what you have here is perhaps a reasonable distinction between what one calls high or serious art and vulgar art of mass culture – or whatever you wish to call it.[19] For one cannot simply tell these things apart according to their so-called standard, since the concept of standard is something extremely problematic in art. There are works of art that were once located at a very high standard but can no longer uphold this standard at all, while others were not at such a high standard objectively speaking but managed through the unfolding of some inner forces to leave so-called high-class art far behind. I need only remind you of Johann Peter Hebel[20] in this context; then you will know what I mean. But the less one can rely on the dogmatic notion of standard in such distinctions, the more important it is to find such criteria within the matter itself, as I have attempted to do for you in one such case. But here I would say that this ability really to perceive the individual aspects as functional aspects of the whole is constitutive of aesthetic experience and that, on the other hand, a work of art exists only where there is indeed such a – yes, let me say it – dialectical relationship between the individual aspects and the whole. And when I speak of a dialectical relationship, what I mean is precisely that the whole comes together from such relations as the one I attempted to show you using the example of the 'Eroica', while, on the other hand, each individual element gains its meaning only from the whole.

This reciprocal production of the whole and its parts in a dynamic progression, then, is the meaning one can assign to the dialectical form of the work of art in itself. I would say that this aspect of breaking apart into so-called beautiful passages or individual sensual stimuli has, in fact, accompanied art time and again, that it could be seen as the constant temptation to which the works have always been subject, and that this aspect inheres in art as an element of danger just as, on the other hand, the element of abstract or idealistic unity can also threaten the work.[21] Regarding this aspect of the individual sensual stimulus that threatens to breach the work of art, however, one can say that, because the works of art have only rarely developed as autonomous constructs in the world we inhabit and have almost always been to some degree elements of the market, the market has always asserted itself in a certain preponderance of these aspects. And the great artists have always submitted to this circumstance in some way. I think it would be a philistine and narrow view to reproach the artists for this, as it were from the vantage point of a *poésie pure* or a *musique pure* or *peinture pure*.[22] Rather, it seems to me that the greatness of art in history until today – when these things are admittedly starting to become a little extreme and a little precarious – has really always consisted in the fact that art has yielded to this temptation yet nonetheless preserved the force of its spiritualization, the force of its integration, at the very point where it was lost.[23] It is not at all in the nature of the work of art to be in control of itself and commanding its elements at every moment; it is surely an equal part of its nature that it becomes lost in its individual aspects and, in following the motto 'throw away in order to gain',[24] namely surrendering to that danger, it demonstrates its strength all the more – the strength to find itself again. A work of art that does not succumb to temptation – one could almost say a work which, in modern terms, does not contain the potential of kitsch as something sublated – is probably not a work of art at all.[25] Let me just add that the aspect of the sensual, culinary particular, which threatens to rupture the unity of the work, is clearly at its most legitimate where it immediately declares itself without masquerading as something higher. In certain revues or film revues, for example, where there is hardly any claim to present a context of meaning, and the work of art instead abandons itself unreservedly to these sensual aspects, a second spiritual context can compose itself precisely from these unleashed sensual elements, while elsewhere – let us say, in the music of Tchaikovsky or other great bad composers – where the work claims to be art, but one realizes it is actually only a matter of connecting themes that the ladies and gentlemen can take home with them, such aspects are infinitely less bearable than where they reveal themselves with a certain air, I would say an air of great shamelessness.

Here you must not forget that the work of art is truly an interplay between the individual impulse and the whole, and that even these heteronomous individual impulses, if you will, always contain an element of truth, namely that here, that same nature breaks through which is suppressed, and whose renewed honouring through its integration is what gives the work of art its own honour. But if I now return to our own aesthetic experience, it must be said that the whole constituted by the work of art – the context of meaning, that element which can be termed the carrier of the work's spiritual aspect – is initially its concealed side, that which is not immediate, and that therefore, at least for us in our situation today, the path of aesthetic experience is largely the path to the whole, and that one must not misuse the things I have told you about the retrieval of the sensual individual stimulus as an ideological justification to stop at that sphere, unless one wants to end up appreciating works of art in the manner of the provincial uncle who takes a trip to the metropolitan theatre. I would argue, then, that a work of art is experienced by someone who experiences the whole, for it is only the whole that lends meaning. And this experience tends to be an experience that leads away from the individual sensual phenomenon. Here you come across a strange paradox in the experience of art, just as the sphere of art in general – I have tried to elaborate for you as to why this is so – is the sphere of paradox *par excellence*. For the more adequate the sensual experience of works of art, the more perfectly you will perceive a work of art sensually and the more you will also distance yourself from the merely sensual element of the work of art. That is to say, if you truly listen to a complex symphonic movement in such a way that you genuinely relate all its sensual aspects to one another, that you hear and sensually perceive them in their unity and their mediatedness, if you thus hear what you hear not simply in the way it appears to you now but also in its relation to what has already passed in the work and to what still lies ahead of you in the work, and finally to the whole, then this is surely the highest degree of precise sensual experience that can be achieved. By the same token, however, you also distance yourself from sensual experience because this mode of perception takes you way from the mere 'this thing here', the mere moment in which you hear the individual element; because, in other words, adequate aesthetic experience is always one that simultaneously transcends the mere given, the momentary given of which it is composed. And from this necessarily follows the question of the nature of aesthetic experience itself and the question of whether, after what I have told you here, the correlate of the subjective concept of aesthetic beauty is tenable at all or, to formulate it very radically, whether it is actually possible for the enjoyment of art to be an adequate aesthetic experience.

LECTURE 12

8 January 1959

Our train of thought had developed in such a way that, in order to come closer to the problematics of the concept of beauty, we had attempted to follow on as directly as possible from grasping what aesthetic experience means; and here my prime intention was to show you first of all in what concrete ways the concept of beauty is problematic in the representation of art. I decided to show you this through an analysis of so-called aesthetic experience itself. When we are finished, however, I will carry out the opposite exercise with you: I will try to show you that, on the other hand, aesthetics cannot dispense with a concept of beauty, and then attempt to show how these two opposites can be unified. Now, our investigations will not merely have this methodological value; as must be the case in any dialectical procedure, I will try to ensure that the ideas necessary in order to make this central train of thought clear to you also convey something about aesthetic questions that is vaguely worthwhile and substantial in its own right.

At the end of the last session we came across the question of the so-called enjoyment of art and its problematics. Here one undoubtedly touches a form of consensus, a fixed clichéd notion with which probably few people would like to part, simply because they are so used to it. Now, certainly the phrase 'enjoyment of art' has itself become so old-fashioned and harmlessly good-natured that no one except persons of a very advanced age would use it so readily. But the seemingly more subjectively tinged and – how should one put it? – more experienced formulations, for example that a person wishes to be 'given' something by a work of art, and that they assess the work's entire value depending on what it offers them as a consumer, so to speak: these are no more than shamefaced paraphrases of that old-fashioned 'enjoyment of art'. I would therefore rather take the bull by the horns and, for now, give less thought to the question of whether a work of art has anything to give people than to the question of the enjoyment of art. Here, however, it strikes me that – and I say this in the full awareness that it goes against widespread habits – genuine aesthetic experience, the experience of a work of art that does justice to this work itself and, on the other hand, is itself in fact aesthetically constituted, really has very little directly to do with enjoyment; that, when one approaches a work of art in a truly living way, one is doing something entirely different. In order to explain this to you, I would like to draw on the definition we formulated at the start and to which we keep being led back: that of the work of art as a special area, as a removed, secularly magical domain that may be connected to empirical reality through its elements and does, after all, refer to them in a highly mediated way, either critically or utopically, but, in so far as it is something aesthetic, in so far as we experience it as aesthetic, is not directly experienced as a piece of physical reality. It seems to me that the artistic experience we are examining at the moment essentially consists in being in this special area – and, if you recall, the definitions of this area should not be considered static, for the removal or positing of the aesthetic area itself rather takes place in a kind of endless process, starting anew at every moment. So I would say that aesthetic experience essentially consists in taking part in this co-enactment, in joining the process of the work of art by being inside it, by – to put it very simply – living in it.

The question of enjoyment – to say this right at the start – is simply discarded here because the kind of experience I am trying to define for you is, in a sense, a path leading precisely away from the subject, whereas every form of enjoyment is in fact something which, as they say, gives the subject something, something that, with regard to the subject, is chalked up as its own – to put it maliciously – 'advantage'. The better someone actually understands art, however – by which I mean the more genuine their relationship to art – the less they will really enjoy art. Let me read you a few lines I wrote almost thirty years ago, and which reappear unchanged in my new book:[1]

> What distinguishes the musician from the bad amateur is the lack of enthusiasm. The amateur enters the realm of music like a stranger wishing to spend their time there; they drift through the city and find

everything beautiful that does not irk them. The native guiding them can only say 'yes, yes' to their words of praise, for the streets and corners are too familiar to require confirmation; perhaps the local even sees their differences in such detail that they can no longer appreciate their totality. But they abstain willingly therefrom, and their love is the even pace at which they check every alley corner and step through the right gate to glimpse the jutting gable of the house just across from them; sometimes they unlatch an unassuming door and enter a court-yard with the most perfect inner facade. If the stranger wishes to reward them with their delight, the local merely responds with the name of the courtyard.[2]

So that, to me, is the form of behaviour we are dealing with here. Incidentally, when people in certain movements, for example the youth music movement,[3] said that doing is better than feeling, or when Hindemith once stated that making music is better than listen-ing to music,[4] there was some truth in it from this perspective. And, to be fair, I would like – especially after being very critical of this attitude of blind doing[5] – to underline this element of truth, namely that the relationship with the work of art is not merely that of passive acceptance, which would be enjoyable in all its aspects, but that this question of enjoyment no longer even arises at first, in so far as artistic experience consists in a particular form of 'doing' or 'making', namely in co-enacting. Except that this making should be understood not as a technical busyness, as minstreldom, as somehow joining in, but rather as a spiritual, imaginary enactment, as an act of following the work of art, of the inward spiritual co-enactment of what the work of art, as a sensual manifestation, decides of its own accord. By contrast, the form of behaviour towards art that generally parades itself as the so-called naïve and immediate approach – based on enjoy-ment, in a word – actually strikes me as the opposite, namely an alienated form of behaviour borrowed from that of the consumer, the customer who experiences the world only in categories of commodi-ties and – as commodities happen to be exchanged with their equiva-lents – asks with each such commodity whether it is worth its money,[6] whether it returns as much as they have put into it of themselves. But – if we assume that a work of art is indeed an objective context of meaning, not a mere accumulation of sensual stimuli – the behaviour towards the work itself is naturally the opposite, and it was once rightly stated that it is less a matter of what the work 'gives' us than what we give to it. That is, whether, in a particular form of active passivity or effortful surrender to the matter, we give it what it actu-ally expects of us. One could perhaps encapsulate that negatively in the rule of thumb that the enjoyer – namely, the person with the culinary attitude which, last time, I termed atomistic – not only fails to grasp the whole but in fact always perceives the wrong things in the work of art precisely because this attitude of enjoyment – which aesthetics still generally posits quite unreflectingly as the attitude towards art[7] – ignores from the outset the very things that are present in the work.

Now, here you could admittedly enquire as to the purpose of this. You could ask: 'If I do not enjoy a work of art, what is the point of the whole business?' It must somehow have a meaning within the human world too, otherwise it is nothing but a fetish. If, as history certainly teaches us, works of art do contain fetishes, among other things, at least in their genealogy,[8] then I think there are initially worse charges than that of fetishism. Just as one cannot imagine an act of artistic production that does not involve the work appearing to the artist as something absolute, truly as a manifestation of truth, however much they might know about the relativity of the aesthetic sphere, so too one can hardly imagine any artistic experience that views the work from the outset merely as a means to an end. Perhaps it would make more sense to say, rather paradoxically, that the work only comes to mean anything, to have a function and thus prove its *raison d'être* in the world, where it does not fulfil any immediate purpose but instead appears as a being-in-itself. Only through this being-in-itself, only through this constitution of its objective inner laws, can it hope to achieve that provision of joy which the guileless consciousness simply expects immediately from the work of art here and now, at every moment. Works of art have certainly preserved enough of their sacred origins that, as Benjamin once put it very aptly, they are not directly intended for an audience.[9] No painting is there for the viewer, no symphony for the listener, nor even any drama for the audience, as they are first of all for their own sake; and only through this aspect, which must be described as a secularized theo-logical one, so only with reference to the absolute, and not in some immediate relationship with humans, do [the works] exist, do they speak at all. As soon as one violates the distance that lies in them, as soon as one relates the works directly to what one wants from them, one already 'de-artifies' them and destroys the very thing one hopes to get from them. It also strikes me as one of the most characteristic inconsistencies in the current vulgar aesthetic consciousness that, while there is constant talk of 'bonds' and the supposed metaphysical meaning or, as people so wonderfully put it, the 'statement' of the work, there are at once incessant demands that the work should be there for people's sake; this exposes that demand for a 'bond' as precisely what one should suspect: an expression of administrative manipulation. But ultimately – you could say, the same way one lets sleeping dogs lie – one can also let the work of art lie. And if it indeed no longer has any connection to happiness, why should I be compelled to have any dealings with works of art? I spoke to you earlier of such a connection, using the example of *Romeo and Juliet* to show that, even in negativity, and especially in negativity, every work of art contains the idea of the complete fulfilment of utopia.

But now I would like to examine this question of the connection of the work of art to happiness, or to enjoyment, from a slightly different angle in keeping with what we are dealing with, namely actual aesthetic experience. Certainly there is something resembling happiness or enjoyment derived from works of art, and it would go against the simplest common sense if one simply denied that based on the metaphysical speculation I have carefully touched on, and indeed idolized the works quite primitively as absolutes. Works of art are not divine manifestations but the work of humans, and this gives them both their limits and their connection to human matters. What I wish to say, however, is that the happiness emanating from works of art, or I suppose even the enjoyment they provide, is not directly one with the aesthetic experience of them; this aesthetic experience itself does not directly provide enjoyment in its individual aspects, as imagined by the amateur and the bourgeois, who turn the work into a plate of pork rib and sauerkraut. Rather, the work of art offers happiness because it succeeds in drawing us into it in the way I have tried to show you; that it forces us to accompany it on the paths it traces within itself; and that, at the same time, it thus alienates us from the alienated world in which we live, and through this very alienation of the alienated in fact restores immediacy or undamaged life. If there is such a thing as happiness coming from the aesthetic, or aesthetic enjoyment, then this enjoyment therefore lies in that to which the work succeeds in subjecting us by absorbing it, by the fact that we enter it and follow it. But the work's aesthetic quality plays a substantial part in this achievement.[10] Now you might think: 'Well, what you are telling us – happiness through a work of art – is something rather abstract and general; so this means that the removal from the everyday sphere applies equally from the most inferior light novel to the greatest works of art, and what you are serving up here is really pretty stale, abstract and empty stuff.' But I think it would be a little too hasty if you argued in this way. For it is precisely the work's ability to absorb the viewer or the listener so strongly, to draw them into itself so far and, as I put it, to alienate them from the alienated world, which strikes me as the idea of the work of art – this itself depends on the power and greatness of the work, on its autonomy, the extent to which it can embody within itself its own formal law down to the smallest details. In this sense, one could say – if I may return to the categories I laid out for you in the last session – that happiness through the work of art concerns the work as a whole, whose power ultimately decides how far it takes us out of mere existence, even if only temporarily, or whether it does not. To that extent, the description of being elevated through the work of art which is still found in earlier aesthetics,[11] but scarcely exists today, is certainly as superior to the description of so-called enjoyment as it is to the question of what the work has to give us. I would like to mention, at least in passing, that you can indeed find here quite a fundamental connection to the problematics of art itself. For, ultimately, this power of the work of art to alienate us once again from the alienated world is itself an aspect of illusion; this real world from which we become alienated is not negated in its alienated character but, in a certain sense, left in precisely that state because we withdraw from it.[12] And this is indeed where we find that conflict – if I may put it somewhat grandiloquently – between the moral, namely the aim to change the world, and the specifically aesthetic, namely the intolerability of the world as it is. If I correctly understand Tolstoy's novel *The Kreutzer Sonata*, which, despite certainly somewhat embarrassing ascetic tendencies of his, I consider an extremely important creation, then the idea essentially developed in this novel – and it is a theoretical novel concerned with the critique of art, and great art in particular, for he very consciously chooses a highly significant work of art, and what he says about this work, incidentally, testifies to an extraordinarily penetrating and subtle understanding – so what Tolstoy says in this novel about the work of art amounts to the statement that, the more significant a work of art, and the more adequate the artistic experience, the more the context of delusion is reinforced in a sense, and the more one leaves reality in the ghastly state one intended to flee through all this.[13] I think that this antinomy must be named, at least, and that we are indeed dealing with a phenomenon of which – if one wishes to avoid burying oneself in a kind of naïve aestheticism, especially in the current period of restoration – one must say that there are periods in which art has exactly this value, that it pushes itself – and does so all the more, the more serious and perfect it is – as a substitute in front of other things that are ruled out in such a situation. And especially if one espouses what are termed avant-garde and very extreme positions in art, as I do, then one must also be aware, and tell those who trust one, that this radicalism also contains something very un-radical, one could almost say something resigned, and that there are situations in which precisely such radical

art can become an alibi for an eschewal of an interventional practice.[14] But I do not consider it my task to pursue this argument further
here. I only wish to tell you – as nothing is isolated, as there is no
sentence that, in the world we inhabit today, cannot be transformed
into a lie through the function it assumes, no matter how true it might
be – that even this idea I am touching on has become a lie in the
entire eastern area, for example, where all art is being subordinated
to so-called practice, which means being reshaped into a practical
tool. And what this does to art, namely the obvious insufficiency and
stupidity and primitivity of the art thus produced, at least shows that
the problem I have described to you does not involve a simple duality
in which, as it were, the moral human could simply triumph in
Kierkegaardian fashion over the aesthetic one,[15] but that what we
have is rather an antinomy that probably cannot be resolved in the
world we inhabit, and where all one can do is to take it into account.

But, to remain on the subject of aesthetic experience, I would argue
that, even with what I have said to you – that the so-called liberating
or elevating quality one attributes to art lies in the totality of the
work and in its power to remove us from the immediacy of a bad
and questionable existence – that even that does not truly describe
the whole but is still something abstract. I think some of you will
already have been bothered by this abstractness, and rightly so: bothered that the experience of the concretely aesthetic and that liberation
which is only meant to follow indirectly through the whole do not
face each other as directly, as simply as it would seem. If I may speak
of my own experience for a moment, which is perhaps not as singular
as one would think: I am inclined to take an extremely democratic
view in these matters and always to presuppose that – if I can only
succeed in getting hold of my own experience genuinely and very
precisely – with this in particular, I am uttering something that does
not belong only to me privately, but which is more or less human; I
do not believe in the absolute right of individuation here. So if I may
refer to my own experience once again, I have the impression that,
in actual artistic experience, where it is genuine and the relationship
with the work of art is intensified to the utmost degree – one could
almost say, where one becomes entirely one with the life of the work
in the pulse, the rhythm of one's own life, where one is taken up in
it – that there are then moments of breakthrough. What I mean by
breakthrough is that there are moments – they could be chance
moments, but it could also be the highest and most intense moments
of a work of art – in which that feeling of being lifted out, that feeling,
if you will, of transcending mere existence, is intensely concentrated
and actualizes itself, and in which it seems to us as if the absolutely

mediated, namely that idea of being freed, is something immediate after all, where we think we can directly touch it. These moments are probably the highest and the most decisive which artistic experience can achieve; and it is certainly conceivable that the notion that works of art can be enjoyed is taken from them, for those moments truly have a form of delight to them that – I will not say outshines, but definitely matches the highest moments of happiness one experiences elsewhere; they have the same power as the highest real moments that we know. Yet, strangely enough, these very moments in which – how shall I put it? – the spirit of the work of art or its meaning actualizes itself and it seems as if we were experiencing it directly and almost physically in ourselves, these moments are far less ones of enjoyment than of being overwhelmed, of forgetting oneself, really the annihilation of the subject in a very similar sense to the way Schopenhauer – under the preconditions of his metaphysics, of course – describes these effects of the work of art in Book III of *The World as Will and Representation*. It is then as if, in that moment – one could call them moments of weeping – the subject were collapsing, inwardly shaken. [They are] really moments in which the subject annihilates itself and experiences happiness at this annihilation – and not happiness at being granted something as a subject. These moments are not enjoyment; the happiness lies in the fact that one has them.[16]

I would say that art, which is so often associated with hedonism and has always been viewed with suspicion, especially by the puritans of all religions and all so-called worldviews, for supposedly seeking pleasure, is – in the sense we have discussed – something anti-hedonistic. That is, the experience of art is not one that benefits the subject in the usual sense but, rather, one that leads away from the subject. From this perspective, artistic experience is indeed a form of temporary suspension, as Schopenhauer would have it, a temporary suspension of the *pricipium individuationis* in the idea,[17] if I may say it in the old idealistic language, and by no means the path directly taken by sensual fulfilment – though I would note here that even the distinction between the so-called sensual and the so-called spiritual work of art is far more difficult, far more dialectical, than the cliché of northern-metaphysical and southern-sensual art, a cliché of which I can hopefully rid you along with a number of others in the course of these lectures.

I do not want to occupy myself with this tempting task now, however, but wish rather to follow on from what I explained to you about the concept of enjoyment by saying something about the concept of understanding works of art, in so far as understanding works also means establishing some relationship of appropriation or participation. For the theory of understanding, the work becomes something that belongs to oneself, something one makes one's property – which is also present in the notion of enjoyment – and I by no means desire to deny this aspect of artistic experience; I will discuss in what ways it is justified. But, first of all, I think – and perhaps this can also help you a little in your own relationship with works of art – the genuine relationship with works of art is not really one of understanding, because art categorically, by its very nature and constitution, if I may put it thus, initially contains an element of incomprehensibility; because art itself, as a piece of secularized magic, eludes any attempt to make it like ourselves and like the subject, which is what the concept of understanding essentially demands. If the definition I tried to give you earlier applies, namely that artistic experience is a co-enactment or being-inside, then this type of behaviour towards the work of art would indeed do away with the distance, the thing-ness, that is inherent in the concept of understanding. But the works themselves have an enigmatic aspect to which one can initially do justice only by refraining from asking 'What does it all mean?' and rather oneself entering the matter itself. So one could almost say for now: the less one 'understands' art, meaning the less one reduces it to some abstract, underlying general concepts which it supposedly conveys, and the more one instead surrenders to its happening, the better one will understand it, grasp its context of meaning, which means following the work of art without guessing what it means. When Hegel once responded to the accusations that his philosophy was so hard to understand, and that people often did not know what they were supposed to think of when reading about his concepts, by saying that one should not think of anything but the concept itself,[18] he was describing an experience that specifically corresponds to the relationship with art. And, indeed, the experiences with which Hegel's philosophy is saturated have a great deal in common with the type of aesthetic experience I am seeking to define – though this should not lead one to aestheticize his philosophy, of course. Understanding a work of art does not mean understanding what is behind it, as it were, what the work means, but rather understanding the work of art as it is: understanding the logic that leads it from one chord to the next, from one colour to the next, from one line to the next. And only when this understanding of the matter itself is fully achieved, albeit without yet touching on the work's riddle character, only then does one come close to the work. On the other hand, the works of art – and this will perhaps show you in closing how essential a part of the work is that aspect of the riddle, the enigmatic element, which I have tried to describe to you – are completely helpless and exposed at the moment when someone who knows nothing about the artistic sphere, the philistine, asks: 'So, what is that, what does it say, what is it all about?' Attempting to convey to a person who is radically amusical, who suffers from amusia in the clinical sense, what a work of art is for, what it means, what it is – aside from what the work says immediately and of its own accord – is a completely hopeless undertaking. And in reality, as soon as one breaks free of its spell and faces it as one faces a piece of reality, all art has an element of perplexity and helplessness that spreads to those who regard it. But let me say one more thing: the experience of art must not stop at this level of experience but must, rather, insist, in a higher and far more mediated sense, on comprehending the work as something incomprehensible – if I may formulate it so paradoxically. And let me try at least to outline this exact mediation of the concept of aesthetic understanding to you at the beginning of the next session.

LECTURE 13

13 January 1959

In the last session, in our critical analysis of subjective behaviour towards the work of art, we arrived at the problem of so-called understanding. In the course of that I attempted to show you that, first of all, specifically aesthetic experience has nothing to do with the experience of understanding in the usual sense; one is within a work, and participates in its enactment, but does not enter it from without and unlock it, as talk of understanding would suggest, for this quality of being in the work of art is closer to the way one lives in a language, lives immediately without reflecting on its so-called meaning, and reflection on the meaning of a work of art really constitutes a higher level than primary aesthetic experience. I think I owe it to you to say that I did not mean to propagate the view that the adequate mode in which to approach the work of art is one of incomprehension. I hope I am more or less safe from this misunderstanding from the start. But I only wanted to prevent you from thinking that the adequate relationship with the work of art resembles that of the philistine towards a contemporary picture or a contemporary composition or a contemporary poem, who asks: 'What am I supposed to think of?' And I reminded you what Hegel wrote when confronted with his own philosophemes: 'What am I supposed to think of with this concept?' And he replied that one should not think of anything but the concept itself.[1] Aesthetic behaviour, to the extent that I have characterized it as such a co-enactment of the work of art, naturally does not stop at this co-enactment, which is rather a self-aware co-enactment in each case. This means that, only by co-enacting the different aspects of the work to which you surrender, whose discipline you share, if I may put it like this, by floating along with it while also reflecting on its aspects, contrasting them with one another, recalling past ones and awaiting the coming ones – only then can you arrive at a true understanding of the construct you have before your eyes or in your ears. A reflective behaviour towards the work of art, I would say, is first of all nothing foreign to the work that comes from without, a philosophical behaviour in the true sense. It is not the philosophy of art that first causes such reflection but, rather, the co-enactment of the work of art itself. This means that this act of being in the work of art, of co-enacting it, already demands that you go beyond its mere immediacy and become aware of those aspects of the work that are not immediately evident to you as sensual elements. And there you can already see what I keep trying to convey to you from the various perspectives: that the conventional notion of the work of art as something merely sensory is not quite sufficient, but that you can only experience those works fully – to put it in the most emphatic terms – not by simply observing, but always by thinking at the same time. That is because this element of what is thought, the mediated element, is necessarily contained in the specific substance of the work of art – which should be all the less amazing and shocking after what I have already attempted to elaborate to you, as we have already developed, I hope, a concept of the work of art as something substantially spiritual.

You may also reach, for a second, a dimension of art that is generally withheld somewhat by conventional aesthetics, and which I would therefore like at least to point out to you: the dimension of the aesthetically intelligent and the aesthetically stupid. There is a kind of aesthetic stupidity, that is to say an aspect of mere unthinking, perfunctory happening in the material, in which one can hear that the artist was drifting along in the material without this reflection on the necessity for the work lying within that material – which is necessary. If, for example, in countless older compositions, in concertos, you listen to the cadenzas usually played by the soloist towards the end of the first movement, you will immediately detect a certain quality of stupidity, of a lack of reflection. In significant works of art, on the other hand, if you truly immerse yourselves in these works, you will experience time and again a feeling like 'Oh, how clever of him, he really did something very shrewd there!' In some passages in late Beethoven, for instance, where he uses a zeugmatic approach – that is, having the end of one phrase overlap with the beginning of a new phrase – to create an especially concentrated and abbreviated effect, a stretto effect: that falls precisely into this category.[2] You can

perhaps get an idea of the dimension in question, which, as far as I
know, has scarcely been examined in theoretical aesthetics, if you
think of the journalese term 'minstrel-like', which is constantly
attached to some composition or other – and even as praise; what is
meant is that a composition is unreflecting in itself, in its material,
and in a sense just rattles off its notes, and that the respective composer simply yields blindly to the piece by abandoning themselves to
the mere direction of their material. And on closer inspection, I might
add, this material does not transpire so much as does the direction
of the material itself, but rather the direction of convention, which
has already preformed the material in one way or another. This
minstrel-like quality – and there are certainly analogous things in a
particular quickness of the painter's eye,[3] and in language there is an
analogy in that ghastly phenomenon which used to be praised using
phrases like 'fluent style' – consists in the fact that exactly this congestion process of reflection which enables the work to become a
work of art at all did not take place in the work itself.

And I consider it a substantial aspect of aesthetic quality as such
that it possesses this aspect of congestion, of self-reflection, but that,
on the other hand, it does not stop at this self-reflection, for this
reflection in turn translates into the pure logic of the matter, the pure
enactment of the work. But once such a concept of reflection is
brought into play – and I think I am touching on something that by
no means applies only to art but is much more far-reaching and
applies to all rationality – then this process of reflection can no longer
be stopped, one cannot somehow force it to a halt; rather, such a
reflection process necessarily leads further. So if you enact this process
in the work of art itself, these reflections in the matter itself of which
I have provided a few examples, a few models – or for whose absence
I have given you various such models – then your experience will
necessarily turn into a reflection on the work of art itself and its
meaning. So I would like to continue what I said in the last session
by telling you that the primary experience is not that of the so-called
meaning, of course; it is not an understanding experience in the usual
sense but rather a surrendering. But this surrendering, being a blind
act, also holds an aspect of negativity: precisely that aspect of the
stupid, the minstrel-like, which then necessarily pushes beyond itself.
And what lies at the end of this process is an understanding, ultimately a comprehension of the meaning of all aspects, a comprehension whose canon is the experience of the necessity underlying the
relationship between all aspects of the work of art. So once this
reflection on the work of art is brought into play, it returns to the
work. And when it returns into the work, having first left it and

viewed it from without, as it were, it then becomes constitutive of true artistic experience, which ultimately presents itself as something mediated and spiritual after all. I think that there is some use for this line of thought, because it points you to the fact that certain forms, such as that of translation, but most of all commentary and critique, are not parasitic forms that proliferate like weeds growing on art and exploit the primary elements, namely the works, but that these forms too are actually constitutive of art's essence.[4] This means that only through commentary and critique, only through the reflection brought into play by the work of art through its own logic, is a full experience of the work possible, and only through these aspects does the work of art return to itself, or only through them can you really understand the work of art.[5] Accordingly, you must imagine understanding the work of art as a process that is demanded by the work itself but does not take place in the sense that one faces it and suddenly, as if by a wave of a magic wand, this understanding is realized. But this may also show you that art, which, as the antithesis of mere existence, has a deep affinity with philosophy anyway – through this special structure of which I attempted at least to give you an intimation – now proceeds towards philosophy, and demands of its own accord something like philosophy.

But now I would like to return to the matter at hand, namely the dialectic that forms a substantial part of the concept of beauty. With reference to the deliberations about the experience of the work of art – in which I showed you that these experiences are not hedonistic, that one therefore does not directly enjoy the work in a culinary sense, as it were, that the concept of 'enjoying art' is generally very questionable – I tried first of all to introduce you from the perspective of the matter itself to the growing allergy, the increasing sensitivity to the concept of the pleasurable in art, meaning the allergy to an internally unbroken – in terms of what I explained before, one could also say an internally unreflecting – concept of beauty. I might add that, with the allergy towards beauty, towards beauty that is merely given, the problems of art also increase. It is already some forty years since Kandinsky, as you all know, wrote that famous manifesto, the book *Concerning the Spiritual in Art*,[6] in which, contrary to the all-pervading notion of art as sensually immediate, he turned the old theory from idealistic, speculative-idealistic philosophy of the essentially spiritual character of art into a programme of actual artistic creation, which he claimed should henceforth be an expression only of something spiritual and more or less entirely abandon its sensual immediacy. This was a development that was continued in the whole complex with which you are familiar under the name – not a very useful one, incidentally – of 'abstract art'. But the more dominant spirit becomes in the work of art, and the more the sensual aspects are really defined only as carriers of something internal, the more problematic the work of art will become, in a certain sense, a sense that Hegel already anticipated – long before this development began, almost a hundred years earlier – in espousing the theory that a spiritualized art, meaning an art in which the relationship between sensual immediacy and spirit is no longer predefined, or 'substantial', as he calls it, and instead becomes problematic anew for each artist, that this becomes something which can only be created by the respective work, and that the sphere of art itself thus transpires as a problematic one precisely because it lacks that aspect of substantiality, the predefined unity of sensual and spiritual aspects – which Hegel, however, very much in keeping with the classicism of 1800, sought to equate with classical antiquity. The problem one faces in the modern phase of the allergy towards mere sensual beauty in art, which is synonymous with its spiritualization, is slightly different from the problem Hegel detected. Hegel – undoubtedly thinking of the syncretism of the Romantic educational efforts of his time, which assembled their aesthetic forms from all conceivable cultures and conditions – saw the danger of this self-reflective, entirely spiritualized art in the fact that all forms were now open to the artist, which meant that no form was binding any longer. In arguing thus, he indeed superbly anticipated, theoretically and critically, the stylistic syncretism that came to dominate the nineteenth century. And I also want to use this opportunity to point out that dialectical philosophy is not, as the ignorant would have it, a night in which all cats are grey and nothing is really true or untrue: rather, it is a critical philosophy in an eminent sense and, in this respect too, represents the fulfilment of Kant's philosophy. But this syncretism has most certainly continued into our own time. Yet the problems faced in the precise area we are discussing by new art, whose experiences are our fundamental point of departure in these lectures, are of a slightly different and even more serious nature. For one can say that the artists themselves have become aware of this danger, even though, God knows, there is no lack of artists in our time as well, and by no means all of them bad, who thought that the artistic spirit's mastery of its material allows one to play with and make use of every conceivable form. What has become clear today, however – and I think this indeed touches on a very advanced point of artistic development itself – in all areas of art, in so far as I am entitled to pass judgement, that this openness is a questionable matter. The decisive lesson which artists have learned in the last thirty or forty years is that this arbitrariness, as still found recently in the

influence of exoticism in the most diverse forms on modern art, is a
questionable matter; that it genuinely amounts to a non-binding state,
and everything depends on the fact that, today, when this substantiality – the predefinition of a formal canon in the whole of culture – has
been lost, the only thing that can help art is if every single work
immerses itself unreservedly in its own formal law, without glancing
outwards; that art, precisely in the face of the harmful abundance
opened up by education, the harmful wealth of possibilities, limits
itself and abstains from these abstractly possible things in favour of
what its own specific conditions demand concretely, here and now.
But, even then, this does not solve the problem for art that we
encountered here. For time has shown that, the more the aforementioned spiritualization of the work of art grows – and it must grow,
as an allergy to the pleasurable forced on us by the culture industry,
advertising and the commercial system of the contemporary world in
general – that even in this spiritualization, an extraordinary difficulty
remains, namely what one might call the mediation between the
spiritual aspect of art and the carriers of expression, the sensual
aspects of art. What I mean is the aspect that emerged so clearly in
the early manifestos of modern painting, where people spoke of
colour symbolism, for example, and said: 'Now colours, they are not
merely sensual gradations, but all mean something as carriers of a
spiritual element, and if I do not see this meaning – evil is red, while
peaceful or even cosmic things are blue,[7] or whatever else – then I
am not really seeing properly.' All of these relationships, in so far as
they refer to some isolated artificial materials, have an arbitrary
aspect to them, or you could equally call it an element of convention,
of something which has been dictated, as it were – that this colour
must correspond to that term – and it was also very present in expressionist poetry, where Heym, Trakl or Stadler, with a kind of rigidity,
truly associated certain colours with particular expressive meanings
that are not necessarily found in the nature of the colours as such.[8]
The degeneration of these tendencies, one could perhaps call it the
parody of the spiritualization of art, then leads to decorative art,
whose practitioners believe that so-called noble materials or some
particular forms of ritual gestures, taken out of their specific contexts,
or other elements of a similar kind, especially symbolic colours, effect
that spiritualization by themselves. So in other words – and here too
I want to draw your attention to a problem in new art that may help
you a little to find your critical bearings: that inescapable process of
spiritualization undergone by the sensual aspects of art with which
we are dealing here can never – I think this is something that experiences in modern art have imposed on us – orient itself by some

individual sensual element. No individual sensual element in itself is absolutely spiritual, an absolute carrier of expression, or sufficient in itself to produce the spiritual.[9] When we worked with the new, extraordinarily dissonant chords for the first time thirty or forty years ago, we also believed that every single one of these chords, by virtue of its complexity, its crafting, its multi-layered and, above all, unused character, was already something spiritually new in and of itself, something that manifested the intended expressive content in the most compelling way. And I would not even go so far as to deny that completely. The situation was such that, in the era of new art's emancipation, painting as well as music, when these extremes were used for the first time, this power of the first time was also accompanied by some of that spiritual element on which we relied. But after the overall artistic developments had increasingly caused these extremes to change into what, in all forms of art, one speaks of as 'material' – which one does not need to like but can scarcely evade – it transpired that all these individual materials, even the most beautiful twelve-note chords or unheard-of nuances of a Noldian red or unheard-of colour contrasts, cannot bring about that spiritualization by themselves, that the power of spiritualization – which is absolutely vital for all art today if it aspires to be more than Coca-Cola – rather lies only in the configuration of these aspects, in the status these aspects have in the context of a work of art, and no longer as isolated phenomena.[10]

I have added this reflection because here you can perhaps understand in a very simple fashion something that otherwise, if you do not specifically live in aesthetic contexts, sounds slightly outlandish and sinister, namely the problem of so-called constructivism in art. This constructivism in art does not mean some external transfer of construction ideals like those that have developed through the New Objectivity and functionalism in architecture, with the result that now the purposeless, autonomous arts must behave in a similarly constructive way, as demonstrated by the functional arts, especially architecture, but also the genuinely technical disciplines. Rather, this demand for construction – which will surely cause very many of you, assuming you have not really thought these things through at a theoretical level, to say: 'My goodness, why should I be confronted by some absolutely constructed materiality, when what I really demand from art is for it to be my own voice, my native domain in which I myself speak' – this necessity of construction, as I wish to convey to you, originates from the actual artistic problematics, from the intra-aesthetic problematics itself.[11] This means that, after certain binding norms of artistic crafting imposed from without ceased to exist for art – traditional, conventional elements, topical elements, to take up a concept from classical philology[12] – but at the same time the demand that the artistic should be a carrier of the spiritual became inescapable, and this spiritualization of art could no longer come from any individual sensual element, all of this can only be achieved if the various individual aspects of a work of art form part of a structural context that is, in each individual work of art, fully crafted in itself and completely consistent in the sense of a particular logic that is truly specific only to art, and in such a way that, within this specific context of the work, every single aspect proves necessary in the fabric of the whole. And this endeavour is expressed by the concept of construction in art, which really says only that the spiritualization of a work is brought about by the individual aspects being embedded in a stringent, necessary framework that lends them the power of the spiritual which is absent from the individual element as such in isolation.[13] I think I told you in a different context, and have said often enough elsewhere, that this construction principle is very vulnerable and that, instead of spiritualization, it can also result in mere tinkering.[14] Here I will go only so far as to show you how much the problems of construction in modern art stem from its peculiar historico-philosophical situation, as well as from the necessity of that spiritualization, because none of the individual aspects of a work are spiritual – because, as Kant put it, nothing merely sensual can be sublime. Therefore, everything that was formerly provided by style and predefined forms can now only be provided by the inner organization of the work of art; and the quintessence of this inner organization of the work is the concept of its construction.[15]

Let me add that the concept of the pleasurable, to which I told you that we are becoming increasingly allergic, but must never chase the aspect of sensual appeal out of the work of art entirely, has its own historical status and undergoes change. Recall, for example, that, when Manet first introduced the use of extreme colour contrasts into painting, it was not yet taken in conjunction with the sometimes shocking, and at that time repulsive subject matter used by Manet, and was considered exorbitantly ugly and dissonant. For us, however, after all the aesthetic experiences we have had in the meantime, it is scarcely possible to imagine something more sensually appealing than the colour compositions of Manet, which replaced traditional, so-called picture composition.[16] And that is exactly how it is in music too, with the individual sounds. There are countless such individual sounds that would still have been considered harshly dissonant forty or fifty years ago and which – because they are refracted in themselves, because of certain sonic qualities or all manner of technical things I cannot discuss now – today actually convey the impression of something sensually appealing; there are, of course, also other sounds that do not do this at all, and which are even in deliberate opposition to it. Which of these aspects are introduced into a particular work of art is entirely subject to the artist's autonomy – or, to be more precise, the autonomy of the artistic law of form which a work essentially follows. But I do want to add one thing, having spoken to you today – primarily with reference to the allergy to the pleasurable element – about the dialectic between sensual and spiritual aspects in the work of art, which ultimately became the focus of the lecture almost against my will. For you will very often hear – and it is a very widespread theory – that one can speak of two types of works of art: on the one hand the spiritual work, which one often ascribes to the north, and on the other hand the so-called sensuous work, associated with the south. The theories, whose art-historical origins I do not need to examine now,[17] have become so pervasive that one imbibes them like mother's milk, even if one initially fails to do justice to their specific origins. Now, I have no intention of denying the validity of these things; one really need only look at a Bellini Madonna[18] and the Stuppach Madonna by Grünewald[19] to see that there is initially some truth, in a very tangible and drastic sense, to this distinction. I am only concerned to show you that here too, as in many other things, this kind of antithesis between the spiritual and artistic work of art – as a philosophical antithesis, at least – is actually untenable, because the metaphysical content of a work of art is not limited to its being a so-called spiritual work of art. To claim, for example, that a Nordic work is superior to a southern work because the former has an immediately metaphysical content and the latter is based on a fundamentally sensual relationship with the world, that the metaphysics of art really applies only to metaphysical art, strikes me as an extraordinarily simplified view of the matter at hand. For it could be that precisely the absence of the spiritual aspect in art in a particular sense, a particular kind of immersion in the sensual and also a particular form of hedonism in the work, if you will, which cuts off any kind of spiritual transcendence, itself becomes an expression of a metaphysical content: an expression, if I might make a very bold claim, of metaphysical sorrow or God-forsakenness. And it is conceivable that precisely this metaphysical expression of sorrow, as found in the great so-called sensual works of art, might ultimately have a greater metaphysical content than the metaphysics manifested positively in works. I simply wanted to show you this possibility, in closing, so that, after I so emphatically underlined the primacy of the so-called spiritual aspect, you would not assume that this offers a simple canon.[20]

LECTURE 14

15 January 1959

Two questions have reached me from your circles – and, let me say, from the most competent area – to which I would like to respond, especially because it is a matter of clarifying probably the most central concept with which we are dealing in these lectures. And although I have endeavoured in the most varied contexts to articulate this concept to you, it is perhaps advisable for us to say a little more by way of summary. This is none other than the question of the spiritual content of the works of art. I think I am being a good Platonist if I begin by summarizing what, as far as I can see, we should *not* think of here: namely not what an author, a writer, a musician, a painter put into the work in the way of so-called ideas of feelings, or whatever else. Certainly those aspects which are placed into the work of art by the productive subject, whether by artistic intention or indirectly through unconscious processes, are also central, and certainly its objectivity is mediated by these subjective aspects. If one did not posit this, one would indeed arrive at the notion of works that fall from heaven, which is generally espoused by amateurs and philistines in particular. What counts in the work of art, however, is only that which is embodied in the matter itself. And spirit exists in the work as spiritual content, as something binding, only in so far as it manifests itself objectively, without any consideration for its producer, through the work of art itself – one could say, in so far as it is realized by the work. By comparison, what the author places into the work, including so-called spiritual motives, whatever they were thinking, as the phrase goes, or whatever intentions they were following – yes, I must formulate it paradoxically – is really only a material aspect. In literary works it is the thoughts that appear in them, and nothing that takes place in language, and thus in the concept, is radically separate from the thought. The thoughts that are inserted so directly, however, are a piece of material just like the words that are used, or like colours in a painting or notes and note relationships in a composition. I think I can emphasize this aspect because I have the impression – and here I am addressing the Germanists among you in particular – that very many of the current interpretations of literature indeed modestly content themselves with working out what has been put in, so to speak. And the result is certainly a modest one, namely the insight that the author puts so many ideas, worldviews and intentions into a work of art, and the interpreter or arts scholar – the person who adopts the attitude of understanding towards it – takes out again what the author previously put in. One could ask as to the point of the whole enterprise, which is truly somewhat reminiscent of the story about the two farmers who both ate the famous toad.[1] One should scarcely imagine that one can access the substance of a work of art by such cheap methods. This is by no means some dystopian vision of academia that I am entertaining; it is a description of a genuinely widespread state of affairs. If you look at the range of literature on Thomas Mann, for example, you will find that these interpretations are generally content to pick out neatly the philosophical motifs that Mann, shall we say, sprinkled into or embedded in his works.[2] And, having done that, people truly think they have grasped the work's substance. There are works, especially from Thomas Mann's later period – the second half of his productive phase, which starts with *The Magic Mountain*[3] – in which, with very good reason, he did indeed engage with philosophical matters, and these are accordingly manifested there. Someone who is chasing dissertation material and determines these things more or less convincingly will be richly rewarded; there is no telling how many doctoral theses might be written as time goes on.[4] But this does not yet have anything to do with the real spiritual content of a work of art, of course, including that of Thomas Mann. So even if one does not limit oneself directly to the ideas uttered by all manner of figures in Mann's works – especially the adversarial brothers Naphta and Settembrini,[5] of course, who are especially popular for that, as well as countless discussants in *Doctor Faustus*[6] – but also if one draws one's conclusions from this and believes, for example, that the sentence in boldface type[7] from the snow chapter in the second part of *The Magic Mountain* about the master of opposites[8] constitutes the substance of these novels, then all this is essentially just a glorified piling up of information. The question of the true substance of the work of art only begins in the sphere where even these seemingly spiritual elements are understood as mere elements of material content.[9] This is a question which, as far as I can tell, has hardly been addressed so far; and I generally think that, with Thomas Mann, it would be important to emancipate oneself thoroughly from all these almost officially prescribed categories taken from the philosophy of life – such as opposites: life and death, decline, decadence and, on the other hand, spirit, or whatever all these things are called – and to look at these things, for once, as if they had not already been taken up into Baedeker's guide. But, aside from that, I think that the spiritual content of a work of art is not limited to – using a genuinely very compromised word that very few of you would dare to utter – the 'worldview' [*Weltanschauung*] of a work of art. If this is supposed to constitute anything beyond the most superficial, most rhetorical idea such as what a work wants, or what sort of mentality spawned it, then this so-called worldview can scarcely mean anything but – as in earlier art, as in the Middle Ages – the fundamental preconditions from which a work of art originally developed. And that could surely be extrapolated to bourgeois times, for in a sense the bourgeois worldview, with its categories of individual, responsibility, autonomy and the conflicts that are an inescapable part of bourgeois society – between social norms on the one hand and the demand for individual freedom on the other – is as much a precondition for the great bourgeois novels of Flaubert or Fontane[10] as a substantial idea of Christianity was for art during the Middle Ages. But the spiritual content of the work of art is surely constituted only in the specific way in which its crafting goes beyond these general preconditions, or in which they become concrete in the work itself. Otherwise, the spiritual content would be something indescribably impoverished and monotonous; for then all works of art carried by the same worldview, the same substantial overall categories, would also have the same spiritual content. Then the question of the work's spiritual content would indeed be reduced to what the question of a spiritual element must never become: the question of the general concept underlying every one of its determinate manifestations in more or less the same form. But even if one speaks of worldview in the sense of the different so-called worldviews that exist in our time – such as the worldview of existentialism, as presented in the novels of Sartre or Camus,[11] or a certain kind of Catholic worldview novels, which are also very common – I am thinking especially of Graham Greene,[12] who is probably better known in Germany than in the countries where his language is at home – then,

here too, it will become apparent that, compared to something genuinely crafted, the so-called worldview is a supplement, something that
is relatively external to the matter itself and is treated in the matter.
In these novels, then, the spiritual content is not primarily a specific
aspect of Catholicity; the authors simply like to talk about faith. Faith
becomes thematic, one could say, and, in becoming thematic and
being treated, it becomes something material. And I would add that,
when it comes to this problematic, the difference in our time between
the religious worldview novels and the irreligious worldview novels
is really not as great as the daily debates and polemics on both sides
would suggest. Even with a man such as Camus, whose creative
power at the specific level I certainly acknowledge, his work is for
the most part a kind of thesis literature where the worldview, even if
it is not a particular one of his own, is nonetheless demonstrated by
the things that happen there, rather than springing from the things
themselves as a spiritual content and something substantial. In the
work of […][13] you find a great power of concretization, but still the
work more or less illustrates the question – or the attempt at an
answer – of how it is possible to act as a moral person even in a state
of unbelief, to use an old-fashioned term. In all these matters, then,
the spiritual content of a work of art is something far more closed
up, something far less accessible. And if there is any sense in not
surrendering to art as a mere experience but, rather, engaging in
philosophical reflections about art, then I think this is precisely what
justifies it: that the spiritual content of the work of art itself, first of
all the definition of what such a spiritual content even is, does not
simply present itself directly but requires strenuous consideration. I
already outlined this for you in the previous session by telling you
that interpretation and critique, and thus philosophy itself, constitute
a necessary element in the objective unfolding of works of art – a
point of view that, I can assure you, is not simply that of a philoso-
phizer who has gone wild and been seized by hubris, but one that
Paul Valéry espoused with the greatest possible force in the artistic
process itself.[14]

Regarding all this, I would argue that the content of the work of
art, which is not abstractly separated from it, is constituted by the
here and now of the work, by its specific configurations, by the
aspects contained in the work, and by the totality which these aspects
combine to form. You might say that this points, to an extent, to
where the spiritual content of a work of art is to be found; but this
is as inadequate as it is to say in which room, in which area a criminal
is located in order to arrest them and, as it were, say their name. But
I think you can come closest to understanding the concept of the

work of art's content if you try to grasp it, to get hold of it as the very aspect that results from the specific configuration of the work. So what I am saying – and I will try once again to convey this to you as clearly as possible – is that the spiritual content of a work of art is not its mere appearance, not its sensual side, nor is it something expressed as intention through this sensual side, as signs generally convey a meaning to us in languages, in significative languages. Rather, the spiritual content of the work of art is the relationship between its sensual aspects in such a way that, through their connections, their relationship with one another, the material aspects or the sensual aspects of the work go beyond themselves. If one loves to speak in such abstract terms, one could also say that the spiritual content of the work of art is essentially the transcendence of all its interrelated sensual aspects. When one speaks of the structure of a work, after all, one does not really mean a description of the typical sensual forms being used – let us say a merely geometric underlying structure, or an impressionistic structure, or the like. Rather, what aestheticians were seeking to determine in the work of art with the term 'structural context', with reason and also from different perspectives, was really always defined as a context of meaning. In other words, when several different aspects within a work of art enter a relationship with one another that unites them and creates a synthesis, but also distinguishes between them and does not hide their contrasts – indeed, that might even place them expressly in opposition to one another – then the work of art is experienced directly as something meaningful. And the concept of the spiritual that is at issue here can genuinely – and concretely, I would almost say – be defined. For concerning this structural aspect, the reason why we can speak of something spiritual that goes beyond the merely sensual is that it cannot be pinpointed in any isolated sensual element, because it is not a matter of some sensual aspect of the work on its own, but because it is really a relational concept, something which only becomes tangible through the relationship between the different sensual aspects – or, as I love to say in the Hegelian language of philosophy, because it is something mediated. I think now you can see fairly precisely what is meant here: on the one hand, something that is not contained in the work of art as something separate and independent from the sensual form of the work itself, like the nut in its shell; but, on the other hand, also something that is not limited to the sensual appearance but [is] rather that aspect which goes beyond the sensual appearance through the pull of that same sensual appearance. That is, it is the embodiment of the phenomena in the work of art, which is more than merely these phenomena, and hence not pure immediacy. But I would warn you not to equate this spiritual aspect of the work of art – the temptation is a natural one, and a complacent aesthetic is especially willing to succumb to it – with such concepts as totality or *gestalt*,[15] as the psychological fashion, the restorative psychological fashion of today, suggests. This context is not simply a gestalt-like one; it is not an unbroken context. A work of art is not simply a totality, even though it is a totality among other things. Or, at least, it is not necessarily a totality; or, if I may use the language of gestalt theory for a moment, it is not necessarily what is known in gestalt psychology as a 'good' or 'closed' gestalt[16] but can be an open one, even a bad one; it can be an internally fragile gestalt. In other words, the divergent aspects contained in a work of art are not necessarily united seamlessly by structural unity – least of all in current art and its current situation; rather, because the meaning, the power and the substantiality of the work really depend on how far it can incorporate the contradictions afflicting humans, how far it can uncover these contradictions, in so far as they are concealed, and, by uncovering and uttering them, anticipate their resolution. To the extent that the work of art is subordinated to this idea, then, its aspects should not be understood simply in the sense of a synthesis, a unity of the manifold, as promoted by the harmonistic notion of beauty. Rather, it strikes me as a substantial element of art – openly of contemporary art, and latently probably of all art – that this so-called manifoldness that the work encompasses, and from which it forms its structural contexts, its contexts of meaning, is internally antagonistic and divided.

Perhaps I might elaborate here on something I said in passing: it strikes me as central to the relationship between new and traditional art that new art truly, in a genuinely dialectical sense, is simultaneously entirely different and not entirely different from traditional art. Its difference is especially obvious to someone who has not grown up with the new art; to me, however, the difference in fact seems to be that aspects, states of tension, closed – or 'subcutaneous', as Schoenberg put it[17] – structures that did not emerge within traditional art through dictated formal schemata, through τόποι that determined how one treated artistic structure, how one treated it in advance according to some fixed formal canons, whereas in modern art, these tensions, which are all also present in traditional art, but now themselves become thematic and directly become objects of shaping. Thus the naïve mind which believes that an expressionistic work of art is one in which the inside is turned outwards may ultimately, in philosophical reflection, not seem as foolish as such a statement initially sounds when presented naïvely. Now, if this unity which provides the context of meaning is not such a harmonic unity of existent, adjacent aspects but, rather, a unity of contradictory or divergent, perhaps even chaotic ones, then the question of the unity of the work of art must really be understood as a dynamic question, as a becoming, and not as a static relationship or form of harmony. And if I polemicized earlier against the attempt by Heidegger and the Heideggerian school to reduce the work of art to the concept of being, I think I can give you the precise reason for that polemic: that the work of art necessarily consists of antagonistic aspects, not of ones that exist in a form of prearranged unity. Because the unity of the work is a self-producing one, the work itself – even if it is there, however internally static it seems – is in reality a force field and a process. And I would say it is one of the most profound matters in aesthetics that the work remains true to its ideal the more it transforms this process, this character of a tension field, into the appearance of being. When the work of art emerges directly as a mere becoming, we will say that it is not objectified, it has not reached the sphere of something which is-in-itself in the appearance, which has certainly belonged to the concept of art up to a specific threshold. If this constitutive-dynamic aspect is missing, however, then this unity itself is mere semblance and not binding at all but, rather, external to the work. Here, as so often in aesthetics, we see once again the return of a definition which dialectic essentially gained for logic, just as dialectical logic could generally, in a certain sense, be represented in the medium of artistic experience: the spiritual content of a work of art would thus, in so far as this interplay of forces reaches a sort of balance in it – we shall return to this – be the result of the antagonistic forces driving the process that takes place within it. At the same time, however, it is always this process whose totality comes together to form the work of art. And the thing that strikes us time and again as the life of the work, which we experience as something living – and works of art are not creatures, after all, and the concept of life has only a refracted, mediated meaning in this context – is really nothing but the fact that, even in its congealed, objectified state, it utters the process contained within it; but that in a sense, by uttering it and rounding it off, by making it take its form, it in turn transcends it. To experience or co-enact a work would then mean no more or less than co-enacting in the work all these aspects of the force field which the work constitutes, which it simultaneously is and exceeds. In that sense, one can say that aesthetic experience itself is really a spiritual experience, even though this spiritual experience must fall short of the work's essence if it is not the most intense and precise experience of its sensual attributes.

Now I would like to add something that takes us back to a category I treated in the previous sessions, but which perhaps gains new light in the context of what I have said today in order to grasp things more deeply and precisely than before: the allergy to the so-called sensual aspect, to the sensually pleasurable element of the work of art. The reasons I initially gave – perhaps some of you noticed this – namely the increasing resistance that the work of art has developed, for the sake of its substantiality and its truth, to being defaced by commercialism, transformed into a medium of communication and all such things, would – and here I must be self-critical – still be external to the work of art. Certainly, you could ask me: 'What does it matter to a great artist – a Picasso, Joyce, Schoenberg or Kafka – what atrocities the culture industry commits?' On the contrary: is it not beneath us to associate with these atrocities, and does it not constitute a kind of dependence on Mr Disney,[18] or Technicolor, if one imitates in one's own work the sweet colours and forms with which those money-makers usually operate? But I think this aspect of an allergy to the sensually pleasurable does stem from the matter itself, and my reason for pointing out its increasing presence in relation to the increasing transformation of art as such into a consumer product was less to identify the inner motive for this allergy than to show you something that might otherwise have been unduly neglected in these deliberations: namely, that this allergy is something historical. For I think this allergy is quite simply a sensitivity to a particular kind of deception. Recall for a second that I tried to present the idea of the work of art as a force field that is both its own embodiment and its reconciliation. Then one could say that the sensually pleasurable falsely anticipates this reconciliation, as it were, that it pretends this reconciliation of contradictions, whose highest idea is surely that of the work of art as such, has already taken place here and now, such that the individual aspects of their work are already carriers of this resolution in their immediate form. It is precisely because the idea of the work of art is, if I may put it this way, utopia, meaning absolute fulfilment, that this idea is allergic, is sensitive in the extreme to any attempt at smuggling in its true meaning as something already here and now, as something immediate, thus smoothing over all the antagonisms and suffering which are to blame for this utopia remaining unfulfilled. The real object of the allergy to the pleasurable, the sensually pleasant in art, is the deception that the work of art, which is the image and sign, is a direct fulfilment in the here and now, the sensual fulfilment denied to humans by reality. So one could call it the sensitivity, if I may speak in psychological terms for a moment, to the degradation of the work of art to a substitute gratification.

What I am referring to, by way of dissonance in the broadest sense, which is central to all our art, is consonance. But consonance is intolerable, for it mirrors nothing other than the yet unresolved dissonance of reality. The sensual aspect of art itself may, to engage in metaphysical speculation, be the very highest aspect that is possible in art – in the sense in which sensual fulfilment is that which comes closest to what one calls metaphysical experience, just as the deepest sympathies have rightly been observed between utopia and materialism. But that is precisely why it is no longer tolerated, and must no longer be tolerated, that this perfect utopia, which the spirit – which is itself always partly a pointer towards things sensual, not present, not yet in evidence – only anticipates, as it were, without claiming already to be it, that this utopia of total, unadulterated sensual experience be betrayed to something provisional, to something which it has not yet attained.

After all I have said, I think you will perhaps find it less outlandish than you might have in the last session – now that we have established in detail and, I hope, with some degree of conscientiousness, in what sense art progressively opposes the concept of beauty, or at least does not restrict itself thereto – if I add that this cannot mean one should renounce the theory of art, aesthetics and the concept of beauty. Otherwise one will truly arrive at the sphere that recalls catchphrases like 'psychology without soul' – that is, a science which has really lost its own substrate[19] – a construction to which I was forced to add, in critical agreement, an analogous concept in sociology, namely that of a 'sociology without society'.[20] It indeed belongs to the signature of the positivist spirit dominating our time that progressive enlightenment takes over the decisive concepts of individual disciplines and dissolves them, in a sense; but, in dissolving those concepts, it dispenses with the power that fuelled enlightenment itself in the first place, meaning that enlightenment is in extremely grave danger of settling for a capitulation to whatever is merely the case. There is, for example, a particular type of positivist aesthetics that seeks to describe the aesthetic experience without even mentioning a concept such as that of beauty.[21] But the result of this would indeed be no more than a factual report on some relations between aesthetic objects and the subject and would amount to an application of theory and a renunciation of spirit, which simply happens to be the medium of art, hence necessarily that of any theory of art. In all fairness, I must point out that this tendency of an aesthetics without beauty is not limited only to positivistic stupidity but is also found where subtle and sensitive nerves can rightly no longer tolerate all the chatter about beauty as harmony, the invocation of truth, beauty and goodness along with similar Sunday sound bites, and would rather resort to a kind of defiantly abstinent silence than enter that sphere. As close as these experiences I have described may be to me, I do think that one of the duties one accepts the moment one acts philosophically is to dispense with squeamishness about fixed concepts, not to have a mortal fear of cuts and bruises or of bringing some other misfortune on oneself when handling concepts, but rather to hold on to those concepts. And only by holding on to them can one refine them sufficiently to do justice to experience – not by abandoning them and believing that one now directly possesses something spiritual, elevated, refined and more subtle in the form of the conceptless. And this is really my motive for speaking to you about the idea of beauty in the next session, and I will proceed by showing that the concept of truth in its immediacy, which recent aesthetic theories[22] generally place in opposition to that of beauty, simply falls short of what is specific in the work of art – assuming one is speaking directly about this truth.

LECTURE 15

20 January 1959

Once again, I have received a communication from among you which I would like to discuss for two reasons: firstly, because it offers an opportunity to clarify certain things that may have remained too vague in the previous lectures, but also, secondly, because the questions posed to me lead into or belong to the context we are currently developing. This time, however, they are questions specifically about visual art, and I would like to take this opportunity to say that I naturally cannot pretend to speak with the same experience, namely the same technical experience, about visual art with which I can speak about musical or, I like to think, literary matters. I am aware that the problems in the different arts are by no means as directly identical as is generally claimed. I think I have occasionally said to you that the concept of the arts – or of art as a whole, as opposed to the individual arts – already contains an aspect of neutralization and reification. So it is quite clear to me that extrapolations from one area to another are problematic. On the other hand, however, it is unmistakable that, in a situation where the integration of everything spiritual has advanced so far, and where every art has ultimately become such a spokesperson or expression of certain historico-philosophical experiences, the differences between the artistic genres are reduced, even if they always remain insurmountable in the most radical sense. And after the very matter we are dealing with here was confirmed to me by someone I value a great deal, namely Daniel-Henry Kahnweiler in Paris,[1] that the problems I examined in my study 'The Aging of New Music' in *Dissonances* have extremely

precise analogues in visual art, and after also having the opportunity
to pursue these things to a certain extent myself, I do not think I am
especially guilty of overstepping any boundaries if I attempt to say
something about visual art in relation to these matters. I think it
would be best for me to take up a few points from this note and treat
them consecutively, as the complexes are so interwoven that one can
only address them if one accepts certain preconditions underlying the
overall view. The author writes: 'If the special meaning of a work of
art is determined by the specific configuration of its elements, and if
the meaning of visual art as such lies in the seeming and paradoxical
individual and contentual realization of alienation suspended by the
social possibilities of controlling nature', and so forth. Let me begin
by saying – and I hope the interpellant will forgive my slightly schoolmasterly tone – that the definitions to which he is referring were not
intended as such. I did not say that art is only a contentual realization
of alienation; rather, I highlighted an aspect that I feel has withered
away in traditional art theory, and which I therefore felt a particular
need to underline, all the more because it is decisive for our own art
to express exactly this quality of alienation and to overcome it
through its expression. But that is not everything, of course. In addition, I always tried to tell you about a different, very elusive aspect,
namely the utopian aspect of art. I said to you time and again that,
because the elements of the alienated are moved into a context of
meaning, they are transparent and structured as alienated elements
but at the same time transcend this state in a certain sense. And I
think it would not be good, and would indeed fall short of what I
was seeking to tell you, if you now thought that art should be con-
fined to such a definition, and that this could provide a kind of
yardstick which can be slapped onto any given work of art to indicate
its quality. I would say, however, that the relationship between the
categories that really determine the substance of a work of art varies
considerably; but also that it is historico-philosophically predetermined which of these categories is foregrounded, and that one cannot
measure a work of art by any such abstract demand. Otherwise one
would truly be regressing to the level of Gottsched's aesthetics in the
eighteenth century,[2] which good old Lessing went to tremendous
lengths to dethrone[3] or would arrive at such definitions as Aristotle's
notorious decree that tragedy must arouse 'fear and pity',[4] whereas
it is precisely the imposition of such norms on the work from without
that I want to lead you beyond through our mode of investigation.
The point of what I am telling you, from this perspective, is that I
am attempting to hold on to the idea of the objectivity of artistic
quality, the idea of wresting the observation of art from the clutches

of that everyday relativism which still withdraws to the argument that art is a matter of taste; at the same time, however, I am trying to do so not by applying some fixed criteria to art from the outside but, rather, by developing this objectivity from the matter itself, the determinate and unique matter. And if you take anything away for your own relationship with art and understanding of art from the suggestions I am making here, then I would hope it is this: that you co-enact this peculiar movement of the idea but do not ascribe to any individual observations I have made the authority of a fixed standard; it does not exist in this form, as every work of art has such a measure only within itself and in its own movement.

In addition, perhaps I can correct a small misunderstanding. It is always good when such interventions give cause to check how much of what one says during slightly difficult reflections is understood, and to explain it where necessary. I did not say that society's possibilities for controlling nature do away with alienation. On the contrary, it would be more accurate to say that control over nature, along with the associated forms of domination in society, has actually increased the alienation of humans from one another and from nature, and that art, at every level, has the task of revoking this process. First of all, however, I wish to emphasize that the other aspect, namely the creation of a context of meaning – in the sense I explained very precisely, I hope, in the last sessions – is, as the intention of the works of art, at least as much or inalienably the same as the other aspect which we discussed, namely the relationship with the alienated. Now the interpellant continues: if this precondition which he posited, and which I tried to show you cannot be posited as a precondition in the sense he thought, 'would one of the preconditions for the possibility of this individuation not be the binding existence of a sensual materiality that we experience as identical, and which corresponds to the identity of the individual?' If one puts these formulations and my own in slightly more down-to-earth[5] terms, and strips away some of their highly cryptic terminological character which I was originally guilty of using, and which I undoubtedly seduced the interpellant into adopting, then they surely mean the following: that the aforementioned aspect of the expression of alienation – or the resistance to alienation posited in the work of art – is really one with a social resistance that the work must express, and whose fundamental conditions include the fact that it contains empirical reality more or less as directly as each individual does. So what lies behind this, if I may take the liberty of this interpretation, is something like the question of the work's commitment, which was read into the theory of the resistance towards alienation. And the question proceeds quite consistently from here: if the work of art necessarily adopts such a polemical stance towards empirical reality, then does what I have said not require that this empirical reality itself appear in the work in the same way as it is generally open to non-artistic experience among individual humans? That, at least, is how I understand what was said. I think there is actually a specific error at the heart of this. For this incorporation of immediate sensual materiality has two aspects that are really both irreconcilable with the things that have been considered fundamental in our deliberations so far. For if they genuinely sought to claim that they are commensurable with the aesthetic subject, and hence truly capable of carrying in the work of art itself those experiences which the work imposes on them, then they would indeed not be alienated; but the situation is that empirical reality itself faces us as something alienated. Here I would like to recall a very eloquent formulation by Helmuth Plessner, who once said that the defamiliarization [*Verfremdung*] of the work of art is a response to the alienation [*Entfremdung*] of the world.[6] It is only because the alienated form in which we encounter the so-called natural world is suspended by the work of art itself and shifted into another form that it is likewise defined as alienated by the work, which thus teaches us, as it were, to look back with unfamiliar eyes at the world, which already forces us to look at it with unfamiliar eyes. And only thus, through this translation, can the groundwork be laid for us to experience the alienated after all. Owing to this experience of alienation, however, the empirical elements of reality that face us are heteronomous in relation to the formal law, and today – precisely because they are alienated, because in a sense they no longer reach our experience – in their present state, namely in their immediacy, they no longer enter the formal law and can no longer be mastered. [For] the formal law demands that all façades, all superficial connections that we experience as seemingly closed, be dissolved and replaced by a configuration that is both a critique of this alienated superficial form and an attempt to build a non-alienated reality, a reality in which we critically find ourselves, out of the elements of that same reality.

If the process of the history of visual art in the last centuries can accurately be described overall as a process of progressive subjectification, then this process of subjectification today – which cannot simply be halted by reflecting on collectives or objectivities, and cannot be sublated into a form of new objectivity through some arbitrary act – then this process means not only that the way things and objects are observed in art is changed and is subjectively shaped; it also means that the decisive rupture which has taken place is that the essential, the matter itself, continues to be the matter itself in art only if it is mediated, if it no longer faces us as something defined first of all for itself but, rather, contains all its defining attributes through the things we do with it. Any attitude that evades this mediation through the subject in art, and pretends that the work of art still knows anything about reality in an immediate sense, any such behaviour in art, however politically progressive it might consider itself, is in fact reactionary with regard to the immanent developmental process of productive forces in art and is therefore impossible. Art no longer interacts directly with reality, but only in the way in which it is filled with subjective experience, and only in the way that its elements then come together to create forms and constellations of forms. And that is precisely what leads to the circumstance that a consciousness which mistakenly considers itself socially correct by thinking that it can directly incorporate social aspects from reality is quite the opposite, namely the socially false consciousness, because it omits and undoes the very dialectical process that lies within the state of alienation between the subject and the object in society.

Now the interpellant, whose interpellation deals essentially with the question of so-called abstract painting, continues as follows. I would, incidentally, like to take this opportunity to say that the term 'abstract painting' is an especially foolish one, simply because a work of art, if it is indeed a work of art, is concrete: the picture I am dealing with is concrete in the highest sense, and if it is abstract then it is a bad picture. One must not confuse the question of a work's concreteness, which is one of the first demands levelled at a work of art, with the question of how far the work is identical to an objective materiality facing it, or how far it abstracts from this materiality. I think this term has contributed inestimably to the general confusion, almost as much as the word 'atonal', and the only positive thing about it that I can think of is that it at least has a certain shock value, a certain polemical force which has to a certain extent given it something good, something powerful at times, although today, in the state of general neutralization in which everything is swallowed up, this polemical blessing is also a thing of the past. The question posed here by the interpellant is this: 'Would the dissolution of these topoi of sensual experience' – more crudely put, that of the concrete world – 'which already seems technologically complete through the possibility of an unlimited manipulation and variability of this experience, which can be carried out beyond the sensitivity threshold' – he is thinking of the objective construction, in contrast with the construction mediated by the subjective sensorium – 'and the consequence of this arbitrariness of the individual experiential world in the realm of visual art, namely abstract constructivism, reduce the idea of visual art to absurdity, as one can no longer speak of a particular, specific content here of aesthetic experience, as the individual sensual element of the aggregate system, the picture, entirely becomes a function of the respective arbitrary construction principle?' At this point I would like to anticipate something we will address in earnest only in the next sessions, namely that the true criteria for what we are discussing lie not in the subjective experience of works of art but, rather, in the nature of the work itself. And here I would mitigate the objection raised by the interpellant to the lecture – and, I would almost say, to his own artistic intentions as well – by saying that, in so far as we are dealing with the mere subjective modes of experience or reaction in relation to works of art, this aspect of randomness which he criticizes in 'abstract art' is found everywhere. The seemingly established nature of reactions based on certain given objects is itself a superficial matter. And if one were examining subjective experiences of works of art, one would find exactly the same arbitrariness in traditional art that becomes apparent here in modern art. Indeed, it is generally the case – I am almost embarrassed to repeat this, but I keep returning to this one point – that modern art may be something different from traditional art, but it is simultaneously identical to it; the difference is that all the problems and difficulties which were previously subcutaneous, concealed by the closed surface of communication, now emerge actually and substantially. Aside from that, I think that the charge of arbitrariness in the constellations and the arbitrariness of their connection to the concrete world does not really bear scrutiny. I will deliberately pass over literature where the conceptual element, which it necessarily uses even in the most extreme manifestations, always draws a certain degree of determinate concreteness into the work of art. Here I will genuinely try to keep to visual art in the strictest sense, for it seems to me that so-called abstraction has certain boundaries. It is an error in artists' conception of themselves – a very widespread error for which I do not hold the artists responsible, as they are not inherently obliged to have a philosophical, theoretical awareness of what they do – that they keep thinking that the categories they employ, or the forms on which they base their construction, come from nature. That was the error made to a particular degree by cubism, for example, which genuinely believed that the reduction to geometric figures constituted a reduction to certain very simple natural phenomena; in fact, contexts of the kind created by cubist painters are found not in nature but far more readily – to the extent that there are any models – in a landscape such as that of Spain and the Moroccan cultural landscape, whose effect on Picasso can hardly be overestimated. But, quite aside from that, even in its so-called natural material, even where it comes as close to nature and circles, cubes and geometric figures, art is always dealing with something that is already eminently historical. This means that these cubes actually contain the history of all art, just as Picasso once said that Cézanne is 'the father of us all', and that all this had in fact come from Cézanne.[7] It is not my task to describe in detail the historical process that led from impressionism via pointillism on the one hand and on the other hand via Cézanne to cubism and finally to abstract painting; there are more competent people who can do a better job. All I wish to say is that this historical process is nothing external to the works of art, for everything that happens in these works is a testimony, a trace, a monument to this historical process, and I would almost presume to indulge in a speculation that is not so far-fetched in relation to what I intend to tell you about these matters in other contexts: that the force, the substantiality, of modern art depends very significantly on how far it embodies this historical experience through its own forms – how far the forms it uses express this historical aspect even as they are objectified. The phenomena of loss of tension, on the other hand, which occupy us all and also worry the interpellant, are evidently very closely connected to the moment at which the materials and forms become so independent that the same historical experiences they document can no longer be felt but, rather, disappear from them. I think you need only look at pictures from Max Ernst's so-called abstract period – I mention a surrealist here simply because his name occurred to me in this context – and you will see to what an eminent degree the so-called abstract forms in his work all stem from the *Jugendstil* ornament. Here I can note only in passing that the significance of *Jugendstil*'s repertoire of forms is incomparably greater than we admit. Indeed, *Jugendstil* is one of those phenomena that are subject to a sort of process of suppression. People think they can deal with this very strange, traumatic phenomenon by smiling, but, in reality, this smiling shows precisely that one has not dealt with it.[8]

There are really – if I may take this opportunity to formulate this as dogmatically, as starkly, as I possibly can – no so-called formal aspects in art which are not themselves sedimented content, which were not once contentual, just as it has been shown that, with the everyday objects we use, the ornamentations are usually rudiments or residues of necessities from earlier phases of production that have survived. The ornament, as it were, is the scar that appeared on a vase at the point where it could not be made at the potter's wheel without such an interruption. So, following this analogy, it should be the case for all so-called artistic forms that they were once content and, through a process of sublimation, of spiritualization – which is after all the process of artistic development as such – took on that peculiar independence. And I would say it is virtually the central criterion for any non-representational art, or any that rejects the harmony of the surface, that, by going through this process – this process of the content's sedimentation, or the sublimation of the content to become form – it still senses some of the power of that content in the form itself. When we artists speak of a sense of form, a feeling for form, that is what we really mean: we want to express that, in the use of formal means, we still register, realize and take into account whatever contentual impulses once resided in them. And higher forms of critique, critiques of works of art that do not follow abstract rules, only their immanent necessity, almost always end up asking for the hidden contentual justification for whatever seems to be purely formal about them.[9] So what I mean is that the interpellant definitely pointed out a danger, one that I had by no means hidden from you, namely that of a loss of tension, which appears wherever the aspects I have attempted to describe to you are truly forgotten, where they no longer assert themselves, or, in popular parlance, where art turns into decorative art, or where what I have called the 'danger of the dangerless'[10] holds sway – where alienation from the concrete world becomes a wallpaper pattern. But I think we should be aware that all this is not something that can simply be attributed to the process of abstraction, and that could even be eliminated, as the Sedlmayrs[11] and totalitarian guardians of culture[12] would like, by returning to the 'centre', the concrete object or some such thing. For, in reality, we are dealing here with aspects within so-called abstract works of art that can very much be named by critique, primarily a certain lack of the power to create a true context of meaning between the elements instead of applying construction principles only mechanically and externally.

Here, however, we reach the point at which I must confess to my technical incompetence in matters of painting. All I can do is to tell you that, where I feel most at home in terms of my skills, namely in music, I can point out very precisely those elements where the construction has been slapped on from the outside rather than developed from the matter itself, and that the same structures which exhibit this are also those that give the impression of lacking any tension. In addition, there is the aspect that those so-called abstract constructs in which we observe the loss of tension are generally those that have been removed from the dialectical relationship with tradition. Today I can give you only an intimation of this. To me, the great products of the new art almost always seem to have been those which still had tradition as an essential force within them and then negated it on their own strength. The great revolutionary artists of the period – such as Picasso, such as Braque,[13] such as Schoenberg and so forth – were all within tradition, and, by locking horns with it, they essentially brought about something like an induction of tension. The loss of tension and the problems we are discussing here – and this is very closely connected to the lack of historical experience in the matters themselves, in the forms – appear wherever this resistance is no longer enacted and instead, in what Kafka calls the 'gay empty ride',[14] one truly has at one's disposal those things that gain their meaning only within tension, in the act of art repelling themselves from tradition. Where tradition no longer exists as an aspect, however sublimated, the power of true revolutionary art does not really exist. But I can only hint at this. I would just like to note in passing, without drawing any grandiloquent conclusions, how thought-provoking it is that – let me be very cautious – precisely the most significant of modern painters stopped short of complete abstraction, of severing all connections to concrete representation, Klee as much as Picasso. And it seems to me that, in Klee's late period, when that decreased, but most of all in Kandinsky's development, this progression would not necessarily have been a blessing. This hesitation is not, as some of my Darmstadt friends occasionally charge, a hesitation out of cowardice or weakness or inconsistency; rather, these great artists were evidently driven by the knowledge that it requires a kind of resistance to the heteronomous to make the concept of autonomy meaningful in the first place. This means that, at the moment when the autonomy of creation becomes absolute and idles, as it were, it cancels itself out and no longer becomes freedom if this freedom cannot exert itself in relation to something from which it differs.

The interpellant finally emphasizes, very rightly in my opinion – and this is probably where he gets to what he really means: 'It seems to me today that a striving in visual art to advocate the demand for specific representation, in whatever manner, amounts to a reversal of the orientation towards the future, towards utopian possibility that is actually native to the realm of art, in memory of historically past experiences.' I think that the antinomy he mentioned in his interpellation can actually be resolved in the sense I attempted to show you in this session, and that then this utopian intention – and with it the positive attitude towards a radically advanced art – is justified after all. Finally he asks whether the truth of abstract works of art or radically constructivistic works is possible without the support of the viewer. This question is extremely difficult to answer, as it really depends on one's technical specialization. But in a certain sense, I would say, all art actually requires the assistance of theoretical insight. Here too, as I have pointed out so often, the difference is that something becomes explicit in modern art which remains hidden in traditional art. It is one of the superstitions of the typical approach to art, which makes art pure intuitive observation and nature something immediate, that the work of art acts purely from within itself, with no preconditions. This precondition is certainly untenable. There is probably no work of art at all that does not have specific preconditions, starting with the preconditions of the so-called cultural setting, if we accept such a term, in which a work is embedded – for example, it is barely possible for us to listen to, understand or realize Chinese music in any remotely adequate sense – but also in the sense that, in order to understand a work of art at all, we must speak its idiom, its language. If we do not, it will simply slide away from us. And finally, to understand a work, we must in a certain sense already know where it is located. Benjamin once formulated this very provocatively when he said that he could only really evaluate a picture if he knew who had created it.[15] This is naturally a slap in the face of the usual notion that quality acts purely from within itself, but it points exactly to what we are dealing with, namely that a plethora of theoretical preconditions of all kinds – I do not mean historical, but genuinely theoretical preconditions – necessarily contribute to the experience of any work of art so that we can understand this work at all. If we do not know something, however second-hand, about the concept of the human being, the concept of humanity, the concept of autonomy and freedom and such categories, then we can register all manner of sensual things in Beethoven's music, but it is completely out of the question that we might understand a piece of his. And just as we must say of this art, which is viewed within the pantheon as particularly vivid, that it has implicit theoretical preconditions, so too does this apply to all art. In that sense, modern art simply takes the bull by the horns – or embraces an otherwise ideologically concealed situation – by not being entirely vivid but also, as a spiritual thing, by having spiritual preconditions. I would therefore say the following: we should not find it daunting that one needs more than merely one's eyes and ears to understand modern art, for we cannot understand any art at all purely with our eyes or our ears.

LECTURE 16

22 January 1959

[...]¹ take up the thread again after two extended interpellations. But let us try at the same time – if I may use this bold image – to skim the cream off the top of these interpellations, by which I mean making the things we have developed from them useful for our primary concerns. The overall course of the investigation was that I attempted to lay out for you the dialectic of the concept of beauty, which must be at the centre of an aesthetics, and had started by showing you the difficulties to which the concept of beauty inevitably leads if it is introduced as a positive, dogmatic concept. In doing so – and this will be of no small significance for our method – I referred mostly to aesthetic experience, and we will have to return to this concept from a very different perspective. We then went on to reflect on what aesthetics means without a concept of beauty, and then in the last session we treated the objection or problem of the connection to the object in visual art. You will then, I hope, see that these reflections belong directly to the matter we must now deal with, namely the question of whether, and indeed in what way, aesthetic reflections can be carried out meaningfully without including the concept of beauty. One could start with this answer: if a work of art is not beautiful – that is to say, if it does not somehow justify itself before an observer, listener or reader, however ideal – then what is the point of it all? If there is no standard by which to measure aesthetic experience, what good is any of this? Does art then have anything resembling a *raison d'être*? I think this objection does not hold water, because – as I could not help implying in my formulation, for it forced me to do so – it presupposes something like an observer who has to get something out of it, someone to whom, as they say, the work 'gives' something (I will mention only in passing the loathsome exchange idea implicit in this). So the observer does the work of art the honour of devoting their time, their eyes, their ears and the precious strength of their nerves, and they expect to receive something in return, whether as enjoyment, as an enrichment of their worthy inner life or in some other form: a notion whose vulgarity should really exclude it *a priori* from aesthetic reflection. But let us not dwell on that. So, I do not intend to take the approach of developing the concept of beauty in terms of its positive aspect, from the perspective that a work of art would not 'give' anything without it. For it is quite conceivable – and we will indeed have very good reason to assume so – that the quality of a work of art comes from the work itself, not its relation to some observer of whatever kind, and then the question of beauty as a *terminus ad quem* – that is, what good it all is – would be moot. For then the only use for the work of art would be to embody as purely, as consistently and as perfectly as possible whatever it has been chosen to embody. So I want a take a different approach, namely to consider briefly how things stand with the category that is used in some form, and which people think, in the reflection on and – if you will forgive the vulgar term – the evaluation of works of art, they can use in place of beauty: this is almost always the concept of truth. It is a returning theme in aesthetic discussions through the ages that the thing one should demand from works of art is not its beauty, for that is something superficial, deceptive, illusory – whatever you wish to call it – but that what counts in the work is rather its truth.

Let me try first of all to separate, in good Platonic fashion, the different meanings of the concept of truth in art and to use them to assess the validity of this demand that art should be true and nothing else. First of all there is the notion of natural truth. I think – and this is what I would like to carry over from the last session – I criticized in ample depth the argument that the object of art must be commensurate with the experience of the subject, even identical to it. If the work of art indeed had no other purpose than completely to reproduce external, concrete nature – and I am really only repeating something long known, repeating it more out of pedantry than because I feel it is genuinely necessary to say it – then the photograph or all such things would be identical to the work of art. But there are periods in which great works of art were created more or less under the name of naturalism. Here we need think only of Flaubert, whom one can essentially view – at least in the two works that are relevant here, *Madame Bovary* and *Sentimental Education* – as the founder of modern naturalism.[2] But if one looks at the so-called naturalistic works, and in a broader sense the great realist works – those of Balzac, for example[3] – then one will see that this naturalism may have been eminently justified as a battle cry against a Romanticism that had meanwhile become conventional and a rigid cliché, but that naturalism qua naturalism does not convincingly sum up these works either, as they have countless aspects that deviate from naturalism. To return to Flaubert in particular, one should not only recall the extremely artful and subtle composition whereby our random life, which points in different directions towards senseless details, is somehow brought into a form of unity without deceptively concealing the senseless of this life; but, especially in Flaubert's case, we must also recall the function of language. It is generally known that Flaubert was one of the greatest prose artists, and you will also all have heard something about the indescribable and chimerical effort he went through to polish his prose to the utmost degree and bring it close to a particular ideal of purity that was musical, very far removed from meaning. My intention here is to discuss not these aspects but rather something else: I want to ask whether, in such so-called naturalistic novels as those of Flaubert, this integrity of language does not have a decisive function for the constitution of the form itself – and surely the only way to describe this function is that, through the utter purity of expression, the fact that this expression shows its incorruptibility in the face of the temptations of communication and sloppiness, and does nothing except present what it presents in, by the standards of a highly developed formal tradition, the most perfect form – whether, I am saying, a very specific content is not achieved precisely through this medium of an incredibly highly articulated form, whether the very fact that this form [stands in stark contrast] to the triviality, senselessness and God-forsakenness of what Flaubert described in his modern novels is not meant to be highlighted precisely against the background of this loss of meaning. After all, a very substantial part of the programme of a naturalistic art, namely an art that makes the truthful reproduction of events its ideal, is something that later became programmatic in science too, and which overlaps with the whole direction of European positivism: the demand that the work of art abstain from value judgements, as they say, or at least from statements of opinion,[4] which repeatedly appeared to varying degrees in novels up to the threshold of this period. Flaubert was the first who, with absolute rigour and a certain asceticism, went so far that nobody can tell, for example, whether he sympathizes with Madame Bovary or not. Paradoxically, one could say that the kind of sympathy he has for his heroine, who is not a heroine, lies precisely in refraining from any expression of sympathy – that he simply presents it with a gesture of 'Look, this is how it is', *ecce homo*, as it were – and that this is what makes it possible to identify with her at all. But the medium through which this can happen is language alone. That means: only through language can the naturalistic work of art become a work of art in the first place. And it is central that, at the very start, when the modern concept of naturalism was conceived, this extreme conception of formal integrity existed in parallel, while as soon as this Flaubertian demand for rigour of presentation is sacrificed, as soon as it is relaxed in the slightest, the work of art degenerates into trash or photography. Let me just add that things are quite different with Balzac, who was historically ahead of Flaubert. This realistic work of art is completely infused with Romantic notions that are connected to, and in a strange sense overlap with, the opacity of life in early high capitalist society as a whole, which presents the writer with so many riddles that they find it more adventurous than the greatest adventure. So, to summarize: wherever one finds a striving for truth in the naturalistic or realistic sense – this also applies eminently to Thomas Mann, whom many consider one of the most realistic writers – one will see that, if works of art are truly significant, they will go, and indeed must go, substantially beyond a representation, a photographically faithful representation of what they depict. And if I were to make a suggestion to the German and Romance scholars among you, it would be systematically to examine products of so-called realism and naturalism in terms of the non-realistic and non-naturalistic attributes; the naturalism that is not found in Baedeker's guide, as it were. [...] [If one][5] accuses a naturalist writer such as Gerhart Hauptmann of being untrue to himself and betraying his radical naturalistic impulses to neo-romanticism,[6] then this is inconsistent, for one can show very easily that the decisive categories which appear in his work as Romantic categories are also present in the naturalistic plays. For example, the basic habitus of a Romantic-historical drama, as *Florian Geyer*[7] could be considered to a certain extent, is really not so different from *The Weavers*: a portrayal of the hopeless rebellion of the oppressed – in both cases, the formal elements result from this gesture. You can perhaps best identify the way in which naturalism moves towards so-called Romantic elements, as well as the resulting aesthetic problems, in a play such as *The Assumption of Hannele*,[8] whose first part incidentally strikes me as one of, or even the most ingenious thing Gerhart Hauptmann ever wrote – so, that is what I want to say here. Perhaps I can note in this context than an element, an aspect, of what one calls naturalism is also central to our contemporary modern art. And especially now, having spoken about those aspects of modern art that take it further away from the surface of something depicted, it is perhaps appropriate, not least as part of a dialectical investigation, to recall this. Lukács even went so far as to accuse radical modern art, very strangely – and among many other things – of 'naturalism', in the sense of presenting genuinely existent emotional states or similar things.[9] I have an inkling that I am not entirely without blame for this claim by Lukács – which is only peculiar for being presented as an accusation – because I tried to show in the *Philosophy of New Music* that radical expressionism in music is actually connected to a certain documentary character of music, in that this radically expressionistic music, without feeling constrained by formal conventions, registers emotional states like a seismograph, as it were, and replaces a preconceived, merely formal framework with the framework of such emotional states.[10] And, if one likes, one can see this same documentary character, which is found in a great deal of modern art – for example the automatic writing of the surrealist programme[11] – as a sort of transformation of naturalistic elements. I would almost say – and I can really touch on this only briefly – that this is really where the dialectical salt lies, the materialistic salt that connects very radical art, the art that moves furthest away from the surface of real existence, back to this existence after all.

Aside from this concept of concrete truth, however, there is also another that one could describe as the concept of psychological truth, or perhaps even truth of expression, as Schoenberg – who was quite far from naturalism in the overall tendency of his art – may have intended when he once wrote in the early days of the expressionist phase: art should not be decorative, it should be true.[12] This too is a somewhat difficult matter. What this kind of truth might mean in art is really none other than the mimetic impulse – which is to say that art, instead of pursuing a concretized intention, contains something of those reactions whereby one something makes itself similar to another something, as it were, without this similarity becoming a material thing. In relation to this form of truth, which lies in expression, in relation to this mimetic impulse, the concept of truth is at the very least extremely difficult because establishing what is true about expression is extremely problematic. The truth of works of art that consist mainly in expression does not lie primarily in this mimetic action. On the contrary: by the standard of the concrete world, of the *adaequatio* of the *cogitatio* that is called art, so to speak, in relation to the empirical world, expression – the mimetic aspect – always has something exaggerated about it. Especially in art that immerses itself entirely in inner expression – that is, which attempts to reproduce inner states faithfully precisely by surrendering to these inner states rather than following ingrained procedures – there is always also an element of exaggeration. And it is no coincidence that Nietzsche, who was eminently perceptive and sensitive in these matters, accused Richard Wagner, the first great expressive artist – in German culture, at least – of play-acting, so in a certain sense of being untruthful, by the standard of this immersion in expressive content.[13] At the same time, the concept of this expressive truth cannot be unquestioningly upheld, because – and you will find a detailed exposition of this in a forthcoming, extended study of mine entitled 'Criteria of New Music'[14] – something like expression is actually impossible unless the work of art employs something that has so far received too little attention, namely expressive conventions of a kind, tacit agreements that certain configurations of material, certain sounds, certain colours are meant to express something particular. And where these expressive conventions are not respected, there is no expression, as it were. This is, incidentally, closely connected to what I referred to in the last session as the theoretical preconditions that necessarily belong to every work of art. If one is not aware of the rules of expression in advance, theoretically as it were, then the entire question of expression is something highly problematic.

Finally, there is also a concept of truth that has only recently begun to play a significant part in the artistic discourse. It was formulated by the musicologist Eimert, who said that a work of art must be 'right'.[15] Such a statement is on the one hand self-evidently true, but on the other hand it is false. It is self-evident to the extent that, if a work of art is not coherent in itself, if it is not internally organized in a consistent fashion, then the work naturally cannot have any objectivity; if a work of art proves something internally fragile, inconsistent and aesthetically illogical, it does not count. On the other hand, the rightness of a work in the sense of a mathematical problem, the fact that all aspects of its construction can be traced back to a basic process, does not in itself guarantee that it is even a work of art. A work of art can be entirely correct and cogent in terms of an underlying mathematical calculus, the underlying manipulation of the material used in it, yet amount to a dreadful gibberish or nothing at all, a complete nonsense. So this too is not enough.

Please do not misunderstand me; I have no wish to do away with the concept of truth – to 'trash' it, as they say – which I began by criticizing as something pre-aesthetic. Certainly there are always aesthetic situations in which this concept of truth is necessary, especially as a polemic against some kind of rigid conventions. For wherever an expressive need is stronger than the aesthetic agreements that inhibit it, one will always be able to point out that the work of art must follow its inner laws and not those conventions, and this will take the form of truth. But this polemical sense that lies in the concept of the work of art's truth should not be taken to mean that a work of art must be directly true in the manner of a direct agreement of the work with something that it means or depicts. Nonetheless, the concept of truth does have some sense in art, and very good sense; it simply cannot be isolated. One cannot interpret it as if aesthetic truth were something concrete and not subject to the aesthetic laws of form, and by which one could genuinely assess the formal constitution of a work of art. This truth – that which enables a work to manifest itself as truth at all in the only sense I can give a work of art, namely as the unconscious, as it were blind historiography carried out by every period – the work cannot attain this concept of truth through an immediate adaptation to something internal or external, or through its mere correctness, but only through mediation by its own formal law, by the fact that there is a meaningful relationship between all its aspects. And to postulate any truth in art that falls short of this would ultimately amount to a misguided shifting of art towards science. In a situation where the primacy of art is perceived as overbearing, it would be better for art to fall silent and better to dispense with all art than for art to try, by eagerly running after science, to secure some paltry right to exist in the disenchanted world. I think that, if it attempts that, it is all the more certain to dissolve and turn into pure materiality. Now, what strikes me as decisive here is that this concept of truth which one can ascribe to the work of art, and which consists in what I tried to describe in one of the previous sessions as both the work's process and its result, this concept of the truth of the work of art would be in agreement with the concept of its beauty. This kind of truth, which consists in the fact that, even in its contradictory nature, the work of art proves so necessary in all its aspects that this necessity is experienced as being compelled by truth, is at once the context that one can envisage when invoking the concept of beauty. What is true about art is its substance, not its mere materiality or some particular aspect of it, and this substance crystallizes only under its formal law. So the truth of the work of art, to put it a little more precisely, is perhaps not directly identical to its beauty, perhaps that was too hastily said; but the truth of the work is, at any rate, tied to the precondition of its being beautiful, in the sense of forming such a meaningful context as I have tried to explain to you.

So we find ourselves in a somewhat paradoxical and difficult situation: on the one hand, I showed you that all finite, limited, so-called positive criteria for beauty fall short of the work of art, that they hedonistically confine it, degrade it to a mere source of pleasure, and that precisely this insistence on beauty introduces something inartistic into art that needs to be resolved. On the other hand, I hope I have shown you with a degree of stringency that a work of art is entirely inconceivable without the idea of beauty, whether because it simply falls back into chaos otherwise or because it tends towards science in a misguided, rash and primitive way. The conclusion to be drawn from this is probably that one must cling to the idea of beauty, but not as an ontological category, not as a particular form of being that emerges specifically in the work of art and comes into itself, but rather only as something dynamic, something in a state of becoming and always internally in motion.[16] Let me remind you – and I do so as an express polemic against an essay in opposition to modern music that Mr Wellek in Mainz[17] recently saw fit to publish – let me remind you expressly that this concept of an overarching totality of beauty in contrast to particular beauty must not be equated with what, in a psychologizing manner and with a clever-sounding term, people like to call a 'holistic view'. It is not dictated by reality that the contradictions in a work of art come to rest in a totality. I told you in one of the previous sessions that the aesthetic unit or the aesthetic phenomenon cannot be equated with the so-called good or closed gestalt, and that it quite possibly goes beyond that, because all these concepts are still too simple and, above all, much too static compared to the nature of the work of art. All I mean to say is that the work of art, at least in the state that strikes me as the only one still accessible to our experience today, is always an internally contradictory thing.[18]

Now, in this context, I cannot refrain from telling you about a conception that comes from a very important artist of our time, namely Arnold Schoenberg, from one of his late works, and it amounts to something that does look like a positive conception of beauty for modern art. I would like to refer to this concept of beauty with a term that Schoenberg did not use, but which I feel conveys the intention of his theory, as the idea of 'homeostasis'.[19] What I am thinking of is the following – and allow me now to speak of music, simply because I am more secure here than in the realm of visual art: Schoenberg thinks – and this is initially very much in keeping with a dialectical theory – that a work of art, so in this case a composition, enters into a form of obligation with its very first bar, its very first notes.[20] These notes create a form of tension. Through the very act of positing something at the start of a work of art – and you can take the musical work of art as an example here – I commit myself both to pursuing what I have posited and to following the contradictions or tensions implicit in this positing.[21] The idea Schoenberg formulated – and this is the last great theory of traditional aesthetics of which I am aware, and which is truly drawn entirely from the material – Schoenberg's theory is this: by entering into a form of obligation with the first bar, it unfolds – and this is a profoundly bourgeois conception – in an uninterrupted relationship of give and take. One obligation is fulfilled, another follows; the work of art is, in a sense, a never-ending exchange ratio. And only at the last moment, so to speak, do things work out in the achievement of balance. According to this theory, then, beauty would consist in the fact that, on the one hand, these tensions are developed as a facet of artistic truth, if I may introduce this concept again, but at the same time the work of art goes beyond the unresolved state by achieving a kind of reconciliation between these tensions – not merely an external reconciliation, this is what is new about it; not the kind that is described in the usual theories, where the reconciliatory idea emerges at the end of the work of art. Rather, it envisages the immanent process of the work itself resolving its own tensions in a way that reveals the totality as something reconciled, just, almost pacified. It is very interesting – I cannot refrain from pointing it out to you – that Schoenberg in particular, who will perhaps be known to many of you as the one who espoused the omnipotence of dissonance and chased conventional consonances out of music, that in his theory he actually recuperates the concept of harmony or consonance in a very peculiar fashion. The difference is that there is now no one aspect that is harmonious, reconciled, pacified, for all individual elements in the work are in a state of tension; but, through the configurations formed by these individual elements, the result of the whole is intended to be harmony, balance, absence of tension, in short: homeostasis,[22] just as – and that is why I chose the term 'homeostasis' for this – the theory of drive dynamics in modern depth psychology claims that a particular state of balance between libidinous, instinctive forces, a kind of equilibrium, is something for which the organism strives and which fulfils it.[23] It is not without interest that, from an entirely different perspective which is as distant from radical New Music as one could imagine, namely that of the music historian Georgiades in his highly interesting analysis of the last movement from Mozart's Jupiter Symphony,[24] one finds a very similar train of thought; Georgiades shows that this final movement, which famously contains an extremely complex fugal construction, actually incorporates a kind of tension or demand from the first bar and only truly resolves it in the last.

Here I will only touch on a problem without presuming that I can solve it. For it is very strange with this theory: a work of art that does not bring about something of this aspect of homeostasis, the creation of an equilibrium through the process initiated within itself, is indeed always on the verge of becoming senseless. And when Schoenberg, referring to certain compositions that came after his own, asked, 'But is that even music?' – he meant precisely this fact that, in a work of art which does not succeed in bringing about this homeostasis, the concept of the context of meaning that I developed a moment ago itself becomes problematic, because something resembling meaning can only be constructed at all through the creation of this homeostasis, this balance of forces. On the other hand, this demand for homeostasis ultimately reintroduces a harmonistic, affirmative aspect even into dissonant, critical and radical modern art. Whether this aspect is an indispensable part of the utopian, of that aspect of reconciliation which is meant by all art, or whether there is actually an adaptation to dominant notions behind it, and whether Schoenberg was not as much of a traditionalist in this regard as someone such as Einstein, who I am told is still a purveyor of traditional physics – this is a question that I do not dare answer here, but which I would at least point out as the most central and difficult question in modern art.[25] The dispute in painting between rigorous constructivism and surrealism, I would add, seems to me to boil down to exactly the same question; for all surrealist art strikes me substantially as art which even does away with the concept of homeostasis.

LECTURE 17

27 January 1959

Perhaps you recall that, when we attempted to develop the dialectic in the concept of beauty as something at once problematic and indispensable, we drew on the concept of aesthetic experience. In our treatment of aesthetic experience, I made a tacit assumption – as a criterion for the analysis of this aesthetic experience – that, if one reflects on it, should probably be termed the adequacy of this experience to the aesthetic object. This entails something that initially, when you first hear it, probably sounds quite plausible to you, but which nonetheless stands in quite stark contrast to what the official aesthetic tradition – except for Hegel and a few phenomenological aestheticians – has considered self-evident for almost two hundred years, namely that the concept of beauty must have a subjective basis, and that aesthetic experience, if I may put it thus, constitutes the validation of the concept of beauty and not, as I dogmatically argued at the start of my reflections, the other way around.[1] I therefore adopted a clearly opposing stance to established aesthetics and thus introduced what, in a certain sense, forms the centrepiece of Hegel's aesthetics, namely its very objective view based on the nature of the work of art and its own laws and problematics – in contrast to an approach that presumes to unfold all these things from within the subject. In our present discussion, we can leave aside the fact that this objective direction of aesthetics in Hegel remains subjective in the highest sense, because, for him, the Kantian transcendental subject ultimately remains the carrier of the category of beauty too. For here, I would say, we are already dealing with the constituted sphere of the

aesthetic, of art, and not with the most general questions of constitution as such. And, within the framework of something thus constituted, Hegel's reflection, to which I am aware of being fundamentally
indebted, is very much objectively directed. I am therefore obliged
– if we seriously mean to go beyond a merely rhapsodic, and thus
ultimately opaque treatment of aesthetic objects to reach something
like a binding theoretical position – to explain to you what leads me
to adopt this stance and, at once, to say something about the entire
dispute between subjective and objective aesthetics. The appeal of
aesthetic subjectivism in the broadest sense for traditional philosophy
is that it promises to offer something like a uniform context of justification of the kind that was first formulated in Kant's *Critique of
the Power of Judgement*. That is to say, beauty is derived from certain
conditions which are intended to be absolutely binding as conditions
of a consciousness as such, a subject as such, and to remove the work
of art from the ephemeral domain; so, among other things, they are
also meant to provide *a priori* standards – if not for judgement itself,
then certainly as regulatory principles – by which to judge works of
art at all. Basing aesthetics on subjectivity in the broadest sense in
this way means claiming to be largely independent of the supposed
randomness of the object and to have recourse to something that is
firm and binding because it is immutable, namely the self-identical
structure of such a consciousness. And that is fundamentally the
traditional understanding of theory: the belief that, if one can name
some firm, immutable, rule-like principles from which the rest follows,
one has already fulfilled the desideratum of a binding theory, and
anything that is different does not correspond to this notion of theory.
It is impossible to address everything in a single lecture that would
be necessary to illuminate every last corner of this – even if it means
leaving certain things unsaid that should really be said. So, in so far
as we are dealing with the contrast to this traditional understanding
of a theory, including an aesthetic theory, from which all individual
definitions can then be drawn within a closed deductive context, I
must point out the fundamental elements as well as the things I have
said about them that stand resolutely in opposition to the entirety of
tradition, in particular the introduction to *Against Epistemology*[2] and
the study 'The Essay as Form',[3] which further develops the problematics of that introduction in a specifically aesthetic sense. I will
say only one thing about this, namely that – as is already implicit in
Kant's concept of judgement, as the link between the most general
categorial forms and the appearance – even according to Kantian
theory, one can hardly speak of any such deductive theory because
the subject assigned to art, the subject on which one tends to rely in

traditional theory, is not at all the transcendental subject but rather the full, concrete subject with all its attributes, and the pure Kantian 'I think'[4] is entirely inadequate to the work of art from the outset, which means that such a grounding does not actually have the ground on which it relies. I meant only to touch on this in passing. Aside from that, I would like to take a different path from that of such a comprehensive philosophical, theoretical critique, from which I must refrain here, and will try instead to show you that, conversely, a grounding in subjectivity is inadequate to the work of art itself. So I will not proceed from a critique of the concept of subjectivity, of its whole problematic; I intend simply to show you how such an attempt to have recourse to subjectivity vis-à-vis the work is doomed to failure because of the work's particular definition. The aspect we must address first of all is the arbitrariness of the subject's reaction to any work of art; for, in general, subjectivist forms of aesthetics claim to reveal something about the nature of the work itself based on the reactions of the observer, the emotions a work of art supposedly arouses in the observer, using the convenient argument that we know nothing about the work itself independently of these subjective reactions and that, in order to gain access to [the work of art] at all, we must take exactly the same step of subjective reflection that is also required for scientific insights.

One could say that this entire way of looking at things, which attempts to elaborate the meaning of beauty and art from subjective reactions, stands below an uppermost category on which the whole dispute about this is focused. This is the same category that plays a similar role for Kant: taste and the judgement of taste. To appeal to the observer as a final authority on the nature and quality of the work of art is always tantamount to making taste the arbiter of the work's nature. I would therefore like to speak to you today about the concept of taste, and in the process, as is my custom in these lectures, I will try to use this critique or dialectic of taste as a vehicle to unsettle the subjectivist view of art that I suspect potentially resides in all of you, but also to tell you some factual things about an aesthetic category as central as that of taste. I shall refer to a text by Hegel, and here I will repay for the first time a small part of the debt of gratitude I feel I owe Hegel; not simply to read you this Hegel passage and follow it with a few reflections but, primarily, from the perspective that I want – fully aware that I can really only provide impulses and name individual aspects, and how impossible it is in such a lecture to penetrate the whole, even in a fragmentary fashion – to encourage you to read the book, which, especially in its fundamental parts, I consider the most important and substantial product of the tradition of aesthetic writing, namely Hegel's *Aesthetics*, which will develop an endless number of things I have presupposed here, or at least have not really been able to develop. At the same time, there are also a number of things to which you can object in productive outrage, especially in matters that contradict the theorems I have shared with you. The passage in question, which constitutes a critique of taste, is in the introduction to Hegel's *Aesthetics*, and he mentions a number of – today one would probably say rococo-like – texts about the forming of taste, such as Home's *Elements of Criticism*, the writings of Batteux and *Introduction to the Fine Arts* by Ramler:

> Taste in this sense concerns the arrangement and treatment, the aptness and perfection of what belongs to the external appearance of a work of art. Moreover they drew into the principles of taste views which were taken from the old psychology and had been derived from empirical observations of mental capacities and activities, passions and their probable intensification, sequence, etc.[5]

I would add that the famous definition of drama in Aristotle's *Poetics*, of which you, as Germanists, will all have heard via Lessing, namely that the purpose of tragedy is to evoke fear and pity,[6] was the first document of such a subjectively oriented aesthetics. And you will perhaps recall in this context that the emancipation of German literature in particular from a certain kind of immature formalism went hand in hand with the critique of that same Aristotelian poetics. Hegel continues:

> But it remains ever the case that every man apprehends works of art or characters, actions, and events according to the measure of his insight and his feelings; and since the development of taste only touched on what was external and meagre, and besides took its prescriptions likewise from only a narrow range of works of art and a limited training of the intellect and the feelings, its scope was unsatisfactory and incapable of grasping the inner meaning and truth of art and sharpening the eye for detecting these things.[7]

Before I address this passage, I will note in passing that Hegel, as he often did, turns the tables here; so he does not say, 'I only know about the work of art in a mediated fashion, through the feelings it triggers in me, not immediately; the work of art in itself is an unknown, and therefore I must keep to the subject.' Rather, in this passage, he is saying: 'It is precisely the subjective reaction that is arbitrary in the face of the work', and we will hear more about that. He follows this reflection with these words:

In general, such theories proceed in the same kind of way as the other non-philosophical sciences. What they take as their subject matter is derived from our perception as something really *there*; [but] now a further question arises about the character of this perception, since we need closer specifications which are likewise found in our perception and, drawn thence, are settled in definitions.[8]

And now you can see how close what I have told you so far is to the spirit of this Hegelian aesthetics.

But thus we find ourselves at once on uncertain and disputed ground. For at first it might seem that the beautiful was a quite simple idea. But it is soon obvious that several sides may be found in it, and so one author emphasizes one and another author another, or, if the same considerations are kept in view, a dispute arises about the question which side is now to be treated as the essential one.[9]

Let me add a few things to this Hegel passage. So first he discusses what I already tried to point out to you, namely that the very thing which subjectivist aesthetics takes as the most secure starting point, where it believes it is standing on firm ground – the subjective reaction to works of art – is something random. Later on, when we have taken our treatment of the concept of taste a little further, we will have occasion to discuss where this randomness is to be found. Let me add that this is no entirely random randomness, for, in the discrepancy between the observer or perceiver of the work of art and the nature of the work itself, certain mechanisms and necessities win out that almost inevitably distort the awareness of someone who goes to the work of art unreflectingly. What I consider more important is Hegel's statement that the forming of taste addresses only what is external and meagre. I think this truly brings us to a central fact of aesthetics. For the work of art initially shows the observer its exterior, and the reactions of taste with which we are initially dealing are precisely those that refer mostly to this exterior. But as soon as you experience the work of art as something that is alive in itself, and recognize that this exterior is merely an aspect which you must penetrate in order to access the work at all, the security of this so-called taste becomes problematic. Human beings – if I may offer a slight historico-philosophical variation on this Hegelian thought and relate it more to our own situation – human beings, for whom, in the world of today, the concept of taste is central in aesthetic matters, are what, in a derogatory sense, I would call 'refined', in the same way one might find embodied in a particular type of book-collector. These are generally people who essentially experience education – what one calls education – in terms of property, for whom education amounts to an accumulation of possessions, for whom the bourgeois concept of property continues into matters of the spirit, and who accordingly survey the realm of beauty like a bourgeois apartment, going from the salon to the kitchen to see what they can find piled up there and then somehow consume. If you look at the art psychology or aesthetics – I'm no longer even sure of the name for it – of the Austrian aesthetician Othmar Sterzinger[10] (I don't know if he is still alive) then you will immediately find this concept of sophisticated refinement involuntarily displayed in all its indescribable ridiculousness. If we speak of the 'aesthete' in a disparaging fashion, we must take care not to undertake this disparagement like a player in a marching band and think that the refinement of the aesthetic sensorium which fate has bestowed on certain individuals is already a moral taint. Next to this sphere of vigorous folk art, which is presented in opposition to so-called aestheticism, even the kitsch of good old Oscar Wilde is still good enough.[11] Nonetheless, there is something much more earnest to be said against the notion of the aesthete, namely that the aesthete is the one who truly reduces the work of art to those of its aspects that are sensually appealing, that immediately appear on its outer surface; in significant works of art, however, these sensual stimuli always derive their legitimacy from the matter itself – no dissonance, no appealing colour is appealing if it does not receive its justification from the substance of the work – but have little to do with artistic experience as such. I think I can reveal to you that, of the true artists with whom I have had dealings in my life, barely any of them – I must say – have been so-called aesthetes. The stance of the so-called aesthete, if one examines it, is essentially this: a person who approaches the work of art with the mentality that they do not want to be hurt by anything about it. And I would say that the idea of the externality and superficiality of taste, as described by Hegel in the passage I read out, is really based on the fact that, by containing the simultaneously critical and utopian intention I pointed out to you, the work of art is simply always something hurtful and that, where it no longer hurts anyone but, rather, blends completely into the closed surface of experience, it essentially ceases to be a living work of art at all. And indeed this type we call the aesthete, the person who is dominated by the category of taste, is usually the type of fearful person who is excessively at pains to be protected from stimuli, who enters the sphere of art not because the miserable life outside is not enough but in order to be sealed off from life, and who might also castrate this second life by removing anything hurtful, anything – to quote Hegel – that is not 'apt', anything offensive, anything scandalous. In current parlance, the whole realm of art that is subordinate to this category of taste can be referred to as 'decorative art'. The concept of decorative art has long gone beyond the products of arts and crafts in the narrower sense and also includes countless items that do not fulfil any commercial[12] function in life in terms of their genre, and instead pretend to be aesthetic constructs in their own right, but whose inner composition nonetheless obeys the laws of decorative art. You will recognize the inanity of taste in this sphere most clearly if I draw your attention to certain controversies that are characteristic of the sphere of taste, for example whether a tie is tasteful, or whether a room is painted in a tasteful hue. I will not deny that there are certain extremes, and that there are truly awful ties and also very pretty ties. But it is also the case that, firstly, these questions are of a very secondary nature alongside the experience of beauty and, secondly, there are countless ties where it is completely irrelevant whether one finds them tasteful or not. And as for the famous shades of possibly hand-painted rooms, the judgement of taste is quite clearly a matter of absolute decorative-artistic arbitrariness, since the aspects presented here have lost all connection to the life of the matter. From this perspective, one could almost say that the significant works of art are always those that transcend the category of taste and can thus scarcely be assessed according to the standards of taste – works that, as we will see shortly, by no means ignore or dismiss taste, yet always have something in them that passes over these taste aspects. Then Hegel speaks of the abstract one-sidedness of taste formation. And the passage in question is one I would especially recommend to you, for here you can already see the decisive difference between Hegel's position, as well as – if I may say this without being immodest – the ideas I attempted to lay out to you, on the one hand, and aesthetic subjectivism, on the other. In the reflections in question, it is argued that beauty is precisely not the thing that attracts subjective aesthetics, for it is not – in Hegel's words – a 'simple idea';[13] it is a complex one. Here I can perhaps reach into our storeroom again, for this idea presented by Hegel is one I developed for you in detail in quite different contexts when I was trying to show you that the work of art is substantially a force field. If that is the case, however, if every work of art is a process in itself, then this contains the very point I tried to underline: that the idea of the work cannot be reduced to a 'slogan' – as Hegel sardonically put it – that the concept of beauty, as Hegel rightly underlines with irony, cannot be defined. Rather, determining the meaning of beauty can consist only in unfolding these aspects, and only, I would add, in the way they constitute themselves in the immanent life of the works of art and the life of the relationships between them. So aesthetics must grasp this process, must elaborate this process from the work of art, and not reduce beauty to a simple term. And thus the intention of aesthetics, the thing aesthetics is actually meant to achieve – compared to the underlying motive of subjective aesthetics, which is to encapsulate beauty in preferably simple, sloganesque, conclusive assertions – is abandoned, and this intention is replaced by a diametrically opposed intention, namely the one with which I will acquaint you in the course of this investigation and to which, if I may say so, I would like to convert you.[14]

But at this point you will all have a question on your minds, and rightly so, for you will say, 'For God's sake, do you want to abolish taste in art? First you go to Paris and even write essays on Parisian art,[15] which any decent person should keep quiet about if they have no understanding of taste; and then you come here and want to wean us off taste, to take away the very thing that enables one to prove that one is a cultivated person in artistic matters. Now that's really below the belt!' I think that, by presenting it in these terms, I am already safe from the suspicion that this is what I meant. And it was not for nothing that I chose my words carefully enough to tell you that significant works of art transcend taste, but – I hasten to add – do not ignore it. What we should demand of the work is that it be above taste, and not beneath taste or even against it. I already told you that taste, *goût*, is a constitutive category, especially in the whole area of French art, and it would not be fitting simply to dismiss it. But I would say this much: if one tries to do justice to a concept such as that of taste, one must examine it very closely. To this day, for example, there is undoubtedly no precise idea, no precise theoretical investigation, of that highly peculiar quality in French painting, or also in French music of worth, that one perceives as taste, and which [is connected to] that feeling of something pleasant and apt or, as in the Hegel passage, 'the aptness and perfection of what belongs to the external appearance of a work of art'.[16] Here one would really need to have first a concrete phenomenology of this *goût*, and then one would see that it has rather little to do with general subjective principles about how one should perceive works of art, or how they should be created in an apt way.[17]

Having said various negative things to you about the phenomenology of taste, I would like at least to make a few positive points about it. First of all, it seems to me that this concept of taste, which one needs but must not fetishize or immobilize – if it means anything substantial, it is really the aggregate of the accumulated experience that has been stored up in art in general – so, in a sense, the potential of tradition, which stands behind every work of art, even in a negated form, even when it does not directly appear, and which gives every work its 'manners', one could almost say, its way of life – just as what we call manners in human interactions has been shaped by the whole of history. We know that everything we might call manners are rudiments of earlier courtly or knightly ceremonials within culture. In short: if, in God's name, art is one day viewed as the prototype for what developed as 'culture' – and I think one can say that the concept of culture in general takes art as its model – then one will have to state that taste encompasses all those aspects of works of art whereby they legitimize themselves as culture, so to speak, in which they show that they have learned their manners in history, or that they show through their taste that they speak the idiom, speak the language that history conveyed to them. One could almost say that, in this sense of the accumulation of the historical, the concept of taste is extremely close to that of style – just as one will always say of a tasteful work of art in this sense that it is also a stylish one – and here the concept of taste from historical experience is always meant in its sedimented, self-evident form. By comparison, abstract education, which falls back on tradition or thinks it can take something similar from bygone eras as a model, inevitably stands out for its lack of taste, whereas one can only speak of taste where this traditional aspect is contained substantially unquestioned in the work of art, and – I would add – where, precisely for the sake of this self-evidence, it may not be respected but rather attacked and altered in a great many aspects.

Beyond this, however, there is something else to say about this concept of taste. One can indeed say reasonably whether a work of art is tasteful or not, in the sense of whether or not it embodies the technical standard reached at the respective point in history – that is, the most advanced language that can be spoken within the appropriate artistic medium. In this sense, Picasso is a tasteful painter and Hans Thoma[18] is a tasteless one. It is precisely the ephemerality that inheres in taste, this aforementioned non-binding quality that is not tied to anything objective, this negativity of taste, its deficiency, that makes it especially qualified – and this is the virtue of its vice – to have these innervations for the most advanced standard reached by artistic technique and language during a particular time. Having taste necessarily entails having sufficiently good manners as an artist that one will resist doing anything démodé, anything that is out of fashion. In Germany we are generally taught to view the concepts of fashion and art simply as opposites; I think that is an overly primitive and undialectical view. I think that what becomes apparent in the innervations of fashion, in what is modern and what is not modern, in the category of taste is that one can only say anything substantial as an artist if one has the most advanced tools of one's own period at one's disposal. By contrast, if one believes that one can say anything more substantial, more authentic and more fundamental with older, backward tools, one will always become utterly powerless and decline into unconvincing Romanticism. The absolute, individual originality of the work of art is mere illusion and residue, for what is original in the work of art can only be that which grows as something new from what preceded it; this is precisely what is registered and guarded by taste.[19]

LECTURE 18

29 January 1959

In the last session, as you may recall, I attempted an analysis of the subjective category which aesthetics, in so far as it is subjectively oriented, generally takes as its starting point and tried both to criticize the prevailing notion of the concept of taste and to extract the elements of truth contained in this concept. What I told you about the concept of taste should really be taken more as a prelude, in the sense of a phenomenology of this category, than as an attempt to contribute anything truly radical and decisive about this problem, which, for very many of you, is probably central to your own stance towards the problem of aesthetics in general. So let me try to take the bull by the horns, if I may put it like that, and give you some fundamental reasons why aesthetic subjectivism in the broadest sense strikes me as inadequate. I think I do not have to fear being misunderstood, in the sense that you might think I took aesthetic subjectivism to mean the so-called subjective work of art, namely a work that is very subjectively oriented compared to, shall we say, a classicist approach – as if I were about to unleash a philippic against Jens Peter Jacobsen[1] or Peter Altenberg.[2] That is certainly not my intention. On the contrary, I think that, if you have followed the tenor of these lectures, you will have noticed that the notion of an unmediated objectivity in art which has not passed through the subject is precisely not what I have in mind. So, to avoid any misunderstandings, what I am presenting is an attempt to base an aesthetics and a set of criteria of art on the reactions of the subject.[3] Here one would usually start – following the idea of an analysis of aesthetic experience, which is equated with

something like progress in the experience of knowledge, of non-
aesthetic knowledge – from the analysis of the recipient, the one who
perceives art, and hence of what one calls the 'experience of art'. My
thesis is that this recipient – whether as an individual or an abstracted
recipient – cannot provide any fundamental theory of justification. I
remind you of my intention to formulate the critique of aesthetic
subjectivism by showing you to what discrepancies the very concept
inevitably leads.[4] I already hinted that recourse to a general aesthetic
subject of whatever kind is not possible when I pointed out that the
subject, which alone is capable of having aesthetic experiences, is
precisely not a logical subject but, rather, that full subject which
encompasses the essence of its own concrete contentual experience.
Things are no different with the individual subject, however. In the
last session you already heard Hegel's objection that the individual
subject's reactions to the work of art are arbitrary, but this statement
is like all such statements: it does not really go beyond the abstract.
And I think that, for such a statement truly to take on the weight of
an insight, one must look at it more closely. If, when analysing artistic
experience, you completely abstract from an analysis of the work
itself, then the work is reduced to what psychologists call a 'stimulus'.
So then the work of art is something that stimulates the sensory
organs as well as the psyche of the recipient. And aesthetics would
then indeed only have to examine the ensuing reactions, without
making any prejudgements about the nature of this stimulus itself,[5]
for the aim is precisely to base the theory on subjectivity, not objectivity. But – and this truly strikes me as the plausible and central
argument in this controversy – there is no direct relation between the
aesthetic object, that is, the matter to be experienced, and the modes
of reaction that follow from it.[6] I am not ruling out the possibility
that the two have something to do with each other; certainly they
do. And the nature of the relationship between stimulus and response
in art would be something to research in psychology, aesthetics and
also sociology – albeit another question that could not be addressed
without an analysis of the so-called stimulus. I will only point out in
passing that there is already something senseless about the silent
transformation of a work of art into a stimulus in this perspective,
because the work is not comparable to some flickering light in a
psychological laboratory that is followed by this or that reaction;
rather, according to its own ambition and the purpose with which it
is experienced, it means something different from such a stimulus.
And, as I have tried to expound to you, it cannot be understood at
all except as a context of meaning, and, next to this aspect of meaningfulness, the reduction to such a stimulus – that is, a mere means

to an end, an abstract trigger of subjective experiences – already reduces the matter at hand to such a degree that it can no longer be reconstructed from these reactions, for the so-called stimulus, if it causes reactions, is something entirely different from the work of art itself. If I am stimulated in some particular way, by a colour I see or by a sound I hear, then this stimulation by such an aspect is obviously only a quite pitiful residue of what a work of art as a totality actually constitutes. That would be a fundamental point to make about the stimulus theory.

But I do not want to dwell on that and, through an overly radical and premature investigation, forfeit the concreteness of analysis I promised you. To make it clear how little one can deduce the stimulus from the reaction – which is what giving aesthetics a subjective basis amounts to – let me remind you, especially the psychologists among you, of the theorem concerning specific nerve energies, which states that all so-called stimuli we receive are processed according to the criteria of the sensory organs on which they are bestowed.[7] For example, if one gives a person a firm punch on their closed eye, there will normally be sensations of light – a fact that is also confirmed by numerous figures of speech. It is clear that works of art are no mere sensual constructs but something spiritual, and that the theorem about specific sensory energies – about the categorical difference between reaction and stimulus which is thus posited – cannot simply be transferred literally and unrefracted to the work of art. I mentioned it only as an analogy, in order to explain that there is also something spiritual here which corresponds exactly to the things I wish to convey to you now: the subjectively determined nature of our aesthetic experience, which can be completely at odds with the object of experience and even change it entirely and radically. Let me give you an example: there are countless people – I think depth psychology has not yet considered this to an appropriate extent – with a feeling for the grandiose, the pompous. These are generally people – if I may speak psychologically for a moment – who probably have very strong ideas of power and needs for power that have somehow been repressed, which do not properly come to the surface, but which remain intact in an area where one thinks one will be more or less undisturbed, namely the artistic area. Then they can indulge in fantasies of greatness in a form that is not sublimated but, rather, distorted into the pathological, resulting in what is familiar in psychiatry as megalomania. In its more harmless form, one could probably speak of a 'Nero complex' among numerous people.[8] These people have a tendency not only to attach themselves to works of art which are themselves perfect embodiments of the Nero complex – such as the famous prelude in C sharp minor by Rachmaninov,[9] which has probably thundered into all of your ears at some time or other – but actually to perceive art as such in keeping with the Nero complex, and they will fatten their supposed notions of the sublime, which they take directly from the educated sphere, on this Nero complex. There is, for example, a way of reacting to Beethoven that perceives a kind of aggressive, pompous, grandiose abundance in his music from the outset but, as one can see through an analysis of the works, is truly at the expense of the matter itself. I recall an old gentleman – he was a headmaster and I was very young at the time – who told me that he loved Richard Wagner so much because his music was so 'viscous', as he put it. It was somehow the notion of a slowly encroaching mass of lava, a fiery liquid mush that, for reasons that undoubtedly had their basis in his inner life, attracted him to Wagner. Now, one can establish – and here you must concede this to me methodologically, as it were – through a technical, entirely concrete analysis of the works of art themselves, the facts of the matter, which God knows initially has relatively little to do with the spiritual side of the work, that this viscosity unjustly credited to Richard Wagner by that gentleman – whatever one might have against Wagner – has no basis. In fact, Wagner's treatment of the orchestra is extremely transparent; only at certain very carefully judged points does it rise to a voluminous fortissimo, and elsewhere it displays the finest, most unobtrusive shadings. And if one might be allowed to refer to the will of the lawmaker himself, Wagner's own performance practice, which forms an immediate part of his works, involved doing practically everything in his power to counteract any so-called viscosity. As far as I know, he was the only major composer who, at Bayreuth, expressly arranged for the orchestra to be lowered in order to avoid that very quality. So this predetermination, which one can assume to be of a projective kind, is very much at the expense of the matter itself. If one seriously attempts, as is often the case in America, to build up an aesthetics from people's reactions, to base a hierarchy of value on these reactions, one arrives at something completely nonsensical – namely a kind of majority vote which is direct and severely at odds with the matter. The consequences of a subjective aesthetics are those letters which are familiar to every head of music at a radio station, saying that the modern work played the previous day was simply dangerous to one's health and nerves, and that the author of the missive, who is opposed to wasting taxpayers' money on such nonsense, is not alone in this view and in fact knows that they are speaking for many like-minded people who still have something resembling sound judgement. [...][10] It is quite interesting, furthermore, that in this very sphere, where people stand proud before royal thrones[11] and act as if they were speaking from their own particular aesthetic experience, they in fact use completely standardized arguments. In America, where the notion on which I dogmatically, shall we say, based our entire deliberations, but which I think I have shown you from so many different angles that it must be somewhat evident to you by now, namely where the question of a work of art's objectivity, the question of whether there is actually such a thing as an objective spirit, is essentially impossible for people to understand, and where any talk of the objectivity of a work of art is met with the response that this is nothing but a subjective projection – in America, people have caught on to the difficulties of basing an aesthetics on a *volonté de tous*[12] and have instead tried to get out of the matter by using experts as the true authority. Here you will first of all find a simple logical problem: if you set the experts apart from the reactions of the other people, you are implicitly acknowledging the validity of criteria from the matter itself. For an expert can only be a person who knows something about the matter itself and is therefore entitled to say something about it; someone who is experienced in the matter, *expertus*, would be an expert. Otherwise it would be a mere abbreviation of the *volonté de tous*, the majority decision, and would in no way lead beyond the aporia I described to you. But even if you leave aside this problem, it is naturally the case that the experts cannot constitute a truth authority, as they are selected on the basis of certain power constellations with all manner of social factors, where, for example, a critic who uses certain tricks to appeal to the listeners can very easily become an expert. In this context, I cannot refrain from telling you the name of one such very famous expert whom you will very often encounter in such committees, expert committees dealing with the forming of taste in America: the man in question is Sigmund Spaeth, whose fame is based primarily on having written a book called *Great Symphonies: How to Recognize and Remember Them*,[13] and his [notion] is that one can best absorb great symphonic works by assigning verbal descriptions to the most important themes and then remembering the main themes by these words. I can tell you: this is such a fiendish assault on listening that, once you have tried it, it is difficult to get away from those words again. I certainly do not question the effectiveness of Mr Spaeth's method, but I rather doubt that this kind of subjective aesthetic takes us any further into the matter. I recall, for example, a description he assigned to the famous second subject from Tchaikovsky's *Pathétique* Symphony.[14] It is what one would call a lyrical, calm theme; he added the words 'It seems Tchaikovsky now is calm again.'[15] Here you have the wonderful idea of the artist as a kind of wild man who gets terribly worked up and rages about like anything but then, when he writes a quiet theme, calms down again like a lunatic in a straitjacket. I think I am not only pointing this out to you for your amusement; here the saying that one will know them by their fruits truly applies. That is, it starts with the scholarly-sounding assurance that there is no such thing as objective spirit, and that one should concentrate on people's reactions – as we all know, art is only there for human beings – and it ends, if taken to its logical conclusion, with Tchaikovsky being calm again. That is how it is with these experts, who are supposed to teach us what is objectively valuable based on a subjective aesthetics; and you can believe me that most experts are perhaps quantitatively but not qualitatively very different from Mr Spaeth. With this, and with what I told you about the experts, about the social selection mechanisms that determine whether a person becomes an aesthetic expert in the first place – believe me, treat aesthetic experts with suspicion whenever you encounter them! The only ones who are worse than the experts are those who are not experts, namely the amateurs. But the choice between them is a painful one, and the two categories are perfectly suited to one another; they are precisely complementary and show clearly that the genuine experience of art has been disturbed.

This touches on an absolutely central fact of aesthetics: the impossibility of basing aesthetics on subjective forms of reaction. And I would like to say in passing that, if I disdain to draw a strict line separating philosophical aesthetics, the so-called basic questions of philosophy, from sociology, then this is precisely where the reason lies. Here, unlike those of my colleagues who claim that this is therefore not philosophy, I am following Hegel, who is surely highly versed in such matters, and who wrote that, if one is too shy about the concrete social content of phenomena and believes that philosophy is really only that which has no concrete content, one is then debasing philosophy to complete superficiality and emptiness[16] – here I would like to second this expressly as a methodological principle. A rebuttal such as that of subjective aesthetics, that is to say a so-called philosophical or aesthetic question of principle, is – as I hope to show you in a moment – inseparable from certain reflections of a sociological nature. And because, as you know, I always endeavour in my lectures to bring the so-called basic issues and methodological questions together with the contentual problems whereby the general problems can be demonstrated, I will take the same approach in this matter.

The idea in question is that the recipients to which subjective aesthetics refers are in fact considered the ultimate authority in aesthetic judgement – that is, the immediacy on which, according to this view, judgements about art and the relationship with art should be based. In order to act as such a foundation, these judgements are relied on as something immediate, irreducible and final. I explained, after a fashion, my objections to this foundation mania in philosophy – this attempt to trace something back to such a fixed, final given – in the two theoretical studies I mentioned earlier. You will, as it happens, find at least elements of a critique of this foundation mania scattered through Hegel's work, albeit intersecting with different motives, namely those of a *prima philosophia*. But I do not mean to engage in this critique of the first, the immediate, from which everything supposedly comes; instead I will take this claim literally – as I said, taking the bull by the horns – and ask how it is with these aesthetic relations, as such an immediacy to which all that can be said about art can be traced. Here we discover that there is no such immediacy to speak of at all, and that, rather – and this is what I truly consider decisive in a contentual critique of an aesthetics grounded subjectively in the reactions of those who receive works of art – the reactions which are taken here as final and absolute are to a massive extent predetermined, and that – to put this idea in a dynamic-social context – this predeterminacy of the supposedly fundamental aesthetic reactions increases the more tightly the web of socialization is woven, the more we and our entire lives are reduced to intersections of social lines.[17] The immediacy of subjective reaction, which, according to the view I am discussing, is supposedly the source of justification for aesthetics, is in reality something entirely mediated, and the belief that I somehow have a purer source of aesthetic insight, one less disturbed by random factors than if one immerses oneself in the works and the substance of the works themselves, is purely a superstition of traditional philosophy.

I would like to demonstrate this, at least, with reference to three categories. First of all, let me explain that what is consumed in works – if I can take up that point – namely the aspect that is the primary focus of the reactions of people, of the audience, depends to an enormous extent on authority and popularity, as well as on all manner of similar elements. I will not dwell on the highly amusing and highly convincing experiments of my Princeton colleague Hadley Cantril,[18] who showed that, if one plays relatively large groups of people recordings by some provincial musical director and swaps the labels or announcements, making them think they are listening to recordings by Toscanini,[19] they cannot tell the difference, and the hierarchy of value mirrors this. For you could respond to me, without my being able to contradict you very convincingly, that something like the

quality of the conductor is a very problematic matter with highly
organized orchestras, who can generally play the Fifth Symphony just
as badly without the conductor as under his direct instruction. But
perhaps I can point you to the study on the *Missa Solemnis* that I
published in the last issue of *Neue deutsche Hefte*.[20] I mention it
because, with my heavily taxed stone, I wish to kill another bird:
there is a particular type of person who, when they read the things I
publish, thinks that these ideas just come to me and do not have any
particular system, as it were. I have made my views on the concept
of the system sufficiently clear.[21] If, however, these lectures encourage
you to engage with some of my writings, I would like to point out
that these things, even if they seem to deal with very distant, not
directly connected thematic areas, have a very precise status within
the overall structure of the philosophy of which I can show you only
a small part here, and that when I publish a study on the *Missa
Solemnis*, for example, then this is not an excursion into music
history. Believe me: I have no such ambition whatsoever. In reality,
this is part of my systematic intention to show you that there is a
total discrepancy between the reception of a work of art, even the
authority of a work of art, and the matter itself. The *Missa Solemnis*,
if I may say so, is one of the most opaque and enigmatic works to
be found in the whole of our great musical literature. And I think I
even showed in the aforementioned study that it has not really been
understood to this day; and the few people whose judgement in
musical matters I truly value – for example Schoenberg[22] – have
confirmed this opacity and incomprehensibility in the work. This
does not remotely alter the fact that every self-respecting choral
society churns out some version of it every year or every other year,
and that critics write that it was once again an uplifting or not-so-
uplifting evening – depending how much it appealed to the respective
person – and that no one dares to say that it is quite similar to the
emperor's new clothes: for here is something that cannot really be
understood at all without addressing the most unfathomable experiences of the aesthetic problems with Beethoven as such. But through
these unfathomable experiences, the *Missa Solemnis* will probably
reveal itself as one of Beethoven's central works, which is indeed how
he described it himself.[23] At any rate: people go and listen to it, they
applaud; the work has great authority and is acknowledged as a
masterpiece – and people do not even notice, in the most literal sense
of the word, that they do not understand this work at all. In reality,
they consume only the prestige accrued by this work. I would almost
say: they consume the accumulated exchange value of the work,
instead of finding – if I may put it in such vulgar materialist terms

– some utility value in it. I examined this situation from a different side, a mostly theoretical one – focusing on its economic roots – in the study 'On the Fetish-Character of Music and the Regression of Listening'.[24] In the texts on the *Missa Solemnis* and on Toscanini,[25] I attempted to grasp it from the other side, namely through the analysis of two artistic phenomena. And this preformation mechanism based on fetishes – here in Germany we still have fetishes of education, and in America, where things have progressed further, they already have fetishes such as the grinning advertising girls from toothpaste commercials or film stars, pure advertising deities – these categories have come to obscure all aesthetic experience to such a degree that any attempt to ground the nature of beauty in the reactions themselves, the subjective forms of response, strikes me as doomed to failure from the outset. Where would it lead if one tried to reach judgements on the *Missa Solemnis* or the essence of the *Missa Solemnis* by questioning a representative sample of people and found out what this work, acknowledged as a classic yet completely incomprehensible, means to the inner workings of their souls? It does not bear thinking about.

But now let me proceed to the second condition of this kind, namely something that is far less directly subject to social pressure but in which a penetrating analysis will uncover the mechanisms of social mediation no less than in the phenomenon I have just described to you. What I mean is something one could perhaps describe in a catchphrase as the emotional relationship with art. Let me tell you of an experience I had concerning this. Many years ago, in Oxford, I befriended a young Englishman who was exceptionally talented, especially as an aesthetic theorist, and I occasionally played a little piano for him. The strange thing was that any music I played, and by no means music of an especially touching or harrowing nature, made him weep. And let me emphasize that this was an extremely refined, in many ways highly developed person of great intellectual powers.[26] What I mean to say is that, when it comes to the so-called affects triggered by works of art – as shown very clearly here – there is a great range of variations between the object with which one is confronted and the mode of reaction. Let me go a step further: the fact of this reaction, which is also incredibly widespread here – that one searches for emotions in art and reacts to art with the corresponding emotions – is connected to the circumstance that under the so-called reality principle – which I already mentioned in an entirely different context earlier on in these lectures – we are constantly forced to repress our affects. In connection with the discipline demanded by a work ethic and all manner of other things, then, a person who bursts into tears at every opportunity, especially if it is a man, becomes a figure of ridicule. Perhaps many of you will perhaps have gone through what I went through as a child: I was reprimanded in the harshest terms if I cried in any situation. This repression, not only of specific sexual drives but of all affective expressions, is then loosed by art in a certain sense. Recall the definition we arrived at when we said that art is the voice of nature in its unmutilated, not yet ravaged state. In the present context, this aspect of art itself now leads to a peculiar inversion, a peculiar perversion. For now art itself is not experienced in line with the dialectic of nature and its domination, which I tried at least to outline for you, but rather the reverse: art now becomes a receptacle for one's own affects. It becomes a kind of nature reserve in which one can let oneself go, where one can allow oneself to feel anything at all. And the relatively large part which art plays in our present culture – that fact that art is tolerated to such a degree at all in such a rationalized civilization – is connected precisely to this change of function, that it becomes a nature reserve which allows people to act out their affects, to feel something at all, to feel passions at all, without having to repress them – but also without these affects having any consequences for their real-life behaviour. One could call that the satanic parody of the establishment of art as a special area strictly separated from empirical reality. In psychological terms, this is a very strict case of what one calls projection. That is, one simply projects one's own feelings, one's own affects, onto the work of art. The so-called stimulus acts only as a sort of trigger, a sort of lever, and the entire reaction that follows has nothing to do with the matter itself, or at most as a borderline case.

LECTURE 19

3 February 1959

Last time, as you may recall, I tried to show you in detail why the subjective modes of reaction to works of art – and thus, in a broader sense, the basing of aesthetics on the receiving subject – are not binding. After showing you first of all in what sense reactions to works of art are predetermined – that is, mediated by all manner of clichés, fetishes and the like – I then turned to the phenomenon of emotional reactions to works of art and attempted to show you that, for overall cultural reasons, the emotional reactions triggered by works of art are not necessarily connected to the actual content of the works at all and that, in such situations, the work truly acts as a mere stimulus – an aspecific impulse for reactions in general – and that, in this context, the work of art is a sort of receptacle for all manner of emotions that are otherwise repressed, but of which people then, in the face of art, feel they can cheaply unburden themselves. I ended by telling you that one should approach the work of art in a certain very delicately rational manner. I think I am safe from being misunderstood as recommending any calculating or intellectualizing behaviour towards the work of art, by which I mean an approach that reflects on the work before it has experienced the work itself, and which substitutes a judgement about it for a living experience thereof. That is obviously not what I mean. What I mean is adopting a stance towards the work of art that can perhaps best be described as recognitive.[1] That is, one concentrates on the work in all its aspects, in everything that it brings with it, but that this concentration is not merely a passive concentration, not the kind where one just sits there in a 'relaxed' manner, as they say in America, lets things take their course and waits to see what nice things the work will offer; rather, one takes on that same responsibility as a listener – or a viewer or a spectator – which, as I once told you, the work itself bears at every moment, and faces it with such concentration that one is capable of carrying out the same synthesis, the same unification, of diverging yet connected aspects of the work that takes place in the work itself. Because this synthesis, if I may remind you, is a spiritual synthesis. For the aspects as such always remain separate in the work of art, and you can only perceive the work as a spiritual unity, as a context of meaning, as a structure, to the extent that you bring synthesizing power of your own to the work – that is, if I may exaggerate somewhat, in so far as you are prepared to renew in yourself, as an observer, that process which is present in the work in a solidified form.[2] That sounds quite harmless and quite plausible. But I will not hide from you that such a view deviates from official aesthetics – indeed almost all aesthetics – on a very decisive point; in fact, it even opposes it vehemently, and I think I owe it to you to address this point, which is perhaps the most important of all the deviations from conventional opinion that underlie my own position. I am doing so not only because this is truly a central dispute but also because it is usually the case – I have drawn your attention to this in the past – that theoretical aesthetics lags behind the actual development of art and the artistic sensorium. And if this lag on the part of theoretical aesthetics can be pointed out anywhere, then it is in this: the notion that art must be something intuitive, a notion very closely connected to the 'pure feeling' which I discussed critically last time.

It is a peculiar business that a society which progresses ever further in its own constitution, in its rationality – at least in the means it uses – and is thus becoming an increasingly rationalized society, sets up a few such nature reserves of irrationality in which it simply cannot bear for reason to have any say. One example of this is the traditional bourgeois construction of the so-called female character, which is essentially praised for being unaware, naïve and unreflecting, because this image of woman that is shaped by a male society, a dominating male society, mirrors the oppression to which women are subjected as a reconciled state that is approved by nature, as it were. The prevailing conventions treat art much the same as women: art is also meant to be intuitively appreciable, something that absolves us from effort, just as the bourgeois expects that his wife or mistress will provide him with relaxation and free him from all strains – a behaviour that could be said to translate the separation of work and leisure into anthropological categories. The fact that, sociologically speaking, art has been assigned to the realm of leisure, and that our society insists so rigorously on keeping effort and leisure separate – so that leisure, as recovery for the reproduction of labour power, is all the more beneficial for labour – is also mirrored in the aesthetics of 'pure intuition',[3] whose sublime aspiration to be independent of all mere intellectuality always makes me suspect that what is really behind it is the same thing found in an advertising slogan once used for some revue in London or New York: 'The Tired Business-Man's Show'. I think the 'tired businessman' is not the ideal observer of works of art; not only for his sake, because he is not in a receptive state, but because it is part of the work's very nature that it cannot be perceived in this merely passively receiving, purely intuitive manner. And if there is one aspect in which modern artistic production, in all fields, is truly qualitatively different from traditional art, then it is this: it has broken its oath of mere intuitiveness – the oath that any aspect of the work of art which is not apparent to the senses is simply non-existent – and that it has incorporated, for very profound reasons, elements that cannot simply be reconciled with the immediacy of the intuitive. This is substantially connected to the fact that the new art, unlike traditional art, can no longer provide the notion of a self-enclosed and thus directly experienceable context of meaning, because the very context of meaning which the work of art must represent has become problematic for the work itself; this context of meaning can appear only in a refracted form, if you will. And this refractedness of the context of meaning means quite simply that in new art, all areas of art, the work is no longer limited to the intuitive.[4] But here the situation – I pointed it out earlier – is in many ways as it is with new art in general. That is, it simply makes evident things – takes them up openly and makes them thematic, shall we say – that in fact already pervade all art. In other words, one can say that works of art have never been limited to pure intuition in the manner claimed by the aestheticians.

I cannot refrain from sharing with you a little find of which I am very proud: the aesthetician Theodor Meyer, who worked at the Schönthal seminary, wrote a book almost sixty years ago with the title *The Stylistic Law of Poetry* in which he formulated, with the greatest modesty and simplicity, something he had realized: that one of the traditional claims of poetics, one which had become increasingly consuming since Lessing's *Laocoon*,[5] namely the claim that literature evokes sensual images in us, that is to say, inner representations, intuitions – that this claim about the intuitiveness of literature through the evocation of sensory images was untrue.[6] He simply arrived at this insight that, as he himself puts it with charming

Swabian naïveté, upon reading some great literature or other, these sensual images, these almost visual representations, did not appear. And this made him realize that, in literature, the medium of language as a medium of concepts is not simply a supplement but in fact the very medium in which the aesthetic content is constituted – in other words, that the aesthetic content cannot possibly be presented as something purely intuitive. It is similar in painting: in traditional works, the subject matter provided by painting always goes beyond the mere immediacy of intuition and demands something like identification, thus introducing certain intellective elements. Certainly it is even more the case in modern painting, as the various 'optical signs' (as people now call them)[7] with which it operates are meant to be understood precisely as signs, and not simply taken directly. And naturally it is also true in music, in which, as I have already hinted once before, the possibility of understanding always consists in the fact that, in what is present, one simultaneously becomes aware and catches hold of the non-present; that one uses the power of memory or the power of anticipation in order to understand music at all. And this effort involved in making the non-present present, namely remembering or anticipating, is precisely the effort that we normally describe as intellectual effort. Art, the true experience of art, involves all the synthetic functions that we usually ascribe to thought, and which should not be assigned simply to intuition; except that here we are dealing with a kind of thought whose structure has barely been analysed at all, namely a conceptless thought, a conceptless synthesis – and, beyond that, a synthesis without judgement, a synthesis that does not conclude by saying, 'This is so', but rather results in something being placed there with a gesture of 'This is so', without any predication from outside the work of art that this is so. In terms of its structural elements, however, it essentially contains all the elements of logical synthesis, except without any claim that something general encompasses something particular beneath it, and that this constitutes a judgement on anything existent. By imposing such a synthesis or enactment on the observer, art is more than just a passively intuitive thing. It is precisely that merely passive intuition, the ideal of art imposed on us by almost all aesthetics, is – if I may be so blunt – essentially anti-artistic; the upshot of it is that we simply surrender to the individual stimuli conveyed to us by works of art. But as soon as we surrender to these stimuli without embracing the effort of the conceptual or the work of synthesis that is called for by the nature of the matter, we fall short of the work of art itself. We reduce it to that mere materiality, that mere sensuality which, as I tried to show you, is precisely not its true aesthetic content. By carrying out such a synthesis vis-à-vis the work, I would add, instead of devouring it passively, so to speak, our behaviour towards the works of art exhibits that aspect of aesthetic distance which, as I originally sought to show you in the historico-philosophical reflections from which we began, enables the aesthetic domain to exist as something separate from immediate empirical reality in the first place. So this is how I would ask you to understand my words: to experience art essentially means to recognize[8] it.[9] I do not mean puristically excluding the emotional aspects, which are indeed contained in some works of art as their expressive content, and of which the observer can certainly legitimately partake. On the contrary: it is precisely such a purism, which wants to cut off this aspect entirely, that usually debases art to serving a merely disciplinary function and essentially robs it of the very thing that it can mean for living human beings. But I think that the question of this emotional relationship with the work of art is not something that exists simply in the manner I described to you with reference to the person who started crying at every piece of music; rather, this emotional content of the work exists only as something mediated; it only ever results from the synthesis I have attempted to describe to you and does not itself form the basis of that synthesis.

If I am speaking to you now about cognition of art, however, then I am not – let me emphasize this again, to ensure that you do not misunderstand me on this important point[10] – referring to some form of external reflection relating to art. So what I mean is not that, if you find yourselves in a Picasso or Braque exhibition and do not really know what to make of the pictures, you can pore over all kinds of books about Picasso and acquire information about cubism and more, and think that this is the kind of insight into art, the cognition of art, that I am talking about. These educational elements can indeed augment artistic experience, and will perhaps have positive results; but they can also do damage by substituting the mere educational experience, especially mere historical reflection, for the matter itself. But the recognition I mean is genuinely an immanent recognition of the matter itself, that you surrender yourselves entirely to those syntheses, that you actively-passively enact those syntheses which are prefigured in the relationships between the individual sensual aspects of the work of art, as it were, but which come to life only when you go through them yourselves. Let me add – if I may speak of what I call the aspect of immanent reflection, the intellective relationship with the matter itself – that the boundary between the reflective and the intuitive is naturally a fluid one. And perhaps one could even go so far as to say that, the more advanced an artistic consciousness is, the more that consciousness has been trained through experience of the matter itself, then the more of what is seemingly merely intellective will also transpire as intuitive.[11] Let me explain: part of understanding a large symphonic movement, an elaborated musical construct, is that you understand the proportions of the individual parts in time – not only their external proportions but their having been produced from one another, resulting from one another, their intra-temporal logic. Certainly, this may require a form of intellective effort, as when one tries very hard to recall or retain something. And this retention, this heightened attentiveness, is undoubtedly an entirely necessary form of behaviour when one is endeavouring to absorb unfamiliar works of art. It is also possible, however, that, once you have accumulated a wealth of experience, or if you know such a work very precisely, you will feel these things directly, even temporal relations on the largest scale that are as far as imaginable from the momentary events, just as Alfred Lorenz once wrote in his analysis of Wagner's *Ring* – and I think he captured something very beautiful and profound here – that one should ideally be able, and that he himself felt able, to see the whole of this gigantic, four-evening-long monster of a piece before him *in toto* within a single second.[12] But this transformation of an 'extensive totality', to use the phrase from early Lukács,[13] into an intensive totality is an ideal in the exact Kantian sense.[14] This means it is something which we can, in fact, achieve only through what can be termed aesthetic education. And, in so far as one can actually speak of aesthetic education, it probably means that these mediated and, to an extent, arbitrary processes increasingly move towards the possibility of directly perceiving these elements. For it is clear that we come closer to the substance of the work of art by being able to follow everything that happens in it with such an immediacy – in the sense of that one second from the *Ring* which Lorenz mentioned.[15] That is all I will say now about the problem of intuitive perception, and I must expressly leave open and unexplored the question of how this intellective or logical connection to the work of art differs from ordinary logic in detail. It is as if all the formal components of thought – synthesis, differentiation, recollection, recognition, expectation, creation of proportions – as if all of that were returning in the experience and constitution of the work itself, but with a peculiar modification that cuts off what, in the language of logic, is termed an objectifying act.[16] It is as if the logical categories were all at work, but in a way that is not objectifying and thus does not enable a form of concrete objectivity, an intra-worldly objectivity, of which abstraction forms a central part, as we know; rather, what constitutes itself is an object of a completely different nature; I hope that I will be able at some point to define very precisely what that nature is. In fact, that is really what I consider the topic of a true aesthetics: to show what kind of logic works of art possess in comparison to the logic and cognition of the concrete world – this highly peculiar logic where everything is kept but there is no longer a connection to anything predicated, anything stated, to an *is*; a logic with no copula, one could almost say. There have been attempts in this direction, for example in the musical metalogic of Harburger,[17] a book that works with an incredibly mathematical apparatus that is opaque for me; but I cannot really say that – although Harburger somehow felt it, and saw this central problem of aesthetics – his book brought me very much closer to solving the question I have pointed out to you here.

I would also like to address a third aspect in order to show you how little recourse to mere subjective reactions actually offers a basis for aesthetic judgements, or for any aesthetics in general. For those are the defensive reactions that modern art triggers very frequently, and in very many people – defensive reactions that are used not only by advocates of both varieties of totalitarianism – by Lukács and Sedlmayr – to arrive at verdicts about modern art as such – also in the Western area by theoretical exponents of the culture industry such as Mr Alois Melichar,[18] a furious enemy of modern music and modern painting, to arrive directly at a verdict about modern art. The approach is simply to view the resistance which modern art arouses in a particular naïve consciousness already as a judgement on this art, instead of first reflecting on the actual causes of this resistance. And as these reactions are extremely widespread, indeed almost universal, such argumentation harmonizes perfectly with the interests of the culture industry, for then one can say that this constitutes the voice of healthy popular sentiment, or at least the voice of those listeners who – as the American advertising slogan goes – just 'can't be wrong'.[19] I will try to say some things about the unsoundness of this recourse to defensive reactions, although I would say that these reactions, which at least perceive and resist the disconcerting and non-conformist nature of radical new art, are still better than the far more widespread – and far more dangerous, I would say – reaction which quite simply consumes everything that exists and is offered, and which cannot even summon the strength of this resistance and hatred and outrage, because the matter itself is no longer taken so seriously, because art as such is no longer viewed as a manifestation of truth but just as some phenomenon of the time that one registers more or less vaguely and non-committally without reading into it anything that might be obliging for one's own understanding, let alone one's own life. These negative reactions to modern art – let us just accept this term for a moment in the way I am using it, though in the sense of emphatically modern art. That is, pictures by Miró[20] and Tachist pictures, or those of Klee or from a certain phase of Picasso, if you like, music by Schoenberg, music by Schoenberg's successors and the serial school, Joyce's *Finnegan*[21] and so forth – you can only understand what I am talking about to any extent if you truly associate the term with radical things, not so-called moderate modernity, in which case this discussion is superfluous. I think that, first of all, a large part of these defensive reactions comes from the fact that there is a contradiction between the expectations with which people approach the respective works and what people actually do. I have analysed this fairly closely using musical examples in particular,[22] and perhaps you will allow me to do the same here for simplicity's sake. When a person with no specifically musical training hears the song 'Little Hans' – I will pass over the words entirely – they expect the first two lines, 'Little Hans / went alone', to be melodically completed by 'out into the wide world'; this is because the melody is built symmetrically in a particular way, with a rhythm based on equal durations, and because it is built harmonically in such a way that it ends with an imperfect cadence to the dominant in the middle, which directly calls for the perfect cadence to complete it, and the whole thing takes place in the top part. I think it is equally true for painting and literature that, first of all, very primitively, the resistance to new art stems largely from the fact that the 'Litle Hans' schema is applied to works where Little Hans does not go out into the wide world at all, because he has always been entirely alone; in other words, works in which precisely the triviality, the conventionality of this symmetrical disposition, of the connection to an imperfect and a perfect cadence, and the unimpaired simplicity with which the melody proceeds in the top part have all become offensive. This is where artistic ingenuity precisely refuses to provide what that consciousness which still lags behind this development would expect, such that the naïve consciousness of the listener or viewer almost always perceives a series of denials at the very point where the work of art offers a series of fulfilments, which means that an entirely different logic applies – for example, a way of forming melodies that follows entirely different laws, such as using all those pitches which were not present before, or the rule of irregular periods, or such things that stand precisely in opposition to those ingrained structures. Consequently, that resistance to new art, if I am not mistaken, already sins in advance against the demand for an immanent approach that I attempted to justify to you as well as I could. That means it is essentially based on approaching the works from the outset with expectations which these works do not even intend to fulfil, and cannot fulfil, followed by the infantile disappointment that things have not happened the way one is used to and therefore desires; and this results in a negative judgement on the matter itself when encountered in such a situation. But that is not everything, for there is another and more profound element too: the fact that new art – I have already said this to you in an entirely different context – makes itself something that art has actually, in a crucial sense, always been, namely the voice of suppressed suffering. And what appears as suffering will, to a degree, arouse sadism and the urge to inflict suffering on what is suffering already – primarily because the person who is reacting sadistically is directly reminded of their own suffering, which they normally cannot utter. There is a passage in a text by the Marquis de Sade, who received a great deal of attention from the surrealists, and more recently also Sartre,[23] in which he states that it is only enjoyable to cause pain where suffering is already present from the start.[24] And there is indeed an element of such reactions among those people who are induced by an unknown picture or an unaccustomed piece of music to rage and cause some form of mischief. Perhaps I can tell you that an American psychologist, his name was Brunswik,[25] conducted rather interesting experiments in which he showed groups of people portraits that varied in terms of the joviality, sorrow or suffering they depicted and tested the people whom he thus confronted by having them say which of the faces they found appealing and which unappealing. What he found – forgive me for using such a positivistic example – was a very high correlation between the negative judgements, that is to say the verdicts of 'unappealing', and the degree of suffering and despair expressed by such a face. This infantile identification of suffering with the unappealing, with something one wants to wipe away, keep at arm's length, or preferably trample and exterminate, is probably the same mechanism that led to the rage of the brownshirts, or now some other shirts, over so-called degenerate or decadent art. And this rage is rationalized after the event with all sorts of varyingly pathetic cultural-philosophical arguments, with the claim that one is dealing with 'decadence' or 'declined art', something 'alien' to the species or the people, something 'snobbish' and 'deviant', or whatever other terms are used. There is something very strange here; one could call it the counterpoint to what I sought to explain to you in the last session with reference to the emotional, more specifically the false emotional element in relation to art. Wherever the emotional is a cliché – that is, where suffering as such does not actually crop up, but where it is channelled, where kinds of schemata of emotional behaviours are developed, as in all the popular hits, in the cinema, and everything of that kind – emotion, which is not present in the matter at all, is tolerated, and people weep without shame and are happy. But the very moment they are faced with emotion as the real emotion of human beings, where the work of art is, in a higher sense, naturalistic, where it speaks of humans themselves and makes itself the voice of what is normally suppressed by humans yet lies within them, they are not amused; they become enraged, thrash around, and base their damning judgements about new art on this. One could say that the declaration of emotions in art is suppressed precisely when they are not disfigured; on the other hand, when emotion is cultivated and thus – if you will – de-emotionalized, it is tolerated. You should take the relationship I have described very much as a historical-dynamic thing, a cumulative relationship. That is, these forms of reaction have grown with the extent of increasing socialization; the contradiction between the willingness of large numbers of people to submit to these new experiences, on the one hand, and what the experience itself constitutes, on the other hand, seems to become ever greater. Naturally, educational-sociological factors also play a very significant part – for example the fact that, through today's means of communication, infinitely more people and social strata come into contact with modern art than was the case in earlier times, and they can now, both maturely and immaturely, contribute jointly to that resistance to new art. Of course, this is compounded by the problem of semi-literacy,[26] which remains entirely unanalysed to this day.[27] In general, it is sociologically already the case that, when a person – Huxley described this very aptly in *Brave New World* – says about a work of modern art, 'Do you understand that? I don't', this already makes them feel superior, and that, rather than being embarrassed not to understand what they have been confronted with, they actually derive from it a pride in being an especially normal, healthy person who is backed up, as it were, by the *communis opinio* of everyone, and then feel that they have said something especially good.

LECTURE 20

5 February 1959

Let me remind you of the overall course of our reflections: I had
attempted to show you in concrete terms, using various models, how
questionable are the attempts to ground aesthetics as a theory – or
indeed individual aesthetic judgements – in subjectivity, first of all the
subjectivity of the recipient. For the first models I used two aspects
that also strike me as having a certain objective significance for
understanding aesthetic matters: firstly, the preformation of so-called
direct reactions to works of art by social mechanisms and, secondly,
the whole question of so-called emotional reactions to works of art.
I then closed by showing you the unsoundness of invoking such
immediate reactions, discussing the typical cases one encounters of
resistance to modern art through purportedly spontaneous reactions.
The last observation we arrived at was one that I would like to repeat
because I believe that, beyond the aesthetic domain, it has a certain
diagnostic significance for our current spiritual and intellectual situation, namely that people generally view phenomena that are reified,
that are foreign to them and no longer have any direct connection to
them, but where provision has been made for them as customers, so
to speak, as their own concern, and support them; whereas anything
which speaks seriously about, which gives voice to what truly moves
people and what actually lies within them, is resisted by them as
foreign, disconcerting and cold precisely for daring to do so. This is
an extraordinarily widespread mechanism that naturally hides behind
such categories as progress. For, in general, phenomena of reification
and calculation are more progressive – albeit in a particular, very

limited technological sense – than those which speak of people themselves. Naturally a poor composer, equipped with nothing but their own ears and reason, their responsibility and perhaps even talent, will generally have great difficulty competing with a statistical research office in New York that calculates, for example, which ingredients a pop song requires to be successful and to get into one of the charts of most-played pop songs. And I think that phenomena such as jazz,[1] and a variety of analogous phenomena, are connected to the fact that people actually affirm and internalize their own reification in such phenomena, their own transformation into customers, and in a sense enjoy the fact that they themselves are also contained in this mechanism – whereas they resist anything that is not already in it, anything that does not possess this particular immanence within the culture scene.

If I may give you some pedagogical advice, as it were, then it is this: to check your own reactions to art, as far as possible, to see whether they are under the spell of the machinery to a certain extent, and whether, even for you, the experience that something is up to date in this particular sense – that it is filtered through the prevailing mechanisms – wins out over objective reactions. If one observes, for example, how some products of the spirit are prepared and disfigured in the name of so-called journalism in order to become 'consumable', one will also find it virtually demanded that things become tangible, that they are alienated, so that people imagine that they are close to these same things. A further element in these reactions against expressly modern art is naturally the rancour of those who have simply not kept up and who now, because the possibilities to catch up on those experiences which they were denied are limited and problematic, can do nothing but reject that from which they are excluded – just as rancour and resentment generally say about anything which they cannot reach that it is simply snobbish, and therefore devalued. I will try to arouse a certain distrust in you towards this reaction too.

One can therefore say that, in general, art – the more it has reflected on its own formal law, and the more it has consequently been pushed to shape in its own way those things which ultimately transpire, in the course of history, as precisely what remains of works of art, namely their aesthetic manifestation, at the expense of their material's contextual interdependencies – has necessarily been pushed towards an increasing opposition to society. On the other hand, precisely this tendency towards an exclusion of countless people from so-called culture, which is ultimately also the fault of culture itself, which has not been fully realized in people's real lives – this backwardness of people in relation to their own culture has in turn been manipulated and exploited by a separate, indescribably powerful culture whose central and most characteristic form is the cinema, in such a way that this exploitation of backwardness, this exploitation and reproduction of a more or less infantile level of consciousness, may actually have increased the difference between the truly binding spiritual products of our epoch and their reception. In addition, as I have already hinted, there is the educational-sociological factor that the means of mass communication have naturally pulled infinitely more people into the force field of so-called culture, without these people having access to the traditional educational conditions that enabled the so-called educated classes to participate quite readily in advanced artistic production. That was genuinely the case. If one considers, for example, what demands Beethoven's last quartets still make today on the spirituality of their listeners, and if one imagines how small a number of people today are probably at all capable of following such creations with concentration and responsibility, then it is quite amazing to learn that – contrary to the official legend coloured by the culture industry – these five last quartets were extremely successful during Beethoven's lifetime and had to be played again immediately;[2] yet, when people go to listen to them today, it usually takes place out of that fetishism for education which I have already discussed here. I would like to suggest that the phenomenon of semi-literacy, by which I mean people becoming increasingly informed without genuinely experiencing the things about which they are informed, such that one simply learns something about them but has no knowledge of the things themselves – that this phenomenon of semi-literacy is tremendously common today, much the same as a certain type of semi-luxury. So, while the concept of education in the radical sense in which it was not only formulated but also realized in the humanist period is dying out – and there are ever fewer people who are educated in this sense, and something like the vital knowledge of ancient languages, and recently in Germany also French, is dying out – one sees, on the other hand, that the so-called uneducated type of person is likewise dying out; this means that everyone is somehow in the know, and soon there will probably be no more country girls who would not be willing to say of a film which they happened to dislike that it was a film for ordinary Janes. This problem of semi-literacy strikes me as absolutely central for the reception of art today, and for this entire mass of commodities produced by the culture industry, which one also finds in biographical novels; and I think that, if one were to write something like a sociology of art with reference to the reception of works of art, one would have to examine this phenomenon of semi-literacy, the categories of semi-literacy, as it were, far more closely than has hitherto occurred. Perhaps I can especially draw the attention of all educators among you to this problem and encourage you to reflect on it without contenting yourselves in the least with such clichés as those of 'massification'.

It is therefore especially important to point out that the facts outlined here about the subjective stance towards radical modern works of art does not constitute a criterion for them, because there is a very common mechanism that has no doubt met with the approval of some of you too, quite innocently – until the moment I draw your attention to it – namely the fact that the undoubtedly correct identification of the aesthetically, historico-philosophically and also socially predetermined rupture between advanced art and society is now considered the fault of the works of art, and is treated like a form of blasphemy or Fall on the part of art, because artists have moved away from some primal foundations, be they the race, the people, their class or whatever else, and lost themselves in some wayward speculations which so-called healthy public feeling simply cannot follow. The official declarations to this effect, which directly threatened to send the respective artists to concentration camps, or in Russia, as in the case of Meyerhold,[3] to murder them, may no longer be present in the same way, but this way of thinking has certainly survived. And one should say that the mechanisms I have described to you are not to be found in the arbitrariness and failure of aesthetic productive powers, as it were; rather, on the one hand, art – to avoid selling itself, and simultaneously to remain faithful to the demand that it should say what must be said – has been pushed in the direction that causes such animosity today while, on the other hand, the mechanisms that prevent people from experiencing this art at all any more form a social veil which pushes itself between the works of art – those works that are suitable today – and the people themselves. It is a very comfortable mechanism, however, where one simply shifts the blame for not keeping up from society, which is responsible for it, and instead, calling out 'Stop thief!', lays it on the works, thus placing oneself in a regressive situation that ultimately results in one contenting oneself with some staple goods and essentially, through commercial interests in the realm of aesthetic experience, allowing oneself to be cheated of the very thing that aesthetic experience is supposed to provide. I would already be satisfied if I succeeded here in arousing a certain distrust and a certain resistance in you to this mechanism of concealment in aesthetic experience, and indeed the purpose of suggestions such as those I am making to you can only be – as far as a single person can achieve this – to strengthen your resilience, which is under constant threat of being diminished by countless mechanisms, something for which no individual can be blamed. That, if I may speak personally for a moment, is why I occupied myself so thoroughly with the latest book by Georg Lukács, *The Meaning of Contemporary Realism*, and wrote a long polemic against it.[4] Not for the book's absolute meaning, for as a whole – I think I have made that reasonably clear – its level of argumentation is really too low for any fruitful aesthetic dispute to be initiated. What Lukács overlooks, and what is perhaps of interest in this context, is that the alienation of modern art from consumption is itself something social, and that it cannot be revoked through a decision, through mere velleities on the part of the artists. That means he is extremely divided in this, in his stance. When he writes about the dominant practices in the official Soviet manufacture of art, he sees these things very well and expresses them with great courage; but, as long as he remains on theoretical ground, on matters of aesthetic principle, he still parrots the slogans about 'remoteness from the people', 'individualism', and all these things in modern art that people were fed. He did not manage to bring together the experiences he very justifiably had with the so-called artistic production of the Eastern bloc, on the one hand, and his theoretical categories, which he essentially adopted from the ideology of the Eastern bloc, on the other. Above all, he completely missed the fact – if I may just point this out to you – that the state of extreme solitude and the termination of communication, which he criticizes in modern art like a party secretary, is itself an expression of the social situation of a meanwhile radical atomization that, in a sense, is merely the side piece of a collectivization that consists precisely in pressing together something which is essentially a collection of unconnected things, something immediate in the true sense, in such a way that things which are entirely foreign to one another falsely believe they are very close. On the other hand, it is only where this atomized consciousness attains self-consciousness, where it voices itself, that it has a chance to resist the collective violence which actually causes atomization. There are historical situations – and I would think that we are living in such a historical situation today, as we showed in some detail in the *Dialectic of Enlightenment* – in which those ideas aimed at creating a correct society, at giving humans a correct life, are far better served by isolation – however hopeless it currently is – among those who voice or shape it than by a representation of these ideas of solidarity or reconciliation by the collectives which constantly invoke them, yet through their practices – namely, by degrading humans to mere objects – in fact prevent their realization. Here, too, we are ultimately dealing with an aesthetic subjectivism. Lukács would no doubt be enraged to hear this; he would quote the whole of Hegel, on whom he relies, against me and deny any such subjectivism. But I cannot abandon my position, because what he invokes against a reflection on the objective content or objective formedness ultimately remains a contextual interdependence, namely the connection to a possible practice. But the practice to which art is here supposed to refer is none other than that of the people who consume it, which means that this practicism simply makes the receiving subject rather than the matter itself the central authority. So, essentially, the question of the work of art's objective truth is pragmatistically degraded to the question of what a work of art should provide in some political constellations. And that, for its part, is a theory which is quite simply irreconcilable with the fundamentally objectivist stance that Lukács adopts as an aesthetician – that is, the stance that works of art should not simply be subjective declarations but, rather, be shaped objectively in themselves. Just as this aesthetics in general, which for some people has the attraction of a cohesive philosophy, as opposed to that bad, oh-so-uncohesive essayism, damns itself through the fact that it has not really thought through its own conceptual motifs, its theoretical structure, which remains completely arbitrary. If people such as Lukács, or those who fall into his crude trap, claim that, pointedly, modern art takes on a sort of distracting function in relation to the needs of our time because society does not appear in it, then this too strikes me as sophistry. If anything distracts from reality, it is the very diverse types of pseudo-realist creations – be it the heart-warmers that flourish in America and Germany, which seek to convince people that only the human heart matters, or official Soviet state literature, which wants us to believe that socialism has already been realized there, whereas the opposite is true – this kind of so-called realistic literature, whose realism is just as fraudulent and illusory as that of the average film, where every telephone looks exactly as it does in reality, and in which every company's letterhead looks the way a bank's letterhead does, but in which no person is as people really are. So I say that such realism is just as fraudulent as this film realism. It definitely has a distracting function, whereas the shock that comes from advanced works of art and the defamiliarization of the world that they effect can indeed – via whatever mediated routes – turn into practice. It does seem to me, however, that, as soon as art aims directly at practice itself, it immediately manipulates and spoils this relationship, whereas the relationship between practice and the great works of art is a far more mediated one, I would almost say a concealed one. But perhaps we will still have an opportunity to say some more fundamental things about the relationship between art and practice in general in the course of these lectures.

In all these matters, aesthetics is affected by an inadequately considered concept of ideology, namely that concept of ideology which essentially seeks to degrade everything spiritual to a veil, a vehicle of some interests. But instead of criticizing that – as at least occurred in the original conceptions of socialism – instead of defending themselves against it, people even adopt it and assess art according to whether it serves those interests which they personally consider the right ones. In the same way, people have meanwhile stooped to labelling their own theory, which once sought to criticize ideologies, as an 'ideology' itself. But the meaning of the concept of ideology itself cannot [be defined] from without, in terms of how some spiritual constructs, whether works of art or theories, are connected to practical interests; rather, the measure of whether something is ideology or not is ultimately its immanent truth, its content, which it must justify to philosophy. And as soon as one exempts the concept of ideology from the question of truth, as soon as one no longer maintains that ideology is a necessary false consciousness[5] that can be opposed with a correct one, theory in fact degenerates into a bleak relativistic pragmatism and loses all substantiality, which it nonetheless continues to ascribe to itself in opposition to modern decadence.

That brings me to the end of my reflections on the idea of basing an aesthetics on the attitude of the recipient. Let me just say a word about Kant's theory. Regrettably, in these lectures – in which I am trying truly to give you some insight into artistic questions and matters of aesthetic constitution – I cannot give you a history of aesthetic theories and present each in detail, let alone discuss them. But I do at least want to make one point, because my entire deliberations stand in flagrant opposition to the most venerable aesthetic theory – in German tradition, at least – namely that of Kant. For Kant's theory is certainly in agreement with the widespread vulgar understanding, in so far as Kant tried to attribute aesthetics as such to subjective categories, in the form of feelings that arise in the subject and which are now meant to justify the work of art itself. I would like to respond to this as follows: one must first of all make distinctions within the concept of subjectivity itself, and I would think that one needs to make more distinctions than Kant did in his aesthetics. I would go so far as to say that, in the matter of grounding aesthetics in subjectivity and in the formal constituents of consciousness, Kant – if you will forgive my apparent disrespect – fell short of his own approach.[6] The approach of Kant's philosophy in the *Critique of Pure Reason* and the *Critique of Practical Reason* – and these two central

critical works were supposed to be connected to some extent by the
Critique of the Power of Judgement – is that reality is meant to be
constituted through the interplay of sensual givens with forms of
consciousness, whether the so-called forms of intuition or the so-
called categorial forms from which we produce objects.[7] It is obvious,
however, that the analysis of a sphere such as that of art and aesthetic
experience actually takes place in a space which, to use Kantian parlance, is already a constituted space. The works of art that confront
consciousness are not the objects that come about through the interplay between the forms and the contents of intuition in Kant but,
rather, something that already presupposes this constitution. First of
all, they are indeed objectified constructs individuated in space and
time which Kant, following transcendental ideality, referred to as
'empirical reality', which only emerges through the interplay between
transcendental factors and sensual givens in the first place.[8] This is
expressed quite simply in the fact that people do not relate works of
art, in the form in which they normally encounter them, to those
most general of categories, and that they do not come about through
those most general of categories; rather, the works of art are in themselves highly qualified, highly articulated, and – let me add – the
aesthetic subject, namely the subject that, alone, is capable of experiencing works of art in a meaningful way, is likewise a highly organized, concrete subject saturated with historical experiences and
cannot be compared to that general transcendental subject. And I
consider it the true weakness of the *Critique of the Power of Judgement*, and thus of the fundamental philosophical approach of an
aesthetics based on subjectivity, that extremely specific, already constituted categories such as the aesthetic object and the aesthetic
subject seem to be treated here as if they could be directly grounded
in the most general, formally logical subject. But, if you take this
seriously, it has very decisive implications for the question we are
considering here, namely the impossibility of grounding aesthetics in
mere subjectivity, and that is what I really consider the central point
that justifies, or – I must put it like this – forces the objective turn
which I am forced to carry out in the conceptual movements which
I am presenting to you. For, if that is the case, if there is no transcendental relationship of original apperception and constitution between
the object and subject of aesthetic experience, and the two are rather
already part of the constituted world, then the primacy of the subject
over the object comes to an end, since the two aspects produce each
other and have equal status, and – as I hope to show you in the following – the object, for very important reasons, even takes priority
over subjectivity.[9] In my argumentation, then, I am not – as I could

do, believe me – myself dealing with problems of philosophical constitution, though one should also apply a critique of Kant's point of departure to these;[10] rather, my deliberations remain valid even if one fundamentally adopts Kant's idealistic or subjectivist approach.

Let me add that the aesthetic experience which traditional aesthetics claims as its justification is usually described entirely incorrectly and inadequately. Hegel already showed this extremely convincingly in his polemic against Moses Mendelssohn and faith in the so-called beautiful feelings caused by art, a text that is still very much worth reading. Perhaps for now I can simply encourage you to read the corresponding passages in the first part of Hegel's *Aesthetics* for yourselves;[11] I would rather not take up our time with it here. But I think I can say one more thing: aesthetic experience has been described far too primitively, even by the so-called psychologies of art and whatever else one calls them, usually entirely atomistically and not at all in terms of the effect of the work that does justice to the work as a totality which, based on what I have described to you, one can call rational and irrational at once – rational in so far as it is based on a precise, recognitive relationship to the matter, and irrational in so far as the medium of the concept appears in it only in a fragmented form, and the medium of the judgement does not appear at all. If one had to describe the effect that a work of art actually has, one would arrive at a definition so impoverished that it would itself refute the approach based on such a subjective description, but it would at least have the merit of not being quite as untrue as the descriptions that people offer. I am aware of a contamination by dark concepts like the so-called world feeling[12] when I take the risk of telling you that the aggregate of reactions to works of art, the one that could perhaps be considered somewhat suitable, would be that of a world feeling which the work creates, namely the nature of the world in its concrete constitution, not *in abstracto*.[13] If one were seriously carrying out analyses of effects in connection with aesthetic categorical analyses, one would really have to be sure what world feeling was actually being spread by important works of art and would have to try – and this is extremely difficult, almost impossible – to realize this feeling without restricting oneself to individual aspects. A central part of this world feeling, however, is that it does not have the form of a judgement, and even encompasses contradictory elements. Whatever the work of art loses in this world feeling in terms of unambiguity and determinacy, as conveyed to us through the traditional logic of judgement, it gains through a certain concretion and proximity to the essence that is not accessible to the abstracting mechanisms of ordinary judgement.[14]

Let me explain that with a few more concrete statements. I know very well that this is where I am demanding the most of you, which is why I feel compelled, if I am not kind enough to give you bread instead of stones, at least to grind the stones into powders whose consumption will not be too damaging to your health. I mean the following: yesterday I had the opportunity to speak to the outstanding Marburg art historian Usener[15] about Manet, whose pictures I examined very closely again when I was in Paris recently,[16] and there was a surprising agreement between the interpretations by the expert, namely my friend Usener, and the layman, namely myself, that can show you exactly what I mean by the ambiguity of the work of art. Manet's pictures unquestionably contain a certain kind of shock, a certain kind of terror at the reification of the world. What distinguishes Manet from the later impressionists is that he still incorporates the alienated world into a continuum of the sensual apparatus of perception and thus enables it to be reconciled with the subject after all, that he captures it precisely in its foreignness. And the objects he chooses for the purpose, especially the picture of the prostitute as a social type that he certainly portrays in a socio-critical manner – almost like a 'Flower of Evil', like his friend Baudelaire – are extremely revealing of this type of social alienation, which gets as close as possible to people at the same time. But if one wanted, like dear Käthe Kollwitz,[17] to consider someone like Manet a social painter who shows us what comes of vice and absinthe, this would lead to a completely laughable view which utterly missed the depth that lies in the relationship between such an art, with its content, and society; for part of it is that precisely this alienated and threatening element, by getting so close to us, actually develops an attraction. It is only the peculiar unity – of the colours, for example, which express something threatening, frightening and evil through the harshness and sharpness of their contrasts, but are simultaneously experienced very directly as stimulating, as something positive like happiness or exhilaration, only this interplay of negativity on the one hand and the experience of happiness or utopia on the other – this unity of *spleen et idéal*,[18] that alone is what really characterizes Manet. And if one wanted to boil him down to a single judgement – for example that the city has its charms, on the one hand, or, on the other hand, what a bad world we live in, that there are so many fallen women according to the rules of statistics – then any such judgement would not only be wrong but in fact categorically inappropriate to the work of art, whose essence lies precisely in the fact that it knows no such unambiguous judgement but, by creating what I have called a world feeling, at once causes the dialectical intertwining of these elements and sublates, as only great dialectical logic can, that isolation in which each individual judgement of this kind would truly be abstract, limited and narrow-minded; in this sense, art leads beyond the narrow-mindedness of mere isolated elements in much the same way that, aside from art, only the speculative idea truly can.[19] So only if you are capable of understanding what one calls the subjective reaction to works of art in this complexity – where that ghastly, done-to-death word 'multifacetedness' is truly valid for a change, as it conveys its precise meaning – only then do you have any prospects of bringing the subjective aspect to the works through such an analysis. Let me end with this: subject and object – that is, the matter and the viewer – are so closely intertwined in art that it should not be impossible, if one simply throws the whole wealth of objective experience into subjectivity, to learn something about the matter itself from subjective analysis too.

LECTURE 21

12 February 1959

Let us try to take up our threads, meanwhile somewhat tangled, where we left them hanging a week ago. I closed with an attempt to ground aesthetics in the so-called aesthetic experience or the consciousness of the aesthetic observer, and the final motif I introduced was that, in general, defining this so-called aesthetic experience, or defining what one experiences through works of art, is actually something entirely skewed and inadequate because it overlooks the decisive fact that there is really no such thing as determinate, unambiguous reactions, much less unambiguous intellectual judgements, as the conclusion of a work of art. This type of unambiguity, to which we are accustomed from knowledge in the form of judgements – something is or is not the case – is quite simply absent from the sphere of the work of art. Perhaps you recall that I pointed you to the phenomenon of Edouard Manet in order to make this a little clearer, and I tried – admittedly only in the form of propositions, for naturally I cannot develop this adequately in such a theoretically oriented lecture – to show you that, in this work, a critical, a socio-critical aspect, and also an aspect one could describe as the experience of destructiveness or evil, is interwoven in a most peculiar way with a delight at the charms associated with this, and that, even in the form it assumes in Manet, the work of art – as Hegel puts it – does not offer a 'slogan'. One could almost arrive at the heretical notion that the work attempts, in this way, to heal some of what is inflicted on things by the discursive logic that proceeds in concepts and judgements.[1] This means that the world is indeed as complex as the world feeling evoked by a significant work of art. While typical judgements that are for or against something – that say something is so or is not so, and go no further than criticism or a position – in a sense destroy the whole interwovenness of truth and untruth, the interwovenness of what is alive, the work of art, by not arbitrarily separating these aspects and proceeding towards decisions but, rather, by presenting them in their intertwined state, could be said to restore that truth which we lose precisely through the form of the mere judgement.[2] But I think you would be underestimating the epistemic character of works of art or artistic experience if you thought that what I have called – using a phrase whose questionable nature I have already conceded to you, and whose questionable nature I would like to underline again in the strongest terms, and which only gives a small intimation about a very complex issue – if you were to think that what I called a 'world feeling' conveyed by a work were really something entirely vague and undefined. For the world feeling which we gain in artistic experience contains, precisely in that multifacetedness which I attempted to elaborate for you in a somewhat determinate fashion, all sorts of extremely concrete aspects. So you would be entirely mistaken if, for example, as people tend to do in vulgar existentialist interpretations of Kafka – yes, there is such a thing as vulgar existentialism! – you thought, if I too may express myself in vulgar terms, that this depicted the general lousiness of the world, as it were, and that these works, even Kafka's, were ultimately only about the general uncertainty surrounding the heroes of these novels and this general *non liquet*[3] and *non sequitur* which the plots of these works of art repeatedly encounter. Rather, these works contain an infinite number of entirely determinate aspects – be it the sphere of law firms or the sphere of sadism, which plays so infinitely large a part in Kafka's œuvre, or be it a very specific connection to the question of guilt and the guilt context of myth. All of these aspects are evident in Kafka's work in the most unambiguous and emphatic form, and you will only understand it at all if you also note the unambiguity with which these individual motifs appear in his writing. But you must not treat that as the conclusion – and this strikes me as the fundamental error of vulgar existentialism when it addresses these matters – and say, 'Such-and-such reveals itself here'; or, as some also say, 'This or that corresponds to Kafka's world picture or "worldview".' For you, perhaps, the disgusting and repulsive nature of terms such as 'worldview' or 'world picture' already denounces the thing which such atrocious words usually stand for. And the synthesis of these aspects that Kafka brings about is indeed not one which tells us 'That is so'; it does not result in a conclusion, a slogan, a judgement, but rather the judgementless and, if you will, ambiguous intertwining of these aspects that really permits the work of art to incorporate that very wealth of the existent which is otherwise cut off by the logic of judgement.

I have drawn your attention several times to the very profound connection between great speculative philosophy and the approach of art, and God knows I did not intend to suggest with this analogy that – as the vulgar historiography of philosophy claims – Schelling or Hegel erected 'works of intellectual art' [*Gedankenkunstwerke*], meaning self-sufficient products of thought in which there is no longer any real connection to the matter itself. That, of course, is the kind of nonsense that can only be formulated from a position of ossified scientism. One can say nonetheless, however, that there is a far more profound relationship between the character of Hegelian logic and the idea of art, in so far as this Hegelian logic essentially strives for a very similar interweaving of aspects without reducing them to a single slogan, some ready-made judgement or a conclusion or, as some so aptly put it, by 'targeting' an idea, but rather by seeking the idea precisely in the totality of these aspects. So, in this sense, the concept of the idea, which idealistic philosophy in particular associated with art in countless ways, is in fact highly unsuited to the true nature of art. The world feeling that I have mentioned to you is extremely internally articulated. Let me also add that it is itself historical. The world feeling created by Kafka's novels, for example – if I could just insist on this for a moment – is not, as Lukács has insinuated,[4] a feeling of the so-called human condition, a feeling of our God-forsaken, thrown, fear-distorted existence itself; rather, it is a thoroughly modern feeling, a feeling that concerns and reproduces the current state of the world as an experience of its essence, not its façade. Related to this is Kafka's highly peculiar method of giving his novels a certain outdated, obsolete, squalid quality precisely in order to put into relief this historical experience which they strive to incorporate; in a sense it is the obverse, the negative that truly reveals the seeming positive of modern, streamlined high or late capitalist society. And what one could call the determinacy of the work of art as a whole, as opposed to the determinacy of the individual aspects which I have mentioned to you, is the fact that these individual aspects enter a particular kind of synthesis, yet not simply the kind that is familiar from simple cognitive acts – that is, in the synthesis of the judgement with predicate, subject and copula – but rather in a synthesis that connects these different layers and different aspects, placing them in a context by means of the formal law that is native to the work.[5] But this formal law – let me say this too – is not external to the work. Croce showed this with the greatest emphasis, and in the most convincing fashion.[6] So this synthesis does not involve the individual aspects of such a work of art being subsumed under a form which comes to these individual aspects as a finished, already moulded and binding form; this kind of subsumptive synthesis in art is an external synthesis, and a synthesis one can indeed only call inferior. Rather, the essence is that this synthesis itself results from the actual relationship between the individual aspects, while on the other hand these individual aspects are themselves determined by the whole in such a way that, essentially, for example in the first sentence of a good novel, perhaps not every subsequent word, but at least the tendency, the construction of the whole must already be more or less laid out. And naturally that applies all the more to poetry. I think it is also true of painting. That it applies to music – I think I have already tried to show you that. What one could perhaps define as the content of the work of art, if you will grant me the luxury of definition just this once, would perhaps be the way in which this synthesis – this process of the work's aspects in their relationship with one another, which is at once the result of the whole – the way in which this synthesis relates to reality. It would perhaps make sense to call this relationship – this quotient, I am almost inclined to say in positivist fashion – between the living formal law of a work and the reality to which it refers, however mediatedly, the content of the work of art; this would be something different not only from its material content but also from the so-called ideational content, or even the so-called message that, according to vulgar superstition, is conveyed by the work of art.[7]

That brings me to the end of the critique which I have attempted to offer you of any effort to ground the work of art in subjective experience; the function of the last things I mentioned within the construction of the whole is this: the basic error in the common view of a subjective grounding of the work of art in the recipient is that this experience is described too breathlessly, either as if it were concerned only with individual aspects such as sensual stimuli or as if the whole, the idea, were directly and tangibly given, whereas this whole is given only in a mediated form, namely through the aspects, the process and the configuration of aspects from which this whole then grows. Before I continue, however, I cannot refrain from reading you a passage from Hegel concerning this point we have discussed, in which Hegel addresses in the most succinct manner – and entirely

convincingly both in his time and today, I would say – the question
of one's reaction to the work of art – that is to say, the question of
artistic experience: 'If we ask further wherein artistic enthusiasm
consists, it is nothing but being completely filled with the matter,
being entirely present in the matter, and not resting until the matter
has been stamped and polished into artistic shape.'[8] This really takes
us back to the starting point of this reflection, namely that, in order
to describe something like artistic experience at all, to offer something
like a phenomenology of artistic experience, one must always have a
concept of the work of art itself and its objectivity, and that, without
this, it is impossible to access the work itself via the merely psychological aspects of a description of the work. What Hegel says here is
incredibly simple but stands at once – and, please, do not underestimate this – in stark opposition to all the habits which conventional
bourgeois artistic education seeks to instil in us. And I would already
be quite content if I succeeded with my specific analyses in making
this statement by Hegel so evident to you that it genuinely takes on
a certain binding meaning for your own aesthetic experience: that the
subjective feelings which normally form the starting point for homespun vulgar aesthetics – and the more homespun the aesthetics, the
more it likes, as we know, to invoke the authority of the subject –
essentially always miss the mark with the only thing that matters,
namely the connection to the work of art itself, and that whatever
one can describe as 'aesthetic enthusiasm' is quite simply the fulfilled
relationship with the matter itself, that in artistic matters there is
really no other enthusiasm except enthusiasm at being entirely in the
matter – that one dissolves in the matter, I would almost say. This is
the notion that I conveyed to you using that older aphorism of mine
in which I describe the man who knows something about art as a
native who knows his way around a city, while only the amateur
constantly says 'How beautiful, how beautiful, how beautiful!'[9]
True aesthetic enthusiasm, Platonic ἐνθουσιασμός in art, would
probably consist precisely in this 'How beautiful, how beautiful, how
beautiful' being fulfilled and dissolving in the intuitive observation of
the matter itself.

You could now say that, with these reflections, which branched
out in many directions and more or less explained a thesis but at
once treated this thesis as a point of crystallization for all sorts of
things that were said for their own sake – that I made things a
little too easy for myself by restricting myself to a vague, indeterminate and random receiving subject, which surely cannot be used
as grounds for any artistic judgement. For there is a different subjectivity that one can follow, and which is far more binding by

comparison: the subjectivity of the creator, the subjectivity of the artist. I am not sure if many of you would share this view. I would almost assume that it has become a little obsolete today through the spirit of our time, for the cult of the artist and the cult of genius are connected to the belief in the unfettered individual that exists for itself, which was in turn based on very specific social preconditions in the world of late liberalism.[10] In the current world, in which this genius of the Nietzschean type has been more or less replaced by the employee, the image of the artist in this emphatic and pathos-laden sense has paled somewhat, and people will consequently no longer refer to it so much. But I suspect that, in the individual humanities, where Dilthey is still an important name and in which the Dilthey school exercises a very significant influence, more of this reduction of art to the so-called personality of the creator has survived than one would generally assume. By this I mean the notion that, simply put, one understands works if one can reduce them to the experiences by the artist which manifest themselves in them. Let me say in advance that, if one views all of this from a historico-philosophical perspective, it is not entirely invalid. For next to late feudal and absolutist art, which had simply moved away from the living experiential content of the subject and assumed, one might say, a ritualistic objective, an alienatedly objective character, this appeal to the experience was something indescribably new. You need only compare some of Goethe's great youthful poetry, for example 'Über allen Gipfeln ist Ruh',[11] to his Leipzig Anacreontics, and you need only compare this tinge, this violin note one finds there, with this late rococo to see that what was known in the late nineteenth and early twentieth century as the experience [Erlebnis][12] truly introduced here something utterly new and decisive into art – and something, I may perhaps add, that art cannot lose if it is to escape the threat that is probably as constant as that of randomness, namely a regression to Alexandrinism. But that is not what concerns us. For us, the central matter is the epistemological-aesthetic question of whether the work of art is to be understood through the subject of the artist – and even through a so-called understanding, analytic psychology that is directed at the artist; whether, that is, you will know more about Hölderlin or Novalis if you have actually read something like the Novalis or Hölderlin chapters from Dilthey's Poetry and Experience. I don't know if you have all read this book. As many of you want to become teachers, you have probably not been spared it. But, on the other hand, I would like you to consider, if you look at that today, for example where he writes that Hölderlin wraps language around his shoulders like a purple cloak,[13] whether it really helped you a great deal in reaching a better understanding of Hölderlin. I am not saying that to mock the late Dilthey at all; I simply wish to point out something that concerns this entire approach, namely that, if one tries to understand a work of art with reference to its creator, one is on extremely shaky, problematic ground from the outset. This is first of all because it is very difficult to reach any conclusions about the psychology of people who are no longer alive. I can only describe the psychology employed by Dilthey and the human science school as run-of-the-mill psychology. That is, it is a psychology that works with concepts such as 'objective type' or 'subjective type' or similar categories without immersing itself in any specifics – and above all without touching on the driving force, the problematic, dark foundation.

In contrast, this has been attempted by psychoanalysis, whose school has likewise produced a number of seemingly aesthetic reflections, for example Freud's study on Leonardo da Vinci or Laforgue's study on Baudelaire.[14] This psychology is certainly better, deeper and less conformist than the kind of psychology used by the Dilthey school. Yet, although I know that I am greatly indebted to psychoanalysis for its role in my own intellectual development, I feel compelled to say that, while this theory comes closer to the inner lives of artists, it is more capable of decoding works of art as documents of inner life, and it remains no less foreign to the essence of the works of art than the somewhat generalized, common-sense psychological observations usually made by Dilthey. In the work on Baudelaire, for example, you will find Baudelaire's psychology explained largely with reference to his conflict with his mother; in psychoanalytical fashion, he is then presented as a highly neurotic person who simply never overcame this conflict. This book – and I am not making this up – genuinely contains passages which more or less suggest that, if Baudelaire had only had a proper relationship with reality and lost these neurotic love–hate feelings towards his mother, he would have become a perfectly acceptable and normal individual. The question of what would then have become of *The Flowers of Evil* is not even raised in such psychology. The fact that the only thing that matters, namely the quality and dignity of the work of art itself, does not appear at all in such psychology – especially when it is striving quite earnestly to understand the psychology of the artist – speaks directly against the method. One could almost say that, the better the psychology study of an artist is, the less capable it is of providing access to the work itself, for there is something in the work itself that goes beyond psychology, something that is more than psychology. As long as works of art are no more than the fingerprints of psychological individuals, they remain pre-artistic; then they are documents, but not works of art, and in that sense, from a higher perspective, they are irrelevant to aesthetics. And then it must even be said that, thanks to the old fire of constructive philosophy, which continues to burn a little in Dilthey's school, albeit in a very tempered form, it does actually preserve more – of the works themselves, at least – than this psychological procedure.

The category of empathy – that is, the notion that one can understand a work of art by somehow identifying with the artist and putting oneself in their position – is something extremely problematic precisely because it is impossible for one person to empathize with another to such a degree that one can produce the work once again through them. The idea of empathy does have one element of truth, namely that to understand a work of art does indeed, in a certain sense, mean reproducing it – re-enacting for one's own part the process of production that lies within the matter itself, if you will – just as any good actor or any musician with interpretive skill, if they have the task of presenting a work, must, in a sense, personally bring forth this work again in its logicity, in the consistency and necessity and momentum of its elements. But the respective canon that applies to them comprises the texts of the works as given to the performer, not some mediated processes of psychological empathy with the creators who produced the art. Art cannot be grasped through empathy because what makes it art in the first place is that which exceeds what the subject has merely placed into it, that which also goes beyond the randomness of the individual artists.

What probably gives the work of art its binding character, that element which makes the work of art more than merely a random utterance, is the fact that a spirit has been objectified in it, that it is a genuinely objectified spirit, not the mere reflection of a subjective content that expresses itself within it; rather, if something speaks from the work, if the work truly speaks, this speaking quality is precisely that spirit which is objectified in it. One can say – and perhaps it is not immodest to point out that I can confirm this from some of my own artistic experience – that the work of art belongs to the creating subject infinitely less than the consensus would have it; for the more objectified and concretized bourgeois society is, the more it insists that works of art come flying purely to the subject. On the one hand, this expresses a sort of triumph of the concept of property – the work of art is the absolute property of its creator – but, on the other hand, this also maintains the work as the nature reserve of whose notion I have already tried to warn you in various ways. Perhaps one can say that the spirit which speaks from the work of art, once that spirit is truly objectified, is always both the spirit of society and the spirit of a critique of society, but that the dignity of the work depends on how far this sedimented society contained in the work goes beyond the contingency of the individual elements which merely communicate themselves through it.[15]

Let me say a word about the concept of artistic production, which was truly compromised – most of all through the trash novels of Stefan Zweig, Emil Ludwig[16] and all their successors, some adept and some dim-witted – in the most ignominious way because the notion of the creative, which is at home only in theology, but with which humans feel they cannot dispense lest they lose all self-respect, has now been projected onto artists, and people thus imagine that artistic production is something like a *creatio ex nihilo*. This is indeed – I can only return to my old example – a notion that can at most be shared by operetta composers but will quite certainly never be confirmed by any artist or by observing a truly artistic production process. Essentially, producing always means going through something which, as soon as one places it outside oneself by – as people call it – creating it, already faces us as something with objective demands. And what has been referred to as creative agony, for example in the context of art theory and Flaubert's life story – the thing which makes the artistic process in general something so painful and tormenting for countless people – is not so much the birth pangs of the absolute creative process, which is a very superficial view, as the indescribable effort resulting from the fact that the creative process always requires following an objectivity that faces us as if it were already there – and as if it were placing very specific, unalterable demands on us even before it appears. So this means acting in accordance with a law that is not present for us as such, yet nonetheless possesses to the highest degree that character of coercion which, according to Kant, the law always has.[17] Any self-aware artist knows the extent to which they obey. And the decision that must inescapably be made in every process of artistic production – at least today, when there is no longer a fixed canon that is dictated from without – is whether something is right or wrong. Does this thing here have to be so, or should it be different? This uninterrupted process taking place in today's artistic production is really nothing but a way of checking the work against such an imaginary objective element that is not there but which truly influences every moment of production like a magnetic field and demands that we do it in this way and no other, assuming we do not lose our patience and our strength and throw in the towel, or throw the fountain pen onto the piano. Richard Wagner already recorded a little of this in a line from *Die Meistersinger*, where Walther von Stolzing asks, 'How do I begin according to the rule?' Wagner's response: 'You make it yourself, and then you follow it.'[18] This contains the truth that a rule imposed from the outside is not binding. In the current situation of art, however, even Wagner's very profound thought of the self-imposed rule is too harmless. For nowadays, we can no longer even make a rule ourselves if we are to avoid creating a form of automatism, something arbitrary, through the imposed nature of that rule. Rather, we must obey a rule that we could not even make for ourselves – much less have objectively dictated to us – but which rather lies in the matter. We must listen to our own counterpoints, as it were, look at our own colours, observe our own words and follow our own words if we are to produce anything resembling valid or binding works of art at all, and the act of freedom, of drawing freely on what lies within us to create, is of infinitesimal significance by comparison. Please do not misunderstand: there are artists whose temperaments are such that the inhibiting mechanisms I have described – and which I certainly consider highly characteristic of the current objective situation – are absent. There are very many great artists with an incredibly easy hand. Picasso is probably the most extraordinary example, but Schoenberg too worked at amazing speed during his most productive period, though he subsequently rested in very long creative hiatuses and left countless works half-completed because he suddenly lost interest and was unable to finish them. These things are very, very complex today. But I would say that, even in an output such as Picasso's, these aspects can naturally be found objectively everywhere in the fact that he follows something which presents itself to him and wants its aspects to be one way and not another and that, next to this, the so-called free act of creation – 'I want it like this, and that is exactly how it shall be' – retreats entirely. Perhaps – let me just point this out – this is the place to recall a theory that is admittedly very one-sided and crudely ontological, if you will, that constitutes a crude autonomization and hypostatization of aesthetic forms, but which shows a profound knowledge of this aspect I am describing to you, namely the theory of the music aesthetician Halm,[19] who is now almost forgotten. He said that forms such as the sonata or the fugue are indeed products of objective spirit which face the artist as entirely independent factors, and that, in a sense, Bach did not create or invent the fugue but was simply the composer who was adequate to the latent potential of an objective form such as the

fugue. There is certainly some truth in this. If one compares
Bach's fugues with all those that came before and after him, one
truly has the feeling with him of an absolute authenticity of
this form to a degree unmatched by anyone else. Yet, for that objectivity to come about, for that objective spirit to realize itself, one
requires precisely the full force of the subject – which is admittedly
not something that freely posits elements as it likes, but which lies in
the way it dissolves in this latent, non-existent objectivity and,
through this dissolution, turns the non-existent, concealed form into
a visible one.[20]

ADORNO'S NOTES FOR
THE LECTURES

Lecture 1

Problematics of aesthetics. (Refer to Frenzel)

No secure basis as in logic.

Not even continuity of thought as in metaphysics and epistemology.
The consensus of the arbitrariness of judgements of taste, which seems to rule out theory.
but behind that already these questions:

    <u>are</u> judgements of taste arbitrary
    why, in what framework

aesth. principles ask for i.e. <u>require</u> aesth. theory
Further reasons:

    Art as nature reserve for the irrational, meant to rule out reflection.
Answer: the irrationality of a matter does not rule out reflection on it. But it is not really so irrational.
    The supposed randomness of artistic talent.

Its problematics. Talent not an absolute category. Question of jurisdiction.

11 Nov. 1958

a) Dependence on philosophy
   Kant's and Hegel's definitions
b) Impossibility of aesthetics from
   above, insufficiency. Croce.

The operetta composer. –
Theory does not replace
the work. X II. XI

Difference between the outside contemplator and the expert: nothing in the middle.

Through the extremes.
The inartistic and backward nature of official aesthetics (e.g. Volkelt) ^

> The reactionary function of
> supposedly eternal principles

In contrast, basic conception of art as 'appearance of truth'.
Works of art require theory as the medium of their unfolding.
Do not capitulate, do not dogmatize.

Model observations for aesthetic theory, not system, but treatment of a few central categories. – I am not offering any methodology. Method from the matter, not abstract. Refer to 'Darmstädter Beiträge zur neuen Musik'.

Aesthetics as the theory of ~~artistic~~ beauty.
~~Concept of~~ ~~intuition involved here~~: its dignity ~~never an authority.~~

Relationship with _natural_ beauty. In decline since Kant.

Reason: spiritualization of beauty in contrast to the sensually pleasing, which is formal.

Hegel's critique, the indeterminate.
Do not concentrate on it, his theory of natural beauty is still completely absent.
But would be substantial, suppressed, something lies buried there. 'Dignity', the glorification of the human being. Precisely that is problematic.

13.XI.58

2

Hegel confused the fleeting, elusive nature of natural beauty with its abstractness.

Notes on the concept of natural beauty.   Aura

Whoever is unable to perceive natural beauty will not gain any access to art.   This much is true about imitation.

1) Model character for artistic beauty.   Appearance of something objectively meaningful.

Experience: the evening is melancholy, as objective, not

Art ends here. 'Über

a mere mood, is the model for all artistic experience. allen Gipfeln'.

Art, as the opposite of nature, is mediated by it and refers to it,

does justice to what is suppressed, art theory really inseparable from

nature   not merely formal-mathematic

2) Natural beauty also historical, mediated by art. No

absolute opposition between φύσει and θέσει

Alps and sea. La mer est plus belle que les cathédrales.

Renewed experience of the 'cultivated' character of natural beauty through the bombs.

3) substantial experiences of art also influence natural beauty

124-25

Kant's theory of the sublime limited to nature (quote).

This is precisely the anticipation of the new, subjectively contentual

art.

4) 'disinterested pleasure'. Something ceded. Originally greatest interest i.e. desire, this then negated and sublimated.

The validity of that desire. Sexus.   The power of desire evident precisely in the taboo on it.

Yet not definitive, but rather precarious, always threatening again, *naturam*

Longing as the relationship with all beauty: its painfulness.

expellas furca.

Deepest reason: the supremacy of the real over art. Salvation.

the element of nature, which in art is more than art, is what makes it art.   Its pure autarchy sublates art itself.

the inextinguishable nature of sensual happiness.

Sublated in its negation, in dissonance.   this always the pain of a pleasure.

Lenzes Gebet, die süße Not

Art itself as nature's behaviour qua something older that has given way to rationality.

5) Art as mimesis = bringing to bear what is suppressed by control over

Captured in art at the expense of real intervention –

nature.

here to the theory of imitation: the reified, rational form of mimesis.

Art as an imitation, but not of anything.

3

Dialectical relationship between art and nature:

Opposition: Art/world again, separate.

Also play. But not actively

'freed from the lie of being real'.

Secularized sacred sphere.

Hence sensitivity towards the tendency.

A shadow in the 'once again': control over nature.

Identity: art looks after the <u>interest</u> of nature precisely through this opposition, of what is suppressed in the name of the reality principle. It is nature in the alienated world,

'expression'.

as its self-alienated form.

This relationship between art and nature not statically settled once and for all through the constitution of the art sphere. Returns at all levels.

Art, through technology, has a share in the control over nature and is thus part of the overall tendency.

Aspect of enlightenment, de-mythologization, breaking the spell.

In this, it participates in <u>progress</u>, irreversibly. Irretrievability of the obsolete. – Marx and Jochmann, the precarious

But always also has the other aspect, that of an <u>objection</u> to mere domination, of utopia. – appears today in the form of the problem of expression and construction. – On dialectic: expression, as a nature reserve, can precisely prevent utopia. Construction can turn [into expression].

The dignity of works of art depends substantially on whether, and how deeply, these two aspects interpenetrate.   The relationship between φύσει and θέσει dialectical as a whole.

X insert. p. 5.

Lecture 2 (13 November 58)

Try to outline the position using the concept of beauty.

Resist equating art with beauty.

Dialectic knows an aesthetic of ugliness.

Art is not the sensually pleasurable.   Main argument against aesth. subjectivism

X insert p. 8

Refer to the implicit problem of its intuitiveness.

The substantially spiritual character of art is not a construction of speculative aesthetics but rather its basic experience.

Hille Bobbe[1] is not the shattered form, dissonance is not Cage.Qualit.

Has grown stronger.^ Kandinsky. The allergy to beauty   leap

Things become more problematic with this increase: the spirit sought as such is no longer binding. Colour symbolism qua the pleasurable as a function of the polarization towards art and communication.

4

The pleasurable itself has a historical status, it changes.
Colour contrasts (Manet), sounds that were abominated can become sensually beautiful (Pierrot, Lulu). Impressionism becomes sweet.

Critique of the distinction between the sensual and the spiritual work of art.

But: Aesthetics without beauty = psychology without soul, sociology without

against the squeamishness that fears   Admittedly depends on the purpose. Precisely if one

hurting itself with society. –   takes art entirely objectively, no longer as for us, it

fixed concepts / positivism and modernity   can truly cast off the concept of beauty.

Aesthetics then merely a factual report, abdication of

Without beauty =   theory, and thus despiritualization.

what for then?   any more

not a final thing;   Not a terminus ad quem^, mere existence (but maybe

being self-   no terminus ad quem is needed!)

sufficient.

Truth.   On the statement 'Art should be true'.   Its ambiguity   (nat.,

If art is 'true' then not directly so, but through its content,   psychol.)

The concept of   means the anti-ornamental, the logic of the matter itself. Materialistic element.

truth, taken in   which is not a finished thing, for its exterior constitutes

isolation, falls   The idea of beauty inheres

short of art.   itself only through the works.   in this mediation.

Its content is
true and it con-
stitutes itself by
the formal law
i.e. as beauty.

further [?] critique of correctness, not literal.
Otherwise contamination of art and science (Zola etc.),

Instruction for scientific elucidation.
Changes into piling up information (music!)

Task:

Hold on to the idea of beauty, though not as an ontological category but rather as something in motion.

Beauty as totality? Still too simple and static.
against holism (Wellek)

Beauty as a process. Reconciliation and contradiction as a unity.
Category of obligation in the work of art.
The logic of immanence. ~~The prob~~ [?]
Concept of homeostasis, the balance of tension.   Art must
                                    Problem behind this: ∨ expose
                                    and transcend contradiction

Its problematics: not final.
Supply theory of the end of 'criteria'.
Possibility of beauty as an abrogation of the idea of authenticity.
Hence the fragmentation of new art. The allegorical
aspect. Against Lukács. The 'shattered'.

Transition: where I spoke of artistic experience, this was tacitly measured according to the ideal of adequacy. That is, from the perspective of objectivity, not the subject. This, which goes against almost all aesthetics, requires justification

(turn over)

Aesthetic subjectivism is well suited to traditional philosophy because of its unity of justification, the independence from the randomness of the object. It places itself in opposition to the usual concept of theory.

On the basics, refer to the introduction to Against Epistemology and 'The Essay as Form'.   – Also: the subject that belongs to art is not a transcendental but rather a full one, and thus random in the traditional philosophical sense.

The opposite path here: that grounding in subjectivity is insufficient for the matter.   Hegel 38 against

The most drastic argument is the randomness of reaction.   Taste.   X insert p. 13 From the subject's perspective, the work of art is a 'stimulus'; there is no law governing the relationship between the reaction and the matter, though naturally they are connected.

Evidence:

1) the case of the Missa Solemnis. Respect for education instead of the matter, which is not understood. Consumption of prestige, commodity fetishism; hence references to the subject are particularly problematic today.

2) the emotional side: the young Englishman who had to cry at <u>all</u> music (good or bad).

> NB the experience of art demands a certain rationality. To experience art means to recognize it.

3) modern art cannot be grasped through the defensive reactions to it, although they are at least more informative than an indifferent acceptance of everything.

Hence the turn towards the <u>object</u>.

Justification continue p. 7 below – 8

Insertion before p. 3

5

The Platonic doctrine of beauty from the *Phaedrus*.

~~Motif~~ of <u>madness</u> = suspension of the reality principle.

1) XXX. Beauty as a form of madness (p. 63). Conditionality as a precondition of beauty.
    (connected to the sensual).

  Beauty not defined but by its effect: madness = the

start by saying that the 'dogmatic'
palinode gathers together everything that later
    characterizes the phil. of beauty.

Instead of definition, status of beauty in the world of forms. | Starting from erotic beauty: no
alienation from empirical reality. | radical break with nature.
Therein potentially already lies the <u>subjectivism</u> of idealism. But also the opposite, the
The aspect of <u>danger</u> in beauty: the unfathomable rather than the harmonious. [?][2]
    Suffering because of the shell. Beauty and: the body as a prison.

2) XXXI. (64) Beauty as a sensually observable idea.
  This contains both the aspect of intuition and the spiritual.
  The sensual is more than sensual.
  Disinterested pleasure as the result of a <u>process</u>:
  that of 'initiation'. Regarding this, art as a secularized magical
  realm.

The beautiful as the image of beauty (mimesis)

a) its objectivity. (Idea). Image not of an object but of the whole: precisely this is mimetic.

b) beauty as pain (Wedekind, Lulu) Stifter: Heinrich who does not recognize his beloved.

Therefore against 'health'.
Longing as the longing for the absolute: utopia.
The soul's rising up: feathers. – against terre à terre.

3) XXXII. (66) The growth of feathers as an itch.
'Unease'.

Unity of pleasure and displeasure.   67 ~~Suffering as its cure~~

Kant's trembling.   C. o. P. J. 120[3]

viewed objectively: all beauty is itself a process.

From this the theoretical conclusion: work of art as a force field.

Against the notion of the mere being of the work of art.
The basis of this suffering is its cure. (67)

6

on 4 December 1958

Current manifestation of the dialectic of nature and art in art

The relationship between expression and construction.
Proceed from the most modern: develop contrast to the philo-logical view.

The expressive ideal of expressionism is immediate, as the primacy of nature over the hardened, the reified.
The specific quality here is the documentary character of expression

Difference from *Jugendstil*

undiminished by form, ideal of pure immediacy.

Problems here:
1) impossibility of staying on one point, the pure 'this here' as falling silent.
2) experience of absolute immediacy as semblance, always already mediated, conventional elements in the expressive language of expressionism.
3) the problem of aesthetic contingency, the non-binding

to solve these problems construction, i.e. the domination of the material forms

Necessary because ^ no longer naïve, directly dictated.

Construction means the objectification of the subjective from within itself, without borrowing.

The result of expressionism provides the preconditions for this:

1) the material, released and cleansed of preformations.

with relatively little resistance

construction here largely <u>critique</u> of material i.e. discovery of 'linguistic' elements in the expr. material that are no longer reconcilable with its technical-immanent level.

Connection to Schoenberg.

radical control without inhibitions

2) the freedom of the subject as a freedom of infusion.

5. XII. 58

In addition, allergy to speechlike elements.

Shame at expression (vanity of the mere subject; although it ceased long ago

mimetic taboo: don't get excited!

to be a mere subject, and is rather internally mediated!)

Expression can be reactionary: ideology of humans.

Repression of expression. The mimetic taboo in its latest

Fear of touching on what is forbidden by adaptation to rational society.

form. –   Expression falling short of real-life fear.

Critique of expression thus true and false.

False as direct positivity

of the objective. – True as a problem

Situation: the purified material as a crisis of meaning.   of contingency.

Fetishism of means, tinkering.

Today, no longer the question: how can a meaning be realized

(Romanticism: worldview art. Wagner)

in art^, but rather: how can organized material processes

become meaningful.

[This problem corresponds to that of meaning

today in reality (also against Hegel and Marx)

Experience of the limits of construction.

it is neither totally that, in its pure form, nor does it guarantee a meaning.

Problem of chance.

Complementary contrast to construction.

because never purely out of

the material. Problem of

what is suited to the material,

material is not nature.

9. XII.
58

The individual element against construction, but as something bereft of meaning. Breath. Element of play.

Something entirely consistent always has an element of meaning.

But it <u>remains</u>: the reified form of a construction <u>external</u> to the subject and to expression. This is the historico-philosophical reason for the current loss of tension.

The element of arbitrariness in subjectively posited laws themselves, the problem of nominalism.

Return of expression in the <u>violence</u> of the constructed.

11 Dec. 58.   Problem of aesthetic <u>subjectivism.</u>

Not only the concept of the observing but also the creating subject is inadequate.

on p. 4 a   a) ~~Overall critique of idealism, which must here be presupposed~~

~~as already carried out.~~   Art <u>belongs</u> to the subject – the producing and the receiving – incomparably less than most people assume.

Dialectic: the work faces the artist as objectivity,
and for it to become that,   b) specific; the <u>object</u> is spirit (not <u>only</u> spirit) in the work of art
it requires
the subject   the contingency of <u>reactions</u>

8

The inner laws, the meaningful character of the object.
c) approaches towards an objective theory in the midst of Kantian subjectivism

I 35,

d) Hegel's critique of subjectivism.
e) subjectivism as formalism.

<u>Definition</u> of the aesth. subj.: <u>Kant</u>

The questions posed in the C o J are subjective from the outset 10–11

III Connection to feeling of pleasure and displeasure 53

Satisfaction + representation 54

X
Insert p. 3

Method of immanent critique, thus the thesis of the sensually
pleasing is to be examined subjectively
Sensual stimuli are present (refer back)
but only dispersed, as carriers of a meaning (Lulu).
as soon as they are isolated, they become 'culinary', pre-artistic,
i.e. something literal, bodily outside the specifically aesthetic.

The constitution of the special aesthetic realm is itself, as
an undermining of immediacy, spiritualization.

The culinary is the atomistic, i.e. outside of the aesthetic
formal law. Example: one movement and 'beautiful passages'.

This aspect has always accompanied art qua commodity,
is legitimate where it bursts forth associatively (revue etc.), becomes negative
when it hides behind pseudo-form (Tchaikovsky).

Probably interaction of individual impulse and whole.
But: the whole is the concealed, not the immediate.

9

Therefore, the path of aesthetic experience always leads to the whole.
To experience a work of art one must experience the whole, because it bestows meaning.
Example the interrupting figure in the first movement of the Eroica.
This experience tends <u>away</u> from sensual appearance.
Dialectic: the more adequate the sensual experience of works of art, the more perfect, then the further it moves <u>away</u> from the sensual element.
Following on from this the question of how aesthetic experience actually takes place.   6. I. 59

Problematics of 'enjoyment of art'.

It is far more a being-inside-it, co-enacting, living inside it.
This is the truth content of 'making'.
The more someone knows about art, the more precise the relationship, the less they enjoy it. – The one who enjoys is already the alienated listener, the consumer.   Constitutive: that they notice the <u>wrong</u> things.
The example of the resident.
Admittedly <u>without</u> happiness question of what for: so that the work of art is not for its audience.
Happiness – enjoyment – is not directly one with aesthetic experience but rather mediated: <u>that</u> there is an outside; being removed

from mere existence inheres in the whole, and the more highly the work of art is organized, the more it takes one away from immediacy, the more one is outside. – At the same time, this is what the problematics of art refers to.

Only then can this experience break through in the highest moments through its mediatedness. Then it becomes immediate, but those are not moments of enjoyment but of being overwhelmed, of self-forgetfulness – then the subject collapses in tears, one could say.

These moments are not enjoyment: happiness that one has them.

The anti-hedonistic quality of art is the tendency that the experience of it leads away from the subject.

A number of things follow from this concerning the problem of understanding art.

10

This concept is problematic, because an incomprehensible aspect is essential to art itself. Legacy of the magical.

The more/less one understands art, the more one understands it. 'Making' music =

Understanding a work of art means co-enacting the context of meaning, being inside it. following it, not: guessing what it means.

As in Hegel: what one should think of with a concept: the concept itself.

Show this with reference to the unanswerability [?] of the question from outside, the

Only from within: from

without, art is

defenceless.

inartistic: what art is actually for. Helpless.

8. II. 59

Understanding art is the reflection that returns to the matter, and in so doing changes

hence something mediated

it. Philosophy is therefore a constitutive part of artistic experience.

Commentary and critique are thus forms. continue p. 3

15. I. 59.   On the concept of the spiritual content of art.

Not: whatever ideas, meanings the author put into it.

Misunderstanding of Thomas Mann interpretation

This is, paradoxically, something material compared to the design.

not: the so-called worldview of the work of art.

it is either, as in the Middle Ages, the fundamental precondition, condition of possibility, or something supplementary as in most religious art today.

Rather: the content of the work of art, which is not abstract in relation to it but is constituted through the specific configuration of its hic et nunc.

Tied to the appearance without being limited to it.

Its carrier is the structural context, which one can also call the context of meaning, as the aggregate of phenomena that is more than these, not a pure immediacy.

This context is not simply totality, holistic form, but is internally antagonistic, divided, a force field.

11

The spiritual content would need to be defined both as the result of this process and the latter's own totality.

To experience a work of art, to co-enact it, is _identical_ to becoming aware of this spiritual content.

But this process, the more insistent it is, at once leads necessarily to reflection, it is philosophical. Philosophy is not a trade.

Philosophy of art is not subsumption under rules but the conceptual reconstruction – and thus critique – of the spiritual content.

continue top of p. 4 [xxx].

On the allergy to the sensual aspect:

it is against the _falsely_ sensual, the deception, the surrogate.
what is meant by dissonance is consonance; consonance is unbearable as dissonance.
the sensual aspect of art is its _utopia_ and this does not want to be betrayed to anything provisional.

continue top of p. 4.

20 January 1959

Ehrhardt. (1) not <u>only</u> 'contentual realization of alienation'. No
definition. A central <u>aspect</u> – not the whole. Also the
other aspect, creation of a context of meaning
(2) <u>not</u>: identical sensual materiality that would correspond
to the identity of the individual. For it would be:
   a) precisely <u>not</u> estranged
   b) heteronomous in relation to the formal law.
Relationship to experience <u>mediated</u> by the subject.
Art does not directly provide reality, but in the way that individual
experience <u>fills</u> it and how its elements join to create the formal law.

12

3) Abstraction has a threshold.

There are no abstract forms, for art deals not with <u>natural</u> material but rather with a psychological material.

Refer to Max Ernst, *Jugendstil* ornaments.

Every form in art is sedimented content

Loss of tension, mere ornamentation, decorative art as a <u>danger</u>. Yet does not stem from abstraction as such but

a) from the insufficient power of the relation between the elements within a context of meaning, i.e. an external, mechanistic procedure

b) the derived, clichéd character of experience. Lack of <u>resistance</u>.

Abstraction substantial only where it measures itself against tradition. Worldview art against the compulsion to express.

Recall that the greatest painters such as Picasso and Klee did not <u>completely</u> sever the connection to the object, and certainly not out of moderantism

4) Agreement with E. Precisely this marks the aspect that does <u>not</u> exhaust itself in 'defamiliarization'.

5) difficult to answer, probably depends substantially on technical specialization.

In reality <u>all</u> art demands this, it is simply not explicit in other art.

Pseudo-understanding of the ingrained.

Continue p. 4 with   The content is true, and it constitutes itself as
1) critique of 'truth'   beauty
2) the aggregate of the mediations in question <u>is</u> beauty
3) obligation and homeostasis.
4) their problematics.

3   Concepts of true.
    1) Naturally true
    2) expressively true. (problematic, as the mimetic
       not concrete – itself 'untrue'.
       the actor
    3) correct.
    4) polemical sense
                 5) the mediated truth
                    = content = beautiful.

13

Insert p. 4a. Taste.

1) Hegel passage 38–39.[4]

2) Randomness of reactions

3) the external nature of taste.

'Refined', collector-like, accumulation in the sense of education.

'Aesthete' as the opposite of artistic experience, essentially the idea of not getting hurt.

Taste and decorative art; ties, room painted grey. No connection of the appearing aspects to the inner life of the matter. Significant works of art transcend taste, they provoke.

4) the abstractly <u>one-sided</u> nature of taste formation in the 2nd section of the Hegel.

Beauty precisely <u>not</u> – as taught by subjective aesthetics – a 'simple mediation', but rather complex, i.e. not reducible to a slogan. Refer to my definition as a <u>force field</u>. – Aesthetics must grasp this process, not put beauty in a simple nutshell.

5) Taste quand-même.
Be above taste, not against or beneath it.
goût as the constitutive category for all French art.
But this taste is <u>not</u> that empty object of taste formation.
It is:

(turn over)

13a

a) the aggregate of the accumulated experiences of art, what one can grasp as the specific aspect of <u>culture</u> in art. And this in its <u>sedimented</u>, self-evident form.

Aggregate of historical taboos that one must feel in order to violate them. Example of Brecht and didaxis. – Precisely the ephemerality of taste turns it

into a historical <u>agent</u>.

b) the aggregate of the respectively attained <u>standard</u>, with all its idiosyncrasies.
Whoever does not have this is pre-artistic.
Absolute individual originariness as mere <u>illusion</u>, residue.
The original is only that which arises as something new.
This is guarded by taste.
Evidence the Rousseaus at the Jeu de Paume.

14

29 January 1959

on the insufficiency of subjectivism:

A Experience of art = the recipient.

this cannot be its source of justification, since

1) for them, art is a 'stimulus'.
   but there is no direct relation.

Recall the theorem of specific sensory energy.

Also applies spiritually: the ^ documentedness of aesthetic experience can
be entirely at odds with the matter, completely change it

    subjective

e.g. in Beethoven the taste for the pompous, for ostentation can prove
detrimental to the structure.   The headmaster who loved Wagner as viscous.

If one tries to build an xxxx aesthetics from reactions, the result is
complete nonsense, a majority vote against the
matter.   Americ. experience.

    as people want in US, where no one can

      imagine what objectivity of spirit might be

Nor can this be replaced by *expert opinion*, ^ which is itself questionable:
expert preformed by selection mechanisms

2) The recipients are not, as the subjective theory presupposes, the final source but rather completely predetermined, and the more so the tighter the net has become.
The supposed source of validity for aesthetics in the form of immediacy is thoroughly mediated.

Evidence: a) Missa Solemnis
Authority and popularity of an incomprehensible work.
Education pushes itself in front of the matter
Consumption of prestige, commodity fetishism.
Hence recourse to the subject especially problematic today

b) the irrational relationship with art.

The young Englishman who had to cry at all music (good or bad).

All Affects repressed.

Social function of art largely its receptacle.   Nature reserve.

In art affects are projected.

But this has nothing to do with the actual matter, or only in extreme cases.

29. I. 59
X insert a
p. 17

The experience of art demands a certain rationality.

The synthesis demanded by the work of art.

To experience art means to recognize it.

Aesthetic distance, as discussed earlier, consists precisely in this

c) Modern art cannot be grasped through the defensive reactions to it, although they are more informative than the indifferent acceptance of everything:

   1) Expectations are disappointed, against infantile repetition

   2)

Means: being reminded of suppressed suffering.

Experiencing art =
producing naïveté
= liquidating
false expectations

Paradox: what is channelled *allows* projection, letting affects through. its <u>unspoilt</u> expression in art falls <u>prey</u> to its suppression.

Also: estrangement between the technically and spiritually – both, as advanced matter and the audience

shown – inseparable – ∧ increased.

3. II. 59

Art that is the concern of humans themselves is foreign to them.
Art that is estranged from them, a commodity, and treats them as a commodity, is close to them.

Rancour towards new art of those who have not kept up.

X The more autonomous, faithful to the formal law, the more it eludes consumption.

Especially important to point out that this is <u>no</u> source of justification, as the rupture, for which <u>society</u> (culture industry and continuing heteronomy) is to blame, is taken to be <u>art's</u> <u>fault</u> and the reason for its repression.

Hence polemic against Lukács.

L overlooks that the estrangement of art from consumption is <u>itself</u> something social, and cannot be revoked through a decision.

Also educational-sociological reasons. Semi-literacy

16

Atomization as mediated.

Aesthetic subjectivism as practicism∧.^{in Lukács} Purportedly distracting function.

What distracts is the other thing, not the shock.

The concept of ideology affecting this: but ideology is measured against the matter itself, not the mere context of effects.

Followed by Hegel 387   X insert b, p. 17.

B.   Subjectivism of the creator, 19th cent., genius theory, Poetry and Experience.   Usually just folk psychology

First of all the fundamental inaccessibility of the subjective creator, unrecognizable, shaky ground.↓   Depth psychology alone is insufficient. 'Empathy' eludes all discipline. 'Will of the lawmaker'.

Art is precisely what is more. Art is objectified spirit that speaks itself.

Then: art belongs to the creating subject far less than the consensus would have it. Sedimented society.

Producing means enacting, following what is objectively demanded. Only amateurs believe in a creatio ex nihilo, any self-aware artist

knows the extent to which they obey.   Hans Sachs: you make it yourself and
then you follow it

12. II. 59   The act of freedom is infinitesimal.

Helms's claim. Its truth and untruth. The in-itself of forms always already contains S.

Dialectic: the work faces the artist as potential objectivity, but, in order
to make this actual, the subject is <u>required</u>.

Regarding this, the category of the τόπος.

Sublimated, not vanished.

Webern.

Talent even in the most advanced.

Even the artist's creation is not immediacy.

Mediated by the τόπος. Immediacy <u>becomes</u> through the negation of
logical mediation (Mozart).

X insert c. p. 18

C | In the face of this, what can the objective dialectic of art use to support itself?

The fact that the work of art is spirit, and in this sense subject, open,
similar.

But at once also: concretized, manifested, <u>binding</u> spirit. Central.

ctd. p. 18

17

Insert a

Demand for rationality as opposed to the consensus.

Art is supposed to be purely intuitive, just as woman is assumed to be pure feeling.

Insistence of rational society on the irrational.

This is contradicted by art. Here the difference between the arts asserts itself especially.

1) the conceptual elements of literature (Meyer)

2) material layers of painting

3) above all: the mediated, that which goes beyond mere immediacy

Art confronts with the <u>demand</u> for synthesis, enactment; not mere passivity, which is inartistic.

To experience art means to recognize it.

Therein lies aesth. distance, which sublates emotion.

The emotional is mediated.

But recognition of art is not a reflection <u>external</u> to it, rather <u>in</u> it.

Boundary between reflection and intuition fluid (memory and successive form).

Insert b p. 16

Closing critique of grounding in the recipient

in art
feelings have nothing to do with Kantian
constitutive subjectivity but always already
play in the constitution
here have no
primacy over the
lllobjects

Here experience itself is always described
wrongly – atomistically.
Far more complex, rational and irrational at once

the nature of its concrete constitution
a feeling of world, namely   (not against being)

The same amount of <u>unambiguity</u> it loses here as a <u>judgement</u> is gained
as proximity, concretion of the <u>essence.</u>   example <u>Manet</u>
This feeling not merely subjective but means the whole.
Entirely different syntheses copared to the apophantic forms: Brecht's error.

5. II. 59

18

This feeling at once <u>intrinsically</u> highly determinate.
This determinacy is synthesis under the formal law.
Connection of this synthesis to reality, not a reflection of the latter, is the true content of the work of art.

Insert c p. 16.

No regression to the pre-subjective, courtly-hierarchical.
The subject as an objective ferment: freedom.
in this sense progress.
But this subjective element of the objective is to be determined in objective terms, must not be employed psychologically.
Subjectivity essentially a critical category, becomes false through hypostasis.

12. II. 59 Main text contd.

Barrier: the possibility of enactment.

Dying off of the works.

Archaic = what cannot be enacted.

Becoming uninterpretable.

Threshold changing.

With the acceleration of history, even relatively proximate works can become uninterpretable.

Different in the respective arts: music covers itself up more quickly.

Then attitude the construction and recuperation.

The relationship with the living work is the critical one.

Form–content problem.

The critique of subjectivism contains the critique of formalism.

For content is that which cannot be reduced to the constituents.

19

But that does not mean some crude aesthetics of content, as has become dominant today through an abuse of Hegel's critique of Kant.

1) The objectivity of the work contains S and O.

there is no artistic objectivity that has not gone through the subject.

No O without S, otherwise mere material content.

No S without O.

The <u>form</u> is sedimented content.

the two produce each other reciprocally.

explain using novel form.

contingency of concrete material (pointless life)

Fragmentary form against something made from above.

But neither should one directly equate form and content, as the simplistic phrase goes.

The two are dependent on each other, but also always different from one another, against 'form is content'.

this is precisely what characterizes the force field.

finally content is not substance.

The content is necessary in order to be consumed by the form.

this very process is the substance.

<u>Aesthetics Course</u>   Wint. sem. 1958

Topics.

1) Problematics of the topic and its object
2) Outline my position. (using the concept of beauty)
3) Dialectical critique of aesth. subjectivism.
4) "   "   "   formalism. Proportions

Foreground lines

5) Turn against objectivity: Lukács.
6) Semblance and truth.
7) Subject–object dialectic
8) Immanent laws, obligation
9) Technique and technology
10) Work of art and communication.
11) Commitment, tendency etc.
12) L'art pour l'art.
13) The content of art and society.

Further main topics:
Art and intuition.
Imitation and mimesis
  ugliness (NB
    Rosenkranz

Problem of
aesthetic relativism
(ad /?/ 19–20)

the <u>riddle</u> char<u>a</u>cter of art,
its <u>indirect</u> dissolution
(to-wards the end)
art and the category of
<u>play.</u>

14) ~~Art~~ Problem of progress, rationality & mimesis in art. — Problem of aesth. meaning.

15) Art and the arts, culture, neutraliz. — Dispute over the message.

16) Aesthetic nominalism and forms. — Relationship to technology.

17) Critique of the concept of style, justice and injustice — Transcendence and immanence of art.

18) Classicism, Romanticism, Modernity

19) } form-analytical model. Drama, novel,
20) } sonata, symphony

21) } criteria (elaborate using music)
22) }

23) What art actually is, the mediated definition

24) Inside and outside of works of art

25) On the situation of art today.

Social Function of Art

1) changes historically (Büchner, Hugo)
2) not direct today, as always covered from above
3) function in rejecting function
4) not reflection but essence
5) Critical through shifting of elements, defamiliarization
6) Art does not immediately affect practice, no 'slogan'.
7) Incorporation as a function always state-capitalist/totalitarian. (St Simon)
8) precisely art that functions is ideology

    the concept of

9) what L ascribes to ∧ the human condition has a historical status.
10) idealism is realism is mere semblance
11) Utopia lies in negativity.
12) Art vouches for the fact that society is not everything: precisely this is also a piece of ideology, identity philosophy

EDITOR'S NOTES

Lecture 1

1 See Ivo Frenzel, 'Ästhetik', in *Das Fischer Lexikon*, vol. 11: *Philosophie*, ed. A. Diemer and I. Frenzel (Frankfurt: S. Fischer, 1958), p. 35. In the 'Draft Introduction' to *Aesthetic Theory*, Adorno quotes at length from the entry; see Adorno, *Aesthetic Theory*, trans. Robert Hullot-Kentor (London and New York: Bloomsbury, 2013), p. 439. The publicist Ivo Frenzel (1924–2014) studied philosophy and sociology with Nicolai Hartmann, Helmuth Plessner and others. In his review of *Negative Dialectics* ('Ist Philosophie noch möglich?', *Süddeutsche Zeitung*, 2/3 September 1967), Frenzel praised Adorno's book: it had 'given philosophy a possibility of self-assertion, restored a part of its dignity'.
2 Adorno used the tape transcript of this lecture when preparing later lectures and working on *Aesthetic Theory*. When going over the typescript he marked certain passages, in some cases adding handwritten notes. These traces of revision are indicated in the present notes. Here he marked the text from 'If you' to 'vacuum'.
3 See Immanuel Kant, *Critique of the Power of Judgement*, trans. Paul Guyer and Eric Matthews (Cambridge University Press, 2000), §§2–5 (pp. 90–6).
4 Marked by Adorno from 'Kantian aesthetics' to 'definition of beauty'.
5 G. W. F. Hegel, *Aesthetics: Lectures on Fine Art*, 2 vols, trans. T. M. Knox (Oxford and New York: Oxford University Press, 1998–9).
6 See F. W. J. Schelling, *The Philosophy of Art*, trans. Douglas W. Stott (Minnesota University Press, 1989).
7 See Arthur Schopenhauer, *The World as Will and Representation*, 2 vols, trans. E. F. J. Payne (Mineola, NY: Dover, 1969).

8 The definition of beauty as the 'sensual appearance of the idea', which was central for the reception of Hegel's aesthetics, does not feature in any of the surviving transcripts of Hegel's lectures on aesthetics in Berlin (1820/21, 1823, 1826, 1828/29). It is now assumed that this phrase was not coined by Hegel himself but by his student and editor H. G. Hotho; see the editors' introduction in G. W. F. Hegel, *Philosophie der Kunst: Vorlesung von 1826*, ed. Annemarie Gethmann-Siefert, Jeong-Im Kwon and Karsten Berr (Frankfurt: Suhrkamp, 2005), p. 21. The reference to the respective aesthetics of Hegel, Schelling and Schopenhauer is marked by Adorno in the typescript.

9 See Immanuel Kant, *Critique of Pure Reason*, ed. and trans. Paul Guyer and Allen Wood (Cambridge University Press, 1998), p. 409:

> It can be said that the object of a merely transcendental idea is something of which we have no concept, even though this idea is generated in an entirely necessary way by reason according to its own laws. For in fact no concept of the understanding is possible for an object that is to be adequate to the demand of reason, i.e., an object such as can be shown and made intuitive in a possible experience. But we would express ourselves better and with less danger of misunderstanding if we said that we can have no acquaintance with an object that corresponds to an idea, even though we can have a problematic concept of it.

10 Marked by Adorno from 'only then' to 'as effective'.
11 Marked by Adorno from 'the Hegelian approach' to 'of the absolute'.
12 Marked by Adorno from 'beauty itself' to 'on me'.
13 Marked by Adorno from 'let me begin' to 'the aesthetic'.
14 Marked by Adorno from 'that objectivity' to 'works themselves'.
15 In the preface to his *Phenomenology of Spirit* (1807), Hegel explains the relationship between philosophical knowledge and the 'matter' [*Sache*], the recognition of the latter being the task and challenge of philosophy. Responding to the demand to state in advance the aim and result of his philosophical deliberation, he counters:

> This concern with aim or results, with differentiating and passing judgement on various thinkers is therefore an easier task than it might seem. For instead of getting involved in the matter itself, this kind of activity is always away beyond it; instead of tarrying with it, and losing itself in it, this kind of knowing is forever grasping at something new; it remains essentially preoccupied with itself instead of being preoccupied with the matter and surrendering to it. (Hegel, *Phenomenology of Spirit*, trans. A. V. Miller [Oxford and New York: Oxford University Press, 1977], p. 3 [translation modified])

Adorno reads this as a fundamental methodological demand that he adopts as his own and concretizes in *Negative Dialectics*: 'To yield to the object means to do justice to the object's qualitative aspects' (*Negative Dialectics*, trans. E. B. Ashton [New York: Continuum, 1972], p. 43 [translation modified]).

16 According to Hegel, the 'matter' with which thought must occupy itself, on which it must dwell, is the 'movement of the concept' (*Phenomenology of Spirit*, p. 20). In the preface to *Phenomenology* he describes this movement as a fluidization of an initially still rigid, 'fixed thought':

> Thoughts become fluid when pure thinking, this inner *immediacy*, recognizes itself as an aspect, or when the pure certainty of self abstracts from itself – [...] by giving up the *fixity* of its self-positing, by giving up not only the fixity of the pure concrete, which the 'I' itself is, in contrast with its differentiated content, but also the fixity of the differentiated aspects which, posited in the element of pure thinking, share the unconditioned nature of the 'I'. Through this movement the pure thoughts become *concepts*, and are only now what they are in truth, self-movements, circles, spiritual essences, which is what their substance is. (Ibid. [translation modified])

Adorno takes up this basic Hegelian principle in his study on the *experiential content* of Hegel's philosophy:

> Hence the concept that remains true to its own meaning must change; if it is to follow its own conception, a philosophy that holds the concept to be something more than a mere instrument of the intellect must abandon definition, which might hinder it in doing so. The movement of the concept is not a sophistical manipulation that would insert changing meanings into it from the outside but rather the ever-present consciousness of both the identity of and the inevitable difference between the concept and what it is supposed to express, a consciousness that animates all genuine knowledge. (Adorno, *Hegel: Three Studies*, trans. Shierry Weber Nicholsen [Cambridge, MA: MIT Press, 1993], p. 71)

17 Moritz Geiger (1880–1937), a student of Theodor Lipps, Wilhelm Wundt and Edmund Husserl, was professor of philosophy in Munich (1915–23), where his students included Walter Benjamin, and Göttingen (1923–33). He emigrated to the USA in 1933 and taught at Vassar College, New York, until his death. Geiger became known for his phenomenological investigations into aesthetics (see 'Beiträge zur Phänomenologie des ästhetischen Genusses', *Jahrbuch für Phänomenologie und philosophische Forschung I* [Halle: Max Niemeyer, 1913], pp. 567–684) and epistemological works. Here, Adorno is referring primarily to Geiger's book *Zugänge zur Ästhetik* (Leipzig: Der neue Geist, 1928), which deals with amateurism in artistic experience, the surface and deep effects of art, and phenomenological aesthetics.

18 Johannes Volkelt (1848–1930) was professor of philosophy in Leipzig (1894–1921); after his book *Ästhetik des Tragischen* (Munich: C. H. Beck, 1897), which Adorno mentions here as a deterrent example, he wrote the extensive *System der Ästhetik* (3 vols, Munich: C. H. Beck, 1905–12). Adorno had already examined Volkelt intensively in his first aesthetics lectures of 1931; see *Frankfurter Blätter I*, ed. Rolf Tiedemann (Munich: edition text + kritik, 1992), pp. 39–84.

19 Adolf von Hildebrand (1847–1921) was considered the most important German sculptor from around 1880 until the end of the First World War; in his book *Das Problem der Form in der bildenden Kunst* (Strasbourg: Heitz, 1893) he also addressed aesthetic questions. Reprinted in *Gesammelte Schriften zur Kunst*, ed. Henning Bock (Cologne and Opladen: Westdeutscher Verlag, 1969).

20 Marked by Adorno from 'Nor do I' to 'at the start'.

21 Adorno, *Against Epistemology: A Metacritique*, trans. Willis Domingo (Oxford: Blackwell, 1982).

22 In Adorno, *Notes to Literature*, trans. Samuel Weber and Shierry Weber Nicholsen, vol. 1 (New York: Columbia University Press, 1991), pp. 3–23.

23 This lecture was given in the summer of 1957; published in Theodor W. Adorno, *Sound Figures*, trans. Rodney Livingstone (Stanford University Press, 1999), pp. 145–96. It begins thus:

> The question of criteria by which to judge new music calls for reflection not directly on the criteria themselves, but on the methods needed to discover them, if we are to avoid the standard strategies of resistance. But we can scarcely begin by discussing methods in a fundamental sense. For the methods cannot be separated from the subject and treated as something ready-made and external, but must be produced in the course of a process of interaction with their subject.

24 See Kant, *Critique of the Power of Judgement*, §§18–22.

25 Marked by Adorno from 'the deliberations' to 'taste'.

26 Marked by Adorno from 'It is very peculiar' to 'understood'. See also Adorno, *Aesthetic Theory*, p. 363.

27 Marked by Adorno from 'one can see' to 'aesthetic qualities'.

28 *Parsifal*, by Richard Wagner (1813–1883), was premiered at the Bayreuth Festspielhaus in 1882. See Adorno's essay 'On the Score of *Parsifal*', in Adorno, *Night Music: Essays on Music 1928–1962*, trans. Wieland Hoban (London: Seagull, 2009), pp. 71–80. See also Friedrich Nietzsche, 'The Case of Wagner' and 'Nietzsche Contra Wagner', in *The Anti-Christ, Ecce Homo, Twilight of the Idols and Other Writings*, ed. Aaron Ridley and Judith Norman, trans. Judith Norman (Cambridge University Press, 2005).

29 Marked by Adorno from 'Well, if' to 'my lecture'.

30 Marked by Adorno from 'all these aspects' to 'to do so'.

31 Double marked by Adorno from 'I am not' to 'constitutes in itself'.

32 See Hegel, *Aesthetics*, vol. 2, pp. 1236f.:

> For in art we have to do, not with any agreeable or useful child's play, but with the liberation of the spirit from the contents and forms of finitude, with the presence and reconciliation of the Absolute in what is apparent and visible, with an unfolding of the truth which is not exhausted in natural history but revealed in world history. Art itself is the most beautiful side of that history and it is the best compensation for hard work in the world and the bitter labour for knowledge.

33 Marked by Adorno from 'nothing to do' to 'aesthetic logic'. See Adorno, *Aesthetic Theory*, pp. 187–9.
34 This sentence is marked by Adorno with four lines.
35 The *riddle character* of art is one of the central motifs in Adorno's *Aesthetic Theory*:

> All artworks – and art altogether – are enigmas; since antiquity this has been an irritation to the theory of art. That artworks say something and in the same breath conceal it expresses this riddle character from the perspective of language. This characteristic cavorts clownishly; if one is within the artwork, if one participates in its immanent completion, the riddle character makes itself invisible; if one steps outside of the work, breaking the contract with its immanent context, this riddle character returns like a spirit. (p. 160; translation modified)

Adorno already used the term in 1953, in his essay 'On the Current Relationship Between Philosophy and Music' (in *Night Music*, pp. 426–73), and also in 1956, in the essay 'Music, Language and Composition' (in *Essays on Music*, selected with introduction, commentary, and notes by Richard Leppert, with new translations by Susan H. Gillespie [Berkeley and Los Angeles: University of California Press, 2002], pp. 113–26), where he further develops the ideas presented in that text.
36 Marked by Adorno from 'I believe' to 'naïve awareness'.
37 Marked from 'in this philosophical' to 'something reflected'. Marginal note in Adorno's writing: 'Addition to the main text on reflection'. See Adorno, *Aesthetic Theory*, pp. 16ff., 109f.
38 'Fragen des zeitgenössischen Operntheaters', first published in *Neue Deutsche Hefte*, no. 31, January 1957, pp. 526–35; then in 1966, in a revised version, in the programme book of the Bayreuth Festival for Wieland Wagner's production of *Tannhäuser*; now in *Gesammelte Schriften*, ed. Rolf Tiedemann with Gretel Adorno, Susan Buck-Morss and Klaus Schultz (Frankfurt: Suhrkamp, 1984), vol. 19: *Musikalische Schriften VI*, pp. 481–93.
39 Marked by Adorno from 'contemporary opera theatre' to 'Mozart'.
40 Marked with three lines from 'that I generally' to 'character', and marked with three lines from 'and above all' to 'created them'.
41 See Friedrich Schiller, *On the Naive and Sentimental in Literature* (1795/6), trans. Helen Watanabe-O'Kelly (Manchester: Carcanet New Press, 1981).
42 Marked by Adorno from 'the less' to 'dogma'.
43 Marked by Adorno from 'this naïveté' to 'about him'.

Lecture 2

1 Marked by Adorno from 'The second prejudice' to 'this matter'.
2 Marked by Adorno with three lines from 'This is precisely' to 'mere talent'.

3 The Oxford English Dictionary defines 'velleity' (from Lat. *velle*, 'to wish') as 'a wish or inclination not strong enough to lead to action'.

4 See Plato, *Phaedrus*, trans. Robin Waterfield (Oxford and New York: Oxford University Press, 2002), p. 33 (249d–e); also Adorno, *Aesthetic Theory*, p. 435: 'A final intimation of the rationality in mimesis is imparted by Plato's doctrine of enthusiasm as the precondition of philosophy and emphatic knowledge, which he not only demanded on a theoretical level but demonstrated at the decisive point in the *Phaedrus*.'

5 Marked by Adorno from 'So that is what I mean' to 'bourgeois conventions'.

6 See *Schillers Werke: Neue Prachtausgabe*, 2 vols, with 300 illustrations (Berlin: Pass & Garleb, n.d. [c. 1900]).

7 Marked by Adorno from 'I think' to 'clear to them'.

8 See Adorno's essays on Valéry: 'The Artist as Deputy', in *Notes to Literature*, vol. 1, pp. 98–108, and 'Valéry's Deviations', ibid., pp. 137–73.

9 A strictly work-immanent interpretation was the methodological ideal of the dominant schools of art and literary scholarship in the mid-twentieth century, from American New Criticism (with some recourse to the tradition of Russian formalism) to literary hermeneutics. See John Crowe Ransom, *The New Criticism* (New York: New Directions, 1941), René Wellek and Austin Warren, *Theory of Literature* (New York: Harcourt, Brace, 1949), Wolfgang Kayser, *Das sprachliche Kunstwerk: Einführung in die Literaturwissenschaft* (Bern: Francke, 1948), and Emil Staiger, *Die Kunst der Interpretation* (Zurich: Atlantis, 1955). For Adorno, too, the acknowledgement of the works' self-will is the starting point for any productive engagement with art. He does, however, criticize the absolutization of the de-contextualized individual work, which prevents the strictly immanent critics from understanding what is actually going on in each work. See Adorno, *Aesthetic Theory*, p. 247:

> The monadological constitution of artworks in themselves points beyond itself. If it is made absolute, immanent analysis falls prey to ideology, against which it struggled when it wanted to devote itself to the artworks internally rather than deducing their worldviews. Today it is already evident that immanent analysis, which was once a weapon of experience against philistinism, is being misused as a slogan to hold social reflection at a distance from absolutized art.

10 An allusion to Goethe's poem 'Between Both Worlds' (1820), in Siegfried Unseld, *Goethe and His Publishers*, trans. Kenneth J. Northcott (Chicago and London: Chicago University Press, 1996), p. 52:

> To belong to one alone,
> To venerate one alone,
> How this unites heart and sense!
> Lida! Joy of closest nearness,

William! Star of the most beauteous heights,
What I am I owe to you.
Days and years have passed away,
And yet upon those hours together,
Rest my venerable total profit.

11 On Adorno's understanding of *immanent critique*, see 'Cultural Criticism and Society' (1949), in *Prisms*, trans. Samuel Weber and Shierry Weber (Boston: MIT Press, 1983), p. 32: 'Immanent criticism of intellectual and artistic phenomena seeks to grasp, through the analysis of their form and meaning, the contradiction between their objective idea and their pretension. It names what the consistency or inconsistency of the work itself expresses of the structure of the existent.' The translator decided to render *Kritik* as 'criticism', which reflects the German word's potentially negative connotations more than 'critique' (Trans.).

12 Wilhelm Dilthey (1833–1911) was professor of philosophy first in Basel (1867), then in Kiel (1868) and Breslau (1871), and finally in Berlin (1883–1908); he was the founder of the epistemology of the human sciences and one of the main exponents of the 'historical school' of hermeneutical sciences. In addition to the book mentioned by Adorno, *Das Erlebnis und die Dichtung* (1906) (Eng. trans.: *Poetry and Experience*, ed. Rudolf A. Makkreel and Frithjof Rodi [Princeton University Press, 1985]), Adorno was probably thinking of Dilthey's *Von deutscher Dichtung und Musik* (ed. Hermann Nohl and Georg Misch), a selection from his *Studien zur Geschichte des deutschen Geistes* published in 1933, with a second edition published in 1958.

13 The passage Adorno has in mind is from Dilthey's interpretation of *Empedocles* in *Poetry and Experience*: 'The figures stride and speak in solemn sublimity, as if clothed in the flowing robes of archaic Greek statues' (p. 365).

14 Marked by Adorno from 'namely the experience' to 'really arise'.

15 Marked by Adorno from 'one is now outside' to 'to close up'.

16 Marked by Adorno from 'then the justification' to 'what does it say?'

17 Marked by Adorno from 'this state of experience' to 'authentic one'.

18 Marked by Adorno from 'the works of art themselves' to 'must end'.

19 The discipline label 'aesthetics' was first used by Alexander Gottlieb Baumgarten (1714–1762) in his master's thesis at the University of Halle, entitled *Meditationes philosophicae de nonnullis ad poema pertinentibus* (1735), and systematically developed in his unfinished compendium *Aesthetica* (2 parts, Frankfurt an der Oder, 1750–58). The term 'aesthetics' became especially popular through another, more widely read, compendium, in German – *Anfangsgründe aller schönen Wissenschaften* (3 parts, Halle, 1748–50) – by Baumgarten's former student Georg Friedrich Meier (1719–1777); see also Johann Gotthelf Lindner, *Kurzer Inbegriff der Aesthetik, Redekunst und Dichtkunst* (2 vols, Königsberg and Leipzig, 1771–2).

20 In *Critique of Pure Reason*.
21 Marked by Adorno from 'For the concept of aesthetics' to 'verbal definition'.
22 Double marked by Adorno from 'the absolute validity' to 'literal sense'. He formulates this critique in *Aesthetic Theory*, pp. 129f.
23 Double marked by Adorno from 'If we continue' to 'eighteenth century'. Handwritten annotation at the top of the typescript page: 'Natural beauty'. *Aesthetic Theory* examines natural beauty at length: see pp. 85–106.
24 Marked by Adorno from 'can be arrived at' to 'are sublime'.
25 In the introduction to his *Aesthetics* (p. 2), Hegel argues:

> By adopting this expression ['philosophy of fine art'] we at once exclude the beauty of nature. Such a limitation of our topic may appear to be laid down arbitrarily, on the principle that every science has authority to demarcate its scope at will. But this is not the sense in which we should take the limitation of aesthetics to the beauty of art. In ordinary life we are of course accustomed to speak of a beautiful colour, a beautiful sky, a beautiful river; likewise of beautiful flowers, beautiful animals, and even more of beautiful people. We will not here enter upon the controversy about how far the attribute of beauty is justifiably ascribed to these and the like, and how far, in general, natural beauty may be put alongside the beauty of art. But we may assert against this view, even at this state, that the beauty of art is *higher* than nature. The beauty of art is beauty *born of the spirit and born again*, and the higher the spirit and its productions stand above nature and its phenomena, the higher too is the beauty of art above that of nature.

26 Marked by Adorno from 'At the same time' to 'inadequate form'.
27 This statement is marked with three lines.
28 Hegel, *Aesthetics*, vol. 1, p. 123. This and subsequent Hegel quotations are marked in the typescript.
29 The conference of the German Hegel Society mentioned here took place in Frankfurt on 25 October 1958.
30 Hegel, *Aesthetics*, vol. 1, p. 123 (translation modified).
31 Ibid.
32 Ibid., p. 134.
33 Adorno reproduces the original in an abridged form. In context, the full text (ibid., p. 134) reads:

> Regularity as such is in general sameness in something external and, more precisely, the same repetition of one and the same specific shape which affords the determining unity for the form of objects. On account of its initial abstraction such a unity is poles apart from the rational totality of the concrete Concept, with the result that its beauty is a beauty of the abstract Understanding; for the Understanding has for its principle abstract sameness and identity, not determined in itself.

34 The opposition between 'form-oriented' and 'content-oriented' approaches to aesthetics (now understood as the 'philosophy of beauty'), which Adorno traces back to Hegel's separation from the earlier aesthetics of Baumgarten, emerged only in the later nineteenth century and polarized the discourse on art and literature in the twentieth century (New Criticism–formalism dispute; see note 9 above). This is also the context in which one must view the possibility of conceiving an *aesthetica formalis*, which Adorno here associates, somewhat misleadingly, with Baumgarten. It is true that A. G. Baumgarten sought to expand the rationalist philosophy of the Leibniz–Wolff school with his aesthetics, but Adorno – following Hegel – misrepresents the thrust of his project. Baumgarten's concern was not to establish rationalism in the area of taste and forms of design too, in the sense of a 'formalist' 'aesthetics of abstract understanding', as attempted by Johann Christoph Gottsched in the field of poetics with his *Versuch einer critischen Dichtkunst vor die Deutschen* (Leipzig, 1730) (see also Lecture 15, note 2). Rather, Baumgarten's aesthetics aimed to cultivate something that had been neglected in the rationalist school, namely the feeling for the content of sensual insights and notions, as well as the possibilities of representation and communication of non-conceptual ideas (on this, see Dagmar Mirbach's introduction in A. G. Baumgarten, *Ästhetik*, 2 vols, Latin and German [Hamburg: Meiner, 2007], vol. 1, pp. xv–lxxx). The concept of an *aesthetica formalis* does not appear in Baumgarten's writings, nor would there be any systematic place for it within the framework of his aesthetics.

35 Hegel, *Aesthetics*, vol. 1, p. 142.

36 This parenthesized remark, with which Adorno interrupts his reading of the Hegel quotation, is marked with three lines in the typescript, with the marginal note: 'On this: artistic beauty wants what nature promises – at what cost.' See *Aesthetic Theory*, pp. 86 & 101ff.

37 Hegel, *Aesthetics*, vol. 1, p. 152.

38 Marked by Adorno from 'That is roughly' to 'no such theory'.

39 Marked by Adorno with three lines from 'At the same time' to 'unfinished here'.

40 Marked by Adorno with three lines from 'in a concept' to 'mere material'. See *Aesthetic Theory*, p. 85. On the concept of 'dignity' in Kant, see Immanuel Kant, *Groundwork of the Metaphysics of Morals* (1785), ed. and trans. Mary Gregor (Cambridge University Press, 1997), p. 41. See also Friedrich Schiller, 'On Grace and Dignity' (1793), trans. George Gregory, in *Friedrich Schiller: Poet of Freedom* (Washington, DC: Schiller Institute, 1988), vol. 2, pp. 337–95, and *On the Aesthetic Education of Man, in a Series of Letters* (1795), ed. and trans. Elizabeth M. Wilkinson and L. A. Willoughby (Oxford: Clarendon Press, 1967), especially Letter XV. The adoption of Kant's or Schiller's concept of 'dignity' by Hegel, which Adorno names here as the reason for the inadequacy of idealistic aesthetics in relation to natural beauty, is difficult to find in Hegel's philosophy. The only passage in Hegel's

Aesthetics where the concept of 'dignity' is employed actually suggests that Hegel was already reflecting critically on the opposition of 'nature' and 'spirit', which strips the world of the aesthetic presence and abundance of natural beauty and, invoking the 'dignity' of the spirit, merely establishes a violent power relationship between the modern subject and the now available natural materials:

> For on the one side we see man imprisoned in the common world of reality and earthly temporality, borne down by need and poverty, hard pressed by nature, enmeshed in matter, sensuous ends and their enjoyment, mastered and carried away by natural impulses and passions. On the other side, he lifts himself to eternal ideas, to a realm of thought and freedom, gives to himself, as will, universal laws and prescriptions, strips the world of its enlivened and flowering reality and dissolves it into abstractions, since the spirit now upholds its right and dignity only by mishandling nature and denying its right, and so retaliates on nature the distress and violence which it has suffered from it itself. (*Aesthetics*, vol. 1, p. 54)

Adorno was probably thinking less of this passage, which greatly accommodates his argument from the *Dialectic of Enlightenment*, than of the arguments for excluding natural beauty from the 'science of artistic beauty' at the start of the introduction to Hegel's *Aesthetics* (pp. 2f.).

Lecture 3

1 Marked by Adorno from 'this natural beauty' to 'as it were'.
2 Double marked by Adorno from 'that a motif' to 'this philosophy'.
3 Adorno had given a course during the summer semester of 1958 entitled 'An Introduction to Dialectics'. See *An Introduction to Dialectics*, ed. Christoph Ziermann, trans. Nicholas Walker (Cambridge: Polity, 2017).
4 Marked by Adorno from 'but that' to 'not-quite-graspable'.
5 Marked by Adorno with four lines from 'But with regard' to 'its vital principle'. Written in the margin: 'very important' and (likewise in Adorno's hand, but with different ink) 'also Valéry'.
6 Marked by Adorno with three lines from 'the fact that' to 'should begin', with the handwritten marginal note 'very important'. See *Aesthetic Theory*, p. 104: 'By rejecting the fleetingness of natural beauty, as well as virtually everything non-conceptual, Hegel makes himself obtusely indifferent towards the central motif of art, which probes after truth in the evanescent and fragile.'
7 Marked by Adorno, partly double, from 'I do not wish' to 'nature itself'.
8 In the winter semester of 1958/59, Adorno held a seminar on the 'sociology of art' to which Rolf Tiedemann contributed a paper on Walter Benjamin's sociology of art.
9 See Walter Benjamin, 'The Work of Art in the Age of its Technological Reproducibility, Third Version', trans. Edmund Jephcott and Harry

Zohn, in *Selected Writings*, ed. Howard Eiland and Michael W. Jennings, vol. 4: *1938–1940* (Cambridge, MA: Harvard University Press, 2003), pp. 251–83. The third version of this essay, completed in 1936, was the only known one in 1958 owing to its publication in the two-volume edition of Benjamin's *Schriften*, overseen by Adorno (Frankfurt: Suhrkamp, 1955), here vol. 1, pp. 365–405. Benjamin had already introduced his concept of 'aura' in 'Little History of Photography' (1932), trans. Edmund Jephcott and Kingsley Shorter, in *Selected Writings*, vol. 2: *1927–1934* (Cambridge, MA: Harvard University Press, 1999), pp. 507–30.

10 Marked by Adorno from 'The Work of Art' to 'landscapes'.

11 Benjamin, 'The Work of Art in the Age of its Technological Reproducibility', p. 255.

12 Marked by Adorno from 'This character' to 'in agreement'.

13 Marked by Adorno from 'is that one' to 'lifts up its eyes'. See Benjamin, 'On Some Motifs in Baudelaire' (1939), in *Selected Writings*, vol. 4: *1938–1940* (Cambridge, MA: Harvard University Press, 2003), p. 354.

14 Marked by Adorno from 'the threshold' to 'viewing the work'.

15 This sentence is marked by Adorno with three lines. See *Aesthetic Theory*, p. 100: 'The pain in the face of beauty, nowhere more visceral than in the experience of nature, is as much the longing for what beauty promises but never unveils as it is suffering at the inadequacy of the appearance, which fails beauty while wanting to make itself like it. This pain reappears in the relation to artworks.'

16 Marked by Adorno with three lines from 'I think' to 'melancholy'.

17 The concept of a 'freedom to the object', which Adorno often cites as a Hegelian one (see *Negative Dialectics*, pp. 28 and 48, also *Aesthetic Theory*, pp. 25 and 370), does not actually appear in Hegel; see also the editor's note in *Nachgelassene Schriften*, vol. IV.16: *Vorlesung über Negative Dialektik*, ed. Rolf Tiedemann (Frankfurt: Suhrkamp, 2003), p. 302, n. 148. Adorno's understanding of the idea of a *freedom to the object*, which he attributes to Hegel, goes beyond placing a 'positive' (or, as Hegel says, 'affirmative') concept of freedom, in the sense of a freedom *to something*, in opposition to the classically liberal 'negative' understanding of freedom as a freedom *from* certain restrictions. Concerning this opposition, see the Oxford inaugural address given by Isaiah Berlin on 30 October 1958, in *Two Concepts of Liberty* (Oxford: Clarendon Press, 1958). Adorno writes in 'Opinion Delusion Society' that the freedom to the object is 'the freedom of thought to lose and transform itself in its encounter with the subject matter' (Adorno, *Critical Models: Interventions and Catchwords*, trans. Henry W. Pickford [New York: Columbia University Press, 2012], p. 110). Its paradigm is aesthetic behaviour; see *Aesthetic Theory*, p. 25:

> Prior to total administration, the subject who viewed, heard, or read a work was to lose himself, forget himself, extinguish himself in the artwork. The identification carried out by the subject was ideally not that

of making the artwork like itself, but rather that of making itself like the artwork. This identification constituted aesthetic sublimation; Hegel named this comportment freedom to the object. He thus paid homage to the subject that becomes subject in spiritual experience through self-relinquishment, the opposite of the philistine demand that the artwork give him something.

18 Marked by Adorno from 'the barbaric' to 'works of art'. See *Aesthetic Theory*, pp. 357ff., as well as his introduction (1969) to Adorno et al., *The Positivist Dispute in German Sociology*, trans. G. Adey and D. Frisby (London: Heinemann, 1976).

19 Max Kommerell (1902–1944), professor of German philology at the University of Marburg from 1941 onwards, was the author of two books that were especially influential in the field of post-war German studies: *Lessing und Aristoteles* and *Geist und Buchstabe der Dichtung* (1940), in which he exemplarily demonstrated and sought to lay the theoretical foundation for the method of 'pure' interpretation; a collection of his essays was published posthumously in 1952 under the title *Dichterische Welterfahrung*. In his earlier book *Der Dichter als Führer in der deutschen Klassik* (1928), heavily influenced by Stefan George's circle – of which Walter Benjamin wrote in his 1930 review: 'If there is any self-respecting German conservatism, it should take this book as its Magna Carta' (Benjamin, *Gesammelte Schriften*, vol. III: *Kritiken und Rezensionen*, ed. Hella Tiedemann-Bartels [Frankfurt: Suhrkamp, 1972], p. 252) – Kommerell wrote the following about Klopstock: 'For the first time in Germany's recent history, the content of a statement of faith is turned into a mood through language, and thus belongs to the legacy of the soul beyond the duration and limits of this credo' (Kommerell, *Der Dichter als Führer in der deutschen Klassik*, 3rd edn [Frankfurt: Klostermann, 1982], p. 36). In his 'reflection on Heinrich von Kleist', entitled 'Die Sprache und das Unaussprechliche', Kommerell writes the following in his comments on the first monologue by the Prince of Homburg in Kleist's play of the same name: 'Its mood is more important than its content' (Kommerell, *Geist und Buchstabe der Dichtung* [Frankfurt: Klostermann, 1991], p. 287).

20 Marked by Adorno from 'philosophically rehashed' to 'natural beauty'. Adorno added and later crossed out a note at the top of the typescript: '*A.[rt] + n.[ature] not absolute opposites but also mediated. Initially to n.*'. Later annotation (in different ink): 'central'.

21 Marked by Adorno from 'The unthinking view' to 'as opposites'. Adorno had already criticized the 'antithesis of nature and history' in his lecture 'Die Idee der Naturgeschichte' (1932); see *Gesammelte Schriften*, vol. 1, pp. 345–65.

22 See Adorno's criticisms of Benjamin's essay 'The Work of Art in the Age of its Technological Reproducibility' in his letter of 18 March 1936. See Adorno and Benjamin, *The Complete Correspondence 1928–1940*, ed. Henri Lonitz, trans. Nicholas Walker (Cambridge: Polity, 1999), pp. 127–34.

23 Marked by Adorno with three lines from 'I will pass' to 'both directions'.

24 See Walter Benjamin, *The Origin of German Tragic Drama*, trans. John Osborne (London and New York: Verso, 1998), p. 177: 'The word "history" stands on the stands written on the countenance of nature in the characters of transience. The allegorical physiognomy of the nature-history, which is put on stage in the Trauerspiel, is present in reality in the form of the *ruin*.'

25 Adorno understands the opposition of φύσει and θέσει not only with reference to the language-philosophical controversy over the 'natural' or purely conventional foundation of semantics, as introduced by Plato in the *Cratylus* (383 a ff.) or even earlier in the sophistic enlightenment, but rather from a broader culture-philosophical perspective; see, for example, 'The Essay as Form', in *Notes to Literature*, vol. 1, p. 11: 'The essay quietly puts an end to the illusion that thought could break out of the sphere of *thesis*, culture, and move into that of *physis*, nature.' This sentence is marked by Adorno.

26 Marked by Adorno from 'So the beauty' to 'the first time'.

27 Paul Verlaine (1844–1896), a French symbolist poet; the opening quoted here is from poem number XV in the collection *Sagesse III* (1880); see Verlaine, *Selected Poems*, trans. C. F. MacIntyre (Berkeley and Los Angeles: University of California Press, 1948), pp. 166f.; see also *Aesthetic Theory*, p. 90.

28 Marked by Adorno from 'A statement like' to 'historical status'.

29 Marked by Adorno from 'freedom to the object' to 'artistic domain'.

30 In the second part of his *Aesthetics*, the historico-philosophical conception 'Development of the Ideal into the Particular Forms of Art', Hegel defines the tasks of modern art using the ideal-typical notion of the 'romantic art form', which he contrasts with the 'symbolic art form' of archaic and primitive societies and the 'classical art form', demonstrated using the model of ancient Greece:

> For at the stage of romantic art the spirit knows that its truth does not consist in its immersion in corporeality; on the contrary, it only becomes sure of its truth by withdrawing from the external into its own intimacy with itself and positing external reality as an existence inadequate to itself. Even if, therefore[,] this new content too comprises in itself the task of making itself *beautiful*, still beauty in the sense hitherto expounded remains for it something subordinate, and beauty becomes the *spiritual* beauty of the absolute inner life as inherently infinite spiritual subjectivity. (p. 518)

31 Marked by Adorno from 'that, in the name' to 'as the new'.

32 Kant, *Critique of the Power of Judgement*, trans. Paul Guyer and Eric Matthews (Cambridge University Press, 2000), p. 144.

33 Marked by Adorno from 'But the central element' to 'characteristic of beauty'.

34 From Martin Luther's hymn 'A Mighty Fortress Is Our God' (1528) in the translation by Frederic H. Hedge (1853).
35 Kant, *Critique of the Power of Judgement*, p. 145.
36 Marked by Adorno from 'Namely: in nature' to 'in the process'.
37 See Kant, *Critique of the Power of Judgement*, p. 141: 'The mind feels itself moved in the representation of the sublime in nature, while in the aesthetic judgement on the beautiful in nature it is in calm contemplation. This movement (especially in its inception) may be compared to a vibration, i.e., to a rapidly alternating repulsion from and attraction to one and the same object.' Adorno returns to this passage in *Aesthetic Theory*, p. 155.
38 See Sigmund Freud, *The Uncanny*, trans. David McLintock (London: Penguin, 2003).
39 Adorno returns to Plato's *Phaedrus* in greater detail in lectures 9 and 10; the 'definition' of beauty as ἐϰφανέστατον ϰαὶ ἐϱασμιώτατον is located in the *Phaedrus*, 250d. Concerning the 'interplay of forces between desire and the prohibition of desire' which Plato articulates in his interpretation of the experience of beauty in psychologically powerful images, see especially Lecture 10.
40 Adorno refers repeatedly to 'the saying that nature always returns, even if one drives it out with a pitchfork' – for example in Lecture 4; the saying comes from Horace: 'Naturam expellas furca, tamen usque recurrat' (*Epistulae* I, 10, 24).

Lecture 4

1 See Donald Brinkmann, *Natur und Kunst: Zur Phänomenologie des ästhetischen Gegenstandes* (Zurich and Leipzig: Rascher, 1938).
2 The concept of aesthetic semblance was introduced by Friedrich Schiller in *On the Aesthetic Education of Man, in a Series of Letters*, Letter 26: 'The only kind of semblance I am here concerned with is aesthetic semblance, which we distinguish from actuality and truth, and not logical semblance, which we confuse with these: semblance, therefore, which we love simply because it is semblance, and not because we take it to be something better' (p. 193, translation modified). On the further use of this basic concept of modern aesthetics, see Peter Bürger, 'Zum Problem des ästhetischen Scheins in der idealistischen Ästhetik', in Willi Oelmüller (ed.), *Kolloquium Kunst und Philosophie*, vol. 2: *Ästhetischer Schein* (Paderborn: Schöningh, 1981), pp. 34–50. Marked by Adorno from 'there is no sensation' to 'aesthetic semblance'; see also Lecture 3, note 15.
3 See, for example, Sigmund Freud, 'Leonardo da Vinci and a Memory of His Childhood', in *The Uncanny*, pp. 43–120. For Adorno's criticisms of the psychoanalytical theory of art, see also *Aesthetic Theory*, pp. 9–15.
4 See Kant, *Critique of the Power of Judgement*, trans. Paul Guyer and Eric Matthews (Cambridge University Press, 2000), pp. 144f.

5 Marked by Adorno from 'One can say' to 'mere immediacy'.

6 Freud uses the term 'sublimation' in 'Three Essays on the Theory of Sexuality' (1905), in *On Sexuality*, trans. James Strachey (London: Penguin, 1991); see also Freud, 'Instincts and their Vicissitudes' (1915), in *The Standard Edition of the Complete Psychological Works of Sigmund Freud*, trans. James Strachey in collaboration with Anna Freud, assisted by Alix Strachey, Alan Tyson and Angela Richards, vol. 14 (London: Hogarth Press and the Institute of Psycho-Analysis, 1957), pp. 111–40.

7 See Lecture 1, note 8.

8 See Søren Kierkegaard, *Either/Or: A Fragment of Life*, trans. Alastair Hannay (London: Penguin, 1992), p. 81.

9 It is not always easy to reconstruct what specific theories Adorno means when he refers to the 'usual forms of aesthetics' from which he sought to set himself apart; some of them were probably these: Eduard von Hartmann, *Aesthetik* (1886–7) (Berlin: Friedrich, 1924); Theodor Lipps, *Ästhetik: Psychologie des Schönen und der Kunst* (1903–6) (Leipzig: Voss, 1923); Johannes Volkelt, *System der Ästhetik* (Munich: C. H. Beck, 1905–12); Benedetto Croce, *Aesthetic: As Science of Expression and General Linguistic*, trans. Douglas Ainslie (New Brunswick and London: Transaction, 1995); Moritz Geiger, *Zugänge zur Ästhetik* (Leipzig: Der neue Geist, 1928); Nicolai Hartmann, *Aesthetics*, trans. Eugene Kelly (Berlin and Boston: de Gruyter, 2014).

10 Marked by Adorno from 'So there is nothing' to 'no longer of concern'.

11 See Lecture 3, note 40.

12 Concerning the 'prehistory of art', see *Aesthetic Theory*, p. 198: 'The myth of Procrustes recounts something of the philosophical prehistory of art' (translation modified).

13 Marked by Adorno from 'sublimation' to 'the sensual in art'.

14 The Gothic cathedral of Reims, the coronation site of the kings of France, was severely damaged by German artillery in 1914 during the First World War. In response, a conference on the protection of art was held in Brussels in 1915, and a convention was signed to enforce the protection of art monuments from the ravages of war. One of the justifications given by the German military for firing at the cathedral was that the French army had placed artillery directly in front of it and used the spire as an observation post. It is unknown what intervention Adorno had in mind in which the lives of endangered soldiers were weighed against the preservation of the cathedral.

15 Marked by Adorno from 'And then one' to 'by exclusion'.

16 In his essay 'Aldous Huxley and Utopia' (1942/1951), Adorno writes: 'Even the selfless passion of Romeo and Juliet [...] does not exist autarchically, for its own sake, but becomes spiritual and more than mere histrionics of the soul only in pointing beyond the spirit to physical union' (*Prisms*, trans. Samuel Weber and Shierry Weber [Boston: MIT Press, 1983], p. 108).

17   This phrase was often used during the Cold War to denigrate forms of politically committed theatre that were criticized for drawing the audience's interest purely because of agreement with their political-ideological concerns, not any artistic value of their own.

18   The gap in the text resulted from a change of tape.

19   Shakespeare, *Romeo and Juliet*, Act 3, scene v: [Juliet] Wilt thou be gone? It is not yet near day. / It was the nightingale, and not the lark, / That pierced the fearful hollow of thine ear.' See also *Prisms*, p. 108.

20   Aubade: a medieval form of poem or song dealing with the parting of lovers in the morning after spending the night together.

21   *L'art pour l'art*: the catchphrase for the doctrine that art should be completely free of any practical purpose, avoid all social or political involvement, and find meaning purely in the perfection of its products. Adorno views Baudelaire as the originator of the concept (see *Notes to Literature*, trans. Samuel Weber and Shierry Weber Nicholsen, vol. 2 [New York: Columbia University Press, 1992], p. 87, and *Aesthetic Theory*, pp. 304 and 421). Recent research generally believes Théophile Gautier, who introduced the phrase programmatically in the foreword to his epistolary novel *Mademoiselle Maupin* (1835), to have coined it. See Michael Einfalt, 'Autonomie' (IV–VI), in Karlheinz Barck et al. (eds), *Ästhetische Grundbegriffe: Historisches Wörterbuch in sieben Bänden*, vol. 1 (Stuttgart and Weimar: Metzler, 2000), pp. 460f.

22   See *Aesthetic Theory*, pp. 309 and 321ff.; see also 'The Artist as Deputy', in *Notes to Literature*, vol. 1, pp. 98–108.

23   Marked by Adorno from 'And I would say' to 'extremely justified'.

24   Marked by Adorno from 'Let me add' to 'vice versa'.

25   Edouard Manet (1832–1883), French painter and graphic artist. On his significance for the development of modern art, see (among others) Julius Meier-Graefe, *Manet* (Munich: Piper, 1912); Paul Valéry, 'The Triumph of Manet,' in *The Collected Works of Paul Valéry*, ed. Jackson Mathews, vol. 12: *Degas, Manet, Morisot*, trans. David Paul (New York: Pantheon, 1960), pp. 105–14.

26   See Adorno, 'The Position of the Narrator in the Contemporary Novel', in *Notes to Literature*, vol. 1, p. 34:

> Among the extremes – and we can learn more about the contemporary novel from them than from any 'typical case' – belongs Kafka's method of completely abolishing the distance. Through shocks, he destroys the reader's contemplative security in the face of what he reads. His novels, if indeed they even fall under that category, are an anticipatory response to a state of the world in which the contemplative attitude has become a mockery because the permanent threat of catastrophe no longer permits any human being to be an uninvolved spectator, nor does it permit the aesthetic imitation of that stance.

27   The writer Klaus Mann (1906–1949), son of Thomas Mann, moved to Paris in 1933 and then to Amsterdam, where one of his activities was editing the exile journal *Die Sammlung*, published by Querido. From

1936 onwards he lived mainly in the USA. He died of an overdose of sleeping pills on 21 May 1949 in Cannes.

28 See Klaus Mann, 'Europe's Search for a New Credo', in *Tomorrow* 8/10 (June 1949), pp. 3–11.

29 See Klaus Mann, *Pathetic Symphony: A Novel About Tchaikovsky* (New York: Markus Wiener, 1985).

30 Richard Wagner, *Die Meistersinger von Nürnberg* (premiered in Munich in 1868), Act 2, scene iii. See also *In Search of Wagner* (1939/1952), trans. Rodney Livingstone (London and New York: Verso, 2005), p. 56: 'To illustrate, we may think of the characteristic chord with the allegorical rubric "Spring's command, sweet need" in *The Mastersingers*, which represents the element of erotic passion and hence summarizes the whole action. It tells both of the poignant pain of non-fulfilment and of the pleasure that lies in the tension: it is both sweetness and need' (translation modified).

31 Marked by Adorno from 'One could say' to 'all these aspects'.

32 See Max Horkheimer and Theodor W. Adorno, *Dialectic of Enlightenment*, trans. Edmund Jephcott (Stanford University Press, 2002), pp. 13ff.

33 This sentence is marked by Adorno. See *Aesthetic Theory*, p. 74: 'The sentimentality and debility of almost the whole tradition of aesthetic thought is that it has suppressed the dialectic of rationality and mimesis immanent to art.'

34 See *Dialectic of Enlightenment*, pp. 1ff.

35 See ibid., pp. 35–62.

36 See lectures 3 and 4; see also *Minima Moralia: Reflections on a Damaged Life*, trans. Edmund Jephcott (London and New York: Verso, 2005), pp. 89 and 126ff.

37 This sentence is marked by Adorno.

38 See Giorgio Vasari, *The Lives of the Artists*, trans. Julia Conaway Bondanella and Peter Bondanella (Oxford and New York: Oxford University Press, 2008). Vasari deals with the doctrine of the imitation of nature – and the resulting necessity of an intensive study of nature to improve the visual arts – especially in the introductions to the first, second and third parts.

39 Marked by Adorno from 'I would say' to 'find today'. See *Aesthetic Theory*, pp. 381f.; see also Walter Benjamin, 'Doctrine of the Similar', in *Selected Writings*, vol. 2: *1927–1934* (Cambridge, MA: Harvard University Press, 1999), pp. 694–8.

40 In his foreword to the published score of Webern's Six Bagatelles for String Quartet, op. 9 (Vienna: Universal Edition, 1924), Arnold Schoenberg wrote: 'These pieces will be understood only by those who share the faith that music can say things which can only be expressed by music.'

Lecture 5

1 See Friedrich Schiller, *On the Naive and Sentimental in Literature* (1795/6), trans. Helen Watanabe-O'Kelly (Manchester: Carcanet

New Press, 1981), p. 104: 'The ideal, in which perfect art returns to nature.'

2   See Ludwig Friedländer, *Darstellungen aus der Sittengeschichte Roms in der Zeit von Augustus bis zum Ausgang der Antonine*, 4 vols (Leipzig: Hirzel, 1922). In vol. 2, pp. 90–5, he writes:

> Theatrical performances also took place in the arena, especially pantomimes, except that the actors were condemned criminals who had been taught especially and trained not to simulate death and torment, but genuinely to suffer it. [...] In the whole of Roman literature, we scarcely encounter any expression of the revulsion which the world of today feels towards these inhuman entertainments. [...] Ovid saw nothing terrible in recommending the spectacle in which one delights in the sight of murder as especially beneficial to amorous relationships.

3   Emil Ludwig, real name Emil Cohn (1881–1948): a German writer of Jewish descent whose psychologically interpretive biographies of historical personalities were very successful. Selected works: *Bismarck: Ein Psychologischer Versuch* (Berlin: Fischer, 1911), *Goethe* (Stuttgart: Cotta, 1920), *Rembrandts Schicksal* (Berlin: Rowohlt, 1923), *Napoleon*, trans. Eden Paul and Cedar Paul (London: George Allen & Unwin, 1927), *Kaiser Wilhelm II*, trans. Ethel Colburn Mayne (London and New York: G. P. Putnam's Sons, 1926), *Hindenburg und die Sage von der deutschen Republik* (Amsterdam: Querido, 1935), *Barbares et musiciens, les allemands tels qu'ils sont* (Paris: La technique du livre, 1940), *The Germans* (London: Hamish Hamilton, 1942).

4   Herbert Eulenberg (1876–1949) was one of the most performed playwrights on German stages in the 1920s; his biographical novels include *Anna Boleyn* (Berlin: Gurlitt, 1920) and *Heinrich Heine* (Berlin: Aufbau, 1947).

5   The works of the Austrian writer Stefan Zweig (1881–1942) include *Triumph and Disaster: Five Historical Miniatures*, trans. Anthea Bell (London: Pushkin Press, 2016) and *The Royal Game*, trans. B. W. Huebsch (London: Pushkin Press, 2007), as well as the biographical novels *Joseph Fouché: The Portrait of a Politician*, trans. Eden Paul and Cedar Paul (New York: Viking Press, 1930), *Marie Antoinette: The Portrait of an Average Woman*, trans. Eden Paul and Cedar Paul (New York: Viking Press, 1933), *Erasmus of Rotterdam*, trans. Eden Paul and Cedar Paul (New York: Viking Press, 1934), *Mary, Queen of Scotland and the Isles*, trans. Eden Paul and Cedar Paul (New York: Viking Press, 1935), *Conqueror of the Seas: The Story of Magellan*, trans. Eden Paul and Cedar Paul (New York: Viking Press, 1938).

6   Sputnik 1, launched into orbit by the Soviet Union on 4 October 1957, was the first artificial Earth satellite; further ones followed in the subsequent months. In the propagandistically heightened atmosphere of the Cold War, the Sputniks were viewed as a demonstration of technical superiority by the Soviets and triggered a strong sense of threat in the West ('Sputnik shock').

7   The philosopher and psychologist Karl Groos (1861–1946), author of
     Einleitung in die Ästhetik (Giessen: J. Richer'sche Verlagsbuchhand-
     lung, 1892) and the widely read *Das Seelenleben des Kindes* (Berlin:
     Reuther & Reichard, 1911), among other books. He espoused a devel-
     opmental-psychological theory of play, which, on the one hand, traced
     the basic forms of playful activities back to particular behaviours among
     animals but, on the other hand, ascribed a decisive role in anthropo-
     genesis to play and emphasized the function of games for the develop-
     ment of vitally important human abilities. See *Die Spiele der Tiere* (Jena:
     Gustav Fischer, 1896), *Die Spiele der Menschen* (Jena: Gustav Fischer,
     1899) and *Das Spiel* (Jena: Gustav Fischer, 1922).

8   Marked by Adorno from 'that art' to 'empirical reality'. On the polarity
     of semblance and play in mimesis, see Benjamin, 'The Work of Art in
     the Age of its Technological Reproducibility, Second Version,' trans.
     Edmund Jephcott and Harry Zohn, in *Selected Writings*, ed. Howard
     Eiland and Michael W. Jennings, vol. 3: *1935–1938* (Cambridge, MA
     and London: Belknap Press, 2002), pp. 101–33, in particular n. 22, p.
     127f., as well as Adorno's letter of 18 March 1936 to Benjamin about
     it in *The Complete Correspondence 1928–1940*, ed. Henri Lonitz,
     trans. Nicholas Walker (Cambridge: Polity, 1999), pp. 127–34. See also
     Aesthetic Theory, p. 139: 'The rebellion against semblance did not,
     however, take place in favour of play, as Benjamin supposed, though
     there is no mistaking the playful quality of the permutations, for
     instance, that have replaced fictional developments. The crisis of sem-
     blance may engulf play as well, for the harmlessness of play deserves
     the same fate as does harmony, which originates in semblance.'

9   See the excursus 'Theories on the Origin of Art', in *Aesthetic Theory*,
     pp. 429–38.

10   In the Polynesian, Melanesian, Micronesian and other Oceanic lan-
     guages, *mana* means 'power' or 'effectiveness' and is ascribed especially
     to supernatural forces. The term was introduced into anthropology and
     the study of religion by R. H. Codrington (1830–1922) in *The Mela-
     nesians: Studies in Their Anthopology and Folk-Lore* (1891) (New
     Haven: Behavior Science Reprints, 1957). Adorno and Horkheimer use
     it in the *Dialectic of Enlightenment* (p. 32) with reference to, among
     other sources, Marcel Mauss, *A General Theory of Magic*, trans. Robert
     Brain (London and New York: Routledge, 2001); see also Mauss, *The
     Gift*, trans. W. D. Halls (London and New York: Routledge, 1990),
     Émile Durkheim, *The Elementary Forms of Religious Life*, trans. Carl
     Cosman (Oxford and New York: Oxford University Press, 2001), and
     Friedrich Rudolf Lehmann, *Mana: Der Begriff des 'ausserordentlich
     Wirkungsvollen' bei den Südseevölkern* (Leipzig: Otto Spamer, 1922).

11   This sentence is marked by Adorno.

12   The sentence 'music is the world once again', which is often quoted as
     allegedly coined by Schopenhauer, does not appear verbatim in the
     philosopher's writings. One can find a similar thesis in, for example,
     §52 of his central work *The World as Will and Representation* (2 vols,

trans. E. F. J. Payne [Mineola, NY: Dover, 1969]): 'In fact, music is an *unmediated* objectivation and copy of the entire *will*, just as the world itself is, just as in fact the Ideas themselves are, whose multiplied appearance constitutes the world of particular things' (vol. 1, p. 285). Adorno, who repeatedly refers to Schopenhauer's alleged dictum (see *Aesthetic Theory*, pp. 190 and 421; also *Mahler: A Musical Physiognomy*, trans. Edmund Jephcott [Chicago and London: Chicago University Press, 1992], p. 83), is apparently following a reception tradition dating back to the late nineteenth century. Examples of works in which this definition of music is attributed to Schopenhauer include Fritz Mauthner, *Beiträge zu einer Kritik der Sprache*, vol. 1: *Wesen der Sprache* (Stuttgart and Berlin: J. G. Cotta'sche Buchhandlung Nachfolger, 1906), p. 103; and Gustav Landauer, 'Durch Absonderung zur Gemeinschaft' (1900), in *Die Botschaft der Titanic: Ausgewählte Essays*, ed. Walter Fähnders and Hansgeorg Schmidt-Bergmann (Berlin: Kontext, 1994).

13 See *Minima Moralia*, p. 222: 'Art is magic delivered from the lie of being truth.'

14 The entire section from 'I think one can say' to 'unfolding of the truth' is marked in the left margin; the Hegel paraphrase 'art is neither a pleasant nor a useful plaything but, rather, itself an unfolding of the truth' is also underlined in the text (on the Hegel passage, see Lecture 1, note 32).

15 See *Dialectic of Enlightenment*, pp. 6ff.

16 Aristotle, in *Metaphysics* III, 4, 1000 b 6, attributes the doctrine that one can only know like by like to Empedocles; see also Sextus Empiricus, *Adversus Mathematicos*, VII, 121: ἡ γνῶσις τοῦ ὁμοίου τῷ ὁμοίῳ. The doctrine is older, admittedly; it is said that Pythagoras already propagated it (see *Adversus Mathematicos*, VII, 92), and it can be found as early as the Upanishads (see the entry 'Erkenntnis' in Rudolf Eisler, *Wörterbuch der philosophischen Begriffe*, vol. 1 [Berlin: E. S. Mittler, 1904], p. 285).

17 In Greek philosophy, the idea that knowledge can be set in motion by a confrontation with something that is noticed as being different first appears in the work of Anaxagoras. See Theophrastus, *De sensibus*, 27.

18 This sentence is marked in the left margin. See also *Aesthetic Theory*, pp. 89–97.

19 See Walter Benjamin, 'On the Concept of History', in *Selected Writings*, vol. 4: *1938–1940* (Cambridge, MA: Harvard University Press, 2003), p. 392. The image of brushing against the grain was popularized by Joris-Karl Huysmans in *Against Nature* [also translated as *Against the Grain*], trans. Robert Baldick and Patrick McGuinness (London: Penguin, 2003). See also 'Short Commentaries on Proust', in *Notes to Literature*, vol. 1, p. 181.

20 See Benjamin, ibid. Adorno repeatedly refers to this key motif; see *Aesthetic Theory*, p. 266.

21 See Lucian's tale of the bull of Phalaris, to which Kierkegaard refers in his explanation of what a poet is: *Either/Or: A Fragment of Life*, trans.

Alastair Hannay (London: Penguin, 1992), p. 43. Adorno also quotes this passage in *Kierkegaard: Construction of the Aesthetic*, trans. Robert Hullot-Kentor (Minneapolis: University of Minnesota Press, 1989), p. 63.

22 Marked by Adorno from 'This is, of course' to 'truly do this'.

23 This sentence – like the two subsequent ones – is marked by Adorno.

24 Marked by Adorno in the left margin from 'On the other hand' to 'find today'.

25 See Herbert Marcuse, 'The Affirmative Character of Culture' (1937), in *Negations: Essays in Critical Theory* (Boston: Beacon Press, 1968), pp. 88–133.

26 Pablo Picasso (1881–1973) was undoubtedly one of the most famous contemporary artists during the 1950s, but there were certainly still differing opinions. The mention of his name as that of a 'great painter' could only be taken as a demonstrative expression of partisanship in the dispute over modern art. One can no longer reconstruct which paintings in particular Adorno had in mind. He presumably saw Picasso's 'most recent works' in the spring of 1957 at the Galerie Leiris in Paris, where works from 1955–6 were being exhibited. In addition, there were much noticed Picasso exhibitions in Munich, Cologne and Hamburg.

27 Marked by Adorno in the left margin from 'So you should' to 'precarious thing'.

28 Marked by Adorno from 'this overall process' to 'central aspect'.

29 Jean-Jacques Rousseau, 'Discourse on the Origin and Foundations of Inequality among Men' (1755), in *The Basic Political Writings*, 2nd edn, ed. and trans. Donald A. Cress (Indianapolis: Hackett, 2011), p. 104: 'What then! Must we destroy societies, annihilate mine and thine, and return to live in the forests with bears?'

30 This sentence is marked by Adorno in the left margin.

31 Marked in the left margin from 'In other words' to 'first place'.

32 Marked in the left margin from 'technique' to 'describe to you'.

33 See Hegel, *Aesthetics*, vol. 2, p. 1135: 'As little as epic does lyric tolerate, in general, either the caprice of the ordinary man's thinking, or purely logical inferences, or the progress of philosophical thinking, expounded speculatively, in its necessity. On the contrary, it demands that the single parts shall be free and independent.'

34 See Carl Gustav Jochmann, *Die Rückschritte der Poesie und andere Schriften*, ed. Werner Kraft (Frankfurt: Insel, 1967). Walter Benjamin drew Adorno's attention to Jochmann in March 1937 (see Benjamin, *Gesammelte Schriften*, vol. II.3: *Aufsätze, Essays, Vorträge*, ed. Rolf Tiedemann and Hermann Schweppenhäuser [Frankfurt: Suhrkamp, 1977], p. 1392), and in 1940 the *Zeitschrift für Sozialforschung* (8(1/2), pp. 92–114) printed an excerpt from Jochmann's text *Die Rückschritte der Poesie* with an introduction by Benjamin, now in *Gesammelte Schriften*, vol. II.2, pp. 572–98.

35 See Karl Marx, *Grundrisse: Foundations of the Critique of Political Economy*, trans. Martin Nicolaus (New York: Vintage, 1973), p. 111:

[...] is Achilles possible with powder and lead? Or the Iliad with the printing press...? Do not the song and the saga and the muse necessarily come to an end with the printer's bar, hence do not the necessary conditions of epic poetry vanish? But the difficulty lies not in understanding that the Greek arts and epic are bound up with certain forms of social development. The difficulty is that they still afford us artistic pleasure and that in a certain respect they count as a norm and as an unattainable model.

36 Marked in the left margin from 'there is such a thing' to 'peculiar way'.
37 See 'Vorschlag zur Ungüte' (1959), in Adorno, *Gesammelte Schriften*, vol. 10.1, p. 332: 'Hotel paintings and modern ones: there is really no other possibility anymore. Tertium non datur.'
38 Franz Defregger (1835–1921) was professor of historical painting at the Munich Academy of Art; he especially liked painting portraits, motifs from everyday rural life, and dramatic scenes from the Tyrolean Rebellion of 1809.
39 Marked in the left margin from 'On the other hand' to 'the whole'.

Lecture 6

1 Emphasis through underlining in the typescript.
2 Adorno first met the Irish writer Samuel Beckett (1906–1989) in November 1958 in Paris, where he was giving lectures and seminars at the Sorbonne from 24 to 26 November. Concerning the meeting with Beckett on 28 November to which Adorno is referring here, see Rolf Tiedemann, ' "Gegen den Trug der Frage nach dem Sinn": A Documentation on Adorno's Reading of Beckett', *Frankfurter Adorno Blätter III*, ed. Rolf Tiedemann (Munich: edition text + kritik, 1994), pp. 18–77 (here pp. 22f.).
3 Loss of text owing to change of tape.
4 See Lecture 1, note 32.
5 The French composer and conductor Pierre Boulez (1925–2016) was one of the outstanding exponents of the musical avant-garde from the 1950s onwards. He began studying composition with Olivier Messiaen in 1943, then in 1945 studied counterpoint with Andrée Vaurabourg-Honegger and twelve-note technique with René Leibowitz in Paris. From 1950 on, his works were performed in Paris, Donaueschingen and elsewhere; he first attended the Darmstadt International Summer Course for New Music in 1952 and worked there as a tutor and conductor from 1955 to 1967. In 1957 he gave the premiere of his Third Piano Sonata in Darmstadt; in 1958, two of his *Improvisations sur Mallarmé* were premiered in Hamburg; *Le soleil des eaux*, on two poems by René Char for soprano, mixed choir and orchestra (1948, revised version with choir in 1958), was premiered in Darmstadt on 9 September 1958. Adorno already saw the young Boulez at the vanguard of the serial avant-garde in his lecture 'The Aging of the New Music' (1954, pubd

1956) (in *Essays on Music*, pp. 181–202). In particular, Adorno repeatedly refers to his early masterpiece *Le marteau sans maître* (1952–5); see *Aesthetic Theory*, p. 294; *Alban Berg: Master of the Smallest Link*, trans. Juliane Brand and Christopher Hailey (Cambridge University Press, 1991), p. 66; *Introduction to the Sociology of Music*, trans. E. B. Ashton (New York: Continuum, 1988), p. 99; 'Zemlinsky', in *Quasi una Fantasia: Essays on Modern Music*, trans. Rodney Livingstone (London and New York: Verso, 1998), p. 121; 'Vienna', ibid., p. 219; 'Vers une musique informelle', ibid., p. 70. Boulez contributed an essay to the festschrift for Adorno's sixtieth birthday in 1963 entitled 'Nécessité d'une orientation esthétique', in *Zeugnisse: Theodor Adorno zum sechstigsten Geburtgstag*, ed. Max Horkheimer (Frankfurt: Suhrkamp, 1963), pp. 334ff.; after Adorno's death in 1969, Boulez dedicated a choral piece to him: *'Über das, über ein Verschwinden' (in memoriam Theodor W. Adorno)*.

6 See Georg Lukács, *The Theory of the Novel: A Historico-Philosophical Essay on the Forms of Great Epic Literature*, trans. Anna Bostock (Boston: MIT Press, 1971), p. 97.

7 *Die Asiatische Banise, oder das blutig-doch muthige Pegu*, by Heinrich Anshelm von Ziegler und Kliphausen (1663–1697), was the most successful novel of German baroque literature well into the eighteenth century. By 1764, the first edition of 1689 (Leipzig: Gleditsch) had been followed by a further ten, as well as translations into several European languages and various stage adaptations.

8 The following deliberations were important to Adorno; the typescript is marked in the left margin from here to the end of this lecture.

9 See *Aesthetic Theory*, p. 34: 'The painfulness of experimentation finds response in the animosity toward the so-called isms: programmatic, self-conscious, and often collective art movements. This rancour is shared by the likes of Hitler, who loved to rail against "these im-and expressionists", and by writers who out of a politically avant-garde zealousness are wary of the idea of an aesthetic avant-garde.'

10 In Henrik Ibsen's play *Rosmersholm* (1886), the former chief pastor Rosmer, now estranged from his faith, set himself the goal of 'winning the minds and the wills of men. Creating [...] a nobility ... in ever wider circles. Noble men.' In Ibsen, *An Enemy of the People, The Wild Duck, Rosmersholm*, trans. James McFarlane (Oxford and New York: Oxford University Press, 1999), p. 270.

11 Adorno knew the term *principium stilisationis* from Lukács's *The Theory of the Novel* (p. 40). Admittedly, the way in which he uses it here serves not so much to set apart the principle of a particular form of stylization from another possible one; rather, it serves more fundamentally as the principle of stylization as such, which was called into question by expressionism.

12 The French surrealist André Breton (1896–1966) introduced the term *écriture automatique* around 1919 to refer to a 'mental dictation without any control by reason' that supposedly reproduced the 'stream of

thoughts' in an 'uncensored' state. This was most likely to occur, he claimed, if one sat down at one's desk directly after waking up, still half asleep, and wrote down the words formulated 'unconsciously' in this twilight state 'on the threshold of dream'. Together with Philippe Soupault (1897–1990), Breton first explored the principle of automatic writing in 1919, in their joint text *The Magnetic Fields* (see Breton and Soupault, *The Magnetic Fields*, trans. David Gascoyne [London: Atlas Press, 1985]). As documented by the facsimile edition of the manuscript, however, the 'automatic writings' were certainly edited for their publication in 1920.

13 In 1912, the composer Anton von Webern (1883–1945) contributed, together with his teacher Arnold Schoenberg and Alban Berg, to the expressionist almanac *Der blaue Reiter* with a song: *Ihr tratet zu dem Herde*, op. 4, on a poem by Stefan George (1909). Adorno's essay 'Anton von Webern' (in *Sound Figures*, trans. Rodney Livingstone [Stanford University Press, 1999], pp. 91–105) was published in March 1959 in the journal *Merkur* (issue 3). On Webern's Six Bagatelles for String Quartet, op. 9 (1911), which Adorno probably had especially in mind here, see *Der getreue Korrepetitor* (1963), in *Gesammelte Schriften*, vol. 15, pp. 277–301.

14 Whereas the polyperspectival dissolution of the object in the multiplicity of its irreducible views was the central concern during the 'analytically' oriented early phase of the cubist paintings of Pablo Picasso and Georges Braque (starting in 1907), the cubist painters (including Juan Gris, who contributed decisive ideas alongside Picasso and Braque) turned more emphatically towards a 'reconstruction' or 'recovery' of the object in a second, 'synthetically' oriented phase from 1912 onwards. The compositions were built up from a few large surfaces with very clear outlines and stronger colours, partly with collaged materials, but these now seemed subordinate to the overall form, no longer employed as fragments of the disassembled object or to shatter the pictorial continuum. The overlapping of surfaces and very slight shadings show physicality without denying the objects' confinement to the two-dimensionality of the picture's surface. Juan Gris described his understanding of synthetic cubism in an essay written in 1921:

> I work with the elements of the spirit, with the imagination; I try to make the abstract concrete; I proceed from the general to the particular, i.e. I start from an abstraction to arrive at a concrete reality; my art is an art of synthesis, a deductive art. I want to find a way of creating new individual things by starting from general basic forms. (Quoted in Walter Hess, *Dokumente zum Verständnis der modernen Malerei* [Reinbek: Rowohlt, 1956, p. 60)

Regarding Picasso's transition to synthetic cubism, see also *Aesthetic Theory*, p. 295.

15 See Theodor W. Adorno, *Philosophy of New Music*, trans. Robert Hullot-Kentor (Minneapolis: University of Minnesota Press, 2006), pp. 37–41.

16   On loneliness as the signature of failed modernity, see Adorno, *Kierkeg-aard: Construction of the Aesthetic*, trans. Robert Hullot-Kentor (Minneapolis: University of Minnesota Press, 1989); on *Jugendstil* as the 'paradoxical universality of loneliness as a style', see *Aesthetic Theory*, p. 416.

17   See Kurt Mautz, 'Die Farbensprache der expressionistischen Lyrik', *Deutsche Vierteljahrsschrift für Literaturwissenschaft und Geistesgeschichte* 31 (1957), pp. 198–240. Adorno here varies an idea he had presented in 1957 in his Kranichstein lecture 'Criteria of New Music'; see *Sound Figures*, pp. 177f. He also takes it up again in *Aesthetic Theory*, p. 283. Kurt Adolf Mautz (1911–2000), one of Adorno's oldest students, was a secondary school teacher in Mainz from 1950 until his retirement in 1972. In addition to other texts on literary history, he wrote a study that went into several editions: *Georg Heym: Mythologie und Gesellschaft im Expressionismus* (Frankfurt: Athenäum, 1961). After the end of his teaching career he began publishing literary prose and concrete poetry. In 1996 he published *Der Urfreund*, a *roman à clef* about the career of a fellow student and former friend, the German Wilhelm Emrich (1909–1998), between 1930 and 1950, which also features Adorno (under the name Amorelli) as a 'left-wing assistant' and young Frankfurt outside lecturer in the early 1930s.

18   In his essay 'George and Hoffmannsthal', written in 1939/40 and published in 1955 in *Prisms*, Adorno took Arthur Rimbaud's (1854–1891) poem 'Vowels' as a starting point for the 'colour theory of words' that preoccupied Hugo von Hofmannsthal; see *Prisms*, trans. Samuel Weber and Shierry Weber (Boston: MIT Press, 1983), p. 190: 'The endowment of sounds with colours, depending solely on the gravitation of language away from meaning, liberates the poem from the concept.'

19   In the third part of his *Aesthetics*, in which he conceives a 'system of the individual arts', Hegel first of all defines sculpture as an 'art of the classical ideal' (Hegel, *Aesthetics*, vol. 2, p. 718) and sees its central task in representing the human form as an embodiment of 'substantive individuality':

> Thus it turns out that the task of sculpture essentially consists in implanting in a human figure the spiritual substance in its not yet subjectively particularized individuality, and in setting this figure and this substance in a harmony in which what is emphasized is only the universal and permanent element in the bodily forms corresponding to the spirit, while the fortuitous and the transient is stripped away, although at the same time the figure must not lack individuality. (Ibid.)

Hegel's 'system of the individual arts' ends with the chapter on dramatic poetry, and here too he calls for a realization of 'fundamental human interests': 'In general, therefore, it may be maintained that whatever other excellence a dramatic work may have it will become all the more obsolescent the more, instead of dealing with fundamental human interests, it selects as subject-matter non-typical characters and passions, determined by the specific national tendencies of their own period' (ibid., p. 1177).

20 See Martin Heidegger, *Being and Time*, trans. John Macquarrie and Edward Robinson (New York: Harper & Row, 1962), pp. 44ff.; see also *Against Epistemology*, p. 15; *Negative Dialectics*, pp. 111f.

Lecture 7

1 From here, the text is marked in the left margin for the next two pages – until the paragraph ending 'becoming the executor of what the material demands in every single one of its aspects'.

2 Emphasis in the lecture; highlighted by the secretary in the typescript by underlining.

3 An essay by Gustav René Hocke, 'Homer und Raffael: Zur Physiognomie des Klassischen', appeared in *Akzente*, no. 6 (1958), pp. 496–506. Adorno was thinking of this passage (pp. 503f.):

> Raphael is understood once more as one of the most outstanding conquerors of the surface, as a painter of combinatorial spatial and chromatic logic. Symmetries of space and colour vibrate on the surface of the picture like fugues. It seems as if Raphael were whispering to us today [...] that the 'content' is not the decisive element. What Raphael himself loved most of all was the masterful conquest of the surface, the harmony of colour hues, the rhythmic, almost metric balance of tensions [...]. He was 'objective'. One of the greatest 'art' mathematicians and aesthetic engineers of all time.

4 See for example Milton C. Nahm, *The Artist as Creator: An Essay of Human Freedom* (Baltimore: Johns Hopkins University Press, 1956).

5 Marked in the left margin from 'have talent' to 'its own accord'.

6 The entire page from 'I already pointed out' to 'hostility to expression' is marked in the left margin.

7 See *Dialectic of Enlightenment*, pp. 13ff.

8 See Donald Mitchell and Andrew Nicholson (eds), *The Mahler Companion* (Oxford and New York: Oxford University Press, 2002), p. 581.

9 Marked by Adorno from 'Firstly' to 'expressive sphere'. See *Aesthetic Theory*, pp. 160f.

10 See Anatole France, *Les Opinions de Jérôme Coignard* (1893), in *Œuvres*, ed. Marie-Claire Banquart, vol. 2 (Paris: Gallimard, 1987), p. 302: 'The history of men [...]: they are born, they suffer, they die.'

11 Marked in the left margin from 'If one levels' to 'lost again'.

12 It is impossible to reconstruct which specific plays Adorno had in mind. Some of the most successful post-war plays on West German stages included *The Devil's General* by Carl Zuckmayer (premiered at the Zurich Schauspielhaus in 1946) and Wolfgang Borchert's homecoming drama *The Man Outside* (premiered at the Hamburg Kammerspiele in

1946). In Hansjörg Schmitthenner's *Every One of Us* (premiered at the Deutsches Theater, Berlin, in 1947), the murder of prisoners of war becomes an ethical problem; Zuckmayer's *Song in the Fiery Furnace* (premiered at the Deutsches Theater, Göttingen, in 1950) shows a French resistance group burning to death in a castle set on fire by the German field police. Walter Erich Schäfer brought the interrogations by the Gestapo of the failed conspirators of 20 July 1944 to the stage in his play *The Conspiracy* (premiered at the Berlin Schlossparktheater in 1948). Heinrich Goertz's deserter drama *Peter Kiewe* (premiered in the studio of the Deutsches Theater, Berlin, in 1946) received a more critical response.

13 The stage adaptation of *The Diary of Anne Frank* by Frances Goodrich and Albert Hackett (1955), which led to the book's international success and to the American film version (directed by George Stevens, 1959), was often performed, for example at the Berlin Schlossparktheater (premiered on 1 October 1956, directed by Boleslav Barlog) and during the 1957/58 season also in Wuppertal.

14 In his essay 'Cultural Criticism and Society' (1949, pubd 1951), Adorno wrote: 'To write poetry after Auschwitz is barbaric. And this even eats away at the knowledge of why it has become impossible to write poetry today' (*Prisms*, p. 34 [translation modified]). This statement triggered an intense controversy. The poet Hans Magnus Enzensberger responded to Adorno in his essay 'The Stones of Freedom' (in *Merkur*, 13/7 (1959), pp. 770–5): 'If we want to go on living, this statement must be refuted.' Adorno replied to this in 1962, in his essay 'Commitment':

> I do not want to soften my statement that it is barbaric to continue to write poetry after Auschwitz; it expresses, negatively, the impulse that animates committed literature. The question one of the characters in Sartre's *Morts sans sépulture* [The dead without tombs] asks, 'Does living have any meaning when men exist who beat you until your bones break?' is also the question whether art as such should still exist at all; whether spiritual regression in the concept of committed literature is not enjoined by the regression of society itself. But Hans Magnus Enzensberger's rejoinder also remains true, namely that literature must resist precisely this verdict, that is, be such that it does not surrender to cynicism merely by existing after Auschwitz. [...] The excess of real suffering permits no forgetting [...]. But that suffering [...] also demands the continued existence of the very art it forbids; hardly anywhere else does suffering still find its own voice, a consolation that does not immediately betray it. (*Notes to Literature*, vol. 2, pp. 87f.)

See on this debate also Petra Kiedaisch (ed.), *Lyrik nach Auschwitz? Adorno und die Dichter* (Stuttgart: Reclam, 1995).

15 The 'recent works' to which Adorno is referring here are the forms of 'aleatory' music developed by such composers as John Cage, Pierre Boulez and Karlheinz Stockhausen, which were presented and vigorously discussed at the Darmstadt Summer Course for New Music in 1957 and 1958. See note 34 below and Lecture 8, notes 27–9.

16 Adorno had already formulated the observation of a 'crisis of meaning' in New Music, resulting from an unlimited compositional control over the musical material, in the essay 'Music and Technique' (1958):

> The absolute necessity that weaves a note group here and now from these specific notes, this rhythm, these pitches, volumes, colours, and perhaps even modes of playing – a successful subsumption – confers something of an arbitrary character on the individual phenomenon, without which music explicit in time cannot survive. The less it can be anything other than it is, the more it sounds as though it could be different. It is this, and not any ideological loss of extramusical content, that defines the crisis of meaning in which the integration of meaning with technique becomes conscious of itself. (*Sound Figures*, trans. Rodney Livingstone [Stanford University Press, 1999], p. 203)

17 In the essay 'Those Twenties' (1962), Adorno further develops his diagnosis and interpretation of modernity's 'crisis of meaning': 'In every one of its elements contemporary artistic production must bear in mind the crisis of meaning: the meaning subjectively given a work of art as well as the meaningful conception of the world. Otherwise artistic creativity barters away its services to legitimation. The only legitimately meaningful artworks today are those opposing the concept of meaning with the utmost recalcitrance' (*Critical Models*, trans. Henry W. Pickford [New York: Columbia University Press, 2012], p. 45). See also *Aesthetic Theory*, p. 210: 'While the crisis of meaning is rooted in a problematic common to all art, the failure in the face of rationality, reflection cannot suppress the question of whether art does not perhaps, through the demolition of meaning – the very thing that strikes ordinary consciousness as absurd – throw itself into the arms of the reified consciousness, of positivism' (translation modified).

18 See 'Music and Technique', p. 202: 'The whole official musical culture is moving in the direction of the fetishizing of means, and it is even celebrating a triumph among its enemies in the avant-garde.' See also *Aesthetic Theory*, p. 59.

19 Marked in the left margin from 'the criticism of expression' to 'within modern art'. In his lecture 'The Aging of the New Music' (1954), Adorno himself had already noted a 'loss of tension' that should not be viewed merely as a 'symptom of aging' but, rather, could 'be traced all the way back to the origins of New Music' (*Essays on Music*, p. 188). See also *Aesthetic Theory*, p. 72: 'The loss of tension [...] is the strongest objection to be made against some contemporary art'; and p. 78: 'The loss of tension in constructive art today is not only the product of subjective weakness but a consequence of the idea of construction itself [...].'

20 In addition to *The Ring of the Nibelung* (1848–74, premiered at the Bayreuth Feststpielhaus in 1876), the late 'sacred festival drama' [*Bühnenweihfestspiel*] *Parsifal* (see Lecture 1, note 28) is an especially good example of Richard Wagner's 'worldview art'.

21   The playwright Friedrich Hebbel (1813–1863) wrote *The Nibelungs* (1861), among other works. Adorno's understanding of Hebbel's work as 'worldview art' becomes clear in a comparison with Frank Wedekind in which Adorno emphasizes that Hebbel encompassed 'the whole tragic breadth of our despiritualized existence' ('Frank Wedekind and his Genre Painting, *Musik*', *Notes to Literature*, vol. 2, p. 267).

22   It is surprising that Adorno names the French novelist Gustave Flaubert (1821–1880) as an exponent of 'worldview art', as he is reputed to have cultivated, in his novels *Madame Bovary* (1857) and *Sentimental Education* (1869), an ascetic, maximally distanced attitude of observation that many of his contemporaries considered morally reprehensible. But this attitude too, this view of moral conflicts, displays a worldview of its own – admittedly the opposite of what self-assured bourgeois generally claimed as their 'worldview'.

23   Marked in the left margin from 'Today, by contrast' to 'become meaningful'; Adorno had already written down the question in his notes for this lecture, see pp. 172f. in this volume.

24   See Hegel, *Aesthetics*, vol. 1, p. 70:

> It has already been said that the content of art is the Idea, while its form is the configuration of sensuous material. Now art has to harmonize these two sides and bring them into a free reconciled totality. The first point here is the demand that the content which is to come into artistic representation should be in itself qualified for such representation. For otherwise we obtain only a bad combination, because in that case a content ill-adapted to figurativeness and external presentation is made to adopt this form, or, in other words, material explicitly prosaic is expected to find a really appropriate mode of presentation in the form antagonistic to its nature.
>
> Ibid, pp. 299f: Now, in more detail, the forms of art, as the actualizing and unfolding of the beautiful, find their origin in the Idea itself, in the sense that through them the Idea presses on to representation and reality, and whenever it is explicit to itself either only in its abstract determinacy or else in its concrete totality, it also brings itself into appearance in another real formation. This is because the Idea as such is only truly Idea as developing itself explicitly by its own activity; and since as Ideal it is immediate appearance, and indeed with its appearance is the identical Idea of the beautiful, so also at every particular stage on which the Ideal treads the road of its unfolding there is immediately linked with every inner determinacy another real configuration.

25   This question is fundamental to Adorno's understanding of modern art; see *Aesthetic Theory*, p. 120:

> The spirit of artworks is objective, regardless of any philosophy of objective or subjective spirit; this spirit is their own content and it passes judgement on them: it is the spirit of the matter itself that appears through the appearance. Its objectivity has its measure in the power with which

it infiltrates the appearance. Just how little the spirit of the work equals the spirit of the artist, which is at most one element of the former, is evident in the fact that spirit is evoked through the artifact, its problems, and its material. Not even the appearance of the artwork as a whole is its spirit, and least of all is it the appearance of the idea purportedly embodied or symbolized by the work; spirit cannot be fixated in immediate identity with its appearance. But neither does spirit constitute a level above or below appearance; such a supposition would be no less of a reification. The locus of spirit is the configuration of what appears. Spirit forms appearance just as appearance forms spirit: it is the luminous source through which the phenomenon radiates and becomes a phenomenon in the concentrated sense. (Translation modified)

26 This sentence is marked by Adorno.

27 This was the common abbreviation used at the time for 'dialectical materialism', which referred to the Soviet ideology as established in particular in Joseph Stalin's text 'On Dialectical and Historical Materialism' (1938). The anti-Stalinist reform communist Lukács does not use the term 'diamat' to refer to his own position. The fact that Adorno nonetheless mentions his use of this abbreviation, and even describes it as a 'worldview' supposedly espoused by Lukács, implies that he is accusing him of a simplified view of materialist dialectic – simplified especially in comparison to Lukács's own earlier writings such as 'History and Class Consciousness', whose value Adorno acknowledged.

28 See Georg Lukács, *The Meaning of Contemporary Realism*, trans. John Mander and Necke Mander (London: Merlin Press, 1963); see also Adorno, 'Extorted Reconciliation', in *Notes to Literature*, vol. 1, pp. 216–40.

29 See, for example, Karl Marx, *Economic and Philosophic Manuscripts of 1844* (ed. and trans. Martin Milligan [Moscow: Foreign Languages Publishing House, 1961], p. 114:

> But since for the socialist man the entire so-called history of the world is nothing but the creation of man through human labour [...] he has the visible, irrefutable proof of his birth through himself, of his *process of coming-to-be*. [...] but socialism [...] proceeds from the *practically and theoretically sensuous consciousness* of man through and of nature as the essence. Socialism is man's *positive self-consciousness*, no longer mediated through the annulment of religion, just as *real life* is man's positive reality, no longer mediated through the annulment of private property, through *communism*. Communism is the position as the negation of the negation, and is hence the *actual* phase necessary for the next stage of historical development in the process of human emancipation and recovery. Communism is the necessary pattern and the dynamic principle of the immediate future, but communism as such is not the goal of human development – the structure of human society.

30 In *Phenomenology of Spirit* (pp. 487f.), Hegel conceived of the 'world spirit' as both a world-historical process and a process of successive self-appropriation by the increasingly self-conscious spirit:

> For experience is just this, that the content – which is Spirit – is *in itself* substance, and therefore an *object* of *consciousness*. But this substance which is Spirit is the process in which spirit *becomes* what it is *in itself*; and it is only as this process of reflecting itself into itself that it is in itself truly *Spirit*. It is in itself the movement which is cognition – the transforming of that *in-itself* into that which is *for itself* of substance into subject, of the object of consciousness into an object of *self-consciousness*, i.e. into an object that is just as much superseded, or into the *concept*. The movement is the circle that returns into itself, the circle that presupposes its beginning and reaches it only at the end. Hence, so far as Spirit is necessarily this immanent differentiation, its intuited whole appears over against its simple self-consciousness, and since, then, the former is what is differentiated, it is differentiated into its intuited pure Notion, into *Time* and into the content or into the *in-itself*. Substance is charged, as Subject, with the *at first only inward* necessity of setting forth within itself what it is in itself, of exhibiting itself as *Spirit*. Only when the objective presentation is complete is it at the same time the reflection of substance or the process in which substance becomes Self. Consequently, until Spirit has completed itself *in itself*, until it has completed itself as world-Spirit, it cannot reach its consummation as *self-conscious* Spirit.

Adorno criticizes Hegel's concept of the world spirit as an ideological hypostatization of domination:

> Spirit as a second nature is the negation of the spirit, however, and the more thoroughly so the blinder its self-consciousness is to its natural growth. This is what happens to Hegel. His world spirit is the ideology of natural history. He calls it world spirit because of its power. Domination is absolutized and projected on Being itself, which is said to be the spirit. But history, the explication of something it is supposed to have always been, acquires the quality of the ahistorical. In the midst of history, Hegel sides with its immutable element, with the ever-same identity of the process whose totality is said to bring salvation. (*Negative Dialectics*, trans. E. B. Ashton [New York: Continuum, 1972], pp. 356f.)

If there is a movement that shapes the whole of world history, it is that towards destruction. 'The world spirit, a worthy object of definition, could be defined as permanent catastrophe' (Ibid., p. 320). Nonetheless, the historico-philosophical question of the *state of the world spirit* and the stance of individual works towards that overall movement frequently preoccupies Adorno. In *Introduction to the Sociology of Music* (p. 186), for example, he characterizes the difference between the current situation after the Second World War in comparison to the situation in which Schoenberg and the cubists saw themselves before the First World War:

> The generation of Schönberg and his students felt carried by a boundless need to express themselves: not unlike the Cubists before World War I, they knew that what was in them, striving to see the light of day, was one with the world spirit. This concordance with the historic trend that helped artists to bear subjective isolation, poverty, slander, and ridicule is now lacking. In reality the individual is impotent, and nothing he accomplishes by himself and defines as his own can any longer be viewed as so substantial and important.

31 Marked in the left margin from 'In this, the situation' to 'in this way'.
32 See 'The Aging of the New Music', p. 189.
33 Marked in the left margin from 'On the other hand' to 'posits meaning'.
34 The adjective 'aleatory' (from the French *aléa* [in turn from the Latin *alea*, 'die or game of dice'], meaning a chance that leads to success or failure, the unpredictabilities of life, or risk) was first used in a musical context by Werner Meyer-Eppler in 1954, as 'a statistical term to refer to processes whose overall course is roughly fixed, but whose details are dependent on chance' (see Meyer-Eppler, 'Statistische und psychologische Klangprobleme', in *Die Reihe*, no. 1: *Elektronische Musik: Informationen über serielle Musik* [Vienna: Universal Edition, 1955], p. 22). Karlheinz Stockhausen and Pierre Boulez contributed decisively to establishing the term in the vocabulary of the musical avant-garde at the 1957 Darmstadt Summer Course, albeit emphasizing different aspects: for Stockhausen, 'aleatory' is one of the numerous statistical terms he incorporates into his compositional doctrine and with which he seeks to introduce a statistical way of thinking into composition; Boulez uses the term to define the musical form he seeks to achieve. See Wolf Frobenius, 'Aleatorisch, Aleatorik', in *Terminologie der Musik im 20. Jahrhundert*, ed. Hans Heinrich Eggebrecht (Stuttgart: Franz Steiner, 1995), p. 30.

Lecture 8

1 The formulation Adorno attributes to Lukács does not appear in the latter's book *The Meaning of Contemporary Realism* (trans. John Mander and Necke Mander [London: Merlin Press, 1963]).
2 See Hegel, *Philosophy of Subjective Spirit*, vol. 3: *Phenomenology and Psychology*, ed. and trans. M. J. Petry (Boston: D. Reidel, 1978), p. 111:

> [...] through the sublation of the two main stages of development preceding it, of these presuppositions made by itself, spirit has already displayed itself to us as *self-mediating*, as taking itself back into itself out of its other, as *unifying* the *subjective* and the *objective*. Consequently, the

activity of spirit which has *come to itself*, which already contains the object as implicitly sublated within itself, necessarily goes on to also sublate the *semblance* of its own and its general object's immediacy, the form of the object's simply being *found*.

3   See Lukács, *The Meaning of Contemporary Realism*.
4   The German-Bohemian Jewish writer Franz Werfel (1890–1945) wrote, among others, the novels *Barbara or Piety* (1929) and *The Song of Bernadette* (1941), which were especially successful in Catholic circles.
5   See Adorno, 'Notes on Kafka' (1939), in *Prisms*, pp. 243–71; see also Walter Benjamin, 'Franz Kafka' (1934), in *Selected Writings*, vol. 2: *1927–1934* (Cambridge, MA: Harvard University Press, 1999), pp. 794–818.
6   See the third book of Franz Werfel's volume of poetry *Der Gerichtstag* (Leipzig: Kurt Wolff, 1919), pp. 95–121.
7   This sentence is marked by Adorno.
8   See Hegel, *The Science of Logic*, trans. George Di Giovanni (Cambridge University Press, 2010), p. 33:

> The one thing needed to achieve *scientific progress* – and it is essential to make an effort at gaining this quite *simple* insight into it – is the recognition of the logical principle that the negative is equally positive, or that what is self-contradictory does not resolve itself into a nullity, into abstract nothingness, but essentially only into the negation of its *particular* content; or that such a negation is not just negation, but is *the negation of the determined fact* which is resolved, and is therefore determinate negation; that in the result there is therefore contained in essence that from which the result derives – a tautology indeed, since the result would otherwise be something immediate and not a result. Because the result, the negation, is a *determinate* negation, it has a *content*. It is a new concept but one higher and richer than the preceding – richer because it negates or opposes the preceding and therefore contains it, and it contains even more than that, for it is the unity of itself and its opposite.

In his essay 'The Experiential Content of Hegel's Philosophy', which he read out at the Hegel conference in Frankfurt on 25 October 1958, Adorno emphasized: 'The central nerve of dialectic as a method is determinate negation' (*Hegel: Three Studies*, p. 80).

9   In his *Ethics* (1677), Spinoza teaches: 'Just as light reveals both itself and the darkness, so truth is the standard of itself and the false' (Benedictus de Spinoza, *Ethics*, trans. W. H. White [Ware: Wordsworth Editions, 2001], p. 82). The latter statement (*'index sui et falsi'*) is quoted by Hegel in the preface to the second edition of his *Encyclopedia of Philosophical Sciences* (1827), as well as in his *Lectures on the Philosophy of Religion*. Both Karl Marx (in 'Comments on the New Prussian Censorship Instruction') and Lukács (in *The Meaning of Contemporary Realism*) continued this line of thought. Adorno, on the other hand, by inverting the topos and seeing the *falsum* as the *index sui et veri*, is

closer to Kierkegaard: '[...] to reach the truth, one must go through every negativity, for the old legend about breaking a certain magic spell is true: the piece has to be played through backwards or the spell is not broken' (Søren Kierkegaard, *The Sickness Unto Death*, ed. and trans. Howard V. Hong and Edna H. Hong [Princeton University Press, 2013], p. 44). The notion that insight into both the true and the false is gained not by proceeding from a truth that is presumed to be beyond doubt but usually by proceeding from what one has recognized as false in order to move *via negationis* towards what is true is fundamental to Adorno's *Negative Dialectics*; see also *Introduction to the Sociology of Music*, p. 152.

10 The concept of *Verfremdung* [often rendered in English as 'alienation', but translated here as 'defamiliarization' (Trans.)] is central to the programme of an 'epic theatre' advanced by Bertolt Brecht (1898–1956): 'To alienate an event or a character is simply to take what to the event or character is obvious, known, evident and produce surprise and curiosity [...]. The process of alienation, then, is the process of historicizing, of presenting events and persons as historical, and therefore as ephemeral' (Brecht, 'On the Experimental Theatre' [1939], trans. Carl Richard Mueller, *Tulane Drama Review*, vol. 6 [1961], p. 14).

11 In 'Critique of the Minstrel' (1956), Adorno had already postulated in Brechtian fashion: 'Art should obey our own experience so incorruptibly that it breaks through the context of delusion in the administered world: defamiliarization is the only possible response to alienation' ('Kritik des Musikanten', in *Dissonanzen: Musik in der verwalteten Welt, Gesammelte Schriften*, vol. 14: *Dissonanzen; Einleitung in die Musiksoziologie*, p. 71).

12 Adorno often quotes the line 'What has the world done to us!' from Karl Kraus's poem 'Lilac' (in *Ausgewählte Gedichte* [Munich: Verlag der Schriften von Karl Kraus, 1920], p. 20), for example in *Negative Dialectics*, p. 297. The poem is one of those set by Ernst Křenek in his song cycle *Durch die Nacht*, op. 67 (1930–31); Adorno valued Křenek's work highly and presented it to an American audience in a radio concert on 22 February 1940 (see 'Zum Rundfunkkonzert von 22. Februar 1940', in *Gesammelte Schriften*, vol. 18: *Musikalische Schriften V*, p. 580).

13 See Adorno, 'Trying to Understand *Endgame*', in *Notes to Literature*, vol. 1, pp. 241–75, and *Aesthetic Theory*, pp. 338f.

14 Gap in the recording owing to a change of tape.

15 As early as the 1920s, Adorno had reacted sensitively to all talk of 'allnature', whose Spinozist or Goethean pantheism increasingly turned into the 'blood and soil' ideology; see Adorno's review of various concerts in Frankfurt in December 1929, in *Gesammelte Schriften*, vol. 19, p. 163, as well as 'Fussnote zu Sibelius und Hamsun', in *Gesammelte Schriften*, vol. 20.2: *Vermischte Schriften II*, p. 804.

16 This paragraph is marked by Adorno from 'For the alienation of the world' to 'ultimately reduced'.

17   Note in the typescript: 'No more questions'.

18   The composer and writer on music Herbert Eimert (1897–1972) is considered one of the earliest pioneers of twelve-note music. His publications include *Atonale Musiklehre* (Leipzig: Breitkopf & Härtel, 1924), *Lehrbuch der Zwölftonmusik* (Wiesbaden: Breitkopf & Härtel, 1950) and *Grundlagen der musikalischen Reihentechnik* (Vienna: Universal Edition, 1964). He co-founded the studio for electronic music at West German Radio (WDR) in Cologne and was its director from 1951 to 1962. From 1951 to 1957 he was a tutor at the Darmstadt International Summer Course for New Music. Together with Karlheinz Stockhausen he edited the journal *Die Reihe – Informationen über serielle Musik* from 1955 to 1962. In 1965 he was appointed as professor at the Cologne Academy of Music, where he taught composition and was director (until 1971) of the studio for electronic music. In an essay on 'the composer's freedom of choice', Eimert wrote the following about Webern: 'What Webern realized is a functional system of internally coherent pitch and motivic relationships. Its compositional truth no longer lies purely in a spiritually adequate representation, in "similarity", but also in the constructively conclusive, in the "correct"' (Eimert, 'Von der Entscheidungsfreiheit des Komponisten', *Die Reihe*, vol. 3: *Musikalisches Handwerk* [1957], p. 7).

19   In his essay 'Exact Experiments in the Field of Art' (1928), Paul Klee (1879–1940) wrote: 'We construct and construct, and yet intuition still has its uses. Without it we can do a lot, but not everything. [...] Do substantial things, but not bring anything to truthful artistic life. No work of art whose genesis is of notable significance' (Robert Goldwater and Marco Treves [eds], *Artists on Art, from the XIV to the XX Century* [New York: Pantheon, 1945], p. 444. See also Adorno, 'Criteria of New Music', in *Sound Figures*, p. 181: 'Klee's comment that art starts at the point where the system no longer works, a comment which in an artist as methodical as Klee of course presupposes the system, is an insight that has not yet been appropriated by the latest generation of composers.'

20   Marked by Adorno in the left margin from 'Whatever there is' to 'held together'; in the typescript, the secretary underlined the word 'cannot' for special emphasis.

21   See Hegel, *The Science of Logic*, p. 357: 'Internally, therefore, identity is absolute non-identity.' See also Adorno, *Against Epistemology*, p. 38: 'Whoever refuses obedience to the jurisdiction of philosophy of origins has, since the Preface to Hegel's *Phenomenology*, known the mediacy of the new as well as that of the old. It is qualified as already contained in the older form as the non-identity of its identity.'

22   In his lecture 'Difficulties' (1964), Adorno summarizes his criticisms of the serial music of the 1950s – he names Boulez and Stockhausen as its leading exponents – as follows:

> The serial school wanted to radicalize the twelve-note principle, which they regarded, in a sense, as a merely partial reordering of the materials.

They wanted to extend it to all the musical dimensions, to elevate it to totality. Absolutely everything is to be determined, even the dimensions of rhythm, meter, tonal colour, and overall form, which in Schönberg had still been free. In doing so, the serial composers took as their starting point the thesis that because all musical phenomena, including pitch and tonal colour, are, in their acoustical regularity, ultimately temporal relations, they must all be able to be reduced compositionally to a single common denominator – time. (*Essays on Music*, p. 656)

23   Marked in the left margin from 'On the other hand' to 'element of randomness'.

24   Heisenberg's uncertainty principle is the rule in quantum physics that two complementary variables of a particle cannot always be determined precisely at the same time, because measuring the position of a quantum object automatically involves an interruption of its impulse; see Werner Heisenberg, *Physics and Philosophy: The Revolution in Modern Science* (New York: HarperCollins, 2007). In a letter to Eduard Steuermann from 14 October 1955, Adorno refers to a conversation in Darmstadt with the 'awful Stockhausen (no doubt a man of personal integrity, however)' in which the latter claimed that music 'exhibited the uncertainty principle'; quoted in *Adorno: Eine Bildmonographie*, ed. Theodor W. Adorno Archive (Frankfurt: Suhrkamp, 2003), pp. 247f.

25   Marked by Adorno from 'on the one hand' to 'as a whole'.

26   See Lecture 7, note 34.

27   The American avant-gardist John Cage (1912–1992) became perhaps the most influential composer of the second half of the twentieth century by confronting the awareness of sonic form in European art music, as well as the calculations of the serial avant-garde, with non-intentional and unpredictable elements, chance and the abundance of environmental sounds; in so doing, he revolutionized the general understanding of what music can be (see Heinz-Klaus Metzger and Rainer Riehn [eds], *John Cage* [*Musik-Konzepte*, special issue, 2 vols] [Munich: edition text + kritik, 1990]). The composition of his piano piece *Music of Changes* (1951) is the result of drawing lots according to the I-Ching. In his legendary work *4'33"* (1952), the performer(s) sit silently at their instrument(s); the music consists of the sounds in the respective performance setting, including the audience's reactions to the event or non-event. When Cage presented his aleatory composition *12'55.6078* for two prepared pianos at the 1954 Donaueschingen Festival, the reactions in the audience ranged from head-shaking to incredulous laughter and aggressive contempt. Critics spoke of 'amateurish childlike noises', 'sensationalism', 'nonsense', 'nihilistic pointlessness' and 'charlatanry' (see Max Nyffeler, 'Als Cage die Vogelpfeife blies', in *Beckmesser*, 23 November 1999). Cage appeared together with David Tudor at the Darmstadt Summer Course for New Music on 3 September 1958 to perform, among other works, *Music for Two Pianos* (1958) and *Winter Music* (1957), as well as the concept piece *Variations I, for any kind and number of instruments* (1958), a piece which simply posits any possible sonic result as its instantiation (see Gianmario Borio and

Hermann Danuser [eds], *Im Zenit der Moderne: Die Internationalen Ferienkurse für Neue Musik Darmstadt 1946–1966: Geschichte und Dokumentation in vier Bänden* [Freiburg: Rombach, 1997], vol. 3, pp. 513ff.). Cage gave a lecture in Darmstadt on 8 September 1958 entitled 'Indeterminacy', accompanied at the piano by David Tudor. This lecture, admittedly, was not so much an 'explanation' of the principle of indeterminacy as a performative exemplification thereof: 'My intention in putting the stories together in an unplanned way was to suggest that all things – stories, incidental sounds from the environment, and, by extension, beings – are related, and that this complexity is more evident when it is not oversimplified by an idea of relationship in one person's mind.' (See the published version of the lecture in John Cage, *Silence* [Middletown, CT: Wesleyan University Press, 1961], pp. 260–73, here p. 260.) Adorno could assume that at least some of his listeners would be familiar with Cage's piece *TV Köln*, which had been broadcast in September 1958 on WDR television.

28 Pierre Boulez's Third Piano Sonata (1956–7) is indeterminate in a highly determinate fashion, in that it lets the performer choose between different versions of a minutely composed structure. In his lecture 'Alea' (read out in German translation by Heinz-Klaus Metzger at the 1957 Darmstadt Summer Course), Boulez engaged with some of Stockhausen's and Cage's ideas, but also with Mallarmé's poem 'A Roll of the Dice' (1897), and explained various possibilities for incorporating chance elements into the composition and performance of music. Unlike Cage and Stockhausen, Boulez was concerned to employ chance as an element of compositional language. He had already used the term *aléatoire* as early as 1951, though not in a specifically technical musical sense, when he characterized Anton Webern's compositional approach by saying that Webern – because of his stricter need for purity – never aspired to the 'daring' (*aléatoire*) synthesis of a tonal musical language and the note-row principle which Schoenberg and Berg pursued. See Pierre Boulez, 'Bach's Moment' (1951), in *Stocktakings from an Apprenticeship*, trans. Stephen Walsh (Oxford and New York: Oxford University Press, 1991), pp. 3–14.

29 *Klavierstück XI* (1956) by Karlheinz Stockhausen (1928–2007), often discussed as a paradigmatic work of aleatory music, consists of nineteen 'groups', each precisely composed using a complex serial procedure, printed on a single large sheet of paper with the instruction that the performer must choose which fragment to play first and the order in which the rest will follow. The tempo, dynamics and articulation are initially also left to the performer; at the end of each 'group', however, there is a performance instruction which is to be applied to the next (freely chosen) fragment, which leads to significantly varying sonic results depending on the route chosen. For a performance of the whole piece, each 'group' is meant to appear three times. John Cage criticized this piece in one of his Darmstadt seminars in September 1958, arguing that the composer's creative intention is still far too dominant in the

individual modules. David Tudor, to whom Stockhausen had dedicated the piece and who recorded it in several versions, also found the precise notation of durations overly restrictive. In Stockhausen's piece *Zeitmasse* for five woodwind instruments (1956), which made a strong impression on Adorno (see the preface to the third edition of *Dissonanzen*, in *Gesammelte Schriften*, vol. 14: *Dissonanzen, Einleitung in die Musiksoziologie*, p. 12; 'On the State of Composition in Germany', in *Night Music*, p. 407; *Aesthetic Theory*, p. 217), the music alternates between fixed tempi and 'time fields' in which the instruments play in 'individual tempi' between 'as slow as possible' and 'as fast as possible'. This results in regularly irregular structural shifts in the interaction of the five instruments and an overall unpredictability of sonic results.

30 In contrast to Adorno's acknowledgement of the aesthetic relevance of aleatory forms, his later writings largely show a critical stance; see, for example, 'Difficulties', in *Essays on Music*, pp. 658f., and *Aesthetic Theory*, p. 301: '*Action painting, l'art informelle*, and aleatory works may have carried the element of resignation to its extreme: the aesthetic subject exempts itself of the burden of giving form to the contingent material it encounters, despairing of the possibility of undergirding it, and instead shifts the responsibility for its organization back to the contingent material itself.'

31 See *Philosophy of New Music*, pp. 19f.: 'The truth of this music seems to reside more in the organized absence of any meaning, by which it repudiates any meaning of organized society – which it wants nothing to do with – than in being capable on its own of any positive meaning' (translation modified).

32 Ibid., p. 158.

33 The Austrian composer and music theorist Joseph Matthias Hauer (1883–1959) had started developing his own form of twelve-note music in 1912 using his principle of 'building-block technique'. His *Nomos*, op. 19 (August 1919) is considered the first twelve-note composition. In contrast to Arnold Schoenberg's method of 'composition with twelve notes related only to one another', Hauer's theories attracted little attention in the music world; he was, however, awarded the Great Austrian State Prize in 1956. In the context of aleatory procedures, Hauer was rediscovered in the later twentieth century in avant-garde post-serial circles. In 1929, Adorno examined Hauer's Hölderlin settings for the *Zeitschrift für Musik*: see 'Joseph Matthias Hauer, Hölderlinlieder II, op. 23, and Joseph Matthias Hauer, Hölderlin-Lieder III, op. 32, und IV, op. 40', in *Gesammelte Schriften*, vol. 19, pp. 306ff. and 311f.; see also *The Philosophy of New Music*, p. 51). In a concert review from 1927, despite criticizing Hauer's 'amateurism', Adorno admits to being impressed by his Seventh Suite, op. 48; see *Gesammelte Schriften*, vol. 19, pp. 107f.

34 Marked in the left margin from 'For now' to 'in the first place'.

35 John Cage came to the Darmstadt Summer Course for New Music as a tutor in September 1958 (see note 27 above). Following his Darmstadt

appearance, his *Concert for Piano and Orchestra* (premiered in New York on 15 May 1958) was performed in Cologne, then also in Düsseldorf and Stockholm. The score is a collection of experimentally notated materials of the most varied kinds; the instrumental parts bear no relation to one another. The sole function of the conductor is to coordinate the timing. Adorno attended the concert on 19 September 1958 in the small broadcasting hall of the WDR in Cologne and later also listened to the recording of that concert (see his letter to Erich Doflein from 26 February 1960, in *Theodor W. Adorno – Erich Doflein: Briefwechsel*, ed. Andreas Jacob [Hildesheim: Olms, 2006], p. 244). In 1959 Adorno attempted to organize a Cage event at the Amerika-Haus in Frankfurt, which – if it had gone according to his plans – would have included the *Concert* (see his letter to Hans G. Helms from 27 February 1959; Theodor W. Adorno Archive, Br 588/44).

36 Marked by Adorno from 'It really is' to 'works of art'. See also 'New Music Today' (1955), in *Night Music*, pp. 384–400.

37 See Hans Sedlmayr, *Art in Crisis: The Lost Center*, trans. Brian Battershaw (London and New Brunswick, NJ: Transaction, 2006).

38 In *Phenomenology of Spirit*, Hegel mocks 'universal freedom' as a 'fury of disappearance'; see p. 359. Unfortunately, the original phrase *Furie des Verschwindens* is better known in the inaccurate translation 'fury of destruction' (Trans.).

39 Marked in the left margin from 'But at any rate' to 'if at all'.

40 Concerning the 'problem of characters', see Adorno's essay 'Arnold Schoenberg 1874–1951' (1952), in *Prisms*, pp. 147–72, here p. 162; 'In Memory of Eichendorff', in *Notes to Literature*, vol. 1, p. 74; also 'Short Commentaries on Proust', p. 177.

Lecture 9

1 For this lecture, Adorno used the translation of the *Phaedrus* by Constantin Ritter, in *Platon, Sämtliche Dialoge*, ed. Otto Apelt, vol. 2: *Menon – Kratylos – Phaidon – Phaidros* (Leipzig: Meiner, 1922). His personal copy is located in the Theodor W. Adorno Archive (NB Adorno 40). Adorno further consulted the English translation by B. Jowett, *The Dialogues of Plato*, vol. 1 (New York: Random House, 1937); this also includes annotations to the passages from the *Phaedrus* discussed in this lecture (NB Adorno 49, pp. 250–54). The Stephanus pagination, which is normally used for Plato's works, is based on the page and section numbers from the three-volume edition by Henricus Stephanus (Paris, 1578). The chapter numbers given here by Adorno refer not to the Stephanus, however, but to the Apelt; they were presumably also adopted in the paperback edition of the Schleiermacher translation, which most of Adorno's students would probably have used (*Platon, Sämtliche Werke*, vol. 4, ed. Walter F. Otto, Ernesto Grassi and Gert Plamböck [Reinbek: Rowohlt, 1958]). The chapters in the *Phaedrus*

correspond to sections 249d–252c. (In these notes, all references correspond to the edition given in Lecture 2, note 4 [Trans.].)

2 See Plato, *Phaedrus*, pp. 28f. (246a ff.).

3 See Eduard Zeller, *Die Philosophie der Griechen in ihrer geschichtlichen Entwicklung*, Part 2, Section 1: *Sokrates und die Sokratiker; Plato und die Alte Akademie* (Leipzig: Reisland, 1922), p. 537n; also ibid., p. 488n.

4 Adorno is going by Friedrich Ueberweg (ed.), *Grundriss der Geschichte der Philosophie*, Part 1: *Die Philosophie des Altertums*, ed. Karl Praechter (12th edn, Berlin: E. S. Mittler, 1926), p. 189.

5 The establishment of a chronological order for Plato's writings using statistical examinations of words began with Wilhelm Dittenberger, 'Sprachliche Kriterien für die Chronologie der platonischen Dialoge', *Hermes* 16 (1881), pp. 321–45, after Lewis Campbell had already developed first steps towards dating on the basis of linguistic observations in his edition *Sophistes and Politicus of Plato* (Oxford: Clarendon Press, 1867). On the history of dating attempts, see Leonard Brandwood, *The Chronology of Plato's Dialogues* (Cambridge University Press, 1990). Recent research no longer sees the *Phaedrus* as part of the last group of Plato's works (*Laws, Statesman, Sophist, Philebus* and *Timaeus*) but rather (along with *Republic, Parmenides* and *Theaetetus*) considers it to be from the middle period, or a transitional phase between the middle and late periods. See also Michael Erler, *Platon*, vol. 2/2 of the thoroughly revised *Ueberweg: Grundriss der Geschichte der Philosophie: Die Philosophie der Antike*, ed. Hellmut Flashar (Basel: Schwabe, 2007), pp. 22–6.

6 See Zeller, *Die Philosophie der Griechen*, pp. 662ff., and Ueberweg, *Die Philosophie des Altertums*, pp. 329ff. Concerning Adorno's understanding of Plato's theory of forms, see also his lectures on metaphysics (1965), published in English as *Metaphysics: Concept and Problems*, ed. Rolf Tiedemann, trans. Edmund Jephcott (Stanford University Press, 2001).

7 See the speech by Lysias in the *Phaedrus* (227c). In his personal copy, Adorno noted the name 'Proust' next to the sentence quoted here.

8 See Plato, *Phaedrus*, pp. 15ff. (237a ff.).

9 See ibid., pp. 25ff. (244a ff.); concerning the doctrine of anamnesis, see, especially, *Phaedrus* 250a, *Phaidon* 72e–77a and *Menon* 80d.

10 See Plato, *Phaedrus*, p. 33 (250b).

11 See ibid., pp. 34ff. (251a–e).

12 See Søren Kierkegaard, *Fear and Trembling*, trans. Sylvia Walsh (Cambridge University Press, 2006), p. 34: 'To transform the leap of life into a gait, absolutely to express the sublime in the pedestrian – that only the knight of faith can do – and that is the only miracle.' Adorno quotes this passage in *Kierkegaard* (p. 129) and repeatedly returns to it later – for example, in *The Jargon of Authenticity*, trans. Knut Tarnowski and Frederic Will (Evanston, IL: Northwestern University Press, 1973), p. 33.

13 See Plato, *Phaedrus*, pp. 35f. (252a–c).

14 Johann Wolfgang von Goethe, *Faust, Part One* (1808), trans. David Constantine (London: Penguin, 2005), p. 29.

15 In *Phaedrus* 257a, Socrates uses the term παλινῳδία [palinodia] (recantation) for his second, 'euphemistic', speech on eros (*Phaedrus* 244a ff.), which has become necessary for him as a purifying ritual in order to revise his first speech, in which he initially argued that one should favour the non-enamoured over the enamoured (*Phaedrus* 237a–241d), but which he has meanwhile discarded as 'untrue' and blasphemous. As part of his proof that the gods give humans the madness of love for the sake of their greatest happiness, Socrates conceives the 'great parable' of the soul chariot with the winged horses, the departure of the souls to the divine place (*Phaedrus* 246a ff.), and in this context also the classical version of the theory of forms, which is at the centre of Adorno's interpretation of the *Phaedrus*.

16 See, for example, Arnold Ruge, *Die Platonische Aesthetik* (Halle: Buchhandlung des Waisenhauses, 1832); also Stefan Büttner, *Antike Ästhetik: Eine Einführung in die Prinzipien des Schönen* (Munich: C. H. Beck, 2006), especially pp. 26ff and 40ff.

17 The notion that decisive insights cannot be captured in a single term or concept, only in a *constellation* of them, is fundamental to Adorno's understanding of philosophy, from *Kierkegaard* to the late central works *Negative Dialectics* and *Aesthetic Theory*.

18 At the end of Lecture 10, Adorno refers to the poem 'The Tapestry' from Stefan George's cycle *The Tapestry of Life*; see Lecture 10, note 30. See also *Aesthetic Theory*, p. 175: 'Perhaps, in the end, it is even carpets, ornaments, all non-figural things that long most intensely for their decipherment' (translation modified).

19 See Zeller, *Die Philosophie der Griechen*, Part 2, Section 1, pp. 569ff.

20 See Plato, *Phaedrus*, p. 33 (249c–d).

21 See G. W. F. Hegel, *Werke*, ed. Eva Moldenhauer, vol. 4: *Nürnberger und Heidelberger Schriften 1808–1817* (Frankfurt: Suhrkamp, 1983), p. 56: '*Reasoning* reason seeks the *grounds* of things, i.e. their positedness through and in an other, which is the essence that remains in itself, but is at once only *relatively unconditional*, in that the grounded or the consequence has a different content than does the ground.'

22 See Plato, *Phaedrus*, p. 23 (241e).

23 See, in addition to the passage from the *Phaedrus*, also Plato's *Ion* 533d–e and *Timaeus* 71e–72a. See also Hermann Gundert, 'Enthusiasmos und Logos bei Platon', *Lexis* 2 (1949), pp. 25–46.

24 See Plato, *Phaedrus*, pp. 28f. (246a ff.).

25 This association may refer to Hölderlin's hymn 'Patmos' (1802); see Friedrich Hölderlin, *Selected Poems and Fragments*, trans. Michael Hamburger (London: Penguin, 1998), pp. 231–42.

26 See Zeller, *Die Philosophie der Griechen*, Part 2, Section 1, especially pp. 882–6.

27 Plato, *Phaedrus*, pp. 33f. (249d–250c). Adorno's personal copy of the *Phaedrus* contains the note 'Body as prison / Phaedo' next to the quoted passage.

28 Neither the wording nor the occasion of this statement by Josef Hermann Dufhues, a leading member of the Christian Democratic Union (CDU) and interior minister of North Rhine-Westphalia from 1958 to 1962, could be ascertained.

29 Concerning the dialectical method as the 'science of linking concepts', see Zeller, *Die Philosophie der Griechen*, II.1, pp. 614ff.

30 Plato, *Phaedrus*, p. 33 (250b).

31 While it is more common in English to speak of Plato's theory of forms, the German term – *Ideenlehre* – means 'theory/doctrine of ideas'. In passages such as this, where Adorno invokes the idea in its wider sense, the reference to forms has been augmented by the use of 'idea', despite the German using only the single word *Idee*, in order to capture this twofold sense (Trans.).

32 See note 6 above.

33 Here the transcription notes a gap, evidently the result of a disturbance in the recording.

34 Marked by Adorno from 'For it means' to 'objective aspects'.

35 Concerning the 'elimination of desire from the object of beauty' as a basic element of the Christian approach to beauty, see Augustine, *Confessions*, ed. Michael P. Foley, trans. Frank J. Sheed (Indianapolis: Hackett, 2006), Book 4, chapter 13ff.

Lecture 10

1 Plato, *Phaedrus*, p. 34 (250c).

2 Ibid., 250d.

3 The term 'logistics', which in contemporary parlance refers (based on the term for military supply systems) only to the organization of transport services, was used from the early twentieth century to the 1960s as the title of a philosophical discipline, namely the expanded research fields of formal logic (symbolic logic, mathematical logic, algebra of logic, etc.); see Günter Patzig, 'Logistik', in *Das Fischer Lexikon*, vol. 11: *Philosophie*, ed. A. Diemer and I. Frenzel (Frankfurt: S. Fischer, 1958), pp. 160–73, and Joseph M. Bochenski and Albert Menne, *Grundriss der Logistik* (Paderborn: Schöningh, 1954).

4 On the concept of 'shadings', see Edmund Husserl, *Ideas: General Introduction to Pure Phenomenology*, trans. W. R. Boyce Gibson (London and New York: Routledge, 2014), p. 134. See also Adorno, *Against Epistemology*, p. 184 [translated there as 'adumbrations'], as well as 'Zur Philosophie Husserls', in *Gesammelte Schriften*, vol. 20.1: *Vermischte Schriften I*, pp. 59f., and even 'Die Transzendenz des Dinglichen und Noematischen in Husserls Phänomenologie', in *Gesammelte Schriften*, vol. 1: *Philosophische Frühschriften*, p. 22.

5 In Platonic thought, individual things are named specifically only by virtue of their 'partaking' (Gr. μέθεχις) in the forms (see *Phaedo* 102b, *Parmenides* 130e–133d and *Timaeus* 52a). The notion of participation is also meant to convey that a particular content can inhere in a thing

to a greater or lesser extent; this graduality is indirectly expressed in references to 'parts'.

6   Plato, *Phaedrus*, p. 34 (250e).

7   Ibid., pp. 34f. (251a–b).

8   Wolfgang Amadeus Mozart, *The Marriage of Figaro* (1786), K 492; Act 2, scene 2, no. 12, bars. 29–36: 'I feel an emotion full of desire, that is now pleasure, and now suffering.'

9   See Søren Kierkegaard, *Either/Or*, trans. Alastair Hannay (London: Penguin, 1992), p. 87.

10 See Walter Benjamin, *One-Way Street*, in *One-Way Street and Other Writings*, trans. J. A. Underwood (London: Penguin, 2009), p. 81: 'With everything that is justly termed beautiful, its appearing seems paradoxical.'

11 This sentence is marked by Adorno in the typescript.

12 See Lecture 1, note 8.

13 For a critique of the idealistic concept of the symbol, see Benjamin, *The Origin of German Tragic Drama*, trans. John Osborne (London and New York: Verso, 1998), pp. 160ff.

14 Gap in the text due to change of tape.

15 See Adalbert Stifter, *Der Nachsommer* (1857), in *Werke*, ed. Uwe Japp and Hans Joachim Piechotta (Frankfurt: Insel, 1978), vol. 3, pp. 400 and 453.

16 There is no such stage direction in Wedekind's Lulu play *Earth Spirit* (1895) or the later version, *Pandora's Box (1904)*. Possibly Adorno is referring to a version in Wedekind's literary remains which he had already examined closely in 1932; see 'On the Legacy of Frank Wedekind', in *Notes to Literature*, vol. 2, pp. 274–9.

17 Walter Benjamin pointed out an anticipation of tendencies that would become fully manifest only in the *Jugendstil* of the early twentieth century, in the work of the French poet Charles Baudelaire (1821–1867), whom he actually considered more of a modernist antipode to *Jugendstil*. See Benjamin, 'Central Park' (1939–40), in *Selected Writings*, vol. 4: *1938–1940* (Cambridge, MA: Harvard University Press, 2003), pp. 164f. The material Benjamin collected for his *Arcades Project* included, as well as extensive notes and excerpts on Baudelaire (Convolute J), a folder with notes on *Jugendstil* (Convolute S); here one can find further remarks on a 'prefiguration of *Jugendstil*' in Baudelaire (pp. 553ff.).

18 The key phrase to describe the 'loss of the capacity for aesthetic distance' since Baudelaire, as Adorno terms it, is the 'loss' or 'decay of aura'; see Benjamin, 'The Work of Art in the Age of its Technological Reproducibility, Third Version', trans. Edmund Jephcott and Harry Zohn, in *Selected Writings*, ed. Howard Eiland and Michael W. Jennings, vol. 4: *1938–1940* (Cambridge, MA: Harvard University Press, 2003), p. 255, as well as 'Central Park', p. 165, and the corresponding note in the *Arcades Project* Convolute S (p. 557), which refers to the prose poem 'Lost Halo' (first published posthumously in 1869), no. XLVI from Baudelaire's *Paris Spleen*; see Baudelaire, *Paris Spleen: Little*

Prose Poems, trans. Keith Waldrop (Middletown, CT: Wesleyan University Press, 2010), p. 88.

19 Marked in the left margin from 'the capacity for' to 'affinity with death'. Adorno sees particularly effective depictions of the connection between beauty or, most of all, love and death in Wagner's *Ring* and *Tristan*; see *In Search of Wagner*, p. 135.

20 See *Aesthetic Theory*, p. 409: 'Stendhal's dictum of art as the *promesse du bonheur* implies that art does its part for existence by accentuating that part of it which prefigures utopia' (translation modified).

21 Marked in the left margin from 'Let me also' to 'art today'.

22 See Kant, *Critique of the Power of Judgement*, p. 141 (for quotation, see Lecture 3, note 37).

23 Marked by Adorno from 'The difficulty' to 'them together'.

24 In the aphoristic text 'Refutations', published in 1931 in the journal *Die Musik*, Adorno saw 'New Music's claim to truth' in opposition to the 'culinary category of a tasting enjoyment' ('Widerlegungen', in *Gesammelte Schriften*, vol. 18, p. 26); see also 'On the Fetish-Character in Music and the Regression of Listening' (1938), in *Essays on Music*, p. 291, and *Philosophy of New Music* (1949), p. 14.

25 In the scholastic doctrine of the transcendental, beauty – alongside truth, goodness and oneness – was considered one of the supra-categorial definitions that follow from the nature of being, and necessarily apply both for being in general and for each individual entity: '*Ens et unum et verum et bonum et pulchrum convertuntur.*'

26 See Friedrich Nietzsche, *Human, All Too Human: A Book for Free Spirits*, trans. R. J. Hollingdale (Cambridge University Press, 1996), aphorism no. 162, pp. 85f.

27 See *In Search of Wagner*, pp. 74–85.

28 In his essay 'The Origin of the Work of Art' (1936), Heidegger posited that 'the essential nature of art' is 'the setting-itself-to-work of the truth of beings' (Martin Heidegger, *Off the Beaten Track*, trans. Julian Young and Kenneth Haynes [Cambridge University Press, 2002], p. 16). Adorno also engages with Heidegger's thesis in his lecture 'Art and the Arts' (1966), in *Can One Live after Auschwitz? A Philosophical Reader*, ed. Rolf Tiedemann, trans. Rodney Livingstone et al. (Stanford University Press, 2003), pp. 380f.

29 See Hegel, *Phenomenology of Spirit*, trans. A. V. Miller (Oxford and New York: Oxford University Press, 1977), p. 9.

30 Stefan George, 'The Tapestry', from *The Tapestry of Life*, in *The Works of Stefan George*, trans. Olga Marx and Ernst Morwitz (Chapel Hill: University of North Carolina Press, 1974), p. 185; see also *Aesthetic Theory*, p. 241.

31 Marked in the left margin from 'But I think' to 'concept of utopia'.

32 See Eduard Mörike, 'To a Lamp' (1846), in Helga Slessarev, *Eduard Mörike* (New York: Twayne, 1970), p. 72: 'But what is beautiful shines blissfully in itself.'

Lecture 11

1   According to Hegel, 'The *in-itself* is, in the first instance, the *abstraction of essence* in contrast to reality; but an abstraction is precisely what is not true, but exists only *for consciousness*, which means, however, that it is itself what is called real; for the real is that which is essentially *for an other*, or is *being*' (*Phenomenology of Spirit*, trans. A. V. Miller [Oxford and New York: Oxford University Press, 1977], p. 233). 'Everything is essentially "in-itself", but this is not the end of the matter, and just as the germ, which is the plant-in-itself, is simply the activity of self-development, so the thing also generally progresses beyond its mere in-itself (understood as abstract reflection-into-itself) to reveal itself also to be reflection-into-another, and *as a result it has properties*' (Hegel, *The Encyclopaedia Logic: Part I of the Encyclopaedia of the Philosophical Sciences with the Zusätze*, trans. Théodore F. Geraets, Wallis Arthur Suchting and Henry Silton Harris [New York: Hackett, 1991], p. 194). To gain an idea of Adorno's understanding of the relation between 'in itself' and 'for us', one should consider not only these seminal Hegel passages but also a formulation in which Husserl reflects on the problem of relativism: 'There would therefore be no world "in itself", but only a world for us, or for any other chance species of being' (Edmund Husserl, *Logical Investigations*, ed. Dermot Moran, trans. J. N. Findlay, vol. 1 [London and New York: Routledge, 2001], p. 81); see also Adorno, *Against Epistemology*, p. 87, as well as 'Zur Philosophie Husserls', pp. 46–118, especially pp. 91 and 113ff.

2   Concerning the Platonic concept of participation (μέθεξις), see Lecture 10, note 5.

3   See Lecture 9, note 27.

4   See Plato, *Phaedrus*, p. 56 (266b–c). Concerning this epistemological concept of dialectic, see also Friedrich Ueberweg, *Die Philosophie des Altertums* ed. Karl Praechter (12th edn, Berlin: E. S. Mittler, 1926), p. 329, as well as Adorno's *An Introduction to Dialectics* (see Lecture 3, note 3).

5   See Lecture 9, note 27.

6   See *Phaedrus*, pp. 26f. (244c–245c) and 42 (256b).

7   Kierkegaard develops an emphatic definition of the concept of 'appropriation' in *Either/Or*, trans. Alastair Hannay (London: Penguin, 1992), pp. 434 and 458.

8   See Lecture 1, note 39.

9   Karl Rosenkranz, *The Aesthetics of Ugliness: A Critical Edition*, ed. and trans. Andrei Pop and Mechtild Widrich (London and New York: Bloomsbury, 2015). See also *Aesthetic Theory*, p. 63ff.

10   Frans Hals, *Malle Babbe* (c. 1635), oil on canvas, 75 × 64 cm, Gemäldegalerie, Berlin.

11   Adorno had attended a performance of Beckett's *Endgame* in April 1958 at the Theater am Fleischmarkt, Vienna (see his letter of 17 April

1958 to Max Horkheimer, in *Theodor W. Adorno – Max Horkheimer, Briefwechsel 1950–1969*, ed. Christoph Gödde and Henri Lonitz [Frankfurt: Suhrkamp, 2006], p. 500).

12 See Umberto Eco, *On Ugliness*, trans. Alastair McEwen (New York: Random House, 2007).

13 Adorno developed this idea further in his radio lecture 'Schöne Stellen' (1965); see *Gesammelte Schriften*, vol. 18, pp. 695–718.

14 The opera *Lulu*, based on Frank Wedekind's tragedies *Earth Spirit* and *Pandora's Box*, by the Viennese composer Alban Berg (1885–1935), who had given Adorno composition lessons in 1925 and was friends with him until his death (see *Theodor W. Adorno – Alban Berg: Correspondence 1925–1935*, trans. Wieland Hoban [Cambridge: Polity, 2005]), remained unfinished. Adorno had heard Adrian Boult conduct the *Symphonic Pieces from the Opera Lulu* in London in 1935; he was also familiar with the opera fragment premiered in Zurich in 1937, both from reading the score and from various performances (see Adorno, *Alban Berg: Master of the Smallest Link*, trans. Juliane Brand and Christopher Hailey [Cambridge University Press, 1991], pp. 120–35). In 1960 he gave a speech at the premiere of the Frankfurt production under George Solti ('Rede über Alban Bergs Lulu', in *Gesammelte Schriften*, vol. 18, pp. 645–9). In 1968 he was still voicing the urgent hope 'that the remaining portions of the third act' would 'at last be orchestrated' (*Alban Berg: Master of the Smallest Link*, p. 7). He did not live to hear the reconstruction of Act 3 by Friedrich Cerha; it was premiered at the Paris Opera under Pierre Boulez in 1979.

15 See *Alban Berg: Master of the Smallest Link*, p. 122.

16 Adorno does not refer to 'aesthetic attitude' elsewhere. A specifically 'aesthetic attitude' was mentioned by, among others, Moritz Geiger in 'Beiträge zur Phänomenologie des ästhetischen Genusses', *Jahrbuch für Phänomenologie und philosophische Forschung I*, pp. 14 and 50, as well as the Polish phenomenologist Roman Ingarden (1893–1970), in his Paris lecture 'Aesthetic Experience and Aesthetic Object' (1937), published in *Philosophy and Phenomenological Research* 21 (March 1961), pp. 289–313. The art scholar Alfred Werner distinguished between an 'aesthetic attitude' and an 'artistic attitude' (see Werner, *Impressionismus und Expressionismus* [Frankfurt: Kesselringsche Hofbuchhandlung, 1917], pp. 38f.). In Anglo-American aesthetics the phrase was established in particular by the Princeton psychologist Herbert Sidney Langfeld (1879–1958), in his book *The Aesthetic Attitude* (New York: Harcourt, Brace & Howe, 1920). In the post-war period, the American Kantian Jerome Stolnitz was one purveyor of a theory of aesthetic attitude that was not only psychologically but also normatively oriented. For him, this is characterized by a 'disinterested and sympathetic attention to and contemplation of any object of awareness whatever, for its own sake alone' (Stolnitz, 'The Aesthetic Attitude', in *Aesthetics and the Philosophy of Art Criticism* [New York: Houghton Mifflin, 1960], pp. 40ff.).

17   In his essay 'Anton von Webern', which appeared in the journal *Merkur*
     in 1959, Adorno looks in detail at the proximity between Webern and
     Klee:

> It is not for nothing that Webern puts us in mind of Paul Klee. It helps
> us to specify more exactly the idea of absolute lyricism that guided him.
> His affinity with the painter extends more deeply than the mere analogy
> between approaches that led both in the middle years to abandon all
> impasto and everything voluminous and to confine themselves to line. In
> their use of line, too, they are related, both displaying an eccentric graphic
> style, a calligraphy both definite and enigmatic. Its name is scribbling; it
> is how, with a beggar's pride, Kafka chose to describe his prose. Further-
> more, both Klee and Webern explore an imaginary twilight world some-
> where between line and colour. The works of both are tinted, not coloured.
> Never does colour become autonomous, never does it even assert its role
> explicitly as a definite compositional stratum, nor is it a sound pattern.
> But it captures the spirit of scribbling, just as children's drawings feed on
> the delight that springs from the paper they have coloured. The œuvres
> of the two men in their respective media migrate from the established
> genres into the twilight world. (p. 104)

18   This description refers to bar 65 in the first movement of Beethoven's
     Symphony no. 3 in E flat major, op. 55 ('Eroica'); see also Adorno,
     Beethoven: The Philosophy of Music, ed. Rolf Tiedemann, trans.
     Edmund Jephcott (Cambridge: Polity, 2002), pp. 19 and 49.
19   On the relationship between 'serious' and 'light' music, see also Adorno,
     'On Popular Music', in *Essays on Music*, pp. 437–69.
20   The pastor and educator Johann Peter Hebel (1760–1826), from the
     Southern Baden region, wrote poems in Alemannic dialect and, from
     1807 until 1815, numerous 'educational articles and humorous stories'
     for the Lutheran-Baden rural calendar 'Rheinländischer Hausfreund'; a
     collection of the most interesting of these calendar stories first appeared
     in 1811 under the title 'Little Treasure Chest of the Rhenish House
     Friend' and, with numerous new editions, became probably the most
     popular book of German-language literature next to Grimms' fairy
     tales. In *Aesthetic Theory*, Adorno writes: 'The devastation that ideal-
     ism sowed is glaringly evident in its victims – Johann Peter Hebel, for
     example – who were vanquished by the verdict passed by aesthetic
     dignity, yet survived it by exposing the narrow-minded finitude of that
     dignity through their own existence, which the idealists had deemed all
     too finite' (p. 86, translation modified). See also Benjamin, 'Johann
     Peter Hebel 3', in *Gesammelte Schriften*, vol. II.2, pp. 635ff., where the
     author describes Hebel's stories as 'the votive paintings which the
     Enlightenment set up in the temple of the goddess Reason.'
21   Marked in the left margin from 'This reciprocal production' to 'threaten
     the work'.
22   The catchphrase *poésie pure*, coined in 1830 by the French critic Sainte-
     Beuve (1804–1869), stands in contrast to *poésie engagée* as 'pure'

poetry in the sense of *l'art pour l'art* (see Lecture 4, note 21). Following on from this, a distinction also came to be made in music between 'programme music' and 'pure' or 'absolute music' (*musique pure*), and this distinction contributed decisively to the idea, among painters such as Wassily Kandinsky and others in the early twentieth century, of developing a 'pure', 'objectless', 'abstract' form of painting that, as *peinture pure*, was set apart from painting that was traditionally placed in the service of external representations.

23 This sentence is underlined by Adorno in the typescript.

24 'Throw away in order to gain' could almost be considered a leitmotif in Adorno's work; see, for example, *Minima Moralia*, p. 150; *Philosophy of New Music*, p. 156; 'The Mastery of the Maestro', in *Sound Figures*, p. 47; see also Irving Wohlfahrt, 'Dialektischer Spleen: Zur Ortsbestimmung der Adornoschen Ästhetik', in *Materialien zur ästhetischen Theorie Adornos*, ed. Burkhardt Lindner and W. Martin Lüdke (Frankfurt: Suhrkamp, 1980), pp. 310–47, here p. 317, and Philipp von Wussow, *Logik der Deutung: Adorno und die Philosophie* (Würzburg: Königshausen & Neumann, 2007), p. 132. At one point, Adorno terms this exhortation 'biblical' ('Das Erbe und die neue Musik', in *Gesammelte Schriften*, vol. 18, p. 694), but the basis of this claim is unclear. The closest formulation would be in Matthew 16:25: 'For whoever wants to save his life will lose it, but whoever loses his life for me will find it.' A similar message can be found in Matthew 19:21: 'If you want to be perfect, go, sell your possessions and give to the poor, and you will have treasure in heaven. Then come, follow me.' See also Augustine, *Confessions*, ed. Michael P. Foley, trans. Frank J. Sheed (Indianapolis: Hackett, 2006), p. 158: 'Cast yourself upon Him and be not afraid; He will not draw away and let you fall. Cast yourself without fear, He will receive you and heal you.' Adorno's source for the motto was most likely Lukács's *The Theory of the Novel*, trans. Anna Bostock (Boston: MIT Press, 1971), p. 53.

25 Marked in the left margin from 'it is surely' to 'art at all'.

Lecture 12

1 The 'new book' mentioned by Adorno is *Sound Figures*, published in 1959. The plan to incorporate a collection of musical aphorisms first published in 1928–9, which included the lines read out here, was abandoned by Adorno before the book went to press in March 1959.

2 This aphorism was first published in a small collection under the title *Motive II*, in *Musikblätter des Anbruch* 10/6 (1928), p. 199; now in *Gesammelte Schriften*, vol. 18, p. 14; see also the first section of *Introduction to the Sociology of Music*.

3 Concerning the youth music movement, see Dorothea Kolland, 'Jugendmusikbewegung', in Diethart Kerbs and Jürgen Reulecke (eds), *Handbuch der deutschen Reformbewegungen: 1880–1933* (Wuppertal:

P. Hammer, 1998), pp. 379–94. Adorno's perception of this movement, whose central figures were some twenty years older than he was but continued to have important effects on his generation in Germany, and still played a considerable part in music education after the war, was distanced:

> The ideology of readiness to hand, and its counterpart, strips itself bare in the practice of those devotees of the musical youth movement, who swear to it that a proper fiddle is one that a fiddler has rigged up for himself. Since the artisan forms of production have been overtaken by technology, and are superfluous, the intimacy which adhered to them has become as worthless as the do-it-yourself movement. (*The Jargon of Authenticity*, p. 108)

4 Paul Hindemith had collaborated with Bertolt Brecht on the latter's play *Lesson*, the premiere of which at the Baden-Baden Chamber Music Festival in 1929 was accompanied by scandal; its motto was 'making music is better than listening to music.'

5 See 'Kritik des Musikanten', pp. 67–107.

6 The words 'worth its money' appear in English in the original (Trans.).

7 See, for example, Moritz Geiger's 'Beiträge zur Phänomenologie des ästhetischen Genusses', *Jahrbuch für Phänomenologie und philosophische Forschung I*. The question of the legitimacy or dubiousness of a culinary demand in aesthetic behaviour, from which Adorno develops his position here, still defined the reception of his *Aesthetic Theory* after his death. See Hans Robert Jauss, *Kleine Apologie der ästhetischen Erfahrung* (Constance: Universitätsverlag, 1972).

8 In the early modern age, the term 'fetish' (from Portuguese *feitiço*, which in turn comes from the Latin *factitius*: something artificial, an imitation, a false version, especially for objects to which magical effects are ascribed) was initially used in a pejorative sense for West African cult objects; it was then generalized in the eighteenth century by Enlightenment theology and colonialist anthropology (see Charles de Brosses, *Du culte des dieux fétiches* [Paris, 1760]). In his *Lectures on the Philosophy of World History: Introduction*, trans. H. B. Nisbet (Cambridge University Press, 1975), pp. 179f., Hegel describes 'the negroes' as 'sorcerers' (as known since Herodotus) who must 'give this power of theirs [over nature] a visible form [...], making images of it. [...] The first object they encounter which they imagine has power over them – whether it be an animal, a tree, a stone, or a wooden image – is given the status of a genius. [...] It is a fetish [...].' This term, introduced in the context of colonialist criticisms of 'primitive idolatry', was taken up by Karl Marx, who applied it in his analysis of the commodity relationship:

> A commodity appears at first sight an extremely obvious, trivial thing. But its analysis brings out that it is a very strange thing, abounding in

metaphysical subtleties and theological niceties. [...] The mysterious character of the commodity-form consists therefore simply in the fact that the commodity reflects the social characteristics of men's own labour as objective characteristics of the products of labour themselves, as the socio-natural properties of these things. Hence it also reflects the social relation of the producers to the sum total of labour as a social relation between objects, a relation which exists apart from and outside the producers. Through this substitution, the products of labour become commodities, sensuous things which are at the same time supra-sensible or social. [...] I call this the fetishism which attaches itself to the products of labour as soon as they are produced as commodities, and is therefore inseparable from the production of commodities. (Marx, *Capital*, vol. 1, trans. Ben Fowkes [London: Penguin, 2004], pp. 164f.)

Since the late nineteenth century, the term has also been used in sexology to refer to the endowment of partial objects with sexual meaning, enabling them to act as substitutes for real persons and erotic relationships (see the 1886 study by Richard von Krafft-Ebing, *Psychopathologia sexualis: With Especial Reference to the Antipathic Sexual Instinct: A Medico-Forensic Study*, trans. Franklin S. Klaf [New York: Arcade, 1965]; Alfred Binet, 'Le Fétichisme dans l'amour', in *Études de psychologie expérimentale, Bibliothèque des actualités médicales et scientifiques* [Paris: Doin, 1888], pp. 1–85; and Sigmund Freud, 'Fetishism' (1927), in *On Sexuality*, trans. James Strachey [London: Penguin, 1991], pp. 345–58). This made it possible for enlightened Europeans to acknowledge that the fetishization of objects is not simply the outlandish behaviour of 'primitives' but, evidently, an inevitable part of the human ability to give objects meaning. For Adorno, it was beyond doubt that the origin of art was to be found in 'archaic fetishism' (see *Aesthetic Theory*, pp. 24, 310, 429–38, 449). He already drew his aesthetic conclusion from this in *Minima Moralia*: 'Since works are sprung, for better or worse, from fetishes – are artists to be blamed if their attitude to their products is slightly fetishistic?' (p. 222).

9   See Benjamin, 'The Work of Art in the Age of its Technological Reproducibility, Third Version', trans. Edmund Jephcott and Harry Zohn, in *Selected Writings*, ed. Howard Eiland and Michael W. Jennings, vol. 4: *1938–1940* (Cambridge, MA: Harvard University Press, 2003), pp. 255f.; see also the first version of the same essay, in *Gesammelte Schriften*, vol. I.2, p. 441.

10 Marked in the left margin from 'pork rib and sauerkraut' to 'this achievement'.

11 In the framework of his metaphysics in *The World as Will and Representation* (2 vols, trans. E. F. J. Payne [Mineola, NY: Dover, 1969], Schopenhauer understood works of art as outstanding opportunities to rise above the troubles of the present:

We can withdraw from all suffering just as well through present as through distant objects, whenever we raise ourselves to a purely objective contemplation of them, and are thus able to produce the illusion that only those objects are present, now we ourselves. Then, as pure subject of knowing, delivered from the miserable self, we become entirely one with those objects, and foreign as our want is to them, it is at such moments just as foreign to us. Then the world as representation alone remains; the world as will has disappeared. (vol. 1, p. 199)

For if this were not so, if this rising above all the aims and good things of life, this turning away from life and its temptations, and the turning, already to be found here, to an existence of a different kind, although wholly inconceivable to us, were not the tendency of tragedy, then how would it be possible generally for the presentation of the terrible side of life, brought before our eyes in the most glaring light, to be capable of affecting us so beneficially, and of affording us an exalted pleasure? (vol. 2, p. 435)

12 Marked in the left margin from 'I would like' to 'withdraw from it'.

13 The novella *The Kreutzer Sonata* by Leo N. Tolstoy (1828–1910), published in 1889, tells the story of a man who murders his wife out of jealousy after she, under the influence of sensually stimulating music – Beethoven's *Kreutzer Sonata*, op. 47 – commits adultery in an erotic adventure with a young violinist after years of failed marriage. In *Minima Moralia*, Adorno attempts to gain an insight into the 'misshapen bourgeois form of sex' through the vehemently anti-sexual morality of Tolstoy's late work, and thus – contrary to Tolstoy's stated intentions – to find in it, at least indirectly, some prospect of a liberated sexuality (see *Minima Moralia*, pp. 176f.). In *Aesthetic Theory*, Adorno encapsulates Tolstoy's art-critical idea, which he praises here as 'extraordinarily penetrating and subtle', in the following statement: 'The sublime as semblance has its own absurdity and contributes to the neutralization of truth; this is the accusation of art in Tolstoy's *The Kreutzer Sonata*' (p. 270; see also ibid., p. 328).

14 This sentence is marked in the left margin. In *Aesthetic Theory*, Adorno states on this topic: 'Even radical art is a lie in so far as it fails to create the possible to which it gives rise as semblance. Artworks draw credit from a praxis that has yet to begin and no one knows whether anything backs their letters of credit' (p. 116).

15 Kierkegaard's *Either/Or* (1843) is a composition comprising a first part, which gathers the personal testimonies and reflections of the existentially failed aesthetician (and aesthete) 'A', and an antithetical second part containing the papers of the (equally helpless) ethicist 'B' and his letters to A; the whole collection is supposedly edited by a certain Victor Eremita. On the tension between moralism and aestheticism in Kierkegaard, see also Adorno, *Kierkegaard*, pp. 25f.

16 Marked in the left margin from 'These moments are probably' to 'one has them'.

17 See Schopenhauer, *The World as Will and Representation*, vol. 1, §30 (p. 169):

Therefore these Ideas as a whole present themselves in innumerable individuals and in isolated details [...]. The plurality of such individuals can be conceived only through time and space, their arising and passing away through causality. In all these forms we recognize only the different aspects of the principle of sufficient reason that is the ultimate principle of all finiteness, of all individuation, and the universal form of the representation as it comes to the knowledge of the individual as such. On the other hand, the Idea does not enter into that principle; hence neither plurality nor change belongs to it. While the individuals in which it expresses itself are innumerable and are incessantly coming into existence and passing away, it remains unchanged as one and the same, and the principle of sufficient reason has no meaning for it. But now, as this principle is the form under which all knowledge of the subject comes, in so far as the subject knows as an *individual*, the Ideas will also lie quite outside the sphere of its knowledge as such. Therefore, if the Ideas are to become object of knowledge, this can happen only by abolishing individuality in the knowing subject.

By calling an object *beautiful*, we thereby assert that it is an object of our aesthetic contemplation, and this implies two different things. On the one hand, the sight of the thing makes us *objective*, that is to say, in contemplating it we are no longer conscious of ourselves as individuals, but as pure, will-less subjects of knowing. On the other hand, we recognize in the object not the individual thing, but an Idea; and this can happen only in so far as our contemplation of the object is not given up to the principle of sufficient reason, does not follow the relation of the object to something outside it [...] but rests on the object itself. (Ibid., §41, p. 209)

18 In the preface to the second edition (1831) of *The Science of Logic*, Hegel criticizes 'the nasty and uneducated practice of taking for a category under consideration *something other* than this category itself (*The Science of Logic*, trans. George Di Giovanni [Cambridge University Press, 2010], p. 20).

Lecture 13

1 See Lecture 12, note 18.
2 See Adorno, *Beethoven*, p. 131, as well as *Gesammelte Schriften*, vol. 18, p. 185.
3 See Adorno, 'Im Jeu de Paume gekritzelt' (*Frankfurter Allgemeine Zeitung*, 20 December 1958), now in *Gesammelte Schriften* 10.1, p. 324.
4 See *Aesthetic Theory*, p. 264: 'interpretation, commentary, critique'.
5 Marked in the left margin from 'the primary experience' to 'work of art'. See also *Aesthetic Theory*, p. 451.
6 Wassily Kandinsky, *Concerning the Spiritual in Art*, trans. M. T. H. Sadler (Mineola, NY: Dover, 1977).
7 See ibid., p. 24.
8 See the aforementioned study by Kurt Mautz, 'Die Farbensprache der expressionistischen Lyrik' (see Lecture 6, note 17). Marked in the left margin from 'For time has shown' to 'colours as such'.

9   Marked in the left margin from 'So in other words' to 'produce the spiritual'.
10 Marked in the left margin from 'that the power' to 'isolated phenomena'.
11 Marked in the left margin from 'This constructivism' to 'problematics itself'.
12 The Greek word τόπος ('place') was used in classical rhetoric in the sense of a 'commonplace', based on the assumption that, in language, there are certain expressions, phrases, images and quotations that are familiar to everyone and hence universally accessible points of departure from which to develop an idea in an especially intuitive and convincing way; see Aristotle, *Topics*, and, in particular, *Rhetoric* 1358a 10ff., and Cicero, *Topics*.
13 Marked in the left margin from 'after certain binding norms' to 'in isolation'.
14 See 'The Aging of the New Music', p. 193.
15 Marked in the left margin from 'because, as Kant put it' to 'its construction'.
16 See also Adorno, 'Im Jeu de Paume gekritzelt', *Gesammelte Schriften* 10.1, pp. 321–5.
17 See, for example, Fritz Burger, *Die deutsche Malerei vom ausgehenden Mittelalter bis zum Ende der Renaissance* (Berlin: Akademische Verlagsgesellschaft Athenaion, 1913), p. 8:

> In Michelangelo's figures, the facial expressions have grown from the overall motif of the body, the entire appearance. The German, on the other hand, sees the gesture not only as a movement or a motif of the appearance, but as the expression of a supra-sensual idea that, tied to the motif of the gesture, determines the overall appearance of the body or the space and only lets it speak to the extent that it can adapt to the gesture. Raphael only came across these problems very late, and under the influence of Michelangelo. But even then, he still treated the expressive movement as a means to the end of realizing his ideal of unity. For the German, shaping the spiritualizing, supra-sensual idea usually remains the formal problem of representation.

18 It is unclear which specific 'Bellini Madonna' Adorno had in mind. The Städel Museum in Frankfurt houses a Madonna with Child, John the Baptist and Saint Elisabeth (mixed technique on wood, 72 × 90 cm, early sixteenth century) from the workshop of the Venetian painter Giovanni Bellini (c. 1430–1516). Instead of the Frankfurt painting, with its rather aloof, spiritualized air, one that perhaps better embodies the typological contrast mentioned by Adorno would be the Madonna before a red curtain on display at the Metropolitan Museum of Art in New York (oil on wood, 8.9 × 71.1 cm, late 1480s), or also the Madonna before a green curtain at the Galleria Borghese in Rome (oil on canvas, 50 × 41 cm, c. 1505–1510).

19   The large-format Madonna (mixed technique on needlewood, 186 × 150 cm, 1514–1516) that has been at the parish church of St Mary of the Assumption in Stuppach, a district of Bad Mergentheim, since 1812, is one of the main works – along with the Isenheim Altarpiece – of the South German painter Matthias Grünewald (c. 1478–1528).

20   Adorno is referring at the end of the lecture to 'Fantasia sopra Carmen', in *Neue Rundschau*, no. 3 (1955), now in *Gesammelte Schriften* 16, pp. 298–308.

Lecture 14

1   There is a popular South German tale, told for generations – with slight modifications – in which two Swabians see a disgusting toad. One of them makes the other an offer: 'I'll give you ten marks if you eat that toad.' His companion forces down the toad with watering eyes. When they come across a second toad, the latter offers: 'I'll give you back your ten marks if you eat the toad.' Interested in getting back his money, the first man agrees and wins back his ten marks. After a while, he says to the other: 'So what did we both eat a toad for?'

2   The bibliography by Klaus W. Jonas, *Fifty Years of Thomas Mann Studies* (Minneapolis: University of Minnesota Press, 1955) already listed 2,958 books. Some examples showing the state of research to which Adorno is referring are Jonas Lesser, 'Einige Bemerkungen über Thomas Manns Verhältnis zu Philosophie und Religion', *Neue Rundschau* 66 (1955), pp. 518–23; Louis Leibrich, 'Expérience et philosophie de la vie chez Thomas Mann', *Études Germaniques* 9 (1954), pp. 291–307; and Fritz Kaufmann, *Thomas Mann: The World as Will and Representation* (Boston: Cooper Square, 1957).

3   Thomas Mann, *The Magic Mountain*, trans. John E. Woods (New York: A. A. Knopf, 2005).

4   Adorno also referred to his 'discomfort' about the 'dissertations on the influence of Schopenhauer and Nietzsche, on the role of music' in Thomas Mann in his essay 'Toward a Portrait of Thomas Mann' (1962), in *Notes to Literature*, vol. 2, p. 13.

5   The republican humanist Lodovico Settembrini is the representative of 'reason' in *The Magic Mountain*; he attempts to act as a mentor to the young Hans Castorp. His opponent is Leo Naphta, a communist of Eastern Jewish descent and Jesuit schooling, a representative of 'mysticism', asceticism and the revolution. Concerning the significance attributed to the disputes between Settembrini and Naphta in the novel's reception, see, among others, Pierre-Paul Sagave, *Réalité sociale et idéologie religieuse dans les romans de Thomas Mann: Les Buddenbrooks, La Montagne magique, Le Docteur Faustus* (Paris: Les Belles Lettres, 1954), pp. 43ff.

6   Thomas Mann, *Doctor Faustus: The Life of the German Composer Adrian Leverkühn as Told by a Friend*, trans. John E. Woods (New York: Vintage International, 1999).

7   The sentence in question is actually in italics, not boldface (Trans.).
8   See Mann, *The Magic Mountain*, p. 487: 'For the sake of goodness and love, man shall grant death no dominion over his thoughts.'
9   The distinction between a level of 'material content' [*Sachgehalt*] and another, presumably more or less independent one of 'spiritual content' or 'truth content' was most familiar to Adorno from Walter Benjamin, 'Goethe's Elective Affinities', in *Selected Writings*, vol. 1: *1913–1926*, pp. 297f. It can already be found – building on the neo-Kantian distinction between 'objects' and 'values' – in George Simmel's *The Philosophy of Money* (1900).
10 Adorno considered Flaubert's prose – especially in *Madame Bovary* and *Sentimental Education* – the most authentic embodiment of the traditional bourgeois novel (see 'The Position of the Narrator in the Contemporary Novel', in *Notes to Literature*, vol. 1, p. 33). In the German literature of the late nineteenth century – between Goethe and Thomas Mann – Theodor Fontane holds a similar position. In their novels, both Fontane and Flaubert concentrate on portraying the individual's striving for self-realization and emancipation – and the resulting conflicts between the claim to such a free self-realization and the norms of the social whole. For Georg Lukács too, Fontane's late works set the standard for what bourgeois-realist literature could achieve. '*Effi Briest* stands in the line of great bourgeois novels in which the simple tale of a marriage and its necessary violation grows into a portrayal of the general contradictions in the whole of bourgeois society' (Lukács, 'Der alte Fontane', *Sinn und Form* 3/2 [1951], p. 71).
11 Existentialism was the dominant intellectual fashion of the post-war years; the philosopher, playwright and novelist Jean-Paul Sartre (1905–1980) and the writer Albert Camus (1913–1960), who received the Nobel Prize for Literature in 1957, were considered its leading exponents.
12 The British writer Graham Greene (1904–1991) had converted to Catholicism in 1926 and lived mostly in Paris and on travels from the 1920s on. In his novels, including international successes such as *It's a Battlefield* (1934), *The End of the Affair* (1951) or *Our Man in Havana* (1958), he frequently examines dogmas and Catholic religiosity. The novel *The Power and the Glory* (1940) describes the special vocation of the Catholic priest, but it aroused the suspicion of the Congregation for the Doctrine of the Faith in Rome, which temporarily put it on the index of banned books.
13 Owing to a gap in the text caused by a change of tape, it is impossible to say which author Adorno is referring to.
14 See Lecture 2, note 8.
15 The German word *Gestalt* here poses the problem that, while it has entered English in the context of psychology, it is not originally limited to that context at all. In this passage, because Adorno uses it evenly in both its non-psychological and its psychological sense – the original meaning can be 'shape', 'figure', 'guise' and the like, making it a common word in

descriptions of motivic elements in music (and the corresponding verb *gestalten* means 'to shape, to craft') – it has consistently been used as an English word in order to reflect this consistency. Elsewhere, however, this is not usually the case (Trans.).

16 See Christian von Ehrenfels, 'Über Gestaltqualitäten', *Vierteljahress-chrift für wissenschatfliche Philosophie* 14 (1890), pp. 249–92; see also Max Wertheimer, 'Untersuchungen zur Lehre von der Gesalt II', *Psychologische Forschung* 4 (1923), pp. 301–50. As a student in Frankfurt, Adorno had attended lectures by the gestalt psychologists Kurt Goldstein (1878–1965) and Adhémar Gelb (1887–1936) (see *Gesammelte Schriften*, vol. 20.1, p. 156).

17 Schoenberg referred to 'subcutaneous' structures in, among other texts, his essay 'Brahms the Progressive', in Arnold Schoenberg, *Style and Idea*, ed. Leonard Stein, trans. Leo Black (Berkeley and Los Angeles: University of California Press, 1975), pp. 435f.: 'In Brahms' notation these subcutaneous beauties are accommodated within eight measures.' The distinction between 'manifest' and 'subcutaneous' structures (the latter being hidden beneath the surface) is taken up by Adorno on several occasions, for example in a 1952 fragment for his Beethoven book (see *Beethoven: The Philosophy of Music*, p. 72); see also 'Arnold Schoenberg 1874–1951', p. 153, and the later essay 'Toward an Understanding of Schoenberg' (1955/1967), in *Essays on Music*, pp. 627–43, here p. 634. As the central thesis for his projected book on the 'theory of musical reproduction', Adorno noted in 1946: 'True reproduction is the X-ray image of the work. Its task is to render visible all the relations, all aspects of context, contrast and construction that lie beneath the surface of the perceptible sound' (*Towards a Theory of Musical Reproduction*, ed. Henri Lonitz, trans. Wieland Hoban [Cambridge: Polity, 2006], p. 1).

18 The American cartoonist and film producer Walt Disney (1901–1966) is considered the 'father' of Mickey Mouse (from 1927) and other world-famous comic figures such as Donald Duck (1936). With *Flowers and Trees* (1932), Disney produced the first Technicolor film. His cartoon version of the fairy tale 'Snow White and the Seven Dwarfs' (1937) became a classic of animation cinema. After the Second World War, Disney also produced numerous adventure films and had worldwide success with documentaries such as *The Living Desert* (1953) and *The Vanishing Prairie* (1954). He appeared on American television in person, presenting his latest films, explaining the art of animation or introducing films and series. Adorno was sufficiently familiar with production conditions in the American film industry to know that the name Walt Disney stood for a company with a high degree of labour division. Accordingly he uses it, *pars pro toto*, to represent the culture industry.

19 The phrase 'psychology without soul' was coined by Friedrich Albert Lange in *Geschichte des Materialismus*, Book 2: *Geschichte des Materialismus seit Kant* (1874), 2nd edn (Leipzig: Baedeker, 1875), p. 381.

20   See Adorno's contribution to the Festschrift for Max Horkheimer's sixtieth birthday (1955), 'Zum Verhältnis von Soziologie und Psychologie', now in *Gesammelte Schriften*, vol. 8: *Soziologische Schriften I*, pp. 42–85, here p. 57.

21   A theory of 'aesthetic experience' in which the concept of beauty is considered superfluous and rejected as meaningless was propagated by, among others, Ivor Armstrong Richards – following on from similar efforts in psychological aesthetics as early as the late nineteenth century – in his influential 1924 work *Principles of Literary Criticism* (London and New York: Routledge, 2003).

22   It is difficult to say what 'recent aesthetic theories' Adorno specifically meant which place the concept of truth in opposition to beauty; in addition to Heidegger ('The Origin of the Work of Art'), who would scarcely have wanted to be viewed as a purveyor of any aesthetic theory, one possibility would be John Hospers, *Meaning and Truth in the Arts* (Chapel Hill: University of North Carolina Press, 1946).

Lecture 15

1   Adorno first met Picasso's long-standing dealer Daniel-Henry Kahnweiler (1884–1979) on 30 October 1949 in Paris, at the home of René Leibowitz (see *Adorno: Eine Bildmonographie*, ed. Theodor W. Adorno Archive [Frankfurt: Suhrkamp, 2003], pp. 208f.), and subsequently visited him several times; in the 1960s he acquired two drawings by Picasso through him (see ibid., p. 255). In 1962 he dedicated the essay 'Those Twenties' to him, and in 1964 he contributed to a Festschrift for Kahnweiler's eightieth birthday with the essay 'On Some Relationships between Music and Painting' (now trans. Susan H. Gillespie, in *Musical Quarterly* 79 [1995], pp. 66–79).

2   The Wolffian philosopher Johann Christoph Gottsched (1700–1766), from 1730 associate professor of poetics and from 1734 professor of logic and metaphysics in Leipzig, propagated the enlightened-rationalist call for a 'scientification' of poetics and a 'reasonable' grounding of the themes of poetic representation in his influential *Versuch einer critischen Dichtkunst vor die Deutschen*. In opposition to the 'bombast' and mannerisms of German baroque literature, he recommended following the rules of Aristotelian poetics and the model of the French classicists (Boileau, Corneille, Racine), whose plays he also translated and staged. As a highly prolific publicist, he was the most important critic of German literature ('Praeceptor Germaniae') during the mid-seventeenth century. Gottsched did not view his own discipline as 'aesthetics'. The project initiated by Baumgarten, and completed by his students in Halle during the 1750s, of reorganizing the 'beautiful sciences' under the new label 'aesthetics' derived its success not least from the opposition to Gottsched's rationalist 'dictatorship of taste', which was increasingly viewed as dogmatic.

3   Gotthold Ephraim Lessing (1729–1781) opposed Gottsched in 'Briefe, die neueste Literatur betreffend' (1759–65, in *Gotthold Ephraim Lessings sämtliche Schriften*, vol. 8, ed. Karl Lachmann, 3rd edn [Stuttgart: Göschen, 1892]) and also in 'Hamburgische Dramaturgie' (1767–8, in *Gotthold Ephraim Lessings sämtliche Schriften*, vol. 9, 3rd edn [Stuttgart: Göschen, 1893]).

4   See Aristotle, *Poetics*, ch. 6, 1449b 24: 'Tragedy is a representation of an action of a superior kind – grand, and complete in itself – presented in embellished language, in distinct forms in different parts, performed by actors rather than told by a narrator, effecting, through pity and fear, the purification of such emotions' (Aristotle, *Poetics*, trans. Anthony Kenny [Oxford and New York: Oxford University Press, 2013], p. 23).

5   See Adorno's study on the astrology columns in the *Los Angeles Times*: Adorno, *The Stars Down to Earth and Other Essays on the Irrational in Culture*, ed. Stephen Crook (London and New York: Routledge, 1994).

6   Adorno himself wrote in 'Kritik des Musikanten': 'The only response to alienation is defamiliarization' (*Gesammelte Schriften*, vol. 14, p. 71). It is unclear what passage in the work of the philosopher and anthropologist Helmuth Plessner (1892–1985) may have acted as an impulse here; it may also have been something said in conversation. Adorno was acquainted with Plessner, who had survived the Nazi regime in the Netherlands, where he taught as professor of sociology at the University of Groningen. After the war, Plessner was elected as the first president of the German philosophical society (Allgemeine Gesellschaft für Philosophie in Deutschland) in 1950 and appointed as professor of sociology at the University of Göttingen in 1951. He stood in for Adorno in Frankfurt as acting director of the Institut für Sozialforschung in 1953 while the latter was on research leave, working at the Hacker Foundation in California. In his 1948 essay 'With Different Eyes', Plessner writes:

> We have to become exiles from the territory of the familiar things we trust before we are able to perceive it anew. Rediscovering new environment, which companionably surrounds us and confronts us as an image, our senses are able to enjoy them afresh, and we can see them again. This alienation is experienced intensely by anyone who has left his home country as a child and returns as a grown man, and perhaps most intensely by the emigrant in the prime of life who becomes aware of the thousand roots sunk in a friendly soil and of his inherited culture strained to breaking point when he discovers anew the whole tradition from which he has sprung – not as his home country would believe, through the spectacles lent him by the friendly country which is sheltering him – but *through different eyes*. [...] Our search for comprehension applied only to what seems incomprehensible; it is the unfamiliar with which we try to familiarize ourselves, and we can only estrange ourselves from what is commonplace in order to view it [...] That is why the estranged vision of the artist fulfils an indispensable condition of all genuine understanding. ('With Different Eyes', in *Phenomenology and Sociology*, ed. Thomas Luckmann [London: Penguin, 1978], p. 30) ...

7   The title 'the father of us all' ('le père de nous tous') for the French painter
    Paul Cézanne (1839–1906) has been anecdotally attributed to both
    Picasso and Henri Matisse since the 1920s, though it is impossible to
    ascertain who used it first. Cézanne himself stated that 'perhaps we all
    come from Pissarro' (*Joachim Gasquet's Cézanne: A Memoir with Con-
    versations*, trans. C. Pemberton [London: Thames & Hudson, 1991]).
8   See Helmuth Plessner, *Laughing and Crying: A Study of the Limits of
    Human Behavior*, trans. James Spencer Churchill and Marjorie Grene
    (Evanston, IL: Northwestern University Press, 1970).
9   Marked in the left margin from 'So, following this analogy' to 'formal
    about them'.
10 See *Philosophy of New Music*, p. 189; see also 'The Aging of the New
    Music', p. 181.
11 See Lecture 8, note 37.
12 Adorno already spoke of Hitler's 'guardians of culture' in his essay 'Die
    auferstandene Kultur' (in *Gesammelte Schrften*, vol. 20.2, p. 460); he
    criticizes the 'Eastern guardians of culture' who, 'beyond the zone border'
    – in the Soviet occupation zone, and after 1949 in the German Demo-
    cratic Republic founded on the territory of that zone – used cultural
    policies 'in the wake of those of the Nazis' equally as a 'means of domi-
    nation', in his essay 'Die gegängelte Musik' (1953) (in *Gesammelte
    Schrften*, vol. 14, p. 51). During the Cold War, the attribute 'totalitarian'
    was used especially to characterize the forms of rule in the Soviet realm
    of influence to the effect that they were no different from those of fascism.
    Even before Hannah Arendt's influential 1951 book *The Origins of
    Totalitarianism* (New York: Houghton Mifflin Harcourt, 1973), Adorno
    and Horkheimer had used the adjective 'totalitarian' to describe the
    tendency towards total control and unlimited domination that culmi-
    nated in but was by no means restricted to the Nazi dictatorship.
13 Together with Pablo Picasso and Juan Gris, the French painter Georges
    Braque (1882–1963) was considered one of the founders of cubism (see
    Lecture 6, note 14).
14 See Franz Kafka, 'The Great Wall of China', in *Shorter Works*, vol. 1,
    ed. and trans. Malcolm Pasley (London: Secker & Warburg, 1973), p.
    91: 'The more horses you put to the job, the faster it goes – that is to
    say, not the tearing of the block out of its base, which is impossible, but
    the tearing apart of the straps and as a result the gay empty ride.' See
    also 'The Aging of the New Music', p. 187, and *Aesthetic Theory*, p. 23.
15 This statement is not to be found in Benjamin's writings; presumably
    Adorno is referring to a conversational remark by Benjamin.

Lecture 16

1   The start of the lecture is missing from the tape transcript.
2   The French writer Émile Zola (1840–1902) is considered the main propa-
    gator of the term 'naturalism' to describe the literary movement of the

modern novel in the nineteenth century, which followed the exact methods of the modern natural sciences in order to achieve the most precise and unprejudiced representation of reality possible. In his manifesto *The Experimental Novel* (1880) he referred especially to Flaubert's *Madame Bovary* and *Sentimental Education* as examples of the new naturalist literature; see Arnold Hauser, *The Social History of Art*, vol. 4: *Naturalism, Impressionism, The Film Age* (New York: Vintage, 1951), p. 86; regarding Flaubert, see also Lecture 7, note 22, and Lecture 14, note 10.

3   The French novelist Honoré de Balzac (1799–1850) is considered – alongside Stendhal and Flaubert – the most important exponent of bourgeois realism in the nineteenth century. In his cycle *The Human Comedy*, encompassing over ninety novels and stories, he paints a comprehensive picture of the society of his time. From Balzac, whom he had read intensively since his youth, Adorno gained fundamental information about power structures and behavioural typologies in bourgeois society. At the same time, it was not least by applying the paradigm of this poetically intensified portrayal of morals that he developed a substantial part of the criteria which he used to assess the productivity of sociological research approaches. He summarized the essence of 'Reading Balzac' in an essay of that title, published in 1961 in the second volume of *Notes to Literature* (pp. 121–36).

4   In his naturalist programme, Zola had referred to the French sociologist and philosopher of science August Comte (1798–1857), who had insisted that all scientific enquiry should be strictly limited to interpreting 'positive findings', which should be acknowledged without bias. For the social sciences, the demand for strictly 'value-free' research in the twentieth century was influentially espoused by Max Weber in such essays as 'The "Objectivity" of Knowledge in Social Science and Social Policy' (1904) and 'The Meaning of "Value Freedom" in the Sociological and Economic Sciences' (1918), both in Weber, *Collected Methodological Writings*, ed. Hans Henrik Bruun and Sam Whimster, trans. Hans Henrik Bruun (London & New York: Routledge, 2012).

5   Gap due to change of tape; 'If one' added by the editor.

6   The playwright Gerhart Hauptmann (1862–1946), who was awarded the Nobel Prize for Literature in 1912, had polarized audiences in the late nineteenth century with socio-critical naturalistic plays such as *The Weavers* (1892). After receiving negative reviews for his thief comedy *The Beaver Coat* (1893), Hauptmann moved away from the naturalist approach and devoted himself to mystico-religious and fairy-tale subjects. The accusation alluded to by Adorno was made by, among others, Georg Lukács in *The Meaning of Contemporary Realism*, trans. John Mander and Necke Mander (London: Merlin Press, 1963), pp. 58f.

7   Hauptmann, *Florian Geyer: A Tragedy of the Peasants' War*, trans. Bayard Quincy Morgan, in *The Dramatic Works of Gerhart Hauptmann*, ed. Ludwig Lewisohn, vol. 9: *Historic and Legendary Dramas: Florian Geyer, Veland* (New York: B. W. Huebsch, 1929); premiered on 4 January 1896 at the Deutsches Theater, Berlin.

8   Hauptmann, *The Assumption of Hannele*, trans. Charles Henry Meltzer, ibid., vol. 4: *Symbolic and Legendary Dramas: The Assumption of Hannele, The Sunken Bell, Henry of Auë* (New York: B. W. Huebsch, 1927); premiered on 14 November 1893 at the Königliches Schauspielhaus, Berlin.

9   See Lukács, *The Meaning of Contemporary Realism*, p. 28.

10 See *Philosophy of New Music*, p. 42: 'Expressionist music had adopted the principle of expression from traditional Romanticism so faithfully that expression acquired a documentary character' (translation modified).

11 See Lecture 6, note 12.

12 Adorno also quotes this phrase in *Philosophy of New Music* (p. 36). There is no formulation with this exact wording in Schoenberg's writings. In the volume *Arnold Schönberg* (Munich: Piper, 1912), edited by his Vienna students – after Schoenberg's departure to Berlin – Karl Linke (1884–1938) relates some of his experiences with Schoenberg as a teacher and mentions that the master once responded to a song composition Linke showed him by saying, 'What you have here is decoration. But music should not be decorative, it should only be true' (ibid., p. 79).

13 See Nietzsche, 'Nietzsche Contra Wagner', in *The Anti-Christ, Ecce Homo, Twilight of the Idols and Other Writings*, ed. Aaron Ridley and Judith Norman, trans. Judith Norman (Cambridge University Press, 2005), p. 267.

14 See Adorno, 'Criteria of New Music', in *Sound Figures*, pp. 164f.

15 See Lecture 8, note 18.

16 Marked by Adorno from 'On the other hand' to 'in motion'.

17 The psychologist and musicologist Albert Wellek (1904–1972) wrote, among other things, a handbook entitled *Musikpsychologie und Musikästhetik: Grundriss der systematischen Musikwissenschaft* (Frankfurt: Akademische Verlags-Anstalt, 1963), which was treated as a standard work until the 1980s. Here Adorno is referring to the essay 'Problematik der modernen Musik', in *Konkrete Vernunft: Festschrift für Erich Rothacker zum 70. Geburtstag*, ed. Gerhard Funke (Bonn: Bouvier, 1958), pp. 335–44.

18 This sentence is marked by Adorno in the typescript.

19 Adorno is here developing an idea he had already touched on in 1957 in his essay 'The Function of Counterpoint in New Music': 'In general, when any element of the music is intensified or becomes more independent, it affects everything else, so that, between the elements, that homeostasis is established which the mature Schoenberg once defined as the desirable goal to be striven for anew in every composition.'(*Sound Figures*, p. 128). See also, from the same year, 'Criteria of New Music', in *Sound Figures*, p. 193: 'At the heart of the morality of the work of art, the determination not to remain in anyone's debt, is a concern to honour the bill of exchange that is underwritten in the very first bar. Homeostasis becomes the goal of an immanent aesthetic economy' (translation modified).

20 See Schoenberg, *Style and Idea*, ed. Leonard Stein, trans. Leo Black (Berkeley and Los Angeles: University of California Press, 1975), p. 411. Concerning Schoenberg's concept of 'motival and harmonic obligations' that a piece enters and must fulfil, see also Adorno, *In Search of Wagner*, p. 108, and *Beethoven*, p. 104.

21 See Schoenberg, ibid., p. 123:

> Every note which is added to the starting note makes the meaning of that note doubtful [...] and the addition of other notes may or may not clarify this problem. In this manner there is produced a state of unrest, of imbalance, which grows throughout most of the piece and is enforced further by similar functions of the rhythm. The method by which this balance is restored seems to me the real idea of the composition. (Translation modified)

22 Marked in the left margin from 'Schoenberg's theory' to 'homeostasis'.

23 The term 'homeostasis' had already been introduced in the mid-nineteenth century by the French physiologist Claude Bernard, in his book *Leçons sur les propriétés physiologiques et les altérations pathologiques des liquides de l'organisme* (Paris: J. B. Baillière, 1859), to describe states of equilibrium of a chemical-physiological nature. Freud occasionally uses the term in his letters to Wilhelm Fliess but does not assign any terminological function to it in his meta-psychological writings. In substance, the drive-dynamic model he developed especially in *Beyond the Pleasure Principle* (1920), with its concept of balance between partly antagonistic drives, is certainly indebted to the idea of homeostasis; see Nigel Walker, 'Freud and Homeostasis', *British Journal for the Philosophy of Science* 7 (1956), pp. 61–72. Modern psychology adopted the term in the 1940s, after the American physiologist Walter Bradford Cannon (1871–1945) had introduced a general principle of homeostasis for states of equilibrium in living systems in *The Wisdom of the Body* (New York: W. W. Norton, 1932) and cyberneticists such as Norbert Wiener (in *Cybernetics, or Control and Communication in the Animal and the Machine* [New York: Wiley, 1948]) had operationalized the term with the principle of the regulatory circuit.

24 The musicologist Thrasyboulos Georgiades (1907–1977) had given a lecture in Frankfurt on 10 February 1954 on, among other things, the Jupiter Symphony (1788, K 551). Adorno repeatedly expressed enthusiasm about the lecture; see also Adorno, *Der getreue Korrepetitor* (*Gesammelte Schriften*, vol. 15), p. 380; 'Alienated Magnum Opus: the Missa Solemnis', in *Night Music*, p. 262; *Beethoven*, p. 119.

25 Marked by Adorno from 'Here I will' to 'modern art'.

Lecture 17

1 Marked by Adorno from 'namely' to 'other way around'.
2 See *Against Epistemology*, p. 12.
3 See *Notes to Literature*, pp. 3–23.

4   See Kant, *Critique of Pure Reason*, pp. 246f.
5   Hegel, *Aesthetics*, vol. 1, p. 16. The seminal eighteenth-century studies on art mentioned by Hegel are Henry Home, Lord Kames (1696–1782), *Elements of Criticism* (Edinburgh, 1762); Charles Batteux (1713–1780), *Les Beaux-Arts réduits à un même principe* (Paris, 1746); Karl Wilhelm Ramler (1725–1798), *Einleitung in die Schönen Wissenschaften* (1756–1758; 5th edn, Leipzig, 1802) (this last is a translation of Batteux's *Cours de belles-lettres, ou principles de la littérature* [Paris, 1747–50]).
6   See Aristotle's definition of tragedy (Lecture 15, note 4).
7   Hegel, *Aesthetics*, vol. 1, p. 16.
8   Ibid.
9   Ibid.
10 Adorno had reviewd Othmar H. Sterzinger's book *Grundlinien der Kunstpsychologie*, vol. 1: *Die Sinnenwelt* (Graz: Leykam, 1938) in the *Zeitschrift für Sozialforschung* 7 (1938), pp. 426f.; now in *Gesammelte Schriften*, vol. 20.2, pp. 505f.
11 The Irish dandy and writer Oscar Wilde (1854–1900) became one of the exponents of aestheticism in the late nineteenth century with his novel *The Picture of Dorian Gray* (1891) and such plays as *Landy Windermere's Fan* (1892) or *Salomé* (1891). Adorno had already mocked Wilde in his essay 'The George-Hofmannsthal Correspondence, 1891–1906': 'The symbolistically beautiful is doubly distorted – through naïve faith in the material and through allegorical ubiquity. Everything can signify everything on the decorative arts market. The less familiar the materials, the less limited their intentionality. Page after page in Oscar Wilde could serve as a jeweller's catalogue, countless interiors from the *fin du siècle* resemble the curiosity shop' (*Prisms*, p. 220, translation modified).
12 The term translated as 'decorative art', *Kunstgewerbe*, literally means 'art trade'; the references to its 'commercial' [*gewerblich*] function are thus directly derived from it (Trans.).
13 Hegel, *Aesthetics*, vol. 1, p. 16.
14 Marked by Adorno from 'In the reflections' to 'convert you'.
15 See Adorno, 'Im Jeu de Paume gekritzelt', *Gesammelte Schriften* 10.1.
16 Hegel, *Aesthetics*, vol. 1, p. 16.
17 Marked in the left margin from 'What we should demand' to 'in an apt way'.
18 The German painter Hans Thoma (1839–1924), who lived from 1878 to 1899 in Frankfurt, where several works of his are on display at the Städel Museum, was one of the most respected German painters around the turn of the twentieth century.
19 Marked in the left margin from 'In Germany' to 'guarded by taste'.

Lecture 18

1   The Danish writer Jens Peter Jacobsen (1847–1885) received great acclaim in the late nineteeth and early twentieth century as a

forerunner of symbolism and neo-Romanticism. His coming-of-age novel *Niels Lyhne* (1880) focuses on the fantasies and unfulfilled sexuality of the young eponymous hero, described with great psychological empathy. His poetry, which offers highly nuanced portraits of the subtlest emotions and moods of nature, had a strong influence on poets such as Rainer Maria Rilke and Stefan George. Schoenberg's *Gurrelieder* (premiered in Vienna in 1913) used texts from Jacobsen's novella *A Cactus Blooms*, posthumously published in 1886.

2　Peter Altenberg (real name: Richard Engländer, 1859–1919) was a Viennese coffeehouse poet. Alban Berg composed *Five Songs on Postcard Texts by Peter Altenberg*, op. 5. Karl Kraus published a selection from Altenberg's books in 1932; see also Adorno's review 'Physiological Romanticism', in *Notes to Literature*, vol. 2, pp. 280–2.

3　The words 'base an aesthetics and a set of criteria of art on the reactions of the subject' are marked in the left margin.

4　Marked in the left margin from 'My thesis' to 'inevitably leads'.

5　The programme of an 'aesthetics from below' that proceeds from empirically psychological surveys of people's sense of beauty, as already developed by Gustav Theodor Fechner in his *Vorschule der Aesthetik* (2 parts, Leipzig: Breitkopf & Härtel, 1876), was continued in the twentieth century in psychological aesthetics and newer approaches towards 'experimental aesthetics'. The positions from which Adorno is distancing himself here include that of Theodor Lipps in *Ästhetik: Psychologie des Schönen und der Kunst* (Hamburg and Leipzig: Voss, 1906), but also the newer psychological research he had examined in the Princeton Radio Research Project.

6　Marked by Adorno from 'direct relation' to 'from it'. See *Aesthetic Theory*, p. 117.

7　The law of specific nerve energies states that the same stimulus will trigger different sensations in different sensory organs, and that different stimuli will conversely trigger similar sensations in the same sensory organ. It was formulated in 1826 by the physiologist Johannes Müller in his study *The Comparative Physiology of the Facial Sense in Humans and Animals*, which was based on experimental studies of the effects of different stimuli on the optic nerve.

8　Erich Fromm had spoken of a 'Nero complex' in his review of the biography of an American newspaper magnate, in *Zeitschrift für Sozialforschung* 5 (1936), pp. 284f.

9　Concerning the Prelude in C sharp minor, op. 3, no. 2 (1892), by Sergei Rachmaninov (1873–1943), see 'Commodity Music Analysed', in *Quasi Una Fantasia*, pp. 38f.

10　Gap due to change of tape.

11　A reference to Schiller's 'Ode to Joy', verse 8 (original words: 'Männerstolz vor Königsthronen') (Trans.).

12　According to Jean-Jacques Rousseau (1712–1778), the *volonté générale*, the 'universal will' – in the sense of what lies in the reasonable interests of the general public and must therefore implement itself politically – is by no means necessarily the same as what the dominant opinion, or the *volonté de tous*, as the sum of inconsequential individual interests, will demand in a given situation; see Rousseau, 'On the Social Contract', in *The Basic Political Writings*, 2nd edn, ed. and trans. Donald A. Cress (Indianapolis: Hackett, 2011), pp. 153–252, especially Book II, ch. 3. Adorno by no means idealized the alleged supremacy of the *volonté générale* over the despised *volonté de tous*: 'We know how much harm was caused by Rousseau's distinction between *volonté générale* and *volonté de tous*, the general will and the will of all individuals, when terrorist dictators usurped the general will for their own purposes' ('Kann das Publikum wollen?' [1963], in *Gesammelte Schriften*, vol. 20.1, p. 344).

13 See Spaeth, *Great Symphonies: How to Recognize and Remember Them* (Garden City, NY: Garden City, 1936). The American musicologist and entertainer Sigmund Gottfried Spaeth (1885–1965) became known to a mainstream audience with his weekly programme 'The Tune Detective' on the American radio station NBC (1931–3); in 1947 he presented 'Sigmund Spaeth's Musical Quiz' every week on the Mutual Network.

14 The Symphony no. 6 in B minor, op. 74 (1893).

15 In 'Theorie der Halbbildung' (1959), Adorno quotes the corresponding lines by Spaeth as follows: 'This music has a less pathetic strain, / It sounds more sane and not so full of pain. / Sorrow is ended, grief may be mended, / It seems Tchaikovsky will be calm again!' (*Gesammelte Schriften*, vol. 8, p. 113).

16 Adorno is here summarizing a thought that Hegel develops in the 'Preface' to *Elements of the Philosophy of Right* (1821):

> As far as *nature* is concerned, it is readily admitted that philosophy must recognize it *as it is* [...] nature's eternal harmony, conceived, however, as the law and essence *immanent* within it. *The ethical world*, on the other hand [...] is not supposed to be happy in the knowledge that it is reason itself which has in fact gained power and authority within this element, and which asserts itself there and remains inherent within it. [...] The chief tendency of this superficial philosophy is to base science not on the development of the thought and the concept, but immediate perception and contingent imagination; and likewise, to reduce the complex inner articulation of the ethical, i.e. the state, the architectonics of its rationality [...] To comprehend *what is* is the task of philosophy [...]. (Hegel, *Elements of the Philosophy of Right*, ed. Allen W. Wood, trans. H. B. Nisbet [Cambridge University Press, 1991], pp. 12–21)

17 Marked in the left margin from 'no such immediacy' to 'social lines'.

18 Adorno had worked with the American social psychologist Hadley Cantril (1906–1969) from 1938 to 1940 in the Princeton Radio Research Project. Together with Gordon Willard Allport, Cantril had published the pioneering study *The Psychology of Radio* (New York: Harper, 1935), and with Hazel Gaudet and Herta Herzog he examined

the panic triggered in 1938 by Orson Welles's legendary radio broadcast 'Invasion from Mars'; see *Invasion from Mars: A Study in the Psychology of Panic* (Princeton University Press, 1940). The study to which Adorno is referring here is 'Experimental Studies of Prestige Suggestion', *Psychological Bulletin* 34 (1937), pp. 528ff. Adorno also refers to this study in his *Introduction to the Sociology of Music*, p. 106.

19   The Italian conductor Arturo Toscanini (1867–1957), who quickly became very successful in the USA and at the most prestigious European concert and opera venues, could be considered the prototype of the classical music superstar. After following Toscanini's work for many years, Adorno summarized his thoughts after the conductor's death in 1957 in a radio lecture published in 1958; see 'The Mastery of the Maestro', in *Sound Figures*, pp. 40–53.

20   Beethoven's *Missa Solemnis* in D major, op. 123 (1823), is considered one of the composer's greatest achievements. Adorno examined the difficult work and its reception history in a 1957 radio lecture; it was published as 'Verfremdetes Hauptwerk' in *Neue deutsche Hefte*, no. 54 (January 1959); see now 'Alienated Magnum Opus: the *Missa Solemnis*', in *Night Music*, pp. 239–66.

21   See, for example, *Minima Moralia*, no. 79: 'One of the tasks of dialectical logic is to eliminate the last traces of a deductive system, together with the last advocatory gestures of thought' (p. 71); see also the preface to *Against Epistemology*, p. 1, as well as ibid., p. 178.

22   No such statement by Schoenberg about the *Missa Solemnis* could be found.

23   See Beethoven's letter of 10 March 1824 to the publisher Schott: 'Although I find it difficult to talk about myself, yet I must say that I consider this to be my greatest work' (*The Letters of Beethoven*, ed. and trans. Emily Anderson [New York: Macmillan, 1961], vol. 3, p. 1114). See also Adorno, *Beethoven*, p. 138.

24   See 'On the Fetish-Character in Music and the Regression of Listening' (*Essays on Music*), pp. 288ff.

25   See note 19 above.

26   Unknown.

Lecture 19

1   This relatively unusual term has been chosen to render the more common *erkennend*. Like its more famous noun *Erkenntnis*, the central category of epistemology [*Erkenntnistheorie*], the verb *erkennen* is difficult to translate in a philosophical context because, although the various English equivalents – such as 'realize', 'know' or 'recognize' – are obvious choices in more straightforward contexts, none of them quite captures that meaning of attaining insight through active engagement which is essential to its German usage. This is doubly true of *Erkenntnis*, which is commonly translated as 'knowledge' despite the far more

static and passive connotations of that word, and which would often be more accurately rendered as 'insight'. Although 'recognitive' may have some empiricist associations, its derivation from 'recognize' makes it a possible, if unsatisfying, choice for *erkennend*, avoiding the participial implication of 'recognizing'. 'Recognizant' would also be conceivable, but it seems less suggestive of that active, insight-seeking approach intended by Adorno (Trans.).

2 Marked by Adorno from 'Because this synthesis' to 'solidified form'.

3 For the neo-Kantian background to the conception of aesthetics with which Adorno is here engaging, see Hermann Cohen, *Ästhetik des reinen Gefühls* (Berlin: Bruno Cassirer, 1912).

4 Marked by Adorno from 'And if' to 'the intuitive'. See *Aesthetic Theory*, pp. 207f.

5 Gotthold Ephraim Lessing, *Laocoon: An Essay upon the Limits of Painting and Poetry* (1766), trans. Ellen Frothingham (Mineola, NY: Dover, 2005).

6 See Theodor A. Meyer, *Das Stilgesetz der Poesie* (Leipzig: S. Hirzel, 1901); see also *Aesthetic Theory*, p. 138.

7 It was impossible to ascertain what exactly Adorno means here. The phrase 'optical sign' was not terminologically introduced into semiotics from Charles Morris to Max Bense; instead, they use such terms as 'iconic sign', or occasionally 'visual sign'. From the 1950s on, visual artists admittedly began to consider the picture an object that addresses primarily the visual sense, and hence aims for an 'optical' effect, but the term 'optical art' (sometimes abbreviated to 'Op art') emerged only in the mid-1960s.

8 See note 1 above (Trans.).

9 The two typescript pages from 'I cannot refrain' to 'recognize it' are marked by Adorno in the left margin.

10 Marked by Adorno in the left margin from 'this emotional content' to 'important point'.

11 Marked by Adorno from 'But the recognition' to 'transpire as intuitive'.

12 See Alfred Lorenz, *Das Geheimnis der Form bei Richard Wagner*, vol. 1: *Der musikalische Aufbau des Bühnenfestspiels 'Der Ring des Nibelungen'* (1924) (Tutzing: H. Schneider, 1966), pp. 291f.:

> What is clear is that the creation of form requires reasonable thought, as we are dealing here with an *ordering* principle. Of course, this work of reason, if there is to be true creative power, can only be the interpreting consequence of an ingenious aspect in which – and this is the fundamental precondition for all true creation – the genius has the power to gather many disparate things in a single moment. [...] Perhaps some do not believe in the possibility of feeling unity across a curve that, like the one here, lasts over two hours. [...] Although I possess only a very modest power of compositional creation, I can tell of that inspired moment – admittedly not one I often experience – in which I simultaneously hear inside myself, in a moment of utmost intensity, everything that in reality occurs consecutively. This is an incomprehensible metaphysical

phenomenon. I cannot say how it occurs; one does not simply hear the beginning and end pushed closely together but literally hears every note of the entire work *at once* within an unspeakably short moment. [...] If one learns a large work *completely* from memory, with all its details, there are sometimes moments in which the sense of time is suddenly gone and the entire work is simultaneously present in what I would call a 'spatial' fashion, all together in the greatest precision.

Adorno also refers to this ideal of internal and external transparency in 'Zweite Nachtmusik', in *Gesammelte Schriften*, vol. 18, p. 52, and 'Wagner und Bayreuth', ibid., p. 219.

13 See Lukács, *The Theory of the Novel*, trans. Anna Bostock (Cambridge, MA: MIT Press, 1971), pp. 46 and 56.

14 See Kant, *Critique of Pure Reason*, pp. 551ff.

15 Marked by Adorno from 'But this transformation' to 'Lorenz mentioned'.

16 See Edmund Husserl, *Logical Investigations*, vol. 2, part I (1901/1913), p. 129: '[...] an intentional experience only gains objective reference by incorporating an experienced act of presentation in itself, through which *the object is presented to it*. The object would be nothing to consciousness if consciousness did not set it before itself as an object, and if it did not further permit the object to become an object of feeling, of desire etc.'

17 See Walter Harburger, *Die Metalogik: die musikalische Logik: Geometrie der Empfindungen* (Munich: Musarion, 1919); see also Adorno, *Gesammelte Schriften*, vol. 18, p. 160.

18 The Austrian composer and conductor Alois Melichar (1896–1976) conducted the Vienna Philharmonic and Vienna Symphony Orchestras from 1945 to 1949, and from 1946 to 1949 he was also musical director of the classical music department of the Vienna radio station Rot-Weiß-Rot. Between 1933 and 1955 he composed the music for over sixty films, including a number of Nazi propaganda films (e.g., *Comrades* [1941]; ... *Riding for Germany* [1941]; *Attack on Baku* [1942]; and *Secret Tibet* [1943]). His polemics against musical modernity appeared in book form in the following volumes: *Die unteilbare Musik* (Vienna: Weinberger, 1952), *Überwindung des Modernismus* (Vienna: Weinberger, 1954), *Musik in der Zwangsjacke* (Vienna: Wancura, 1958) and *Schönberg und die Folgen* (Vienna: Wancura, 1960).

19 It was impossible to establish when a product was first advertised with the claim that the large number of customers who had chosen it could not be wrong. The frequently used slogan was equally frequently parodied; thus the American entertainer Sophie Tucker (1884–1966) had great success as early as 1927 with the hit song 'Fifty Million Frenchmen Can't Be Wrong'. In 1959, Elvis Presley adapted this title for his album *Fifty Million Elvis Fans Can't Be Wrong*.

20 The Catalan painter and sculptor Joan Miró (1893–1983), who belonged to the surrealist circle in the 1920s and 1930s, became popular in the

post-war years with abstract works reminiscent of children's drawings. In 1954 he was awarded the Grand Prize for Graphic Work at the Venice Biennale; in 1955 he exhibited at Documenta I in Kassel; in 1957–8 his pictures were shown in Krefeld, Berlin, Munich, Cologne, Hanover and Hamburg.

21 *Finnegans Wake* (1939) is the last novel by the Irish writer James Joyce (1882–1941), undoubtedly one of the most remarkable but also least accessible works of twentieth-century literature – with no recognizable plot, written in a deliberately polyvalent hotchpotch of some forty languages, and full of puns and allusions to both central and obscure sources in the Western and non-Western educational canons. Referring to the working title the book bore for decades before Joyce decided on *Finnegans Wake*, Adorno also referred to *Aesthetic Theory* as a 'work in progress' (see *Aesthetic Theory*, p. 477).

22 See *Philosophy of New Music*, pp. 10ff.

23 Jean-Paul Sartre writes about de Sade in, among other texts, *Saint Genet: Actor and Martyr* (1952), trans. Bernard Frechtman (Minneapolis: University of Minnesota Press, 2012). On Sartre's engagement with de Sade, see also Robert E. Taylor, 'The SEXpressive S in Sade and Sartre', *Yale French Studies* no. 11 (1953), pp. 18–24.

24 It is unclear which passage in the work of the Marquis de Sade (1740–1814) Adorno is referring to. Max Horkheimer had given him a copy of *Juliette* as a wedding present in 1937. See also 'Excursus II: Juliette or Enlightenment and Morality', in *Dialectic of Enlightenment*, pp. 63–93.

25 It is difficult to say which study Adorno had in mind here; presumably he was thinking of Egon Brunswik, 'Perceptual Characteristics of Schematized Human Figures', *Psychological Bulletin* 36 (1939), p. 553. The Budapest-born psychologist Egon Brunswik (1903–1955) completed his Habilitation in Vienna in 1934 with a work entitled 'Perception and the Objective World' and in 1936 took a position at the University of Berkeley (California), where he taught until his death in 1955. Concerning the significance of his research for twentieth-century psychology, see *The Essential Brunswik: Beginnings, Explications, Applications*, ed. Kenneth R. Hammond and Thomas R. Stewart (Oxford and New York: Oxford University Press, 2001). A report on the 'Congress for the Unity of Science (Logical Positivists)', written by Adorno together with Walter Benjamin for the Institute of Social Research, characterizes Brunswik in less than favourable terms (see *Theodor W. Adorno – Max Horkheimer, Briefwechsel*, vol. 1: *1927–1939*, ed. Christoph Gödde and Henri Lonitz [Frankfurt: Suhrkamp, 2003], p. 566). Brunswik had married the psychoanalyst and social psychologist Else Frenkel (1908–1958) in 1938; she was one of the main contributors to the Institute of Social Research's study on the authoritarian personality; see Adorno, Else Frenkel-Brunswik, Daniel J. Levinson and R. Nevitt Sanford, *The Authoritarian Personality* (New York: Harper, 1950).

26 The literal translation of *Halbbildung* is 'semi-education' (Trans.).

27 See Adorno's lecture 'Theorie der Halbbildung'at the 14th Congress of German Sociologists in Berlin (23 May 1959), now in *Gesammelte Schriften*, vol. 8, pp. 93–121.

Lecture 20

1 See 'Perennial Fashion – Jazz', in *Prisms*, pp. 119–32, and also 'On Jazz', in *Night Music*, pp. 118–76.
2 See Karl Bargheer, *Ludwig van Beethovens fünf letzte Quartette* (Hamburg: J. F. Richter, 1883).
3 Vsevolod Meyerhold (1874–1940), Russian actor, director and theatre manager. His theatre was closed in 1938 because he had refused to submit to Socialist Realism as commanded; he was arrested in 1939 and probably executed in 1940.
4 See Lecture 7, note 28; see also *Aesthetic Theory*, p. 194.
5 The definition of the concept of ideology as 'necessary false consciousness' or 'necessarily false consciousness', for which Adorno repeatedly refers to Marx (e.g., in 'Opinion Delusion Society', in *Critical Models: Interventions and Catchwords*, p. 106, and *Gesammelte Schriften* vol. 20.1, p. 387), does not appear in this wording in Marx, but it does aptly summarize the concept from which Marx and Engels proceeded in their critique of 'German ideology'. See Karl Marx and Friedrich Engels, *The German Ideology*, ed. C. J. Arthur (New York: International, 1970).
6 Marked by Adorno from 'I would go so far' to 'own approach'.
7 According to Kant's *Critique of Pure Reason*, humans have 'two stems of human cognition [...] namely sensibility and understanding' (p. 152). Through the former, objects are 'given to us' but through the latter they are 'thought'. Strictly speaking, objects cannot, as Kant argues in this work, be 'given' to us at all. Constituting the objects by which we may feel sensually affected as specific objects is rather the work of the subject, something that can only occur in our experience through the interplay of sensuality and those transcendental forms of intuition, as well as the various concepts of understanding; 'intuitions without concepts are blind' (p. 194). All experience must contain 'in addition to the intuition of the senses, through which something is given' – though one cannot immediately know where one stands with it – 'a *concept* of an object that is given or appears in the intuition' (p. 224); otherwise it would not be an experience of anything determinate. In addition to the concepts of understanding or 'categorial forms' and the sensitivity to environmental stimuli, what Kant calls the 'forms of intuition' are also involved as conditions of possibility for the constitution of objects; for Kant, these are the ordering dimensions of spatial adjacency and temporal sequence, which can be grasped neither as categories of understanding nor as aspects of sensual affection (B 33–73). Adorno engaged intensively with the *Critique of Pure Reason* in *Against Epistemology*

and finally in his lectures during the summer semester of 1959; see Adorno, *Kant's Critique of Pure Reason*, ed. Rolf Tiedemann, trans. Rodney Livingstone (Cambridge: Polity, 2001).

8   See Kant, *Critique of Pure Reason*, pp. 160f.

9   Marked by Adorno from 'For if that is the case' to 'over subjectivity'. Concerning the primacy of the object, see e.g., *Negative Dialectics*, pp. 188ff., as well as 'Notes on Philosophical Thinking', in *Critical Models*, p. 129, and 'On Subject and Object', ibid., pp. 251ff.

10   See *Against Epistemology*, pp. 139ff.

11   See Hegel, *Aesthetics*, vol. 1, p. 32:

> This reflection has given rise to the consideration that fine art is meant to arouse feeling, in particular the feeling that suits us, pleasant feeling. In this regard, the investigation of fine art has been made into an investigation of the feelings, and the question has been raised, 'what feelings should be aroused by art, fear, for example, and pity? But how can these be agreeable, how can the treatment of misfortune afford satisfaction?' Reflection on these lines dates especially from Moses Mendelssohn's times and many such discussions can be found in his writings. Yet such investigation did not get far, because feeling is the indefinite dull region of the spirit; what is felt remains enveloped in the form of the most abstract individual subjectivity, and therefore differences between feelings are also completely abstract, not differences in the thing itself.

12   See Robert Henseling, *Das All und wir: Das Weltgefühl der Gegenwart und seine Urgeschichte* (Berlin: G. Schönfeld, 1936).

13   Marked in the left margin from 'the aggregate' to '*in abstracto*'.

14   Marked by Adorno from 'A central part' to 'ordinary judgement'.

15   Karl Hermann Usener (1905–1970) became professor of art history in Marburg in 1953. In addition to several other works on the art of the Middle Ages, the Renaissance and modernity, he wrote a study entitled 'Edouard Manet und die vie moderne', published posthumously in *Marburger Jahrbuch für Kunstwissenschaften*, vol. 19 (1974).

16   See Adorno, 'Im Jeu de Paume gekritzelt', *Gesammelte Schriften*, 10.1, p. 324.

17   It is unknown on what occasion the graphic artist and sculptor Käthe Kollwitz (1867–1945) commented on Manet in the manner criticized here by Adorno.

18   *Spleen et idéal* is the title of the first of six parts in Baudelaire's volume *Les Fleurs du mal*; see Charles Baudelaire, *The Flowers of Evil*, trans. James McGowan (Oxford and New York: Oxford University Press, 1993), pp. 9–163.

19   The entire passage from 'Manet's pictures' to 'truly can' is marked in the left margin by Adorno.

Lecture 21

1   This remark should be understood in the context of the thesis which Adorno encapsulates in the following sentence in *Negative Dialectics*:

'Cognition is a τρώσας ἰάσεται' ['he who wounds also heals'] (p. 53). This topos refers to the legend of Telephus: the wound of Telephus could be healed only by the spear of Achilles that had wounded him. For Adorno, the work of art plays a fundamental part in the context of effects of discursive logic and instrumental reason, a context he views as hurtful and damaging; it is, however, the part of this context to which one can, and must, cling in order to achieve something resembling a healing of the resulting damage.

2   Marked by Adorno from 'One could' to 'mere judgement'.

3   This Latin phrase means 'it is not clear', traditionally referring to inconclusive situations brought about by gaps in the law (Trans.).

4   See Georg Lukács, *The Meaning of Contemporary Realism*, trans. John Mander and Necke Mander (London: Merlin Press, 1963), pp. 78f.

5   Marked in the left margin from 'it is a thoroughly modern feeling' to 'native to the work'.

6   See Benedetto Croce, *Guide to Aesthetics*, trans. Patrick Romanell (Indianapolis: Hackett, 1995); see also Benjamin, *The Origin of German Tragic Drama*, trans. John Osborne (London and New York: Verso, 1998), pp. 43ff.

7   Marked in the left margin from 'So this synthesis' to 'work of art'.

8   Hegel, *Aesthetics*, vol. 1, p. 288 (translation modified).

9   See Lecture 12, note 2.

10 See Edgar Zilsel, *Die Geniereligion: Ein kritischer Versuch über das modern Persönlichkeitsideal, mit einer historischen Begründung* (1918), ed. Johann Dvořak (Frankfurt: Suhrkamp, 1990).

11 Johann Wolfgang von Goethe, 'A Wanderer's Night Song II', in *Selected Poetry*, ed. and trans. David Luke (London: Penguin, 2005), p. 35.

12 Wilhelm Dilthey had opposed the naturalistic psychology of the positivistic nineteenth century with the assertion what whatever is 'there for us' can only reach consciousness via the 'inner apprehension of psychic events and activities'. These psychic events and activities create a 'special realm of experiences [*Erfahrungen*] which has its independent origin and its own material in inner experience and which is, accordingly, the subject matter of a special science of experience' (Dilthey, *Selected Works*, vol. 1: *Introduction to the Human Sciences* [1883], ed. Rudolf A. Makkreel and Frithjof Rodi [Princeton University Press, 1989], pp. 60f.) Proceeding from Kant's 'supreme principle of all synthetic judgements' (*Critique of Pure Reason*, p. 281), Dilthey could now argue that this dimension of 'inner experience' [*Erlebnis*], set apart from all extra-psychically observable objects through the concept of the 'experience', should be acknowledged as the 'condition of possibility of objects of experience'. This exploring the structures and autonomous laws of the 'experience' [*Erleben*], which Dilthey identified as the central task of the 'human sciences' [*Geisteswissenschaften*], offered the key to both the 'epistemological principles' and the 'principles of our action' (Dilthey, ibid., p. 61). This task was taken

up by Edmund Husserl's project of a 'phenomenology', with which Adorno occupied himself in his PhD thesis 'Die Transzendenz des Dinglichen und Noematischen in Husserls Phänomenologie' and the later work *Against Epistemology*. In the early twentieth century, the word 'experience' [*Erlebnis*] became an increasingly fashionable term used to express the most varied intentions in psychology and anthropology, epistemology, logic, aesthetics and ethics. 'In a shimmering, manifold interpretation of its hermeneutical-anthropological meaning, "*Erlebnis*" remains a fundamental concept in the philosophy of life and worldview in the first third of the twentieth century, which stem less from the effect of Dilthey than the influence of Nietzsche and Bergson' (K. Cramer, 'Erleben, Erlebnis', in *Historisches Wörterbuch der Philosophie*, ed. J. Ritter et al., vol. 2 [Basel and Stuttgart: Schwabe, 1972], col. 708f.)

13   See Lecture 2, note 13.

14   See René Laforgue, *The Defeat of Baudelaire: A Psychoanalytical Study of the Neurosis of Charles Baudelaire* (London: Hogarth, 1932); concerning Freud's essay 'Leonardo da Vinci and a Memory of His Childhood', see Lecture 4, note 3.

15   Marked by Adorno from 'One can say' to 'themselves through it'.

16   See Lecture 5, note 3.

17   Marked by Adorno from 'indescribable effort' to 'always has'. In *The Metaphysics of Morals* (1798), Kant discusses the binding nature of duties: 'All duties involve a concept of *constraint* through a law. *Ethical* duties involve a constraint for which only internal lawgiving is possible, whereas duties of right involve a constraint for which external lawgiving is also possible. Both, therefore, involve constraint, whether it be self-constraint or constraint by another' (*The Metaphysics of Morals*, ed. and trans. Mary Gregor [Cambridge University Press, 1996], p. 156).

18   Richard Wagner, *Die Meistersinger von Nürnberg* (premiered in Munich on 21 June 1868), libretto (Mainz, 1862), p. 100 (Act 3, scene 2).

19   The theologian, composer and music aesthetician August (Otto) Halm (1869–1929) was considered one of the most important music educators and spokesmen of the musical youth movement. He taught from 1903 to 1906 at the Landerziehungsheim [a type of reform school] in Haubinda, where he taught Walter Benjamin in 1906 (see Benjamin, *Gesammelte Schriften*, vol. VII.1, pp. 86f.). From 1906 to 1919, and again from 1920 to 1929, he was director of music education at the Wickersdorf Free School in Thuringia. His books include *Harmonielehre* (Leipzig: Göschen, 1900), *Von Grenzen und Ländern der Musik* (Munich: G. Müller, 1916), *Einführung in die Musik* (Berlin: Deutsche Buchgemeinschaft, 1926) and *Von zwei Kulturen der Musik* (Munich: G. Müller, 1913). Concerning Halm, see also Adorno, *Introduction to the Sociology of Music*, p. 217; 'Difficulties', in *Essays on Music*, p. 666; and *Aesthetic Theory*, p. 276.

20　Adorno had to end the semester prematurely after Lecture 21 for health reasons. His lecture materials show that a total of 25 sessions were planned. As he had already diverged from his original plan in his structuring of the content in the course of the semester, however, a direct assignment to the topics of individual sessions seems unproductive or even impossible.

Adorno's Notes for the Lectures

1　See Lecture 11, note 10. Hille Bobbe is a less common name for the same figure [Trans.].

2　Two syllables/abbreviations could not be deciphered.

3　Hegel's *Critique of the Power of Judgement* [Trans.].

4　The page numbers refer to Hermann Glockner's edition of Hegel's *Aesthetics* (*Sämtliche Werke: Jubiläumsausgabe*, vol. 12, Stuttgart: F. Frommann, 1927); see the quotations in Lecture 17.

INDEX